1981

The American's Search for Identity

THE AMERICAN'S SEARCH FOR IDENTITY: A READER

edited by
JAMES E. BROGAN
San Francisco State College

HARCOURT BRACE JOVANOVICH, INC.
New York   Chicago   San Francisco   Atlanta

ISBN: 0–15–502602–X

Library of Congress Catalog Card Number: 70–188370

Printed in the United States of America

FOREWORD

WHEN I was a child, I used to go to the newsreel at the Trans-lux Theatre on Sixtieth Street and Madison Avenue, mostly on Saturday afternoons. The show lasted an hour and included both a newsreel (a nineteen thirties' version of the CBS Evening News with Walter Cronkite), an animated cartoon, and various short features. Once, when I was there with my brother, one of the shorts consisted of an "historical mystery," a darkly tinted documentary film concerning a shadowy incident in the France of the Monarchy. By order of the king, a man had been kept confined inside a formidable chateau, his face permanently concealed behind a specially made iron mask. No one, not even his jailors, knew the identity of the face behind the mask. Although a prisoner, he was kept in luxury, waited on like a member of the nobility, but left in total silence. When he finally died, the mask remained on. According to the film, historians speculated that the noble prisoner was one of three highly placed rivals (one a brother of the king) who had to be confined for life yet treated with deference. The historical mystery was never solved. For myself and for Peter, who was three years younger, the film proved unforgettable. That iron countenance filled us with fear and dread. It was not pity we felt, but a profound fear generated by the man in the iron mask, an apprehension that named no object but that iron face itself. Many nights we imagined we were again seeing that brief film—the dungeon, the silent keepers, the touches of luxury, the sea outside, the man with the iron face. Thirty years later, I can still remember every detail of that brief documentary film and can still feel, with startling immediacy, that nameless dread of the immobile iron countenance.

The individual in America is imprisoned in such a mask. His thoughts, his feelings, his needs, loves, and personal beauty, his happiness and pain are all condemned to a life-long concealment. Although he is the most pitiable of living things, his appearance inspires fear in all others, and none of the prisoners can know, or touch, or hear each other, even for a moment.

Every society forces its members into roles and imposes restrictions on their behavior. The primitive tribe, the medieval village, the nineteenth-century American small town all subjected people to external restraints. In the America of the nineteen seventies these external restraints are found everywhere, in the form of laws, school and job regulations, social conventions and customs. But this external prison, common to all societies, is analogous to the dungeon, but not to the mask; it is that second, inner prison that we encounter in this book.

The people we meet here—Mrs. Bridge, the men on Anopopei in *The Naked and the Dead*, the characters in *Going All the Way*—are all like people locked permanently into space suits, from which they view each other's ungainly motions and stereotyped speech with a sense of utter isolation. There is nothing in the way of laws or regulations to keep Mrs. Bridge from expressing her feelings or telling her pain—she is on the verge of doing so in many brief episodes. But always she draws back, and the members of her family and her friends are prevented from seeing what we can see with the help of her biographer—brief moments in which she might have been revealed as truly human. *Mrs. Bridge* might just possibly be the greatest women's liberation book to date, for no current writer has shown us, so delicately, deftly, and compassionately, the mask within which so many American women are imprisoned.

But it is Norman Mailer's American soldiers in *The Naked and the Dead* who show us most clearly the special case of America. The American male has to live with the special American myth of frontier self-sufficiency, competence, and bravery. The myth is kept alive with all the power of the mass media and all the fear that a highly competitive society creates. Yet the stark truth, for an ordinary boy or man from Boston or Brooklyn or a midwest town or the Texas plains, is that in corporate America there is no way for one to control his own destiny, no way to be self-sufficient. He has been taught that if he fails—that is, if he fails to "succeed"—it must be his own fault, his own weakness and inadequacy. And so he blusters and threatens, swaggers and lies, hides his tenderness and his suffering, and follows all through his life what Philip Slater so hauntingly calls "the pursuit of loneliness."

For four years, beginning in the fall of 1967, I taught a course in Yale College entitled "The Individual in America." The students read books like the ones excerpted in this anthology, including some of the same selections reprinted here. The purpose of the course was to get behind those blank appearances of faces in America—the smiles from old *Life* magazines, the frowns from gangster movies, the frosty cool of the Marlboro man—to see what Americans were really experiencing as their country changed from one of small towns and villages to a corporate monolith, with standing armies, computer files on individuals, people organized into systems and hierarchies—a nation of driven workers and driven consumers. From the very start of my course, James E. Brogan, the editor of this anthology, was both a friend and collaborator. His course, at San Francisco State College, goes further and deeper, and so I would like to feel that in the present book some of my own American Studies 36A is embodied and joined with Jim's work and carried on to students beyond Yale and San Francisco State.

What Jim Brogan is saying to American students who read this book is something like the following. We are all strangers—strangers to ourselves and to each other. But if we could only know and express what we really feel, we might find out how much we really have in common. One tough, tight, competent, competitive American might learn that both he and others are capable of tenderness, softness, and true feeling, just as John Lennon has done us all an inestimable service by telling us "can't do you no harm to feel your own pain." A man who has concealed his own feelings of pain and of love for thirty years might find, incredibly, that others who seemed for all those years like dangerous strangers actually conceal feelings just like his own.

My own conviction is that there is no problem of present-day life —poverty, racial injustice, environment, cities, or war—that cannot yield to the efforts of a people who know themselves and each other and therefore can act together as a true community. I believe that our present desperation is brought on not by an absence of plans and planners, but by a lack of the necessary awareness or consciousness that would enable us to take action. So I view this book, although it is about individual people, as a deeply political book. It offers an opening toward a new consciousness and a new community without which a new politics is impossible, but which, if achieved, will make a new politics inevitable. In Graham Nash's song "Teach Your Children" the singer says, "And you, of tender years/Can't know the fears/That your elders grew by." And Neil Young, in his song "Don't Let It Bring You Down," says, "Just find someone who's turning, and you will come around." It is Jim Brogan's hope, and mine, that this book will help people to find others, old or young, who are turning.

CHARLES A. REICH

PREFACE

THIS collection offers accounts of the emotional side of American life that are the most honest and straightforward I have been able to find. While there is no question that all are "good" literature and lend themselves quite readily to traditional literary analysis, most students will probably prefer to treat them in terms of their personal experiences. This may bring up many aspects of individual lives not commonly discussed in the classroom, and, as a result, in some cases the student may well speak with more authority than the instructor. When most of the selections in this volume were tried in the classroom, students showed an eagerness to discuss them that resulted in a rare degree of communication between class and instructor.

It is hard for an instructor to be both a discussion leader and non-authoritarian, and one way of getting beyond such roles is to offer one's own experience to reinforce the impact of a story. When teaching *Going All the Way*, for example, I may give an account of my own anxieties on college football weekends in the early 1960's, or, if the discussion is of *Mrs. Bridge*, reminisce about repressions that were present in my own family. Such comments are meant not to be confessional in nature, but to encourage a sense of shared feelings in a community of equals, which invests discussion of the literature with an invaluable honesty. I have found that such a classroom atmosphere also can have a beneficial effect on a student's writing, often making it more open and divesting it of the stiffness that comes with attempts to write formal "compositions." The nature of the selections also tends to encourage straightforward, personal writing as well as variety in style. I have also followed the practice of allowing students fifteen minutes of "free-association" writing either in class or just after they have finished a reading assignment. This writing has shown a gratifying heightening of intelligence and sensitivity—perhaps a result of being liberated from the demands of formal composition. Longer papers may consist of a journal of the student's impressions of the readings kept throughout the term, or autobiographical papers inspired by the readings.

The questions that follow each selection are intended primarily to encourage close reading and an appreciation of the complex nature of good writing. "Questions for Study and Writing," which follow each of the four major sections, are designed to suggest how the selections can be analyzed and compared according to the traditional conventions of literary criticism.

I wish to thank those who reviewed the original manuscript and offered suggestions for its improvement—Richard M. Ludwig, Princeton University; David F. Hiatt, University of Saskatchewan; M. Thomas Inge, Virginia Commonwealth University; and Robert C. Bannister, Swarthmore College. William Pullin and Philip Ressner, of Harcourt Brace Jovanovich, gave me sound professional advice at every stage. But my deepest gratitude goes to my friend, Charles Reich, and to all the students at San Francisco State College with whom I have shared the struggle for awareness.

James E. Brogan

CONTENTS

I Disillusionment: The Failure of American Myths and Dreams

II The Imprisoned Self

III   Assertions of the Outsider

IV   The Struggle for Self-Awareness

The American's Search for Identity

INTRODUCTION

TO view one's life as a search for self-awareness may be unabashedly romantic, but today in America more and more young people are beginning to do just that. The opportunity has arisen because, to a large extent, the members of the new generation have fewer anxieties and, consequently, are less subject to traditional standards of behavior. They are the benefactors of the prosperity for which their parents worked so hard after enduring the everyday terrors of the Great Depression. Nor do young people today suffer the fears of those Americans with immigrant parents who, often made to feel ashamed of their ethnic origins, became obsessed by the problem of how to act like an "American"; instead many young people today think in terms of what kind of American they would like to be. They are also more liberated from old sexual restraints and want to discover the kinds of experiences that satisfy their inclinations. Many are willing to acknowledge feelings and conflicts their parents had to repress. Finally, they are aware that they *do* have the freedom to choose their own environment, occupation, and relationships; unlike their parents they have a reasonable chance of becoming who they want to become. In short, the young today constitute a generation particularly conscious of the concept of "self."

Perhaps the most helpful way of defining the idea of the "self" in relation to the selections in this volume is to think of it as an individual's innermost identity, the human being we would be were we to act in accordance with our talents and our deepest feelings. Two more premises about the self might be kept in mind while reading these selections. First, development of the self is helped immensely if external living conditions and general environment are congenial—thus the high potential of today's "affluent" generation. Secondly, as elements of the self are brought to awareness one comes to recognize their interrelatedness. Indeed, there is a profound meaning to the current expression "to have it all together." A word particularly applicable to a person of great self-awareness is "integrity," in both its senses—"wholeness" and "honesty"—for the person who achieves a sense of wholeness of self is one who is honest about and tries to become aware of his true feelings.

This sense of self is crucial to concepts—such as individualism—esteemed by Americans. The related idea of "free will" is basic not only to the economic principle of "free enterprise," but also to our belief that the individual is "responsible" for his own behavior. Currently, for many young Americans, the greatest source of anxiety about our society is a sense that its evolution into a highly developed industrial society has brought with it a tendency to deprive the individual of free will. Government is much more a part of our daily lives, and we live in a world of conglomerates, surveillance, and shrinking natural resources, all of which tend to limit free-wheeling movement and activity. Despite their material advantages, the members of the new generation are almost forced to turn inward to the "self" to capture any sense of the wide-open freedom that characterized the early days of our country.

In the middle of the nineteenth century, Americans did seem to have many opportunities to control their individual fates. America was a young country with a fresh start, free from the constraints of the past. There was little custom, tradition, or history to which it felt itself bound. Instead, Americans had a strong belief in their sense of self. They saw no contradiction in envisioning a new society where each man would be free to develop his full potential and yet still become a helpful member of the community. This version of the "American dream" had little to do with wealth or materialism. It was a humanistic and idealistic faith in man's possibilities.

To look upon man so positively, Americans had to possess, above all, a quality of innocence that enabled them to ignore all of history. Though the Old World might well have criticized him as naive, the young American in all likelihood was much envied by the young European, who was bound by family traditions and race and overwhelmed by dismal conditions and a sense of a tumultuous past. The American writer who best captures this sense of native innocence and who most fully celebrates the idea of the self is Walt Whitman. In his poetry Whitman created a mythic self who personifies this sense of American innocence; a man who resembles Adam in the garden before the Fall, free from the taint of original sin. Whitman himself was reacting strongly against the Puritan doctrine—the Christian belief in man's inherited guilt—which prevailed in nineteenth-century America. Whitman insisted that the native American, in his very newness, was fundamentally innocent.

The American self, as described in Whitman's poetry, is never stationary, but is eternally questing. There are always new lands to see, new adventures to experience; there is little longing for the past or for the family and home. This spirit was typical of that of the pioneers, the settlers on America's frontiers who, when they became discontented, could always effectively part with their pasts by moving on to new lands. Such men weren't interested in social progress; instead they insisted on a life which they themselves had the power to mold and change.

We can see this journey of the self viewed through Whitman's mind in the first four sections of his most famous poem, *Song of Myself*. In its first three sections it is a poem of self-celebration and self-acceptance. In section four the poetic narrator declares himself free from any identity imposed from without, any force or influence that would destroy his fluidity or spontaneity. He asserts, at the end of the first stanza, "They are not the Me myself." The American myth of self-reliance receives its most important and attractive expression in *Song of Myself*. It is the song of a man who celebrates the idea that nothing has greater importance to one than one's self. Moreover Whitman's poetic self clearly represents the purest embodiment of the American myth of the self-made man. His version of it can be far more compelling than the more widely held view of the American as a rugged individual who brags of his lowly origins and his tremendous bank account. In his poetry, Whitman's myth has an undeniable grandeur. As he puts it in "One's Self I Sing," it is a story of "Life immense in passion, pulse and power."

One major limitation of Whitman's concept of the self is that it existed essentially in a mythic dimension, not in a social context. In reality there was a harsh side to the myth of self-reliance, one that emphasized self-interest, competitiveness, and success at all costs. This obsession with "winning" led to suspicion of others, corruption in government, and lack of a sense of human community. Whitman himself toned down the lyric optimism of his poems to criticize Americans in his prose essay *Democratic Vistas* (1871), in which he admitted to being deeply disillusioned by the hollow pursuit of materialism and the hypocrisy prevalent in his country.

There is a second major limitation to Whitman's myth of the American self. While it is appropriate to view the self as subject to fewer influences from past events and traditions in a country that is new, such a view applied in an older and more established country precludes the possibility of learning from one's own cultural development. The great American novelist, Henry James, was deeply disturbed that America had a culture with little sense of the past, not because he was opposed to "newness," but because he saw Americans becoming obsessed by the idea of change for its own sake.

James loved the freshness and innocence of Americans, but he also needed a greater sense of cultural depth. Thus, when still a young man he emigrated to Europe to seek out older literary traditions and to get a better sense of his own identity as a writer. (In America he was oppressed by the presence of two well-known scholars in his family—his father, Henry, Sr., and his brother, William.) After an exile of twenty-one years, James returned in 1904 for a visit. In *The American Scene*, full of the drama of reconciling past and present, he recounts his impressions of our country at that time. He sees an America pervaded with materialism and obsessed with "progress." In New York City, scene of many boyhood memories, he discovers that most of the beautiful and distinctive buildings have been replaced with characterless skyscrapers. The city is noisy, crowded, hurried; all personal comfort is sacrificed to the obsession with growth. "To make so much money that you won't, that you don't 'mind,' don't mind anything— that is absolutely, I think, the main American formula." James selects the new high-speed elevators as an apt symbol of how Americans sacrifice personal comfort for material "progress." He is outraged at being told to "step lively" and at being herded into "some tight mechanic receptacle" which, when tolerated, "represents surely, when cherished and sacrificed to, a strange perversion of sympathies and ideals."

But James is most concerned with the sacrifices of self he encounters. Americans, people cut off from their own history, have little idea of what fosters sense of self; their hurried lives and materialistic values permit no time to reflect on such matters. Watching the men pass by on a busy street, James finds a terrible sameness of facial expression. "No impression so promptly assaults the arriving visitor of the United States as that of the overwhelming preponderance, wherever he turns and twists, of the unmitigated business man's face." It was at this time that James wrote "The Jolly Corner," in which his protagonist, returning to his home in New York after many years in Europe, sets out to find his own ghost, his apparitional *alter ego*, which he imagines to possess just such a businessman's mask.

If the faces of American men show only a dreary sameness, the faces of American women clearly reveal the consequences of such a waste of human resources. James thinks that the feminine faces show "a markedly finer texture than the men, and that one of the liveliest signs of this difference is precisely in their less narrowly specialized, their less commercialized, distinctly more generalized, physiognomic character." James can come to only one conclusion—that a great number of Americans feel frustrated and unfulfilled. Moreover, the American woman, sheltered from the man's world and relegated to the more human responsibilities of the home, has qualities she cannot share with her male counterpart.

In the initial section of this volume, F. Scott Fitzgerald's Dexter

Green (in "Winter Dreams") and Evan Connell's Mrs. Bridge are characters who are embodiments of James' American "types." Each plays out his role in the American success myth only to discover that it is empty of personal satisfaction. Each is left at the end with an overwhelming sense of loss, a sense of missed opportunities. In the biographical sketches from his *U.S.A.* trilogy, John Dos Passos expresses the same sense of disillusionment with public figures who misuse their wealth and power to pursue more wealth and power. The shape of each of their lives is tellingly similar and the sound is distinctly hollow.

The selections in Part II deal with the consequences of what James perceived—the suffering that ensues when the sense of self is sacrificed to external values. At first glance the contents of this section may seem singularly dark and pessimistic. But each piece represents the author's attempt to inform us that we ourselves may be suffering the effects of the peculiarly American problems described, and recognition of that fact can be the first step toward remedy. Furthermore, the authors permit us to examine the lives of earlier generations and, thus, identify our emotional ties with the past: Readers may discover a new compassion for parents who had to contend with modes of behavior more circumscribed than theirs. In the extracts from Norman Mailer's *The Naked and the Dead* we may find close parallels between the problems of the soldiers of World War II and those of our fathers. Best of all, these stories confirm that our problems are not unique, but are part of larger patterns of cultural "hangups," from which we can help each other escape.

The conflicted selves of Mrs. Bridge and Dexter Green, in the first section, are manifested only in the sense of emptiness in their lives. In the second section, however, the writers bombard us with images of the anguished frustration of self-imprisonment. They show how the self can be stifled when the individual unquestioningly accepts social values and roles that go counter to deep feelings. Both Herman Melville and Hamlin Garland assure us that, even in the nineteenth century, the lives of a typical Wall Street businessman or Midwestern farmer were heavily circumscribed by narrow materialistic beliefs or extremely rigid social conventions.

Possibly most painful for some are the selections that portray Americans trapped in all-too-typical psychosexual prisons. While we can see clearly that such problems as poverty are often beyond the responsibility of the individual, the tendency is usually otherwise in the case of sexual problems. In these days of relaxed censorship one need only observe various television comedy programs to realize that the urge to degrade sexuality or ridicule sexual inadequacy is deeply imbedded in our culture. The scene of sexual humiliation in *Going All the Way* explicitly points to a theme underlying this entire section—the inability of the individual to reconcile feelings of sexual desire with feelings of "love" and affection. Thus, while Mrs. Bridge imposed one kind of basic limitation on sexuality (that sex belongs only in monogamous marriage), the characters in this section, though their morality is different from Mrs. Bridge's, endure limitations just as severe in that they can approach sexuality only as abrupt, genital contact.

The people whose imprisoned selves are described in Part II cannot be liberated because the beliefs that bind them are unconscious. The third section, "Assertions of the Outsider," presents characters—always members of a minority group—who clearly see belief in American myths as folly. Because they are rejected by established society, they do not hope for typical "success," and so are free to be more honest about how they feel. Such writers as Baldwin, Kerouac, and Ginsberg were virtually ignored when their works were first published in the early 1950's, so that they too, like their characters, were free to say what they felt. They wrote about losers—blacks, Chicanos, homosexuals, drug addicts—who had little to lose by defying society. Although the lives of the "outsiders" are as painful as those who personify the "imprisoned self" of Part II, they have begun to get in touch with deeper forces within themselves, and their stories ultimately attest to the sheer power and worth of life itself. They achieve a terrifying and wonderful intensity that people like Mrs. Bridge, for all their affluence, can never know. Trapped by social conditions, they defiantly assert themselves, even to the point of self-destruction, and thus become at least partially self-aware. The black and brown people described by Baldwin and Kerouac can sustain at least short periods of joy or make at least meaningful gestures under the most severe economic and political oppression. Isherwood's homosexual teacher, though aging and lonely, "hasn't given up." Ginsberg's poetry is suffused with the affection and compassion he feels for his "underground" drug addicts. In fact, all these underground figures of the 40's and 50's are America's twentieth-century version of pioneers, searching out identities and teaching us to question everything around us. Their stories not only tell of emptiness and sordidness, but point the way to liberation from the gross ignorance of reality that permits the continuing persecution of "outsiders." Most important, we may find some of our own feelings being described in these unlikely sources.

Each selection in Part IV, the final section, is a dramatization of some kind of self-confrontation. The authors reveal the peculiar difficulties and excitement of viewing life through a consciousness that attempts to be scrupulously honest in its self-awareness, which brings with it a heavy sense of responsibility for one's self. For such a person it is no longer possible to pursue blindly a rigid plan of life that does not allow for constant re-evaluation and changes in direction in one's work and personal relationships. Many young people, striving to realize such a life, are beginning to be ambitious in an entirely new way, one that places greatest value on the possibility of personal growth and the opportunity to do socially useful and personally satisfying work. They are, in fact, returning to the ideas of free will and individual responsibility that were held in high esteem in an older America.

The literary portraits in this section may provide models with which many of us can confront and assess ourselves. Henry David Thoreau establishes an atmosphere for self-analysis in his chapter "Where I Lived, and What I Lived For" from *Walden*. Henry James' story, *The Jolly Corner*, then begins a dominant theme in this section—that of an older self viewing its past experiences in order to gain insight from them. Ken Kesey's Chief Broom, in *One Flew Over the Cuckoo's Nest*, is able, with help from his friend, McMurphy, to identify the source of his fears and ultimately to overcome them. The selections by Carl Rogers and David Crosby offer a contrast in age and youth, in the academic success of a researcher and the popular success of a rock musician. Both are men with "good egos"—that is, with enough self-acceptance and self-love to be objective about their accomplishments and disappointments. Both see life as a fluid process of constant growth. Crosby combines a kind of instinctive assertiveness with a solid self-conception that is supported by the enjoyment and fulfillment he gets from his music. His professional success clearly allows him to take other kinds of personal risks in the process of self-discovery. His openness and tolerance do seem to represent a highly "evolved" (to use his own term) version of the American self.

Carl Rogers entered a profession where he could both explore himself and help others. Apparently he has been able to work effectively within institutional structures and still experience a sense of personal fulfillment from his own research. He seems to have kept himself receptive to criticism and other people's opinions of his work without being unduly influenced or upset by others' judgments. His professional emphasis on direct communication between people, whether in psychotherapy or in education, seems to have a "real-life" counterpart in David Crosby's own experiences. It's hard to resist believing Crosby when he says, "I see people relating to each other in ways that haven't happened before . . . people who are concerned with being human."

This concern with "being human" is pretty much the motivation behind all the selections in this book. Because they are literature, they do not offer theories of the self or specific cures for our problems. Instead they reveal the richness of the experience of the American individual in all the complexity of everyday life. Perhaps it is only fitting that, after having immersed ourselves in these experiences, we return at the end to the lyrical, childlike world of Whitman's mythic self. The songs of Crosby, Nash, and Young represent a reemergence of this visionary American self. They do not hesitate to acknowledge the pain we feel in a changing world, but they look forward to a time of human community.

Disillusionment:
The Failure of American Myths and Dreams

WALT WHITMAN

WHEN Walt Whitman published the first edition of *Leaves of Grass* in 1855, even though his talent was at once recognized by Ralph Waldo Emerson, he was generally rejected by the American public. His poetry shocked and offended many traditional Christians by its acceptance of everything within the self, without guilt or reference to outside authority. Furthermore, he not only celebrated human sensuality, but insisted on its spiritual dimension. ("Divine I am, inside and out, and I make holy whatever I touch.") For the next hundred years his poetry was read mainly by intellectuals, many of whom—even the once-admiring Emerson—disparaged him for his unwieldy, unmetrical verse, his endless catalogs, and his egotism. But recently there has been a great revival of interest in his poetry from a new generation that can overlook certain kinds of excesses and can respond to his lyricism, his vitality, and his almost undifferentiated childlike wonder at and acceptance of the natural world and the physical aspects of human beings. "There Was a Child Went Forth," for example, focuses on the archetypal American innocent who absorbs and revels in the things without him while Whitman the poet reestablishes contact with the child within.

Another reason for Whitman's current popularity is his frank acceptance of sex as the life force which, freed from the suppressions of our Puritan-dominated culture, revitalizes love in all its forms. In fact, Whitman, in his extremely sensual celebration of America's young men and women, helped establish sexuality as a legitimate subject for American literature. In his volume of poetry called *Children of Adam*, he wrote of "amative love," the love of man for woman, and in a subsequent work, *Calamus*, described "adhesiveness" or "manly attachment," the affection of man for his fellow man. The explicitly sexual nature of such poems as "A Woman Waits for Me" and "Spontaneous Me" is a source of surprise and delight to many today. The latter, in which the sexual urge is extended outward to women, men, and nature, is very frank in its sexual imagery and is certainly a remarkable poem for its time.

Whitman's mood is much more subdued in the two poems printed here from *Calamus*. In "We Two Boys Together Clinging," there is an ideal completeness of male affection as the two boys unconsciously "fulfill" their youthful foray. But in "I Saw in Louisiana a Live-Oak Growing," Whitman, a man powerful but essentially lonely, apparently tries to overcome this condition by populating his poetic landscape elsewhere with lovers and companions.

Another "dark" element, which begins to make itself felt in some of Whitman's later poetry and prose, is his disillusionment with America. He had once hoped that the "fervid comradeship" of the *Calamus* volume would be "the counterbalance and offset of our materialistic and vulgar American democracy." And indeed, it is possible to see in all his poetry a kind of manic effusiveness, a fierce, almost desperate determination to assert the self in the light of the encroaching dehumanization of American life as the country developed.

[FROM Inscriptions]

One's-Self I Sing

One's-Self I sing, a simple separate person,
Yet utter the word Democratic, the word En-Masse.

Of physiology from top to toe I sing,
Not physiognomy alone nor brain alone is worthy for the Muse, I
    say the Form complete is worthier far,
The Female equally with the Male I sing.

Of life immense in passion, pulse, and power,
Cheerful, for freest action form'd under the laws divine,
The Modern Man I sing.

Song of Myself

1

I celebrate myself, and sing myself,
And what I assume you shall assume,
For every atom belonging to me as good belongs to you.

I loafe and invite my soul,
I lean and loafe at my ease observing a spear of summer grass.
My tongue, every atom of my blood, form'd from this soil, this air,
Born here of parents born here from parents the same, and their
    parents the same,
I, now thirty-seven years old in perfect health begin,
Hoping to cease not till death.

Creeds and schools in abeyance,
Retiring back a while sufficed at what they are, but never forgotten,
I harbor for good or bad, I permit to speak at every hazard,
Nature without check with original energy.

2

Houses and rooms are full of perfumes, the shelves are crowded
    with perfumes,

From LEAVES OF GRASS, 1868.

I breathe the fragrance myself and know it and like it,
The distillation would intoxicate me also, but I shall not let it.

The atmosphere is not a perfume, it has no taste of the distillation,
        it is odorless,
It is for my mouth forever, I am in love with it,
I will go to the bank by the wood and become undisguised and
        naked,
I am mad for it to be in contact with me.
The smoke of my own breath,
Echoes, ripples, buzz'd whispers, love-root, silk-thread, crotch and
        vine,
My respiration and inspiration, the beating of my heart, the passing
        of blood and air through my lungs,
The sniff of green leaves and dry leaves, and of the shore and dark-
        color'd sea-rocks, and of hay in the barn,
The sound of the belch'd words of my voice loos'd to the eddies of
        the wind,
A few light kisses, a few embraces, a reaching around of arms,
The play of shine and shade on the trees as the supple boughs wag,
The delight alone or in the rush of the streets, or along the fields
        and hill-sides,
The feeling of health, the full-noon trill, the song of me rising from
        bed and meeting the sun.

Have you reckon'd a thousand acres much? have you reckon'd the
        earth much?
Have you practis'd so long to learn to read?
Have you felt so proud to get at the meaning of poems?

Stop this day and night with me and you shall possess the origin of
        all poems,
You shall possess the good of the earth and sun, (there are millions
        of suns left,)
You shall no longer take things at second or third hand, nor look
        through the eyes of the dead, nor feed on the spectres in
        books,
You shall not look through my eyes either, nor take things from me,
You shall listen to all sides and filter them from your self.

            3
I have heard what the talkers were talking, the talk of the beginning
        and the end,
But I do not talk of the beginning or the end.

There was never any more inception than there is now,
Nor any more youth or age than there is now,
And will never be any more perfection than there is now,
Nor any more heaven or hell than there is now.
Urge and urge and urge,
Always the procreant urge of the world.

Out of the dimness opposite equals advance, always substance and
  increase, always sex,
Always a knit of identity, always distinction, always a breed of life.

To elaborate is no avail, learn'd and unlearn'd feel that it is so.

Sure as the most certain sure, plumb in the uprights, well en-
  tretied,[1] braced in the beams,
Stout as a horse, affectionate, haughty, electrical,
I and this mystery here we stand.

Clear and sweet is my soul, and clear and sweet is all that is not my
  soul.

Lack one lacks both, and the unseen is proved by the seen,
Till that becomes unseen and receives proof in its turn.

Showing the best and dividing it from the worst age vexes age,
Knowing the perfect fitness and equanimity of things, while they
  discuss I am silent, and go bathe and admire myself.

Welcome is every organ and attribute of me, and of any man hearty
  and clean,
Not an inch nor a particle of an inch is vile, and none shall be less
  familiar than the rest.

I am satisfied—I see, dance, laugh, sing;
As the hugging and loving bed-fellow sleeps at my side through the
  night, and withdraws at the peep of the day with stealthy
  tread,
Leaving me baskets cover'd with white towels swelling the house
  with their plenty,
Shall I postpone my acceptation and realization and scream at my
  eyes,
That they turn from gazing after and down the road,

[1] "crossed-braced," a carpenter's term.

And forthwith cipher and show me to a cent,
Exactly the value of one and exactly the value of two, and which is
    ahead?

    4

Trippers and askers surround me,
People I meet, the effect upon me of my early life or the ward and
    city I live in, or the nation,
The latest dates, discoveries, inventions, societies, authors old and
    new,
My dinner, dress, associates, looks, compliments, dues,
The real or fancied indifference of some man or woman I love,
The sickness of one of my folks or of myself, or ill-doing or loss or
    lack of money, or depressions or exaltations,
Battles, the horrors of fratricidal war, the fever of doubtful news,
    the fitful events;
These come to me days and nights and go from me again,
But they are not the Me myself.

Apart from the pulling and hauling stands what I am,
Stands amused, complacent, compassionating, idle, unitary,
Looks down, is erect, or bends an arm on an impalpable certain rest,
Looking with side-curved head curious what will come next,
Both in and out of the game and watching and wondering at it.

Backward I see in my own days where I sweated through fog with
    linguists and contenders,
I have no mockings or arguments, I witness and wait.

[FROM Autumn Rivulets]

There Was a Child Went Forth

There was a child went forth every day,
And the first object he look'd upon, that object he became,
And that object became part of him for the day or a certain part of
    the day,
Or for many years or stretching cycles of years.

The early lilacs became part of this child,
And grass and white and red morning-glories, and white and red
    clover, and the song of the phœbe-bird,

And the Third-month lambs and the sow's pink-faint litter, and the
      mare's foal and the cow's calf,
And the noisy brood of the barnyard or by the mire of the pond-
      side,
And the fish suspending themselves so curiously below there, and
      the beautiful curious liquid,
And the water-plants with their graceful flat heads, all became part
      of him.

The field-sprouts of Fourth-month and Fifth-month became part
      of him,
Winter-grain sprouts and those of the light-yellow corn, and the
      esculent[1] roots of the garden,
And the apple-trees cover'd with blossoms and the fruit afterward,
      and wood-berries, and the commonest weeds by the road,
And the old drunkard staggering home from the outhouse of the
      tavern whence he had lately risen,
And the schoolmistress that pass'd on her way to the school,
And the friendly boys that pass'd, and the quarrelsome boys,
And the tidy and fresh-cheek'd girls, and the barefoot negro boy and
      girl,
And all the changes of city and country wherever he went.

His own parents, he that had father'd him and she that had con-
      ceiv'd him in her womb and birth'd him,
They gave this child more of themselves than that,
They gave him afterward every day, they became part of him.

The mother at home quietly placing the dishes on the supper-table,
The mother with mild words, clean her cap and gown, a wholesome
      odor falling off her person and clothes as she walks by,
The father, strong, self-sufficient, manly, mean, anger'd, unjust,
The blow, the quick loud word, the tight bargain, the crafty lure,
The family usages, the language, the company, the furniture, the
      yearning and swelling heart,
Affection that will not be gainsay'd,[2] the sense of what is real, the
      thought if after all it should prove unreal,
The doubts of day-time and the doubts of night-time, the curious
      whether and how,
Whether that which appears so is so, or is it all flashes and specks?
Men and women crowding fast in the streets, if they are not flashes
      and specks what are they?

[1] edible.
[2] denied.

The streets themselves and the façades of houses, and goods in the
 windows,
Vchiclcs, tcams, thc heavy-plank'd wharves, the huge crossing at the
 ferries,
The village on the highland seen from afar at sunset, the river be-
 tween,
Shadows, aureola and mist, the light falling on roofs and gables of
 white or brown two miles off,
The schooner near by sleepily dropping down the tide, the little
 boat slack-tow'd astern,
The hurrying tumbling waves, quick-broken crests, slapping,
The strata of color'd clouds, the long bar of maroon-tint away
 solitary by itself, the spread of purity it lies motionless in,
The horizon's edge, the flying sea-crow, the fragrance of salt marsh
 and shore mud,
These became part of that child who went forth every day, and who
 now goes, and will always go forth every day.

[FROM Children of Adam]

Facing West from California's Shores

Facing west from California's shores,
Inquiring, tireless, seeking what is yet unfound,
I, a child, very old, over waves, towards the house of maternity, the
 land of migrations, look afar,
Look off the shores of my Western sea, the circle almost circled;
For starting westward from Hindustan, from the vales of Kashmere,
From Asia, from the north, from the God, the sage, and the hero,
From the south, from the flowery peninsulas and the spice islands,
Long having wander'd since, round the earth having wander'd,
Now I face home again, very pleas'd and joyous,
(But where is what I started for so long ago?
And why is it yet unfound?)

To the Garden the World

To the garden the world anew ascending,
Potent mates, daughters, sons, preluding,
The love, the life of their bodies, meaning and being,

Curious here behold my resurrection after slumber,
The revolving cycles in their wide sweep having brought me again,
Amorous, mature, all beautiful to me, all wondrous,
My limbs and the quivering fire that ever plays through them, for
      reasons, most wondrous,
Existing I peer and penetrate still,
Content with the present, content with the past,
By my side or back of me Eve following,
Or in front, and I following her just the same.

A Woman Waits for Me

A woman waits for me, she contains all, nothing is lacking,
Yet all were lacking if sex were lacking, or if the moisture of the
      right man were lacking.

Sex contains all, bodies, souls,
Meanings, proofs, purities, delicacies, results, promulgations,
Songs, commands, health, pride, the maternal mystery, the seminal
      milk,
All hopes, benefactions, bestowals, all the passions, loves, beauties,
      delights of the earth,
All the governments, judges, gods, follow'd persons of the earth,
These are contain'd in sex as parts of itself and justifications of
      itself.

Without shame the man I like knows and avows the deliciousness of
      his sex,
Without shame the woman I like knows and avows hers.

Now I will dismiss myself from impassive women,
I will go stay with her who waits for me, and with those women
      that are warm-blooded and sufficient for me,
I see that they understand me and do not deny me,
I see that they are worthy of me, I will be the robust husband of
      those women.

They are not one jot less than I am,
They are tann'd in the face by shining suns and blowing winds,
Their flesh has the old divine suppleness and strength,
They know how to swim, row, ride, wrestle, shoot, run, strike, re-
      treat, advance, resist, defend themselves,

They are ultimate in their own right—they are calm, clear, well-
    possess'd of themselves.

I draw you close to me, you women,
I cannot let you go, I would do you good,
I am for you, and you are for me, not only for our own sake, but for
    others' sakes,
Envelop'd in you sleep greater heroes and bards,
They refuse to awake at the touch of any man but me.

It is I, you women, I make my way,
I am stern, acrid, large, undissuadable, but I love you,
I do not hurt you any more than is necessary for you,
I pour the stuff to start sons and daughters fit for these States, I
    press with slow rude muscle,
I brace myself effectually, I listen to no entreaties,
I dare not withdraw till I deposit what has so long accumulated
    within me.

Through you I drain the pent-up rivers of myself,
In you I wrap a thousand onward years,
On you I graft the grafts of the best-beloved of me and America,
The drops I distil upon you shall grow fierce and athletic girls, new
    artists, musicians, and singers,
The babes I beget upon you are to beget babes in their turn,
I shall demand perfect men and women out of my love-spendings,
I shall expect them to interpenetrate with others, as I and you
    interpenetrate now,
I shall count on the fruits of the gushing showers of them, as I
    count on the fruits of the gushing showers I give now,
I shall look for loving crops from the birth, life, death, immortality,
    I plant so lovingly now.

Spontaneous Me

Spontaneous me, Nature,
The loving day, the mounting sun, the friend I am happy with,
The arm of my friend hanging idly over my shoulder,
The hillside whiten'd with blossoms of the mountain ash,
The same late in autumn, the hues of red, yellow, drab, purple, and
    light and dark green,

The rich coverlet of the grass, animals and birds, the private un-
     trimm'd bank, the primitive apples, the pebble-stones,
Beautiful dripping fragments, the negligent list of one after another
     as I happen to call them to me or think of them,
The real poems, (what we call poems being merely pictures,)
The poems of the privacy of the night, and of men like me,
This poem drooping shy and unseen that I always carry, and that all
     men carry,
(Know once for all, avow'd on purpose, wherever are men like me,
     are our lusty lurking masculine poems,)
Love-thoughts, love-juice, love-odor, love-yielding, love-climbers, and
     the climbing sap,
Arms and hands of love, lips of love, phallic thumb of love, breasts
     of love, bellies press'd and glued together with love,
Earth of chaste love, life that is only life after love,
The body of my love, the body of the woman I love, the body of
     the man, the body of the earth,
Soft forenoon airs that blow from the south-west,
The hairy wild-bee that murmurs and hankers up and down, that
     gripes the full-grown lady-flower, curves upon her with
     amorous firm legs, takes his will of her, and holds himself
     tremulous and tight till he is satisfied;
The wet of woods through the early hours,
Two sleepers at night lying close together as they sleep, one with an
     arm slanting down across and below the waist of the other,
The smell of apples, aromas from crush'd sage-plant, mint, birch-
     bark,
The boy's longings, the glow and pressure as he confides to me
     what he was dreaming,
The dead leaf whirling its spiral whirl and falling still and content
     to the ground,
The no-form'd stings that sights, people, objects, sting me with,
The hubb'd sting of myself, stinging me as much as it ever can
     any one,
The sensitive, orbic, underlapp'd brothers,[1] that only privileged
     feelers may be intimate where they are,
The curious roamer the hand roaming all over the body, the
     bashful withdrawing of flesh where the fingers soothingly
     pause and edge themselves,
The limpid liquid within the young man,
The vex'd corrosion so pensive and so painful,
The torment, the irritable tide that will not be at rest,

[1] genitals.

The like of the same I feel, the like of the same in others,
The young man that flushes and flushes, and the young woman
      that flushes and flushes,
The young man that wakes deep at night, the hot hand seeking to
      repress what would master him,
The mystic amorous night, the strange half-welcome pangs, visions,
      sweats,
The pulse pounding through palms and trembling encircling fingers,
      the young man all color'd, red, ashamed, angry;
The souse[1] upon me of my lover the sea, as I lie willing and naked,
The merriment of the twin babes that crawl over the grass in the
      sun, the mother never turning her vigilant eyes from them,
The walnut-trunk, the walnut-husks, and the ripening or ripen'd
      long-round walnuts,
The continence of vegetables, birds, animals,
The consequent meanness of me should I skulk or find myself in-
      decent, while birds and animals never once skulk or find
      themselves indecent,
The great chastity of paternity, to match the great chastity of
      maternity,
The oath of procreation I have sworn, my Adamic and fresh
      daughters,
The greed that eats me day and night with hungry gnaw, till I
      saturate what shall produce boys to fill my place when I
      am through,
The wholesome relief, repose, content,
And this bunch pluck'd at random from myself,
It has done its work—I toss it carelessly to fall where it may.

[FROM Calamus]

I Saw in Louisiana a Live-Oak Growing

I saw in Louisiana a live-oak growing,
All alone stood it and the moss hung down from the branches,
Without any companion it grew there uttering joyous leaves of dark
      green,
And its look, rude, unbending, lusty, made me think of myself,
But I wonder'd how it could utter joyous leaves standing alone
      there without its friend near, for I knew I could not,

---

[1] a drenching or immersion.

And I broke off a twig with a certain number of leaves upon it,
     and twined around it a little moss,
And brought it away, and I have placed it in sight in my room,
It is not needed to remind me as of my own dear friends,
(For I believe lately I think of little else than of them,)
Yet it remains to me a curious token, it makes me think of manly
     love;
For all that, and though the live-oak glistens there in Louisiana
     solitary in a wide flat space,
Uttering joyous leaves all its life without a friend a lover near,
I know very well I could not.

We Two Boys Together Clinging

We two boys together clinging,
One the other never leaving,
Up and down the roads going, North and South excursions making,
Power enjoying, elbows stretching, fingers clutching,
Arm'd and fearless, eating, drinking, sleeping, loving,
No law less than ourselves owning, sailing, soldiering, thieving,
     threatening,
Misers, menials, priests alarming, air breathing, water drinking, on
     the turf or the sea-beach dancing,
Cities wrenching, ease scorning, statutes mocking, feebleness chas-
     ing,
Fulfilling our foray.

QUESTIONS

1. How does Whitman use rhythm and meter in "Song of Myself?"
   How does his use of language increase our awareness of his sensuality?
2. What opposition does Whitman suggest in Section 2 of "Song of
   Myself" between indoor and outdoor experience?
3. How does Whitman's diction help establish a mood of exploration
   and wonder in "There Was a Child Went Forth?" What particular
   words increase this effect? What words and phrases strike us as
   stilted or pretentious?
4. What picture of family life is presented in "There Was a Child
   Went Forth?" Does the description of the father seem appropriate

for today? What is thematically effective about Whitman's use of lists in this poem?

5. Characterize the tone of "To the Garden the World." Who is speaking? Does Whitman's use of this myth have an emotional impact on you or does it seem a mere literary device? Explain.

6. Is the feminine figure in "A Woman Waits for Me" real or symbolic? What attitude towards procreation and offspring does Whitman express in the final stanza?

7. "Spontaneous Me" was originally entitled "Bunch Poem" (after its final image). Which title do you prefer?

JOHN DOS PASSOS

JOHN DOS PASSOS (1896–1970) is best known for his epic trilogy, *U.S.A.*, composed of *The 42nd Parallel* (1930), *1919* (1932), and *The Big Money* (1936). The trilogy presents a panorama of American life in the first three decades of the twentieth century; America itself is its subject and protagonist. In it Dos Passos introduces many technical innovations. In the sections that are most traditionally novelistic he traces the lives of nine major characters who lead apparently dissimilar lives but whose total experiences make a statement about the American scene. His technical brilliance displays itself primarily in three other kinds of sections—"Newsreel," "the Camera Eye," and the cameo biography. In the Newsreel he attempts, in a kind of pop art, to capture the essence of the major events of an era. The Camera Eye is an impressionistic device with which Dos Passos picks out telling details about American society. In the biographies, eight of which are reprinted here, he tries not only to analyze the personalities of major public figures in America, but also to show how corruption of the individual by wealth and power actually is emblematic of the state of the country as a whole. As the trilogy progresses, the pace of the action becomes frantic and, in the final novel, *The Big Money*, we find ourselves in a wasteland of materialism and corruption.

Dos Passos is a "naturalistic" writer, placing the responsibility for human development primarily on the forces of heredity and environment. His "average" characters are overcome by these forces; by the end of the trilogy they have proved themselves incapable of effective action and they are on the verge of despair. Dos Passos seems to be anticipating his own loss of faith in the potential of the common man (whom he loved), and thus, his own disillusionment, for a social vision such as his assumes that once problems of social injustice are resolved, there will be a release of certain human powers that the social order has been inhibiting. Not surprisingly, after the trilogy, Dos Passos never recovered his radical vision of society. He de-emphasized social concerns and, in his work, concentrated on his other major concern—the individual. Perhaps this is why his later writing is so politically conservative.

Dos Passos seems at his best in these biographical portraits, perhaps because he is writing about men who *are* capable of effective action. He is probably the most learned and best informed of twentieth-century American novelists and in these selections he uses his highly critical judgment to examine the most famous political and cultural figures in America. His direct journalistic style is a good vehicle for the ironic understatement he uses against those whom he attacks, yet his irony never hides the deep admiration he feels for those reformers who fail to achieve their visions of America. He also makes good use of a typographically-patterned page that approaches a kind of free verse, not too dissimilar from that of Allen Ginsberg. (See Section III.) The selections are divided between those men who pursued their versions of the American Dream—Carnegie, Teddy Roosevelt, Frederick Winslow Taylor, and the banking family of the House of Morgan—and those reformers who pursued a dream they had *for* America—Eugene Debs, Randolph Bourne, and Robert La Follette. In addition there is the "culture" hero, Rudolph Valentino, in a portrait loaded with irony because of the discrepancies between the real-life man and the passionate lover he portrayed on the screen.

Dos Passos' portraits are frankly biased. It is not too difficult to imagine the outrage many people may have felt reading his portrait of Teddy Roosevelt, for example. Dos Passos deliberately emphasizes the supposedly humanitarian strains in the Roosevelt family to expose it as a kind of imperialistically-oriented nobility dominated by an insatiable need for power. He glosses over T.R.'s courage in overcoming his physical handicaps because he is more interested in exposing a certain mentality that he sees as ultimately cruel and utterly depersonalizing. What is most intolerable to Dos Passos is the total lack of principle that he feels Roosevelt shares with practically every other politician. For all the mystique, for all the colorful myths surrounding him, T.R. is just another "dirty politician" to Dos Passos.

Some of the names and events in these portraits may be unfamiliar today; such details are relatively unimportant. The opportunity here is to glimpse a personalized view of American history not available in any textbook.

[FROM U.S.A.]

Lover of Mankind

Debs was a railroad man, born in a weatherboarded shack at Terre Haute.

He was one of ten children.

His father had come to America in a sailingship in '49,

an Alsatian from Colmar; not much of a moneymaker, fond of music and reading,

he gave his children a chance to finish public school and that was about all he could do.

At fifteen Gene Debs was already working as a machinist on the Indianapolis and Terre Haute Railway.

He worked as locomotive fireman,

clerked in a store

joined the local of the Brotherhood of Locomotive Firemen, was elected secretary, traveled all over the country as organizer.

He was a tall shamblefooted man, had a sort of gusty rhetoric that set on fire the railroad workers in their pineboarded halls

made them want the world he wanted,

a world brothers might own

where everybody would split even:

I am not a labor leader. I don't want you to follow me or anyone else. If you are looking for a Moses to lead you out of the capitalist wilderness you will stay right where you are. I would not lead you into this promised land if I could, because if I could lead you in, someone else would lead you out.

That was how he talked to freighthandlers and gandywalkers, to firemen and switchmen and engineers, telling them it wasn't enough to organize the railroadmen, that all workers must be organized, that all workers must be organized in the workers' cooperative commonwealth.

Locomotive fireman on many a long night's run,

under the smoke a fire burned him up, burned in gusty words that beat in pineboarded halls; he wanted his brothers to be free men.

That was what he saw in the crowd that met him at the Old Wells Street Depot when he came out of jail after the Pullman strike, those were the men that chalked up nine hundred thousand votes for him in nineteen twelve and scared the frockcoats and the tophats and diamonded hostesses at Saratoga Springs, Bar Harbor, Lake Geneva with the bogy of a socialist president.

But where were Gene Debs' brothers in nineteen eighteen when Woodrow Wilson had him locked up in Atlanta for speaking against war,
  where were the big men fond of whisky and fond of each other, gentle rambling tellers of stories over bars in small towns in the Middle West,
  quiet men who wanted a house with a porch to putter around and a fat wife to cook for them, a few drinks and cigars, a garden to dig in, cronies to chew the rag with
  and wanted to work for it
  and others to work for it;
  where were the locomotive firemen and engineers when they hustled him off to Atlanta Penitentiary?

And they brought him back to die in Terre Haute
  to sit on his porch in a rocker with a cigar in his mouth,
  beside him American Beauty roses his wife fixed in a bowl;
  and the people of Terre Haute and the people in Indiana and the people of the Middle West were fond of him and afraid of him and thought of him as an old kindly uncle who loved them, and wanted to be with him and to have him give them candy,
  but they were afraid of him as if he had contracted a social disease, syphilis or leprosy, and thought it was too bad,
  but on account of the flag
  and prosperity
  and making the world safe for democracy,
  they were afraid to be with him,
  or to think much about him for fear they might believe him;
  for he said:
  While there is a lower class I am of it, while there is a criminal class I am of it, while there is a soul in prison I am not free.

Prince of Peace

Andrew Carnegie
was born in Dunfermline in Scotland,
came over to the States in an immigrant
ship worked as bobbinboy in a textile factory

fired boilers
clerked in a bobbin factory at $2.50 a week
ran round Philadelphia with telegrams as a Western Union messenger
learned the Morse code was telegraph operator on the Pennsy lines
was a military telegraph operator in the Civil War and

always saved his pay;
whenever he had a dollar he invested it.
Andrew Carnegie started out buying Adams Express and Pullman stock
when they were in a slump;
he had confidence in railroads,
he had confidence in communications,
he had confidence in transportation,
he believed in iron.
Andrew Carnegie believed in iron, built bridges Bessemer plants blast
furnaces rolling mills;
Andrew Carnegie believed in oil;
Andrew Carnegie believed in steel;
always saved his money
whenever he had a million dollars he invested it.
Andrew Carnegie became the richest man in the world

and died.
Bessemer Duquesne Rankin Pittsburgh Bethlehem Gary
Andrew Carnegie gave millions for peace
and libraries and scientific institutes and endowments and thrift
whenever he made a billion dollars he endowed an institution to pro-
mote universal peace
always
except in time of war.

Fighting Bob

La Follette was born in the town limits of Primrose; he worked on a
farm in Dane County, Wisconsin, until he was nineteen.
At the university of Wisconsin he worked his way through. He wanted
to be an actor, studied elocution and Robert Ingersoll and Shakespeare
and Burke;
(who will ever explain the influence of Shakespeare in the last century,
Marc Antony over Caesar's bier, Othello to the Venetian Senate and
Polonius, everywhere Polonius?)
riding home in a buggy after commencement he was Booth and
Wilkes writing the Junius papers and Daniel Webster and Ingersoll de-

fying God and the togaed great grave and incorruptible as statues magnificently spouting through the capitoline centuries;

he was the star debater in his class,
and won an interstate debate with an oration on the character of Iago.

He went to work in a law office and ran for district attorney. His schoolfriends canvassed the county riding round evenings. He bucked the machine and won the election.

It was the revolt of the young man against the state republican machine and Boss Keyes the postmaster in Madison who ran the county was so surprised he about fell out of his chair.

That gave La Follette a salary to marry on. He was twentyfive years old.

Four years later he ran for congress; the university was with him again; he was the youngsters' candidate. When he was elected he was the youngest representative in the house

He was introduced round Washington by Philetus Sawyer the Wisconsin lumber king who was used to stacking and selling politicians the way he stacked and sold cordwood.

He was a Republican and he'd bucked the machine. Now they thought they had him. No man could stay honest in Washington.

Booth played Shakespeare in Baltimore that winter. Booth never would go to Washington on account of the bitter memory of his brother. Bob La Follette and his wife went to every performance.

In the parlor of the Plankinton Hotel in Milwaukee during the state fair, Boss Sawyer the lumber king tried to bribe him to influence his brother-in-law who was presiding judge over the prosecution of the Republican state treasurer;

Bob La Follette walked out of the hotel in a white rage. From that time it was war without quarter with the Republican machine in Wisconsin until he was elected governor and wrecked the Republican machine;

this was the tenyears war that left Wisconsin the model state where the voters, orderloving Germans and Finns, Scandinavians fond of their own opinion, learned to use the new leverage, direct primaries, referendum and recall.

La Follette taxed the railroads

John C. Payne said to a group of politicians in the lobby of the Ebbitt House in Washington "La Follette's a damn fool if he thinks he can buck a railroad with five thousand miles of continuous track, he'll find he's mistaken . . . We'll take care of him when the times comes."

But when the time came the farmers of Wisconsin and the young
lawyers and doctors and businessmen just out of school
   took care of him
   and elected him governor three times
   and then to the United States Senate,

where he worked all his life making long speeches full of statistics,
struggling to save democratic government, to make a farmers' and small
businessmen's commonwealth, lonely with his back to the wall, fighting
corruption and big business and high finance and trusts and combinations
of combinations and the miasmic lethargy of Washington.

He was one of "the little group of wilful men expressing no opinion
but their own"
   who stood out against Woodrow Wilson's armed ship bill that made
war with Germany certain; they called it a filibuster but it was six men
with nerve straining to hold back a crazy steamroller with their bare
hands;
   the press pumped hatred into its readers against La Follette,
   the traitor,
   they burned him in effigy in Illinois;
   in Wheeling they refused to let him speak.

In nineteen twentyfour La Follette ran for president and without
money or political machine rolled up four and a half million votes
   but he was a sick man, incessant work and the breathed out air of
committee rooms and legislative chambers choked him
   and the dirty smell of politicians,
   and he died,
   an orator haranguing from the capitol of a lost republic;
   but we will remember
   how he sat firm in March nineteen seventeen while Woodrow Wilson
was being inaugurated for the second time, and for three days held the
vast machine at deadlock. They wouldn't let him speak; the galleries
glared hatred at him; the senate was a lynching party,
   a stumpy man with a lined face, one leg stuck out in the aisle and his
arms folded and a chewed cigar in the corner of his mouth
   and an undelivered speech on his desk,
   a wilful man expressing no opinion but his own.

Randolph Bourne

Randolph Bourne
came as an inhabitant of this earth
without the pleasure of choosing his dwelling or his career.
He was a hunchback, grandson of a congregational minister, born in
1886 in Bloomfield, New Jersey; there he attended grammarschool and
highschool.
At the age of seventeen he went to work as secretary to a Morristown
businessman.
He worked his way through Columbia working in a pianola record
factory in Newark, working as proofreader, pianotuner, accompanist in
a vocal studio in Carnegie Hall.
At Columbia he studied with John Dewey,
got a travelling fellowship that took him to England Paris Rome
Berlin Copenhagen,
wrote a book on the Gary schools.
In Europe he heard music, a great deal of Wagner and Scriabine
and bought himself a black cape.

This little sparrowlike man,
tiny twisted bit of flesh in a black cape,
always in pain and ailing,
put a pebble in his sling
and hit Goliath square in the forehead with it.

War, he wrote, is the health of the state.

Half musician, half educational theorist (weak health and being poor
and twisted in body and on bad terms with his people hadn't spoiled the
world for Randolph Bourne; he was a happy man, loved die Meistersinger
and playing Bach with his long hands that stretched so easily over the
keys and pretty girls and good food and evenings of talk. When he was
dying of pneumonia a friend brought him an eggnog; Look at the yellow,
it's beautiful, he kept saying as his life ebbed into delirium and fever.
He was a happy man.) Bourne seized with feverish intensity on the ideas
then going around at Columbia, he picked rosy glasses out of the turgid
jumble of John Dewey's teaching through which he saw clear and sharp
the shining capitol of reformed democracy,
Wilson's New Freedom;
but he was too good a mathematician; he had to work the equations
out;

with the result

that in the crazy spring of 1917 he began to get unpopular where his bread was buttered at *The New Republic;*

for *New Freedom* read *Conscription,* for *Democracy,* *Win the War,* for *Reform, Safeguard the Morgan Loans*

for Progress Civilization Education Service,

Buy a Liberty Bond,

Straff the Hun,

Jail the Objectors.

He resigned from *The New Republic;* only *The Seven Arts* had the nerve to publish his articles against the war. The backers of *The Seven Arts* took their money elsewhere; friends didn't like to be seen with Bourne, his father wrote him begging him not to disgrace the family name. The rainbowtinted future of reformed democracy went pop like a pricked soapbubble.

The liberals scurried to Washington;

some of his friends plead with him to climb up on Schoolmaster Wilson's sharabang; the war was great fought from the swivel chairs of Mr. Creel's bureau in Washington.

He was cartooned, shadowed by the espionage service and the counterespionage service; taking a walk with two girl friends at Wood's Hole he was arrested, a trunk full of manuscript and letters was stolen from him in Connecticut. (Force to the utmost, thundered Schoolmaster Wilson)

He didn't live to see the big circus of the Peace of Versailles or the purplish normalcy of the Ohio Gang.

Six weeks after the armistice he died planning an essay on the foundations of future radicalism in America.

If any man has a ghost

Bourne has a ghost,

a tiny twisted unscared ghost in a black cloak

hopping along the grimy old brick and brownstone streets still left in downtown New York,

crying out in a shrill soundless giggle:

War is the health of the state.

The Happy Warrior

The Roosevelts had lived for seven righteous generations on Manhattan Island; they owned a big brick house on 20th Street, an estate up at Dobbs Ferry, lots in the city, a pew in the Dutch Reformed

Church, interests, stocks and bonds, they felt Manhattan was theirs, they felt America was theirs. Their son,

Theodore,

was a sickly youngster, suffered from asthma, was very nearsighted; his hands and feet were so small it was hard for him to learn to box; his arms were very short;

his father was something of a humanitarian, gave Christmas dinners to newsboys, deplored conditions, slums, the East Side, Hell's Kitchen.

Young Theodore had ponies, was encouraged to walk in the woods, to go camping, was instructed in boxing and fencing (an American gentleman should know how to defend himself), taught Bible Class, did mission work (an American gentleman should do his best to uplift those not so fortunately situated);

righteousness was his by birth;

he had a passion for nature study, for reading about birds and wild animals, for going hunting; he got to be a good shot in spite of his glasses, a good walker in spite of his tiny feet and short legs, a fair horseman, an aggressive scrapper in spite of his short reach, a crack politician in spite of being the son of one of the owning Dutch families of New York.

In 1876 he went up to Cambridge to study at Harvard, a wealthy talkative erratic young man with sidewhiskers and definite ideas about everything under the sun,

at Harvard he drove around in a dogcart, collected stuffed birds, mounted specimens he'd shot on his trips in the Adirondacks; in spite of not drinking and being somewhat of a christer, having odd ideas about reform and remedying abuses, he made Porcellian and the Dickey and the clubs that were his right as the son of one of the owning Dutch families of New York.

He told his friends he was going to devote his life to social service: *I wish to preach not the doctrine of ignoble ease, but the doctrine of the strenuous life, the life of toil and effort, of labor and strife.*

From the time he was eleven years old he wrote copiously, filled diaries, notebooks, loose leaves with a big impulsive scrawl about everything he did and thought and said;

naturally he studied law.

He married young and went to Switzerland to climb the Matterhorn; his first wife's early death broke him all up. He went out to the badlands of western Dakota to become a rancher on the Little Missouri River;

when he came back to Manhattan he was Teddy, the straight shooter from the west, the elkhunter, the man in the Stetson hat, who'd roped steers, fought a grizzly hand to hand, acted as Deputy Sheriff,

(a Roosevelt has a duty to his country; the duty of a Roosevelt is to uplift those not so fortunately situated, those who have come more recently to our shores)

in the west, Deputy Sheriff Roosevelt felt the white man's burden, helped to arrest malefactors, bad men; service was bully.

All this time he'd been writing, filling the magazines with stories of his hunts and adventures, filling political meetings with his opinions, his denunciations, his pat phrases: Strenuous Life, Realizable Ideals, Just Government, *when men fear work or fear righteous war, when women fear motherhood, they tremble on the brink of doom, and well it is that they should vanish from the earth, where they are fit subjects for the scorn of all men and women who are themselves strong and brave and highminded.*

T.R. married a wealthy woman and righteously raised a family at Sagamore Hill.

He served a term in the New York Legislature, was appointed by Grover Cleveland to the unremunerative job of Commissioner for Civil Service Reform,

was Reform Police Commissioner of New York, pursued malefactors, stoutly maintained that white was white and black was black,

wrote the Naval History of the War of 1812,

was appointed Assistant Secretary of the Navy,

and when the *Maine* blew up resigned to lead the Rough Riders, Lieutenant-Colonel.

This was the Rubicon, the Fight, the Old Glory, the Just Cause. The American public was not kept in ignorance of the Colonel's bravery when the bullets sang, how he charged without his men up San Juan Hill and had to go back to fetch them, how he shot a running Spaniard in the tail.

It was too bad that the regulars had gotten up San Juan Hill first from the other side, that there was no need to get up San Juan Hill at all. Santiago was surrendered. It was a successful campaign. T.R. charged up San Juan Hill into the governorship of the Empire State;

but after the fighting, volunteers warcorrespondents magazinewriters began to want to go home;

it wasn't bully huddling under puptents in the tropical rain or scorching in the morning sun of the seared Cuban hills with malaria mowing them down and dysentery and always yellowjack to be afraid of.

T.R. got up a round robin to the President and asked for the amateur warriors to be sent home and leave the dirtywork to the regulars

who were digging trenches and shovelling crap and fighting malaria and dysentery and yellowjack

to make Cuba cosy for the Sugar Trust

and the National City Bank.

When he landed at home, one of his first interviews was with Lemuel Quigg, emissary of Boss Platt who had the votes of upstate New York sewed into the lining of his vest;

he saw Boss Platt too, but he forgot about that afterwards. Things were bully. He wrote a life of Oliver Cromwell whom people said he resembled. As Governor he doublecrossed the Platt machine (a righteous man may have a short memory); Boss Platt thought he'd shelved him by nominating him for the Vice-Presidency in 1900;

Czolgocz made him president.

T.R. drove like a fiend in a buckboard over the muddy roads through the driving rain from Mt. Marcy in the Adirondacks to catch the train to Buffalo where McKinley was dying.

As President
he moved Sagamore Hill, the healthy happy normal American home, to the White House, took foreign diplomats and fat armyofficers out walking in Rock Creek Park where he led them a terrible dance through brambles, hopping across the creek on steppingstones, wading the fords, scrambling up the shaly banks,

and shook the Big Stick at malefactors of great wealth.

Things were bully.

He engineered the Panama revolution under the shadow of which took place the famous hocuspocus of juggling the old and new canal companies by which forty million dollars vanished into the pockets of the international bankers,

but Old Glory floated over the Canal Zone
and the canal was cut through.

He busted a few trusts,

had Booker Washington to lunch at the White House,

and urged the conservation of wild life.

He got the Nobel Peace Prize for patching up the Peace of Portsmouth that ended the Russo-Japanese war,

and sent the Atlantic Fleet around the world for everybody to see that America was a firstclass power. He left the presidency to Taft after his second term leaving to that elephantine lawyer the congenial task of pouring judicial oil on the hurt feelings of the moneymasters

and went to Africa to hunt big game.

Big game hunting was bully.

Every time a lion or an elephant went crashing down into the jungle underbrush, under the impact of a wellplaced mushroom bullet

the papers lit up with headlines;

when he talked with the Kaiser on horseback

the world was not ignorant of what he said, or when he lectured the Nationalists at Cairo telling them that this was a white man's world.

He went to Brazil where he travelled through the Matto Grosso in a dugout over waters infested with the tiny maneating fish, the piranha, shot tapirs,
jaguars,
specimens of the whitelipped peccary.
He ran the rapids of the River of Doubt
down to the Amazon frontiers where he arrived sick, an infected abscess in his leg, stretched out under an awning in a dugout with a tame trumpeterbird beside him.

Back in the States he fought his last fight when he came out for the republican nomination in 1912 a progressive, champion of the Square Deal, crusader for the Plain People; the Bull Moose bolted out from under the Taft steamroller and formed the Progressive Party for righteousness' sake at the Chicago Colosseum while the delegates who were going to restore democratic government rocked with tears in their eyes as they sang

> On   ward Christian so   old   gers
> March   ing   as   to   war

Perhaps the River of Doubt had been too much for a man of his age; perhaps things weren't so bully any more; T.R. lost his voice during the triangular campaign. In Duluth a maniac shot him in the chest, his life was saved only by the thick bundle of manuscript of the speech he was going to deliver. T.R. delivered the speech with the bullet still in him, heard the scared applause, felt the plain people praying for his recovery but the spell was broken somehow.

The Democrats swept in, the world war drowned out the righteous voice of the Happy Warrior in the roar of exploding lyddite.

Wilson wouldn't let T.R. lead a division, this was no amateur's war (perhaps the regulars remembered the round robin at Santiago). All he could do was write magazine articles against the Huns, send his sons; Quentin was killed

It wasn't the bully amateur's world any more. Nobody knew that on armistice day, Theodore Roosevelt, happy amateur warrior with the grinning teeth, the shaking forefinger, naturalist, explorer, magazine-writer, Sundayschool teacher, cowpuncher, moralist, politician, righteous orator with a short memory, fond of denouncing liars (the Ananias Club) and having pillowfights with his children, was taken to the Roosevelt hospital gravely ill with inflammatory rheumatism.

Things weren't bully any more;

T.R. had grit;

he bore the pain, the obscurity, the sense of being forgotten as he had borne the grilling portages when he was exploring the River of Doubt, the heat, the fetid jungle mud, the infected abscess in his leg,

and died quietly in his sleep
at Sagamore Hill
on January 6, 1919
and left on the shoulders of his sons
the white man's burden.

The House of Morgan

I commit my soul into the hands of my savior, wrote John Pierpont Morgan in his will, in full confidence that having redeemed it and washed it in His most precious blood, He will present it faultless before my heavenly father, and I intreat my children to maintain and defend at all hazard and at any cost of personal sacrifice the blessed doctrine of complete atonement for sin through the blood of Jesus Christ once offered and through that alone,

and into the hands of the House of Morgan represented by his son,

he committed,

when he died in Rome in 1913,

the control of the Morgan interests in New York, Paris and London, four national banks, three trust companies, three life insurance companies, ten railroad systems, three street railway companies, an express company, the International Mercantile Marine,

power,

on the cantilever principle, through interlocking directorates

over eighteen other railroads, U.S. Steel, General Electric, American Tel and Tel, five major industries;

the interwoven cables of the Morgan Stillman Baker combination held credit up like a suspension bridge, thirteen percent of the banking resources of the world.

The first Morgan to make a pool was Joseph Morgan, a hotelkeeper in Hartford Connecticut who organized stagecoach lines and bought up Ætna Life Insurance stock in a time of panic caused by one of the big New York fires in the 1830's;

his son Junius followed in his footsteps, first in the drygoods business, and then as partner to George Peabody, a Massachusetts banker who built up an enormous underwriting and mercantile business in London and became a friend of Queen Victoria;

Junius married the daughter of John Pierpont, a Boston preacher, poet, eccentric, and abolitionist; and their eldest son,
John Pierpont Morgan
arrived in New York to make his fortune
after being trained in England, going to school at Vevey, proving himself a crack mathematician at the University of Göttingen,
a lanky morose young man of twenty,
just in time for the panic of '57.
(war and panics on the stock exchange, bankruptcies, warloans, good growing weather for the House of Morgan.)

When the guns started booming at Fort Sumter, young Morgan turned some money over reselling condemned muskets to the U.S. army and began to make himself felt in the gold room in downtown New York; there was more in trading in gold than in trading in muskets; so much for the Civil War.

During the Franco-Prussian war Junius Morgan floated a huge bond issue for the French government at Tours.

At the same time young Morgan was fighting Jay Cooke and the German-Jew bankers in Frankfort over the funding of the American war debt (he never did like the Germans or the Jews).

The panic of '75 ruined Jay Cooke and made J. Pierpont Morgan the boss croupier of Wall Street; he united with the Philadelphia Drexels and built the Drexel building where for thirty years he sat in his glassedin office, redfaced and insolent, writing at his desk, smoking great black cigars, or, if important issues were involved, playing solitaire in his inner office; he was famous for his few words, Yes or No, and for his way of suddenly blowing up in a visitor's face and for that special gesture of the arm that meant, *What do I get out of it?*

In '77 Junius Morgan retired; J. Pierpont got himself made a member of the board of directors of the New York Central railroad and launched the first *Corsair*. He liked yachting and to have pretty actresses call him Commodore.

He founded the Lying-in Hospital on Stuyvesant Square, and was fond of going into St. George's church and singing a hymn all alone in the afternoon quiet.

In the panic of '93
at no inconsiderable profit to himself
Morgan saved the U.S. Treasury; gold was draining out, the country was ruined, the farmers were howling for a silver standard, Grover Cleveland and his cabinet were walking up and down in the blue room at the White House without being able to come to a decision, in Congress they were making speeches while the gold reserves melted in the Subtreasuries; poor people were starving; Coxey's army was marching to

Washington; for a long time Grover Cleveland couldn't bring himself to call in the representative of the Wall Street moneymasters; Morgan sat in his suite at the Arlington smoking cigars and quietly playing solitaire until at last the president sent for him;

he had a plan all ready for stopping the gold hemorrhage.

After that what Morgan said went; when Carnegie sold out he built the Steel Trust.

J. Pierpont Morgan was a bullnecked irascible man with small black magpie's eyes and a growth on his nose; he let his partners work themselves to death over the detailed routine of banking, and sat in his back office smoking black cigars; when there was something to be decided he said Yes or No or just turned his back and went back to his solitaire.

Every Christmas his librarian read him Dickens' *A Christmas Carol* from the original manuscript.

He was fond of canarybirds and pekinese dogs and liked to take pretty actresses yachting. Each *Corsair* was a finer vessel than the last.

When he dined with King Edward he sat at His Majesty's right; he ate with the Kaiser tête-à-tête; he liked talking to cardinals or the pope, and never missed a conference of Episcopal bishops;

Rome was his favorite city.

He liked choice cookery and old wines and pretty women and yachting, and going over his collections, now and then picking up a jewelled snuffbox and staring at it with his magpie's eyes.

He made a collection of the autographs of the rulers of France, owned glass cases full of Babylonian tablets, seals, signets, statuettes, busts,

Gallo-Roman bronzes,

Merovingian jewels, miniatures, watches, tapestries, porcelains, cuneiform inscriptions, paintings by all the old masters, Dutch, Italian, Flemish, Spanish,

manuscripts of the gospels and the Apocalypse,

a collection of the works of Jean-Jacques Rousseau,

and the letters of Pliny the Younger.

His collectors bought anything that was expensive or rare or had the glint of empire on it, and he had it brought to him and stared hard at it with his magpie's eyes. Then it was put in a glass case.

The last year of his life he went up the Nile on a dahabiyeh and spent a long time staring at the great columns of the Temple of Karnak.

The panic of 1907 and the death of Harriman, his great opponent in railroad financing, in 1909, had left him the undisputed ruler of Wall Street, most powerful private citizen in the world;

an old man tired of the purple, suffering from gout, he had deigned to go to Washington to answer the questions of the Pujo Committee during the Money Trust Investigation: Yes, I did what seemed to me to be for the best interests of the country.

So admirably was his empire built that his death in 1913 hardly caused a ripple in the exchanges of the world: the purple descended to his son, J. P. Morgan,

who had been trained at Groton and Harvard and by associating with the British ruling class

to be a more constitutional monarch: *J. P. Morgan suggests* . . .

By 1917 the Allies had borrowed one billion, ninehundred million dollars through the House of Morgan: we went overseas for democracy and the flag;

and by the end of the Peace Conference the phrase *J. P. Morgan suggests* had compulsion over a power of seventyfour billion dollars.

J. P. Morgan is a silent man, not given to public utterances, but during the great steel strike, he wrote Gary: *Heartfelt congratulations on your stand for the open shop, with which I am, as you know, absolutely in accord. I believe American principles of liberty are deeply involved, and must win if we stand firm.*

(Wars and panics on the stock exchange,
machinegunfire and arson,
bankruptcies, warloans,
starvation, lice, cholera and typhus:
good growing weather for the House of Morgan.)

The American Plan

Frederick Winslow Taylor (they called him Speedy Taylor in the shop) was born in Germantown, Pennsylvania, the year of Buchanan's election. His father was a lawyer, his mother came from a family of New Bedford whalers; she was a great reader of Emerson, belonged to the Unitarian Church and the Browning Society. She was a fervent abolitionist and believed in democratic manners; she was a housekeeper of the old school, kept everybody busy from dawn till dark. She laid down the rules of conduct:

selfrespect, selfreliance, selfcontrol
and a cold long head for figures.

But she wanted her children to appreciate the finer things so she took them abroad for three years on the Continent, showed them cathedrals, grand opera, Roman pediments, the old masters under their brown varnish in their great frames of tarnished gilt.

Later Fred Taylor was impatient of these wasted years, stamped out of the room when people talked about the finer things; he was a testy youngster, fond of practical jokes and a great hand at rigging up contraptions and devices.

At Exeter he was head of his class and captain of the ballteam, the first man to pitch overhand. (When umpires complained that overhand pitching wasn't in the rules of the game, he answered that it got results.)

As a boy he had nightmares, going to bed was horrible for him; he thought they came from sleeping on his back. He made himself a leather harness with wooden pegs that stuck into his flesh when he turned over. When he was grown he slept in a chair or in bed in a sitting position propped up with pillows. All his life he suffered from sleeplessness.

He was a crackerjack tennisplayer. In 1881, with his friend Clark, he won the National Doubles Championship. (He used a spoonshaped racket of his own design.)

At school he broke down from overwork, his eyes went back on him. The doctor suggested manual labor. So instead of going to Harvard he went into the machineshop of a small pumpmanufacturing concern, owned by a friend of the family's, to learn the trade of patternmaker and machinist. He learned to handle a lathe and to dress and cuss like a workingman.

Fred Taylor never smoked tobacco or drank liquor or used tea or coffee; he couldn't understand why his fellowmechanics wanted to go on sprees and get drunk and raise Cain Saturday nights. He lived at home, when he wasn't reading technical books he'd play parts in amateur theatricals or step up to the piano in the evening and sing a good tenor in A *Warrior Bold* or A *Spanish Cavalier*.

He served his first year's apprenticeship in the machineshop without pay; the next two years he made a dollar and a half a week, the last year two dollars.

Pennsylvania was getting rich off iron and coal. When he was twenty-two, Fred Taylor went to work at the Midvale Iron Works. At first he had to take a clerical job, but he hated that and went to work with a shovel. At last he got them to put him on a lathe. He was a good machinist, he worked ten hours a day and in the evenings followed an engineering course at Stevens. In six years he rose from machinist's helper to keeper of toolcribs to gangboss to foreman to mastermechanic in charge of repairs to chief draftsman and director of research to chief engineer of the Midvale Plant.

The early years he was a machinist with the other machinists in the shop, cussed and joked and worked with the rest of them, soldiered on the job when they did. Mustn't give the boss more than his money's worth. But when he got to be foreman he was on the management's side of the fence, *gathering in on the part of those on the management's side all the great mass of traditional knowledge which in the past has been in the heads of the workmen and in the physical skill and knack of the workman.* He couldn't stand to see an idle lathe or an idle man.

Production went to his head and thrilled his sleepless nerves like liquor or women on a Saturday night. He never loafed and he'd be damned if anybody else would. Production was an itch under his skin.

He lost his friends in the shop; they called him niggerdriver. He was a stockily built man with a temper and a short tongue.

I was a young man in years but I give you my word I was a great deal older than I am now, what with the worry, meanness and contemptibleness of the whole damn thing. It's a horrid life for any man to live not being able to look any workman in the face without seeing hostility there, and a feeling that every man around you is your virtual enemy.

That was the beginning of the Taylor System of Scientific Management.

He was impatient of explanations, he didn't care whose hide he took off in enforcing the laws he believed inherent in the industrial process.

When starting an experiment in any field question everything, question the very foundations upon which the art rests, question the simplest, the most selfevident, the most universally accepted facts; prove everything,

except the dominant Quaker Yankee (the New Bedford skippers were the greatest niggerdrivers on the whaling seas) rules of conduct. He boasted he'd never ask a workman to do anything he couldn't do.

He devised an improved steamhammer; he standardized tools and equipment, he filled the shop with college students with stopwatches and diagrams, tabulating, standardizing. *There's the right way of doing a thing and the wrong way of doing it; the right way means increased production, lower costs, higher wages, bigger profits:* the American plan.

He broke up the foreman's job into separate functions, speedbosses, gangbosses, timestudy men, orderofwork men.

The skilled mechanics were too stubborn for him, what he wanted was a plain handyman who'd do what he was told. If he was a firstclass man and did firstclass work Taylor was willing to let him have firstclass pay; that's where he began to get into trouble with the owners.

At thirtyfour he married and left Midvale and took a flyer for the big money in connection with a pulpmill started in Maine by some admirals and political friends of Grover Cleveland's;

the panic of '93 made hash of that enterprise,

so Taylor invented for himself the job of Consulting Engineer in

Management and began to build up a fortune by careful investments.

The first paper he read before the American Society of Mechanical Engineers was anything but a success, they said he was crazy. *I have found,* he wrote in 1909, *that any improvement is not only opposed but aggressively and bitterly opposed by the majority of men.*

He was called in by Bethlehem Steel. It was in Bethlehem he made his famous experiments with handling pigiron; he taught a Dutchman named Schmidt to handle fortyseven tons instead of twelve and a half tons of pigiron a day and got Schmidt to admit he was as good as ever at the end of the day.

He was a crank about shovels, every job had to have a shovel of the right weight and size for that job alone; every job had to have a man of the right weight and size for that job alone; but when he began to pay his men in proportion to the increased efficiency of their work,

the owners who were a lot of greedy smalleyed Dutchmen began to raise Hail Columbia; when Schwab bought Bethlehem Steel in 1901

Fred Taylor

inventor of efficiency

who had doubled the production of the stampingmill by speeding up the main lines of shafting from ninetysix to twohundred and twentyfive revolutions a minute

was unceremoniously fired.

After that Fred Taylor always said he couldn't afford to work for money.

He took to playing golf (using golfclubs of his own design), doping out methods for transplanting huge boxtrees into the garden of his home.

At Boxly in Germantown he kept open house for engineers, factorymanagers, industrialists;

he wrote papers,

lectured in colleges,

appeared before a congressional committee,

everywhere preached the virtues of scientific management and the Barth slide rule, the cutting down of waste and idleness, the substitution for skilled mechanics of the plain handyman (like Schmidt the pigiron handler) who'd move as he was told

and work by the piece:

production;

more steel rails more bicycles more spools of thread more armorplate for battleships more bedpans more barbedwire more needles more lightningrods more ballbearings more dollarbills;

(the old Quaker families of Germantown were growing rich, the Pennsylvania millionaires were breeding billonaires out of iron and coal)

production would make every firstclass American rich who was willing to work at piecework and not drink or raise Cain or think or stand mooning at his lathe.

Thrifty Schmidt the pigiron handler can invest his money and get to be an owner like Schwab and the rest of the greedy smalleyed Dutchmen and cultivate a taste for Bach and have hundredyearold boxtrees in his garden at Bethlehem or Germantown or Chestnut Hill,

and lay down the rules of conduct;

the American plan.

But Fred Taylor never saw the working of the American plan;

in 1915 he went to the hospital in Philadelphia suffering from a breakdown.

Pneumonia developed; the nightnurse heard him winding his watch;

on the morning of his fiftyninth birthday, when the nurse went into his room to look at him at fourthirty,

he was dead with his watch in his hand.

Adagio Dancer

The nineteenyearold son of a veterinary in Castellaneta in the south of Italy was shipped off to America like a lot of other unmanageable young Italians when his parents gave up trying to handle him, to sink or swim and maybe send a few lire home by international postal moneyorder. The family was through with him. But Rodolfo Guglielmi wanted to make good.

He got a job as assistant gardener in Central Park but that kind of work was the last thing he wanted to do; he wanted to make good in the brightlights; money burned his pockets.

He hung around cabarets doing odd jobs, sweeping out for the waiters, washing cars; he was lazy handsome wellbuilt slender goodtempered and vain; he was a born tangodancer.

Lovehungry women thought he was a darling. He began to get engagements dancing the tango in ballrooms and cabarets; he teamed up with a girl named Jean Acker on a vaudeville tour and took the name of Rudolph Valentino.

Stranded on the Coast he headed for Hollywood, worked for a long time as an extra for five dollars a day; directors began to notice he photographed well.

He got his chance in *The Four Horsemen*

and became the gigolo of every woman's dreams.

Valentino spent his life in the colorless glare of klieg lights, in stucco villas obstructed with bricabrac oriental rugs tigerskins, in the bridalsuites of hotels, in silk bathrobes in private cars.

He was always getting into limousines or getting out of limousines,
or patting the necks of fine horses.
Wherever he went the sirens of the motorcyclecops screeched ahead
of him
flashlights flared,
the streets were jumbled with hysterical faces, waving hands, crazy
eyes; they stuck out their autographbooks, yanked his buttons off, cut a
tail off his admirablytailored dress suit; they stole his hat and pulled at
his necktie; his valets removed young women from under his bed; all
night in nightclubs and cabarets actresses leching for stardom made
sheepseyes at him under their mascaraed lashes.
He wanted to make good under the glare of the milliondollar search-
lights
of El Dorado:
the Sheik, the Son of the Sheik;
personal appearances.

He married his old vaudeville partner, divorced her, married the
adopted daughter of a millionaire, went into lawsuits with the producers
who were debasing the art of the screen, spent a million dollars on one
European trip;
he wanted to make good in the brightlights.
When the Chicago *Tribune* called him a pink powderpuff
and everybody started wagging their heads over a slavebracelet he wore
that he said his wife had given him and his taste for mushy verse of which
he published a small volume called *Daydreams* and the whispers grew
about the testimony in his divorce case that he and his first wife had
never slept together,
it broke his heart.
He tried to challenge the Chicago *Tribune* to a duel;
he wanted to make good
in heman twofisted broncobusting pokerplaying stockjuggling America.
(He was a fair boxer and had a good seat on a horse, he loved the
desert like the sheik and was tanned from the sun of Palm Springs.)
He broke down in his suite in the Hotel Ambassador in New York:
gastric ulcer.

When the doctors cut into his elegantlymolded body they found that
peritonitis had begun; the abdominal cavity contained a large amount of
fluid and food particles; the viscera were coated with a greenishgrey film;
a round hole a centimeter in diameter was seen in the anterior wall of
the stomach; the tissue of the stomach for one and onehalf centimeters
immediately surrounding the perforation was necrotic. The appendix was
inflamed and twisted against the small intestine.

When he came to from the ether the first thing he said was, "Well, did I behave like a pink powderpuff?"

His expensivelymassaged actor's body fought peritonitis for six days.

The switchboard at the hospital was swamped with calls, all the corridors were piled with flowers, crowds filled the street outside, filmstars who claimed they were his betrothed entrained for New York.

Late in the afternoon a limousine drew up at the hospital door (where the grimyfingered newspapermen and photographers stood around bored tired hoteyed smoking too many cigarettes making trips to the nearest speak exchanging wisecracks and deep dope waiting for him to die in time to make the evening papers) *and a woman, who said she was a maid employed by a dancer who was Valentino's first wife, alighted. She delivered to an attendant an envelope addressed to the filmstar and inscribed From Jean, and a package. The package contained a white counterpane with lace ruffles and the word Rudy embroidered in the four corners. This was accompanied by a pillowcover to match over a blue silk scented cushion.*

Rudolph Valentino was only thirtyone when he died.

His managers planned to make a big thing of his highlypublicized funeral but the people in the streets were too crazy.

While he lay in state in a casket covered with a cloth of gold, tens of thousands of men, women, and children packed the streets outside. Hundreds were trampled, had their feet hurt by policehorses. In the muggy rain the cops lost control. Jammed masses stampeded under the clubs and the rearing hoofs of the horses. The funeral chapel was gutted, men and women fought over a flower, a piece of wallpaper, a piece of the broken plateglass window. Showwindows were burst in. Parked cars were overturned and smashed. When finally the mounted police after repeated charges beat the crowd off Broadway, where traffic was tied up for two hours, they picked up twentyeight separate shoes, a truckload of umbrellas, papers, hats, tornoff sleeves. All the ambulances in that part of the city were busy carting off women who'd fainted, girls who'd been stepped on. Epileptics threw fits. Cops collected little groups of abandoned children.

The fascisti sent a guard of honor and the antifascists drove them off. More rioting, cracked skulls, trampled feet. When the public was barred from the undertaking parlors hundreds of women groggy with headlines got in to view the poor body

claiming to be exdancingpartners, old playmates, relatives from the old country, filmstars; every few minutes a girl fainted in front of the bier and was revived by the newspapermen who put down her name and address and claim to notice in the public prints. Frank E. Campbell's undertakers and pallbearers, dignified wearers of black broadcloth and tackersup of crape, were on the verge of a nervous breakdown. Even the boss had his fill of publicity that time.

It was two days before the cops could clear the streets enough to let the flowerpieces from Hollywood be brought in and described in the evening papers.

The church service was more of a success. The policecommissioner barred the public for four blocks round.

Many notables attended.

America's Sweetheart sobbing bitterly in a small black straw with a black band and a black bow behind, in black georgette over black with a white lace collar and white lace cuffs followed the coffin that was

covered by a blanket of pink roses

sent by a filmstar who appeared at the funeral heavily veiled and swooned and had to be taken back to her suite at the Hotel Ambassador after she had shown the reporters a message allegedly written by one of the doctors alleging that Rudolph Valentino had spoken of her at the end

as his bridetobe.

A young woman committed suicide in London.

Relatives arriving from Europe were met by police reserves and Italian flags draped with crape. Exchamp Jim Jeffries said, "Well, he made good." The champion himself allowed himself to be quoted that the boy was fond of boxing and a great admirer of the champion.

The funeral train left for Hollywood.

In Chicago a few more people were hurt trying to see the coffin, but only made the inside pages.

The funeral train arrived in Hollywood on page 23 of the New York *Times*.

QUESTIONS

1. In what ways does Dos Passos see La Follette as different from typical American politicians?
2. "He was a happy man." Does Dos Passos give us any evidence to support this statement about Randolph Bourne?
3. What myths about Teddy Roosevelt does Dos Passos try to devastate? What is your reaction to this version of his life? What has Dos Passos deliberately emphasized? De-emphasized?
4. Does Dos Passos' irony work effectively in his portraits of Teddy

Roosevelt and the Morgans? What are some specific instances of it?

5. Is it accurate, in the light of our current industrial system, to call Taylor's industrial reform "The American Plan"? What personality "type" does Taylor seem to possess? How does Dos Passos call our attention to the particular excesses of this type?

6. How does the rise of Valentino parallel or contrast with the careers of other Americans described in this section? What kind of "masculine" image does Valentino try to live up to? For what was he famous on the screen?

F. SCOTT FITZGERALD

F. SCOTT FITZGERALD (1896–1940) embodied in his own life-time many American myths and dreams. His parents aspired to send him away from his native St. Paul, Minnesota, to school in the afflu-ent East, and he went to boarding school in New Jersey and then to Princeton (1913–17). After leaving college without a degree he en-tered the Army and, while stationed in the South, met his wife, Zelda Sayre. After the war he quit his job in New York to return to St. Paul to write *This Side of Paradise* (1920), a novel about his college experiences. His success allowed him and Zelda to pursue a life of extravagance and glitter, although he was continually in debt and had to keep writing to sustain the ten-year-long party that was the Roaring Twenties. In fact, he and Zelda became symbols of the Jazz Age, a nickname Fitzgerald himself gave to the period. Even-tually he became a heavy drinker and his wife had to be institution-alized after a mental breakdown.

"Winter Dreams," written in 1922, has none of the social ex-travagance and wild parties of *The Great Gatsby* (1925). Dexter Green's story embodies the American myth of the self-made man who succeeds not only because of his intelligence and industrious-ness, but also because he knows the right "forms." Yet, unlike many businessmen, living out this myth is not enough to satisfy him; he has other "dreams." He tries to stay in touch with the repressed romantic side of himself by indulging in fantasies about Judy Jones. To understand Fitzgerald we must understand the complex nature of the dreams that Judy Jones embodies for Dexter.

Intellectually Fitzgerald, like Whitman, disapproves of the Ameri-can emphasis on materialism and social pretensions. But unlike Whitman, Fitzgerald invests money and social standing with ro-mance since, for him, these values in our culture have become ingrained in feelings and unconscious beliefs. For Fitzgerald great wealth and status mystically confer upon their possessor a special glamor and romance. He felt that the very rich were different, that they had exotic and romantic qualities. As with Dexter's attitude toward Judy Jones, Fitzgerald felt that they could do almost no wrong, that they were beyond the common concepts of morality. Thus, in a sense, they were both "better" and "worse" than the average man.

Fitzgerald, sharing this common "romantic" sense about the rich with his character, Dexter, portrays the young man with a warm sympathy as well as an artistic, intellectual detachment. In fact, one fascination of this story is that Dexter, like Fitzgerald (but unlike Gatsby in his pursuit of Daisy Buchanan), is totally *conscious* of his ambivalence towards Judy. But he cannot put her aside—he has a need to pursue a form of romance that he knows to be an illusion. In fact his attraction to her is almost asexual—"he had wanted Judy Jones ever since he was a proud, desirous little boy"—and she represents everything that deprived little boy could never and still cannot have. Her image resides deep inside him, taunting him with dreams and longings he has chosen to forsake in his everyday life, where his urge to succeed dominates and corrupts his romantic side.

Winter Dreams

Some of the caddies were poor as sin and lived in one-room houses with a neurasthenic cow in the front yard, but Dexter Green's father owned the second best grocery-store in Black Bear—the best one was "The Hub," patronized by the wealthy people from Sherry Island—and Dexter caddied only for pocket-money.

In the fall when the days became crisp and gray, and the long Minnesota winter shut down like the white lid of a box, Dexter's skis moved over the snow that hid the fairways of the golf course. At these times the country gave him a feeling of profound melancholy—it offended him that the links should lie in enforced fallowness, haunted by ragged sparrows for the long season. It was dreary, too, that on the tees where the gay colors fluttered in summer there were now only the desolate sand-boxes knee-deep in crusted ice. When he crossed the hills the wind blew cold as misery, and if the sun was out he tramped with his eyes squinted up against the hard dimensionless glare.

In April the winter ceased abruptly. The snow ran down into Black Bear Lake scarcely tarrying for the early golfers to brave the season with red and black balls. Without elation, without an interval of moist glory, the cold was gone.

Dexter knew that there was something dismal about this Northern spring, just as he knew there was something gorgeous about the fall. Fall made him clinch his hands and tremble and repeat idiotic sentences to himself, and make brisk abrupt gestures of command to imaginary audiences and armies. October filled him with hope which November raised to a sort of ecstatic triumph, and in this mood the fleeting brilliant impressions of the summer at Sherry Island were ready grist to his mill. He became a golf champion and defeated Mr. T. A. Hedrick in a marvellous match played a hundred times over the fairways of his imagination, a match each detail of which he changed about untiringly—sometimes he won with almost laughable ease, sometimes he came up magnificently from behind. Again, stepping from a Pierce-Arrow automobile, like Mr. Mortimer Jones, he strolled frigidly into the lounge of the Sherry Island Golf Club—or perhaps, surrounded by an admiring crowd, he gave an exhibition of fancy diving from the spring-board of the club raft. . . . Among those who watched him in open-mouthed wonder was Mr. Mortimer Jones.

And one day it came to pass that Mr. Jones—himself and not his ghost—came up to Dexter with tears in his eyes and said that Dexter was the — — best caddy in the club, and wouldn't he decide not to quit if Mr. Jones made it worth his while, because every other — — caddy in the club lost one ball a hole for him—regularly——

"No, sir," said Dexter decisively, "I don't want to caddy any more." Then, after a pause: "I'm too old."

"You're not more than fourteen. Why the devil did you decide just this morning that you wanted to quit? You promised that next week you'd go over to the State tournament with me."

"I decided I was too old."

Dexter handed in his "A Class" badge, collected what money was due him from the caddy master, and walked home to Black Bear Village.

"The best — — caddy I ever saw," shouted Mr. Mortimer Jones over a drink that afternoon. "Never lost a ball! Willing! Intelligent! Quiet! Honest! Grateful!"

The little girl who had done this was eleven—beautifully ugly as little girls are apt to be who are destined after a few years to be inexpressibly lovely and bring no end of misery to a great number of men. The spark, however, was perceptible. There was a general ungodliness in the way her lips twisted down at the corners when she smiled, and in the—Heaven help us!—in the almost passionate quality of her eyes. Vitality is born early in such women. It was utterly in evidence now, shining through her thin frame in a sort of glow.

She had come eagerly out on to the course at nine o'clock with a white linen nurse and five small new golf-clubs in a white canvas bag which the nurse was carrying. When Dexter first saw her she was standing by the caddy house, rather ill at ease and trying to conceal the fact by engaging her nurse in an obviously unnatural conversation graced by startling and irrelevant grimaces from herself.

"Well, it's certainly a nice day, Hilda," Dexter heard her say. She drew down the corners of her mouth, smiled, and glanced furtively around, her eyes in transit falling for an instant on Dexter.

Then to the nurse:

"Well, I guess there aren't very many people out here this morning, are there?"

The smile again—radiant, blatantly artificial—convincing.

"I don't know what we're supposed to do now," said the nurse, looking nowhere in particular.

"Oh, that's all right. I'll fix it up."

Dexter stood perfectly still, his mouth slightly ajar. He knew that if he moved forward a step his stare would be in her line of vision—if he moved backward he would lose his full view of her face. For a moment he had not realized how young she was. Now he remembered having seen her several times the year before—in bloomers.

Suddenly, involuntarily, he laughed, a short abrupt laugh—then, startled by himself, he turned and began to walk quickly away.

"Boy!"

Dexter stopped.

"Boy——"

Beyond question he was addressed. Not only that, but he was treated to that absurd smile, that preposterous smile—the memory of which at least a dozen men were to carry into middle age.

"Boy, do you know where the golf teacher is?"

"He's giving a lesson."

"Well, do you know where the caddy-master is?"

"He isn't here yet this morning."

"Oh." For a moment this baffled her. She stood alternately on her right and left foot.

"We'd like to get a caddy," said the nurse. "Mrs. Mortimer Jones sent us out to play golf, and we don't know how without we get a caddy."

Here she was stopped by an ominous glance from Miss Jones, followed immediately by the smile.

"There aren't any caddies here except me," said Dexter to the nurse, "and I got to stay here in charge until the caddy-master gets here."

"Oh."

Miss Jones and her retinue now withdrew, and at a proper distance from Dexter became involved in a heated conversation, which was concluded by Miss Jones taking one of the clubs and hitting it on the ground with violence. For further emphasis she raised it again and was about to bring it down smartly upon the nurse's bosom, when the nurse seized the club and twisted it from her hands.

"You damn little mean old *thing!*" cried Miss Jones wildly.

Another argument ensued. Realizing that the elements of the comedy were implied in the scene, Dexter several times began to laugh, but each time restrained the laugh before it reached audibility. He could not resist the monstrous conviction that the little girl was justified in beating the nurse.

The situation was resolved by the fortuitous appearance of the caddy-master, who was appealed to immediately by the nurse.

"Miss Jones is to have a little caddy, and this one says he can't go."

"Mr. McKenna said I was to wait here till you came," said Dexter quickly.

"Well, he's here now." Miss Jones smiled cheerfully at the caddy-master. Then she dropped her bag and set off at a haughty mince toward the first tee.

"Well?" The caddy-master turned to Dexter. "What you standing there like a dummy for? Go pick up the young lady's clubs."

"I don't think I'll go out to-day," said Dexter.

"You don't——"

"I think I'll quit."

The enormity of his decision frightened him. He was a favorite caddy, and the thirty dollars a month he earned through the summer were not to be made elsewhere around the lake. But he had received a strong emotional shock, and his perturbation required a violent and immediate outlet.

It is not so simple as that, either. As so frequently would be the case in the future, Dexter was unconsciously dictated to by his winter dreams.

2

Now, of course, the quality and the seasonability of these winter dreams varied, but the stuff of them remained. They persuaded Dexter several years later to pass up a business course at the State university—his father, prospering now, would have paid his way—for the precarious advantage of attending an older and more famous university in the East, where he was bothered by his scanty funds. But do not get the impression, because his winter dreams happened to be concerned at first with musings on the rich, that there was anything merely snobbish in the boy. He wanted not association with glittering things and glittering people—he wanted the glittering things themselves. Often he reached out for the best without knowing why he wanted it—and sometimes he ran up against the mysterious denials and prohibitions in which life indulges. It is with one of those denials and not with his career as a whole that this story deals.

He made money. It was rather amazing. After college he went to the city from which Black Bear Lake draws its wealthy patrons. When he was only twenty-three and had been there not quite two years, there were already people who liked to say: "Now *there's* a boy—" All about him rich men's sons were peddling bonds precariously, or investing patrimonies precariously, or plodding through the two dozen volumes of the "George Washington Commercial Course," but Dexter borrowed a thousand dollars on his college degree and his confident mouth, and bought a partnership in a laundry.

It was a small laundry when he went into it but Dexter made a specialty of learning how the English washed fine woollen golf-stockings without shrinking them, and within a year he was catering to the trade that wore knickerbockers. Men were insisting that their Shetland hose and sweaters go to his laundry just as they had insisted on a caddy who could find golf-balls. A little later he was doing their wives' lingerie as well—and running five branches in different parts of the city. Before he was twenty-seven he owned the largest string of laundries in his section of the country. It was then that he sold out and went to New York. But the part of his story that concerns us goes back to the days when he was making his first big success.

When he was twenty-three Mr. Hart—one of the gray-haired men who like to say "Now there's a boy"—gave him a guest card to the Sherry Island Golf Club for a week-end. So he signed his name one day on the register, and that afternoon played golf in a foursome with Mr. Hart and Mr. Sandwood and Mr. T. A. Hedrick. He did not consider it necessary to remark that he had once carried Mr. Hart's bag over this same links, and that he knew every trap and gully with his eyes shut—but he found himself glancing at the four caddies who trailed them, trying to catch a gleam or gesture that would remind him of himself, that would loosen the gap which lay between his present and his past.

It was a curious day, slashed abruptly with fleeting, familiar impressions. One minute he had the sense of being a trespasser—in the next he was impressed by the tremendous superiority he felt toward Mr. T. A. Hedrick, who was a bore and not even a good golfer any more.

Then, because of a ball Mr. Hart lost near the fifteenth green, an enormous thing happened. While they were searching the stiff grasses of the rough there was a clear call of "Fore!" from behind a hill in their rear. And as they all turned abruptly from their search a bright new ball sliced abruptly over the hill and caught Mr. T. A. Hedrick in the abdomen.

"By Gad!" cried Mr. T. A. Hedrick, "they ought to put some of these crazy women off the course. It's getting to be outrageous."

A head and a voice came up together over the hill: "Do you mind if we go through?"

"You hit me in the stomach!" declared Mr. Hedrick wildly.

"Did I?" The girl approached the group of men. "I'm sorry. I yelled 'Fore!' "

Her glance fell casually on each of the men—then scanned the fairway for her ball.

"Did I bounce into the rough?"

It was impossible to determine whether this question was ingenuous or malicious. In a moment, however, she left no doubt, for as her partner came up over the hill she called cheerfully:

"Here I am! I'd have gone on the green except that I hit something."

As she took her stance for a short mashie shot, Dexter looked at her closely. She wore a blue gingham dress, rimmed at throat and shoulders with a white edging that accentuated her tan. The quality of exaggeration, of thinness, which had made her passionate eyes and down-turning mouth absurd at eleven, was gone now. She was arrestingly beautiful. The color in her cheeks was centered like the color in a picture—it was not a "high" color, but a sort of fluctuating and feverish warmth, so shaded that it seemed at any moment it would recede and disappear. This color and the mobility of her mouth gave a continual impression of flux, of intense life, of passionate vitality—balanced only partially by the sad luxury of her eyes.

She swung her mashie impatiently and without interest, pitching the ball into a sand-pit on the other side of the green. With a quick, insincere smile and a careless "Thank you!" she went on after it.

"That Judy Jones!" remarked Mr. Hedrick on the next tee, as they waited—some moments—for her to play on ahead. "All she needs is to be turned up and spanked for six months and then to be married off to an old-fashioned cavalry captain."

"My God, she's good-looking!" said Mr. Sandwood, who was just over thirty.

"Good-looking!" cried Mr. Hedrick contemptuously, "she always looks as if she wanted to be kissed! Turning those big cow-eyes on every calf in town!"

It was doubtful if Mr. Hedrick intended a reference to the maternal instinct.

"She'd play pretty good golf if she'd try," said Mr. Sandwood.

"She has no form," said Mr. Hedrick solemnly.

"She has a nice figure," said Mr. Sandwood.

"Better thank the Lord she doesn't drive a swifter ball," said Mr. Hart, winking at Dexter.

Later in the afternoon the sun went down with a riotous swirl of gold and varying blues and scarlets, and left the dry, rustling night of Western summer. Dexter watched from the veranda of the Golf Club, watched the even overlap of the waters in the little wind, silver molasses under the harvest-moon. Then the moon held a finger to her lips and the lake became a clear pool, pale and quiet. Dexter put on his bathing-suit and swam out to the farthest raft, where he stretched dripping on the wet canvas of the springboard.

There was a fish jumping and a star shining and the lights around the lake were gleaming. Over on a dark peninsula a piano was playing the songs of last summer and of summers before that—songs from "Chin-Chin" and "The Count of Luxemburg" and "The Chocolate Soldier"— and because the sound of a piano over a stretch of water had always seemed beautiful to Dexter he lay perfectly quiet and listened.

The tune the piano was playing at that moment had been gay and new five years before when Dexter was a sophomore at college. They had played it at a prom once when he could not afford the luxury of proms, and he had stood outside the gymnasium and listened. The sound of the tune precipitated in him a sort of ecstasy and it was with that ecstasy he viewed what happened to him now. It was a mood of intense appreciation, a sense that, for once, he was magnificently attuned to life and that everything about him was radiating a brightness and a glamour he might never know again.

A low, pale oblong detached itself suddenly from the darkness of the Island, spitting forth the reverberate sound of a racing motor-boat. Two white streamers of cleft water rolled themselves out behind it and almost immediately the boat was beside him, drowning out the hot tinkle of the piano in the drone of its spray. Dexter raising himself on his arms was aware of a figure standing at the wheel, of two dark eyes regarding him over the lengthening space of water—then the boat had gone by and was sweeping in an immense and purposeless circle of spray round and round in the middle of the lake. With equal eccentricity one of the circles flattened out and headed back toward the raft.

"Who's that?" she called, shutting off her motor. She was so near now that Dexter could see her bathing-suit, which consisted apparently of pink rompers.

The nose of the boat bumped the raft, and as the latter tilted rakishly he was precipitated toward her. With different degrees of interest they recognized each other.

"Aren't you one of those men we played through this afternoon?" she demanded.

He was.

"Well, do you know how to drive a motor-boat? Because if you do I wish you'd drive this one so I can ride on the surf-board behind. My name is Judy Jones"—she favored him with an absurd smirk—rather, what tried to be a smirk, for, twist her mouth as she might, it was not grotesque, it was merely beautiful—"and I live in a house over there on the Island, and in that house there is a man waiting for me. When he drove up at the door I drove out of the dock because he says I'm his ideal."

There was a fish jumping and a star shining and the lights around the lake were gleaming. Dexter sat beside Judy Jones and she explained how her boat was driven. Then she was in the water, swimming to the floating surf-board with a sinuous crawl. Watching her was without effort to the eye, watching a branch waving or a sea-gull flying. Her arms, burned to butternut, moved sinuously among the dull platinum ripples, elbow appearing first, casting the forearm back with a cadence of falling water, then reaching out and down, stabbing a path ahead.

They moved out into the lake; turning, Dexter saw that she was kneeling on the low rear of the now uptilted surf-board.

"Go faster," she called, "fast as it'll go."

Obediently he jammed the lever forward and the white spray mounted at the bow. When he looked around again the girl was standing up on the rushing board, her arms spread wide, her eyes lifted toward the moon.

"It's awful cold," she shouted. "What's your name?"

He told her.

"Well, why don't you come to dinner to-morrow night?"

His heart turned over like the fly-wheel of the boat, and, for the second time, her casual whim gave a new direction to his life.

3

Next evening while he waited for her to come down-stairs, Dexter peopled the soft deep summer room and the sun-porch that opened from it with the men who had already loved Judy Jones. He knew the sort of men they were—the men who when he first went to college had entered from the great prep schools with graceful clothes and the deep tan of healthy summers. He had seen that, in one sense, he was better than these men. He was newer and stronger. Yet in acknowledging to himself that he wished his children to be like them he was admitting that he was but the rough, strong stuff from which they eternally sprang.

When the time had come for him to wear good clothes, he had known who were the best tailors in America, and the best tailors in America had made him the suit he wore this evening. He had acquired that particular reserve peculiar to his university, that set it off from other universities. He recognized the value to him of such a mannerism and he had adopted it; he knew that to be careless in dress and manner required more confidence than to be careful. But carelessness was for his children. His mother's name had been Krimslich. She was a Bohemian of the peasant class and she had talked broken English to the end of her days. Her son must keep to the set patterns.

At a little after seven Judy Jones came downstairs. She wore a blue silk afternoon dress, and he was disappointed at first that she had not put on something more elaborate. This feeling was accentuated when, after a brief greeting, she went to the door of a butler's pantry and pushing it open called: 'You can serve dinner, Martha." He had rather expected that a butler would announce dinner, that there would be a cocktail. Then he put these thoughts behind him as they sat down side by side on a lounge and looked at each other.

"Father and mother won't be here," she said thoughtfully.

He remembered the last time he had seen her father, and he was glad the parents were not to be here to-night—they might wonder who he was. He had been born in Keeble, a Minnesota village fifty miles farther north, and he always gave Keeble as his home instead of Black Bear Village. Country towns were well enough to come from if they weren't inconveniently in sight and used as footstools by fashionable lakes.

They talked of his university, which she had visited frequently during the past two years, and of the near-by city which supplied Sherry Island with its patrons, and whither Dexter would return next day to his prospering laundries.

During dinner she slipped into a moody depression which gave Dexter a feeling of uneasiness. Whatever petulance she uttered in her throaty voice worried him. Whatever she smiled at—at him, at a chicken liver, at nothing—it disturbed him that her smile could have no root in mirth, or even in amusement. When the scarlet corners of her lips curved down, it was less a smile than an invitation to a kiss.

Then, after dinner, she led him out on the dark sun-porch and deliberately changed the atmosphere.

"Do you mind if I weep a little?" she said.

"I'm afraid I'm boring you," he responded quickly.

"You're not. I like you. But I've just had a terrible afternoon. There was a man I cared about, and this afternoon he told me out of a clear sky that he was poor as a church-mouse. He'd never even hinted it before. Does this sound horribly mundane?"

"Perhaps he was afraid to tell you."

"Suppose he was," she answered. "He didn't start right. You see, if I'd thought of him as poor—well, I've been mad about loads of poor men, and fully intended to marry them all. But in this case, I hadn't thought of him that way, and my interest in him wasn't strong enough to survive the shock. As if a girl calmly informed her fiancé that she was a widow. He might not object to widows, but——

"Let's start right," she interrupted herself suddenly. "Who are you, anyhow?"

For a moment Dexter hesitated. Then:

"I'm nobody," he announced. "My career is largely a matter of futures."

"Are you poor?"

"No," he said frankly, "I'm probably making more money than any man my age in the Northwest. I know that's an obnoxious remark, but you advised me to start right."

There was a pause. Then she smiled and the corners of her mouth drooped and an almost imperceptible sway brought her closer to him, looking up into his eyes. A lump rose in Dexter's throat, and he waited breathless for the experiment, facing the unpredictable compound that would form mysteriously from the elements of their lips. Then he saw— she communicated her excitement to him, lavishly, deeply, with kisses that were not a promise but a fulfilment. They aroused in him not hunger demanding renewal but surfeit that would demand more surfeit . . . kisses that were like charity, creating want by holding back nothing at all.

It did not take him many hours to decide that he had wanted Judy Jones ever since he was a proud, desirous little boy.

4

It began like that—and continued, with varying shades of intensity, on such a note right up to the dénouement. Dexter surrendered a part of himself to the most direct and unprincipled personality with which he had ever come in contact. Whatever Judy wanted, she went after with the full pressure of her charm. There was no divergence of method, no jockeying for position or premeditation of effects—there was a very little mental side to any of her affairs. She simply made men conscious to the highest degree of her physical loveliness. Dexter had no desire to change her. Her deficiencies were knit up with a passionate energy that transcended and justified them.

When, as Judy's head lay against his shoulder that first night, she whispered, "I don't know what's the matter with me. Last night I thought I was in love with a man and to-night I think I'm in love with you———"—it seemed to him a beautiful and romantic thing to say. It was the exquisite excitability that for the moment he controlled and owned. But a week later he was compelled to view this same quality in a different light. She took him in her roadster to a picnic supper, and after supper she disappeared, likewise in her roadster, with another man. Dexter became enormously upset and was scarcely able to be decently civil to the other people present. When she assured him that she had not kissed the other man, he knew she was lying—yet he was glad that she had taken the trouble to lie to him.

He was, as he found before the summer ended, one of a varying dozen who circulated about her. Each of them had at one time been favored above all others—about half of them still basked in the solace of occasional sentimental revivals. Whenever one showed signs of dropping out through long neglect, she granted him a brief honeyed hour, which encouraged him to tag along for a year or so longer. Judy made these forays upon the helpless and defeated without malice, indeed half unconscious that there was anything mischievous in what she did.

When a new man came to town every one dropped out—dates were automatically cancelled.

The helpless part of trying to do anything about it was that she did it all herself. She was not a girl who could be "won" in the kinetic sense —she was proof against cleverness, she was proof against charm; if any of these assailed her too strongly she would immediately resolve the affair to a physical basis, and under the magic of her physical splendor the strong as well as the brilliant played her game and not their own. She was entertained only by the gratification of her desires and by the direct exercise of her own charm. Perhaps from so much youthful love, so many youthful lovers, she had come, in self-defense, to nourish herself wholly from within.

Succeeding Dexter's first exhilaration came restlessness and dissatisfaction. The helpless ecstasy of losing himself in her was opiate rather than tonic. It was fortunate for his work during the winter that those moments of ecstasy came infrequently. Early in their acquaintance it had seemed for a while that there was a deep and spontaneous mutual attraction—that first August, for example—three days of long evenings on her dusky veranda, of strange wan kisses through the late afternoon, in shadowy alcoves or behind the protecting trellises of the garden arbors, of mornings when she was fresh as a dream and almost shy at meeting him in the clarity of the rising day. There was all the ecstasy of an engagement about it, sharpened by his realization that there was no engagement. It was during those three days that, for the first time, he had asked her to marry him. She said "maybe some day," she said "kiss me," she said "I'd like to marry you," she said "I love you"—she said —nothing.

The three days were interrupted by the arrival of a New York man who visited at her house for half September. To Dexter's agony, rumor engaged them. The man was the son of the president of a great trust company. But at the end of a month it was reported that Judy was yawning. At a dance one night she sat all evening in a motor-boat with a local beau, while the New Yorker searched the club for her frantically. She told the local beau that she was bored with her visitor, and two days later he left. She was seen with him at the station, and it was reported that he looked very mournful indeed.

On this note the summer ended. Dexter was twenty-four, and he found himself increasingly in a position to do as he wished. He joined two clubs in the city and lived at one of them. Though he was by no means an integral part of the stag-lines at these clubs, he managed to be on hand at dances where Judy Jones was likely to appear. He could have gone out socially as much as he liked—he was an eligible young man, now, and popular with down-town fathers. His confessed devotion to Judy Jones had rather solidified his position. But he had no social aspirations and rather despised the dancing men who were always on tap for the Thursday or Saturday parties and who filled in at dinners with the younger married set. Already he was playing with the idea of going East to New York. He wanted to take Judy Jones with him. No disillusion as to the world in which she had grown up could cure his illusion as to her desirability.

Remember that—for only in the light of it can what he did for her be understood.

Eighteen months after he first met Judy Jones he became engaged to another girl. Her name was Irene Scheerer, and her father was one of the men who had always believed in Dexter. Irene was light-haired and sweet and honorable, and a little stout, and she had two suitors whom she pleasantly relinquished when Dexter formally asked her to marry him.

Summer, fall, winter, spring, another summer, another fall—so much he had given of his active life to the incorrigible lips of Judy Jones. She had treated him with interest, with encouragement, with malice, with indifference, with contempt. She had inflicted on him the innumerable little slights and indignities possible in such a case—as if in revenge for having ever cared for him at all. She had beckoned him and yawned at him and beckoned him again and he had responded often with bitterness and narrowed eyes. She had brought him ecstatic happiness and intolerable agony of spirit. She had caused him untold inconvenience and not a little trouble. She had insulted him, and she had ridden over him, and she had played his interest in her against his interest in his work—for fun. She had done everything to him except to criticise him—this she had not done—it seemed to him only because it might have sullied the utter indifference she manifested and sincerely felt toward him.

When autumn had come and gone again it occurred to him that he could not have Judy Jones. He had to beat this into his mind but he convinced himself at last. He lay awake at night for a while and argued it over. He told himself the trouble and the pain she had caused him, he enumerated her glaring deficiencies as a wife. Then he said to himself that he loved her, and after a while he fell asleep. For a week, lest he imagined her husky voice over the telephone or her eyes opposite him at lunch, he worked hard and late, and at night he went to his office and plotted out his years.

At the end of a week he went to a dance and cut in on her once. For almost the first time since they had met he did not ask her to sit out with him or tell her that she was lovely. It hurt him that she did not miss these things—that was all. He was not jealous when he saw that there was a new man to-night. He had been hardened against jealousy long before.

He stayed late at the dance. He sat for an hour with Irene Scheerer and talked about books and about music. He knew very little about either. But he was beginning to be master of his own time now, and he had a rather priggish notion that he—the young and already fabulously successful Dexter Green—should know more about such things.

That was in October, when he was twenty-five. In January, Dexter and Irene became engaged. It was to be announced in June, and they were to be married three months later.

The Minnesota winter prolonged itself interminably, and it was almost May when the winds came soft and the snow ran down into Black Bear Lake at last. For the first time in over a year Dexter was enjoying a certain tranquillity of spirit. Judy Jones had been in Florida, and afterward in Hot Springs, and somewhere she had been engaged, and somewhere she had broken it off. At first, when Dexter had definitely given her up, it had made him sad that people still linked them together and asked for news of her, but when he began to be placed at dinner next to Irene Scheerer people didn't ask him about her any more—they told him about her. He ceased to be an authority on her.

May at last. Dexter walked the streets at night when the darkness was damp as rain, wondering that so soon, with so little done, so much of ecstasy had gone from him. May one year back had been marked by Judy's poignant, unforgivable, yet forgiven turbulence—it had been one of those rare times when he fancied she had grown to care for him. That old penny's worth of happiness he had spent for this bushel of content. He knew that Irene would be no more than a curtain spread behind him, a hand moving among gleaming tea-cups, a voice calling to children . . . fire and loveliness were gone, the magic of nights and the wonder of the varying hours and seasons . . . slender lips, downturning, dropping to his lips and bearing him up into a heaven of eyes. . . . The thing was deep in him. He was too strong and alive for it to die lightly.

In the middle of May when the weather balanced for a few days on the thin bridge that led to deep summer he turned in one night at Irene's house. Their engagement was to be announced in a week now —no one would be surprised at it. And to-night they would sit together on the lounge at the University Club and look on for an hour at the dancers. It gave him a sense of solidity to go with her—she was so sturdily popular, so intensely "great."

He mounted the steps of the brownstone house and stepped inside. "Irene," he called.

Mrs. Scheerer came out of the living-room to meet him.

"Dexter," she said, "Irene's gone up-stairs with a splitting headache. She wanted to go with you but I made her go to bed."

"Nothing serious, I——"

"Oh, no. She's going to play golf with you in the morning. You can spare her for just one night, can't you, Dexter?"

Her smile was kind. She and Dexter liked each other. In the living-room he talked for a moment before he said good-night.

Returning to the University Club, where he had rooms, he stood in the doorway for a moment and watched the dancers. He leaned against the doorpost, nodded at a man or two—yawned.

"Hello, darling."

The familiar voice at his elbow startled him. Judy Jones had left a man and crossed the room to him—Judy Jones, a slender enamelled doll in cloth of gold: gold in a band at her head, gold in two slipper points at her dress's hem. The fragile glow of her face seemed to blossom as she smiled at him. A breeze of warmth and light blew through the room. His hands in the pockets of his dinner-jacket tightened spasmodically. He was filled with a sudden excitement.

"When did you get back?" he asked casually.

"Come here and I'll tell you about it."

She turned and he followed her. She had been away—he could have wept at the wonder of her return. She had passed through enchanted streets, doing things that were like provocative music. All mysterious happenings, all fresh and quickening hopes, had gone away with her, come back with her now.

She turned in the doorway.

"Have you a car here? If you haven't, I have."

"I have a coupé."

In then, with a rustle of golden cloth. He slammed the door. Into so many cars she had stepped—like this—like that—her back against the leather, so—her elbow resting on the door—waiting. She would have been soiled long since had there been anything to soil her—except herself—but this was her own self outpouring.

With an effort he forced himself to start the car and back into the street. This was nothing, he must remember. She had done this before, and he had put her behind him, as he would have crossed a bad account from his books.

He drove slowly down-town and, affecting abstraction, traversed the deserted streets of the business section, peopled here and there where a movie was giving out its crowd or where consumptive or pugilistic youth lounged in front of pool halls. The clink of glasses and the slap of hands on the bars issued from saloons, cloisters of glazed glass and dirty yellow light.

She was watching him closely and the silence was embarrassing, yet in this crisis he could find no casual word with which to profane the hour. At a convenient turning he began to zigzag back toward the University Club.

"Have you missed me?" she asked suddenly.

"Everybody missed you."

He wondered if she knew of Irene Scheerer. She had been back only a day—her absence had been almost contemporaneous with his engagement.

"What a remark!" Judy laughed sadly—without sadness. She looked at him searchingly. He became absorbed in the dashboard.

"You're handsomer than you used to be," she said thoughtfully. "Dexter, you have the most rememberable eyes."

He could have laughed at this, but he did not laugh. It was the sort of thing that was said to sophomores. Yet it stabbed at him.

"I'm awfully tired of everything, darling." She called every one darling, endowing the endearment with careless, individual comradery. "I wish you'd marry me."

The directness of this confused him. He should have told her now that he was going to marry another girl, but he could not tell her. He could as easily have sworn that he had never loved her.

"I think we'd get along," she continued, on the same note, "unless probably you've forgotten me and fallen in love with another girl."

Her confidence was obviously enormous. She had said, in effect, that she found such a thing impossible to believe, that if it were true he had merely committed a childish indiscretion—and probably to show off. She would forgive him, because it was not a matter of any moment but rather something to be brushed aside lightly.

"Of course you could never love anybody but me," she continued, "I like the way you love me. Oh, Dexter, have you forgotten last year?"

"No, I haven't forgotten."

"Neither have I!"

Was she sincerely moved—or was she carried along by the wave of her own acting?

"I wish we could be like that again," she said, and he forced himself to answer:

"I don't think we can."

"I suppose not. . . . I hear you're giving Irene Scheerer a violent rush."

There was not the faintest emphasis on the name, yet Dexter was suddenly ashamed.

"Oh, take me home," cried Judy suddenly; "I don't want to go back to that idiotic dance—with those children."

Then, as he turned up the street that led to the residence district, Judy began to cry quietly to herself. He had never seen her cry before.

The dark street lightened, the dwellings of the rich loomed up around them, he stopped his coupé in front of the great white bulk of the Mortimer Joneses house, somnolent, gorgeous, drenched with the splendor of the damp moonlight. Its solidity startled him. The strong walls, the steel of the girders, the breadth and beam and pomp of it were there only to bring out the contrast with the young beauty beside him. It was sturdy to accentuate her slightness—as if to show what a breeze could be generated by a butterfly's wing.

He sat perfectly quiet, his nerves in wild clamor, afraid that if he moved he would find her irresistibly in his arms. Two tears had rolled down her wet face and trembled on her upper lip.

"I'm more beautiful than anybody else," she said brokenly, "why can't I be happy?" Her moist eyes tore at his stability—her mouth turned slowly downward with an exquisite sadness: "I'd like to marry you if you'll have me, Dexter. I suppose you think I'm not worth having, but I'll be so beautiful for you, Dexter."

A million phrases of anger, pride, passion, hatred, tenderness fought on his lips. Then a perfect wave of emotion washed over him, carrying off with it a sediment of wisdom, of convention, of doubt, of honor. This was his girl who was speaking, his own, his beautiful, his pride.

"Won't you come in?" He heard her draw in her breath sharply.

Waiting.

"All right," his voice was trembling, "I'll come in."

5

It was strange that neither when it was over nor a long time afterward did he regret that night. Looking at it from the perspective of ten years, the fact that Judy's flare for him endured just one month seemed of little importance. Nor did it matter that by his yielding he subjected himself to a deeper agony in the end and gave serious hurt to Irene Scheerer and to Irene's parents, who had befriended him. There was nothing sufficiently pictorial about Irene's grief to stamp itself on his mind.

Dexter was at bottom hard-minded. The attitude of the city on his action was of no importance to him, not because he was going to leave the city, but because any outside attitude on the situation seemed superficial. He was completely indifferent to popular opinion. Nor, when he had seen that it was no use, that he did not possess in himself the power to move fundamentally or to hold Judy Jones, did he bear any malice toward her. He loved her, and he would love her until the day he was too old for loving—but he could not have her. So he tasted the deep pain that is reserved only for the strong, just as he had tasted for a little while the deep happiness.

Even the ultimate falsity of the grounds upon which Judy terminated the engagement that she did not want to "take him away" from Irene —Judy, who had wanted nothing else—did not revolt him. He was beyond any revulsion or any amusement.

He went East in February with the intention of selling out his laundries and settling in New York—but the war came to America in March and changed his plans. He returned to the West, handed over the management of the business to his partner, and went into the first officers' training-camp in late April. He was one of those young thousands who greeted the war with a certain amount of relief, welcoming the liberation from webs of tangled emotion.

6

This story is not his biography, remember, although things creep into it which have nothing to do with those dreams he had when he was young. We are almost done with them and with him now. There is only one more incident to be related here, and it happens seven years farther on.

It took place in New York, where he had done well—so well that there were no barriers too high for him. He was thirty-two years old, and, except for one flying trip immediately after the war, he had not been West in seven years. A man named Devlin from Detroit came into his office to see him in a business way, and then and there this incident occurred, and closed out, so to speak, this particular side of his life.

"So you're from the Middle West," said the man Devlin with careless curiosity. "That's funny—I thought men like you were probably born and raised on Wall Street. You know—wife of one of my best friends in Detroit came from your city. I was an usher at the wedding."

Dexter waited with no apprehension of what was coming.

"Judy Simms," said Devlin with no particular interest; "Judy Jones she was once."

"Yes, I knew her." A dull impatience spread over him. He had heard, of course, that she was married—perhaps deliberately he had heard no more.

"Awfully nice girl," brooded Devlin meaninglessly, "I'm sort of sorry for her."

"Why?" Something in Dexter was alert, receptive, at once.

"O, Lud Simms has gone to pieces in a way. I don't mean he ill-uses her, but he drinks and runs around——"

"Doesn't she run around?"

"No. Stays at home with her kids."

"Oh."

"She's a little too old for him," said Devlin.

"Too old!" cried Dexter. "Why, man, she's only twenty-seven."

He was possessed with a wild notion of rushing out into the streets and taking a train to Detroit. He rose to his feet spasmodically.

"I guess you're busy," Devlin apologized quickly. "I didn't real-ize——"

"No, I'm not busy," said Dexter, steadying his voice. "I'm not busy at all. Not busy at all. Did you say she was—twenty-seven? No, I said she was twenty-seven."

"Yes, you did," agreed Devlin dryly.

"Go on, then. Go on."

"What do you mean?"

"About Judy Jones."

Devlin looked at him helplessly.

"Well, that's—I told you all there is to it. He treats her like the devil. Oh, they're not going to get divorced or anything. When he's particularly outrageous she forgives him. In fact, I'm inclined to think she loves him. She was a pretty girl when she first came to Detroit."

A pretty girl! The phrase struck Dexter as ludicrous.

"Isn't she—a pretty girl, any more?"

"Oh, she's all right."

"Look here," said Dexter, sitting down suddenly, "I don't understand. You say she was a 'pretty girl' and now you say she's 'all right.' I don't understand what you mean—Judy Jones wasn't a pretty girl, at all. She was a great beauty. Why, I knew her, I knew her. She was——"

Devlin laughed pleasantly.

"I'm not trying to start a row," he said. "I think Judy's a nice girl and I like her. I can't understand how a man like Lud Simms could fall madly in love with her, but he did." Then he added: "Most of the women like her."

Dexter looked closely at Devlin, thinking wildly that there must be a reason for this, some insensitivity in the man or some private malice.

"Lots of women fade just like *that*," Devlin snapped his fingers. "You must have seen it happen. Perhaps I've forgotten how pretty she was at her wedding. I've seen her so much since then, you see. She has nice eyes."

A sort of dulness settled down upon Dexter. For the first time in his life he felt like getting very drunk. He knew that he was laughing loudly at something Devlin had said, but he did not know what it was or why it was funny. When, in a few minutes, Devlin went he lay down on his lounge and looked out the window at the New York sky line into which the sun was sinking in dull lovely shades of pink and gold.

He had thought that having nothing else to lose he was invulnerable at last—but he knew that he had just lost something more, as surely as if he had married Judy Jones and seen her fade away before his eyes.

The dream was gone. Something had been taken from him. In a sort of panic he pushed the palms of his hands into his eyes and tried to bring up a picture of the waters lapping on Sherry Island and the moonlit veranda, and gingham on the golf-links and the dry sun and the gold color of her neck's soft down. And her mouth damp to his kisses and her eyes plaintive with melancholy and her freshness like new fine linen in the morning. Why, these things were no longer in the world! They had existed and they existed no longer.

For the first time in years the tears were streaming down his face. But they were for himself now. He did not care about mouth and eyes and moving hands. He wanted to care, and he could not care. For he had gone away and he could never go back any more. The gates were closed, the sun was gone down, and there was no beauty but the gray beauty of steel that withstands all time. Even the grief he could have borne was left behind in the country of illusion, of youth, of the richness of life, where his winter dreams had flourished.

"Long ago," he said, "long ago, there was something in me, but now that thing is gone. Now that thing is gone, that thing is gone. I cannot cry. I cannot care. That thing will come back no more."

QUESTIONS

1. What are Dexter Green's "winter dreams"? In what ways does the opening of the story resemble a fairy tale?
2. How does Fitzgerald make use of the contrast between the East and the Midwest?
3. What effect does being the son of an immigrant have on Dexter? What does he mean when he says he is of "rough, strong stuff"? Why does Dexter accept the "peculiar reserve" and "mannerisms" of his friends from college and leave the "carelessness" for his children?
4. What are the characteristics of Judy Jones which attract Dexter? What is magical, fascinating? What is corrupt about her? How do his desires for her conflict with his business ambition? In what sense do they bring out the best in him?
5. In what way is Judy more of a romantic symbol than an actual girl? Is what she symbolizes unattainable? Is she exciting because she is so different from typical American women of this period?
6. What kind of a girl would make Dexter happy as his wife? Is Irene Scheerer this kind of girl? Is he wise in trading that "old penny's worth of happiness" for a "bushel of content?"
7. Why does Judy marry the kind of man she does? Is she capable of love? Would her opinion of Dexter have changed if he had refused to tolerate her infidelity during their courtship?

EVAN CONNELL

EVAN CONNELL (b. 1924) was born in Kansas City, Missouri, Mrs. Bridge's home, but now lives in Sausalito, California, a suburb of San Francisco. Some of his other works of fiction include *The Anatomy Lesson and Other Stories* (1957), *The Diary of a Rapist* (1966), and *Mr. Bridge* (1969), a sequel to *Mrs. Bridge* (1958).

Connell's epigraph for *Mrs. Bridge* is taken from Walt Whitman's poem, "Facing West from California's Shores."

But where is what I started for so long ago?
And why is it yet unfound?

The implication is that the searcher has lost sight of his dream. In this case India Bridge ("India" is her romantic first name which she tries to disown as if it were somebody else's) somehow loses any sense of purpose in life. She assumes she should be satisfied because, in terms of the typical American Dream, she has everything. Actually what she has is an emotionally sterile husband who channels all his energy into his work and gives her "leisure." The book is, in fact, a documented nightmare about affluence and leisure. Mrs. Bridge closes off her opportunities for self-discovery by marrying early and "well." She concludes at the end of the first chapter ("Love and Marriage") ". . . that while marriage might be an equitable affair, love itself was not." And since *all of* Mrs. Bridge's values are what we have come to label "straight," she cannot even be conscious of the possibility of ever expressing her repressed sexuality in any other way.

Connell, through many pointed episodes, makes it clear that he is not opposed to Mrs. Bridge's values *per se*. What is so poignant about her life is that she *does* occasionally have momentary realizations that the quality of her experiences is wretchedly low. She is a deprived person; she does nothing she really enjoys. She does only those things that are prescribed and accepted by the narrow-minded, white, Anglo-Saxon, Protestant country-club community of which she is a part. One current expression is very appropriate for her—she never really "gets into" anything. Her friends are only superficial acquaintances, her "community" work for her club is silly and shallow. She never really allows herself a chance to explore music or art because her "social calendar" is always too filled with tiresome cocktail parties and other obligations. (Mr. Bridge refers to not "returning" invitations, but "retaliating" them.) She won't even "get into" her recorded Spanish lessons because she is afraid that someone will overhear and she will appear foolish. She is obsessed by the need for "good taste" and "moderation." If she were in the East she would know rich people who either were "eccentric" or allowed themselves to be at least occasionally "outrageous"—but not in Middle America.

The novel itself is composed of 117 short chapters. Each chapter is a vignette which, in a gently ironic and understated way, repeats the same theme over and over—Mrs. Bridge's life is inauthentic because she has no sense of an inner self. Many incidents in the narrative suggest what possibilities she is missing, the possible richness that could be hers if she would only acknowledge her unhappiness.

The twenty-two chapters here are those that tell of her personal life and the ones in which she has some glimmerings of disillusionment and some sense of self-alienation. Other chapters are about the lives of her children and the emotional and sexual "hang-ups" they have inherited from such a repressed family. Still others reveal her racism and prejudice.

Connell is a "soft sell" reformer. He has the good taste to understate everything; he never overtly analyzes or comments. The result is that practically everyone finds this book enjoyable; most see in it only what they want to see. Its appeal is that its point of view is never political or polemical, but always human.

[FROM Mrs. Bridge]

1

Love and Marriage

Her first name was India—she was never able to get used to it. It seemed to her that her parents must have been thinking of someone else when they named her. Or were they hoping for another sort of daughter? As a child she was often on the point of inquiring, but time passed, and she never did.

Now and then while she was growing up the idea came to her that she could get along very nicely without a husband, and, to the distress of her mother and father, this idea prevailed for a number of years after her education had been completed. But there came a summer evening and a young lawyer named Walter Bridge: very tall and dignified, red-haired, with a grimly determined, intelligent face, and rather stoop-shouldered so that even when he stood erect his coat hung lower in the front than in the back. She had known him for several years without finding him remarkable in any way, but on this summer evening, on the front porch of her parents' home, she toyed with a sprig of mint and looked at him attentively while pretending to listen to what he said. He was telling her that he intended to become rich and successful, and that one day he would take his wife—"whenever I finally decide to marry" he said, for he was not yet ready to commit himself—one day he would take his wife on a tour of Europe. He spoke of Ruskin and of Robert Ingersoll, and he read to her that evening on the porch, later, some verses from *The Rubáiyát* while her parents were preparing for bed, and the locusts sang in the elm trees all around.

A few months after her father died she married Walter Bridge and moved with him to Kansas City, where he had decided to establish a practice.

All seemed well. The days passed, and the weeks, and the months, more swiftly than in childhood, and she felt no trepidation, except for certain moments in the depth of the night when, as she and her new husband lay drowsily clutching each other for reassurance, anticipating the dawn, the day, and another night which might prove them both immortal, Mrs. Bridge found herself wide awake. During these moments, resting in her husband's arms, she would stare at the ceiling, or at his face, which sleep robbed of strength, with an uneasy expression, as though she saw or heard some intimation of the great years ahead.

She was not certain what she wanted from life, or what to expect from it, for she had seen so little of it, but she was sure that in some way—because she willed it to be so—her wants and her expectations were the same.

For a while after their marriage she was in such demand that it was not unpleasant when he fell asleep. Presently, however, he began sleeping all night, and it was then she awoke more frequently, and looked into the darkness, wondering about the nature of men, doubtful of the future, until at last there came a night when she shook her husband awake and spoke of her own desire. Affably he placed one of his long white arms around her waist; she turned to him then, contentedly, expectantly, and secure. However nothing else occurred, and in a few minutes he had gone back to sleep.

This was the night Mrs. Bridge concluded that while marriage might be an equitable affair, love itself was not.

2

Children

Their first child, a girl, curiously dark, who seldom cried and who often seemed to want nothing more than to be left alone, was born when they had been married a little more than three years. They named her Ruth. After the delivery Mrs. Bridge's first coherent words were, "Is she normal?"

Two years later—Mrs. Bridge was then thirty-one—Carolyn appeared, about a month ahead of time, as though she were quite able to take care of herself, and was nicknamed "Corky." She was a chubby blonde, blue-eyed like her mother, more ebullient than Ruth, and more demanding.

Then, two years after Carolyn, a stern little boy was born, thin and red-haired like his father, and they named him Douglas. They had not wanted more than two children, but because the first two had been girls they had decided to try once more. Even if the third had also been a girl they would have let it go at that; there would have been no sense in continuing what would soon become amusing to other people.

3

Preliminary Training

She brought up her children very much as she herself had been brought up, and she hoped that when they were spoken of it would be in connection with their nice manners, their pleasant dispositions, and their cleanliness, for these were qualities she valued above all others.

With Ruth and later with Carolyn, because they were girls, she felt sure of her guidance; but with the boy she was at times obliged to guess and to hope, and as it turned out—not only with Douglas but with his two sisters—what she stressed was not at all what they remembered as they grew older.

What Ruth was to recall most vividly about childhood was an incident which Mrs. Bridge had virtually forgotten an hour after it occurred. One summer afternoon the entire family, with the exception of Mr. Bridge who was working, had gone to the neighborhood swimming pool; Douglas lay on a rubber sheet in the shade of an umbrella, kicking his thin bowed legs and gurgling, and Carolyn was splashing around in the wading pool. The day was exceptionally hot. Ruth took off her bathing suit and began walking across the terrace. This much she could hardly remember, but she was never to forget what happened next. Mrs. Bridge, having suddenly discovered Ruth was naked, snatched up the bathing suit and hurried after her. Ruth began to run, and being wet and slippery she squirmed out of the arms that reached for her from every direction. She thought it was a new game. Then she noticed the expression on her mother's face. Ruth became bewildered and then alarmed, and when she was finally caught she was screaming hysterically.

8

Who Can Find the Caspian Sea?

As time went on it became evident that Douglas was the most introspective of the three children, but aside from this—to his father's disappointment—he appeared to be totally unremarkable. Mr. Bridge had hoped for a brilliant son, and though he had not yet given up that hope he was reluctantly adapting himself to the idea that his son was no prodigy. If Douglas amounted to anything in later life, he concluded, it would be less the result of brilliance than of conscientious effort.

Ruth, even more obviously, had no intention of relying on her brains; but Carolyn, as soon as she entered kindergarten, began to make a name for herself, and very shortly was known as the brightest child in the class. Furthermore she appeared to understand her own superiority and when, through some mischance, another child equaled or exceeded her for a moment, Carolyn would grow furiously vindictive, and was not above lying or cheating in order to regain her position at the head of the class, so that by the time she was in the third grade she was beginning to be envied and disliked by her classmates and carefully observed by her teachers. It was no surprise to anyone when she was allowed to skip the second half of the third grade.

The teacher of Carolyn's fourth-grade class was a young lame woman named Bloch, who wore eye shadow and mascara and had one rather strange habit: every day she would call one of the children to her desk, give the child a comb, and then, bowing her head and shutting her eyes, she would instruct the child to take the pins out of her hair. Her hair was thick and greasy and hung down to her waist.

"Who can find the Caspian Sea?" she would murmur, and the child behind her would begin combing.

"Who knows where to find the Caspian Sea?" she would ask again, and without opening her eyes she would say, "Albert Crawford knows."

Then the boy she had named would walk to the great green and blue map pulled down over the blackboard, and with the pointer he would locate the sea.

"Carefully, dear," she would whisper if the comb snarled, but even then she seemed not displeased.

Although the children did not like this curious task they seldom thought of it once they were out of class. Carolyn, however, happened to mention at home that she had been chosen that morning. Mrs. Bridge was aghast; she had never heard of Miss Bloch's habit. After questioning Carolyn and becoming convinced it was the truth, she resolved to telephone the school and report the incident to the principal, and yet, for some reason, she could not do it. Several times she picked up the telephone, shivering with disgust, but each time she put down the receiver with an expression of doubt and anxiety; she decided it would be better to visit the principal's office, and yet this, too, was beyond her. She did not know why. In the end she told Carolyn that if she was ever again called upon to comb the teacher's hair she was to refuse. Having done this, Mrs. Bridge told herself the teacher was no longer a threat and the entire affair, therefore, was closed. And so it was. Carolyn was not called upon for the remainder of the term, and the following September she had a different teacher. There were times later on when Mrs. Bridge wondered if she had done the right thing; she wondered if Miss Bloch was still calling children to comb her hair, and when Douglas entered fourth grade she waited anxiously to learn who his teacher would be. It was not Miss Bloch; if it had been she would have gone to the principal and demanded that something be done. But it was not, and Mrs. Bridge, who disliked making trouble for anyone, was greatly relieved, and found that she was no longer obliged to think about the matter.

20

What's Up, Señora Bridge?

Spanish was a subject she had long meant to study, and quite often she remarked to her friends that she wished she had studied it in school. The children had heard her say this, so for her birthday that year they gave her an album of phonograph records consisting of a lethargic dialogue between Señor Carreño of Madrid and an American visitor named Señora Brown. Along with the records came an attractive booklet of instructions and suggestions. Mrs. Bridge was delighted with the gift and made a joke about how she intended to begin her lessons the first thing "mañana."

As it turned out, however, she was busy the following day, and the day after because of a PTA meeting at the school, and the day after. Somehow or other more than a month passed before she found time to begin, but there came a morning when she resolved to get at it, and so, after helping Harriet with the breakfast dishes, she found her reading glasses and sat down in the living room with the instruction booklet. The course did not sound at all difficult, and the more pages she read the more engrossing it became. The instructions were clear enough: she was simply to listen to each line of dialogue and then, in the pause that followed, to repeat the part of Señora Brown.

She put the first record on the phonograph, turning it low enough so that the mailman or any delivery boys would not overhear and think she had gone out of her mind. Seated on the sofa directly opposite the machine she waited, holding onto the booklet in case there should be an emergency.

"Buenas días, Señora Brown," the record began, appropriately enough. "Cómo está usted?"

"Buenas días, Señor Carreño," Señora Brown answered. "Muy bien, gracias. Y usted?"

The record waited for Mrs. Bridge who, however, was afraid it would begin before she had a chance to speak, and in consequence only leaned forward with her lips parted. She got up, walked across to the phonograph, and lifted the needle back to the beginning.

"Buenas días, Señora Brown. Cómo está usted?"

"Buenas días, Señor Carreño," replied Señora Brown all over again. "Muy bien, gracias. Y usted?"

"Buenas días, Señor Carreño," said Mrs. Bridge with increasing confidence. "Muy bien, gracias. Y usted?"

"Muy bien," said Señor Carreño.

Just then Harriet appeared to say that Mrs. Arlen was on the telephone. Mrs. Bridge put the booklet on the sofa and went into the breakfast room, where the telephone was.

"Hello, Madge. I've been meaning to phone you about the Auxiliary luncheon next Friday. They've changed the time from twelve-thirty to one. Honestly, I wish they'd make up their minds."

"Charlotte told me yesterday. You knew Grace Barron was ill with flu, didn't you?"

"Oh, not really! She has the worst luck."

"If it isn't one thing, it's another. She's been down since day before yesterday. I'm running by with some lemonade and thought you might like to come along. I can only stay a split second. I'm due at the hairdresser at eleven."

"Well, I'm in slacks. Are you going right away?"

"The instant the laundress gets here. That girl! She should have been here hours ago. Honestly, I'm at the end of my rope."

"Don't tell me you're having that same trouble! I sometimes think they do it deliberately just to put people out. We're trying a new one and she does do nice work, but she's so independent."

"Oh," said Madge Arlen, as if her head were turned away from the phone, "here she comes. Lord, what next?"

"Well, I'll dash right upstairs and change," said Mrs. Bridge. "I suppose the garden can wait till tomorrow." And after telling Harriet that she would be at Mrs. Barron's if anyone called, she started toward the stairs.

"Qué tal, Señora Brown?" inquired the record.

Mrs. Bridge hurried into the living room, snapped off the phonograph, and went upstairs.

27

Sentimental Moment

Mrs. Bridge stood alone at a front window thinking of how quickly the years were going by. The children were growing up so rapidly, and her husband— She stirred uneasily. Already there was a new group of "young marrieds," people she hardly knew. Surely some time had gone by—she expected this; nevertheless she could not get over the feeling that something was drawing steadily away from her. She wondered if her husband felt the same; she thought she would ask him that evening when he got home. She recalled the dreams they used to share; she recalled with a smile how she used to listen to him speak of his plans and how she had never actually cared one way or another about his ambition, she had cared only for him. That was enough. In those days she used to think that the long hours he spent in his office were a temporary condition and that as soon as more people came to him with legal problems he would, somehow, begin spending more time at home. But this was not the way it turned out, and Mrs. Bridge understood now that she would never see very much of him. They had started off together to explore something that promised to be wonderful, and, of course, there had been wonderful times. And yet, thought Mrs. Bridge, why is it that we haven't—that nothing has—that whatever we—?

It was raining. Thunder rumbled through the lowering clouds with a constant, monotonous, trundling sound, like furniture being rolled back and forth in the attic. In the front yard the evergreen trees swayed in the wind and the shutters rattled in the sudden rainy gusts. She noticed that a branch had been torn from the soft maple tree; the branch lay on the driveway and the leaves fluttered.

Harriet came in to ask if she would like some hot chocolate.

"Oh, no thank you, Harriet," said Mrs. Bridge. "You have some."

Harriet was so nice. And she was a good worker. Mrs. Bridge was very proud of having Harriet and knew that she would be next to impossible to replace, and yet there were times when Mrs. Bridge half wished she would quit. Why she wished this, she did not know, unless it was that with Harriet around to do all the work she herself was so often dismally bored. When she was first married she used to do the cooking and house-cleaning and washing, and how she had looked forward to a few minutes of leisure! But now—how odd—there was too much leisure. Mrs. Bridge did not admit this fact to anyone, for it embarrassed her; indeed she very often gave the impression of being distracted by all the things needed to be done—phone the laundry, the grocer, take Ruth to the dentist, Carolyn to tap-dancing class, Douglas to the barber shop, and so on. But the truth remained, and settled upon her with ever greater finality.

The light snapped on in the back hall. She heard his cough and the squeak of the closet door and the familiar flapping sound of his brief-case on the upper shelf. Suddenly overwhelmed by the need for re-assurance, she turned swiftly from the window and hurried toward him with an intent, wistful expression, knowing what she wanted without knowing how to ask for it.

He heard the rustle of her dress and her quick footsteps on the carpet. He was hanging up his coat as she approached, and he said, without irritation, but a trifle wearily because this was not the first time it had happened, "I see you forgot to have the car lubricated."

30

The Search for Love

It seemed to Mrs. Bridge that she had done the necessary thing, and therefore the right thing, in regard to the monstrous tower. Again and again she thought about it, and the reason she thought about it so intensively was that she perceived a change in Douglas's attitude toward her. He was more withdrawn.

As time went on she felt an increasing need for reassurance. Her husband had never been a demonstrative man, not even when they were first married; consequently she did not expect too much from him. Yet there were moments when she was overwhelmed by a terrifying, inarticulate need. One evening as she and he were finishing supper together, alone, the children having gone out, she inquired rather sharply if he loved her. She was surprised by her own bluntness and by the almost shrewish tone of her voice, because that was not the way she actually felt. She saw him gazing at her in astonishment; his expression said very clearly: Why on earth do you think I'm here if I don't love you? Why aren't I somewhere else? What in the world has got into you?

Mrs. Bridge smiled across the floral centerpiece—and it occurred to her that these flowers she had so carefully arranged on the table were what separated her from her husband—and said, a little wretchedly, "I know it's silly, but it's been such a long time since you told me."

Mr. Bridge grunted and finished his coffee. She knew it was not that he was annoyed, only that he was incapable of the kind of declaration she needed. It was so little, and yet so much. While they sat across from each other, neither knowing quite what to do next, she became embarrassed; and in her embarrassment she moved her feet and she inadvertently stepped on the buzzer, concealed beneath the carpet, that connected with the kitchen, with the result that Harriet soon appeared in the doorway to see what it was that Mrs. Bridge desired.

45

The Clock

She spent a great deal of time staring into space, oppressed by the sense that she was waiting. But waiting for what? She did not know. Surely someone would call, someone must be needing her. Yet each day proceeded like the one before. Nothing intense, nothing desperate, ever happened. Time did not move. The home, the city, the nation, and life itself were eternal; still she had a foreboding that one day, without warning and without pity, all the dear, important things would be destroyed. So it was that her thoughts now and then turned deviously deeper, spiraling down and down in search of the final recess, of life more immutable than the life she had bequeathed in the birth of her children.

One fathomless instant occurred on a windy, rainy night when Harriet had gone to church, and the children were out, and only she and her husband remained at home. For some time, perhaps an hour or more, they had been reading, separately; he had the financial page of the newspaper and she had been idly reading of the weddings that day. The rain blew softly against the windowpanes, shutters rattled, and above the front door the tin weather stripping began to moan. Mrs. Bridge, with the newspaper in her lap, listened to the rumbling and booming of thunder over the house. Suddenly, in total quiet, the room was illuminated by lightning. Mr. Bridge lifted his head, only that and nothing more, but within Mrs. Bridge something stirred. She looked at her husband intently.

"Did the clock strike?" he asked.

"No, I don't believe so," she answered, waiting.

He cleared his throat. He adjusted his glasses. He continued reading.

She never forgot this moment when she had almost apprehended the very meaning of life, and of the stars and planets, yes, and the flight of the earth.

46

Countess Mariska

The one person she ever met who surely had experienced similar moments was a Russian-Italian-Hungarian countess who passed through Kansas City like a leaf in the wind.

"The Countess Mariska Mihailova Strozzi," was how Lois Montgomery, who was the newly elected president of the Auxiliary, introduced her at luncheon.

"Ladies," the countess began, and went on talking for an hour, but it was an hour that seemed like a minute. No one whispered, no one left the room. The countess was electrifying, and the women who missed hearing her were told about her for months afterward. She was born in Shanghai, the daughter of an elderly Russian diplomat who, until an intrigue at the court, had been a close friend of Czar Nicholas II. The family had been exiled, there had been murders, abductions, espionage, and no one knew what else. At fourteen she was married to an Italian millionaire who claimed direct descent from the great Renaissance family which opposed the Medici, but she had run away from him. Later she married a rich Greek. Now she was divorced and on her way to San Francisco at the invitation of a munitions maker. She talked of her experiences, but mostly of the Nazis, and there was a rumor that just before coming to America she had killed a Nazi colonel with his own revolver. Mrs. Bridge, sitting in the front row, looking up into the glittering violet eyes, could easily believe it.

The countess was quite small and chic, and wore a black sheath dress. Her only jewelry was a large star sapphire that accentuated a strange bluish-white scar across the back of her hand. Mrs. Bridge was certain everyone was dying to know what had caused the scar, but no one dared ask. It was only one of the mysteries of the countess. She was delicate and utterly feminine, but at the same time she was as blunt as a man. It was clear she had been witness to many kinds of folly and wisdom and agony and joy. Once she paused and leisurely fitted a European cigarette into an ebony holder; several minutes must have gone by while she smoked and stared over the heads of her audience, but they were so transfixed that no one moved. Tamping out the cigarette, she continued in her perfect, heavy English, "We must destroy the Fascist. . . ."

Later Mrs. Bridge introduced herself to the countess, for that was what everyone else was doing, and for a minute or so they chatted. Two things Mrs. Bridge remembered about her: the first was a fresh red bruise on the tiny golden throat, a bruise such as a man's mouth would leave, and the second was that husky voice murmuring, "To be afraid is, I tell you, Madame, the most terrible thing in the world."

26

Tower

Douglas did a peculiar thing.

Instead of building a cave, or a house in a tree, as most of his friends were doing, he chose to build a tower of rubbish.

"Sounds awfully exciting," Mrs. Bridge responded somewhat absently when he first told her of his project; then, because she knew children wanted their parents to be interested in what they were doing, she asked how big it was going to be. He was vague, saying only that it was going to be the biggest tower anybody ever saw. She smiled and patted him affectionately. He looked at her for a long moment, shrugged in a singular way, and returned to the vacant lot where he intended to build the tower.

In the lot he had found some two-by-fours and a number of old bricks and half a bag of cement. He did not know where these materials had come from; he waited several days to see if they belonged to anybody. Apparently they didn't, so he claimed them. He got a shovel and went to work.

Having dug a hole about four feet deep, he lined it with brick and cement, planted the two-by-fours solidly upright, and liberally sprinkled this foundation with water. He then waited for his friends, the trash collectors, and followed their truck around the neighborhood. There was a moment between the time a rubbish barrel was rolled to the curb and the time the truck stopped for it that Douglas made good use of; he grabbed anything he thought belonged on his tower. He collected a great quantity of useful objects, and, on the side, about forty or fifty cereal boxtops, which he mailed to such places as Battle Creek, where there was a cereal factory, getting in return all kinds of prizes.

Within a week he had accumulated enough junk to keep the construction going for a long while. Half-hidden in the tall grass and wild shrubbery of the vacant lot lay a bundle of brass curtain rods which the Arlens thought were now in the city dump, a roll of electrician's tape and a bent skillet from the Pfeiffers' trash barrel, a hatchet with a splintered handle, a cigar box full of rusty nails, a broken fishing rod, several lengths of clothesline and wire, coat hangers, bottles, two apple boxes, an old raincoat and a pair of worn galoshes, a punctured inner tube, some very old golf clubs with wooden shafts, the cylinder from a lawnmower, springs from an overstuffed chair, and, among other articles, thanks again to the unconscious generosity of the Arlens, a mildewed leather suitcase.

"My!" said Mrs. Bridge, when he told her he was working on the tower, "I can see you're going to be an architect or an engineer when you grow up. Now we're having an early lunch because this is my day for bridge club, so don't run off somewhere."

Douglas said he would be in the vacant lot.

During the next week he managed to steal a full bag of powdered cement from a house going up in the next block; he broke it open after the workmen left, shoveled the powder into a wheelbarrow, and eventually managed to push the wheelbarrow into the vacant lot, where he dumped the powder in the pit and gave it a thorough watering. Thereafter he stopped mentioning his tower, and if asked what he was doing in the lot he would reply laconically that he was just playing.

With the addition of jugs and stones, tin cans, tree limbs, broken bottles, and all the other trash he could find, tied or nailed or cemented to the uprights, the tower continued to grow, until there came a Sunday morning when a man named Ewing who lived on the far side of the lot saw the tower rising above his hedge. At this point it was nearly six feet high. Ewing went around for a better look, and, discovering Douglas watching him from behind a sycamore tree, said to him, "What have you got here, my friend?"

"Nothing," replied Douglas, coming out from behind the sycamore. "It's just a tower, that's all. It isn't hurting anybody."

Having inspected the tower from all sides, Ewing turned his attention to Douglas, because it was the builder, after all, and not the building which was remarkable; and Douglas, embarrassed by the speculative eyes, picked up a length of pipe and struck the tower a resounding blow to prove it was as substantial as it looked.

Shortly thereafter Mrs. Bridge saw it too—it rose jaggedly above the fence that divided their grounds from the lot—and went out to investigate. She looked at it for a considerable period, tapping a fingernail against her teeth, and that same afternoon she said lightly to her son, "My, but that certainly is a big old tower."

Douglas thrust his hands in his pockets and gazed with a distant expression at his shoes.

"Think what would happen if it fell over ker-*plunk* and hit you square on the head," she continued, ruffling his hair, and reflecting automatically that he needed another haircut.

Douglas knew his tower would stop a truck, so he only sighed and pursed his lips.

Mrs. Bridge was not overly concerned, being under the impression he was going to become bored with the tower and would dismantle it. But about two weeks later she realized he was still working on it, because she could see a cider jug and a chicken coop wired to the top of a broken chair, and she recalled that on her last visit this chair had been on top of everything. She had assumed this chair was his throne; she remembered how he liked to play king-of-the-mountain, and possibly he only built the tower in order to have a throne. Now, wondering how much higher he meant to go, she walked out to the vacant lot for another look, and this time she remained somewhat longer. Tentatively she pushed at the tower and was troubled by its solidity. She pushed again, with her palm, and again, much harder. The tower did not sway an inch. She began to wonder whether or not he would be able to destroy his creation—assuming she could convince him it ought to be torn down.

She intended to speak to him that same afternoon, but she did not know precisely how to begin because, like the tower, he seemed to be growing out of her reach. He was becoming more than a small boy who could be coaxed this way or that; the hour was approaching when she must begin to reason with him as with an adult, and this idea disturbed her. She was not certain she was equal to it. And so a few days, a week, two weeks went by, and though she had not spoken neither had she forgotten.

"Well!" she finally exclaimed, as though she had just thought of it, "I see that ugly old tower keeps getting bigger and bigger." It was, to tell the truth, quite a bit bigger. When he did not say a word, or even look at her, she wanted to grab him by the shoulders and shake loose whatever was growing inside him.

"It seems to me that a big boy like you wouldn't want to go on building a silly tower," she said, hopefully, and then he glanced at her in a way that was somehow derisive, as if he were reading her mind.

"I'll tell you what let's do!" She stooped in order to look directly into his face. "First thing after dinner we'll get some wire clippers and a hammer and a screwdriver and—well, just everything we need, and you and I together will tear it to bits. Won't that be fun?"

He turned his head away and said very softly, "No."

"No? Why not?"

After a while Douglas rubbed his nose and muttered that there was too much concrete.

"Oh, I'll bet we—" Mrs. Bridge hesitated. Her insights usually arrived too late to illuminate the situation, but this one was in time.

"You're probably right," she said, continuing with treacherous frankness, "I doubt if you or anybody else could tear it down."

She watched him almost fall into the trap. He was ready to defy her by saying he could if he wanted to, and if she could get him to say that she knew the battle would be half over. He was on the verge of it; she could see the defiance on his face and in the way he stood. But then, instead of answering, he paused to think, and Mrs. Bridge was dismayed. All her life she had been accustomed to responding immediately when anyone spoke to her. If she had been complimented she promptly and graciously thanked the speaker; or if, by chance, her opinion was asked on something, anything—the cost of butter, the Italian situation—no matter what, if she was asked she answered readily. Now, seeing her son with his mouth clamped shut like a turtle with a seed and his face puckered in thought, she did not know what to do. She gazed down on him expectantly.

After a long silence Douglas said, "Maybe."

And here, for the time being, the matter rested.

29

Nothing Spectacular

At his wife's suggestion Mr. Bridge had walked around to the vacant lot to examine the eccentric and mystifying memorial Douglas had built and which he had not yet abandoned; Mr. Bridge tried to topple it and then simply attempted to shake it. The tower did not move. Satisfied that it would not collapse while Douglas or his friends were clambering about, and that they had sense enough not to impale themselves on the outcroppings, he returned to his evening newspaper and thought no more about it.

Mrs. Bridge, however, was uneasy. She sensed that people in the neighborhood were aware of the tower. Even so, she did not become actively alarmed until a man at a cocktail party, upon being introduced to her, mentioned that he had driven over to see the tower.

"Oh, horrors!" she exclaimed as a means of registering her attitude. "Is it famous all over the city?" And though she was joking she was dead serious.

"A curious form of protest," the man replied, tucking his pipe with tobacco; then, after a sharp glance directly into her eyes, he added, "You *are* aware of the boy's motivation, are you not?"

To which she smiled politely, being somewhat confused, and made a mental note that the man had been drinking.

The next morning as soon as Douglas left for school she telephoned the fire department. Everyone called the fire department when there was a problem that defied classification. Shortly before noon a small red truck parked in front of the house and two firemen—she had never spoken to a fireman before and found the experience rather strange—two of them entered the house as though it were the most natural thing in the world, and listened to what she told them about the tower. Then they went out to have a look. Mildly amused at first, presently they were startled. However they had been called upon by housewives for many unnatural labors, and so they unhooked their tools of destruction and set to work. It took them until almost dark to turn it into a mound of rubble, but at last an area of several square yards was covered with splintered wood, broken glass, wire, great gritty chunks of lumpy concrete, and whatever else had gone into the creation of it, and the air was filled with dust as though there had been a peculiar explosion. The firemen said they would make a report of the tower and its destruction and that the lot would be cleaned up within a day or two.

Douglas, having come home a few minutes before the firemen left, stood watching them in grieved silence. Mrs. Bridge, seeing him from an upstairs window, went out to stand behind him with her hands resting on his shoulders, and occasionally rumpled his hair.

"It was just getting too big," she confided to him gently. "People were beginning to wonder."

71

French Restaurant

To Mr. and Mrs. Bridge it seemed that no matter where they went in Paris they ran into Americans; consequently it was no surprise when a young man named Morgan Hager, who was from Kansas City and whose father had written that the Bridges would be visiting, told them that in addition to tourists there were several thousand Americans who had taken up permanent residence in the city, mostly on the Left Bank.

No, he did not know what all these expatriates did for a living; yes, he thought they were happy in France; he had no idea whether they intended to remain in a foreign country for the rest of their lives. Mrs. Bridge could not imagine anyone wanting to live outside the United States. To visit, yes. To take up residence, no.

"I should think they would get awfully lonely," she said.

"I guess so," said Hager. "I know I do."

"But then why do you stay?"

"Because I'm happier here."

This was puzzling and she wanted to understand. She observed him frankly and saw that he did not look happy; at least he seldom smiled. She did not think he was truly happy.

"If you have the time, Morgan," said Mr. Bridge, "I'd like to see some of this Bohemian life we hear so much about."

Hager looked at him doubtfully, for the request posed a problem. There were many things he could have shown them, but, even as certain murals in Pompeii are not open to casual tourists, so there were various Parisian experiences not listed in the guidebook.

"Well," said Hager modestly, "I really don't know of anything very Bohemian, but you might like to have dinner at a place on Montparnasse where a lot of art students eat. It's sort of dirty," he added thoughtfully.

Mrs. Bridge thought this sounded exciting. "Perhaps we should go back to the hotel and change," she said.

Hager did not know whether she meant to get more dressed up or less dressed up, so finally he said, "I don't think anybody will notice you." This had a peculiar ring, so he added, "You look all right." Somehow this was not what he had in mind either, so he cleared his throat, scratched his nose, and said, "The place is actually a real dump." He tried again. "I mean, you can get in with no trouble." Having run himself into a cul-de-sac he stopped to meditate. "Oh, well," he said at last, "let's go. I'm hungry as a sonofabitch."

It was the smallest restaurant Mrs. Bridge had ever seen. It was not much larger than her kitchen at home, but somehow or other there were a dozen oilcloth-covered tables jammed into it and every table was crowded. It reeked of cheese and wine and smoke and perspiration. Wedged between the door and a coatrack they stood and waited for three vacancies, and finally the waiter, who was a fat boy with crew-cut hair and a dirty apron, called through the smoke and the gabble, "Alors, vite! J'ai trois! Vite!"

"Okay, step on it," Hager muttered. "He's got three but they won't last," and he began pushing Mrs. Bridge into the confusion.

Finding no room on the table for her purse, and no other place to put it, she was obliged to hold it in her lap. The menu was scrawled on a blackboard on the wall and Hager translated and made recommendations and both Mr. and Mrs. Bridge accepted his suggestions. Seated next to her was an unusually ragged person wearing a short-sleeved shirt and a filthy blue beret.

"Bonjour, Claude," said Morgan Hager.

"Ah, mon ami!" said the dirty one. "Comment ça va?"

"Oh, ça va," replied Hager. "Claude, je vous présente Monsieur et Madame Bridge."

"How do you do?" said Mrs. Bridge.

"Enchanté!" said Claude, with his mouth full of bread. He looked at her speculatively. He plucked at his shirt and said, "C'est un cadeau."

"I gave him the shirt," said Hager.

"Oh. How nice."

"Oui," said Claude, still chewing and eyeing her. He saw that her wine glass had not been filled, so he reached across the table for the community bottle and filled the glass for her, saying, "C'est bon, alors."

"Thank you," said Mrs. Bridge. The wine was bright red and had a few specks floating on the surface.

"It tastes like vinegar," said Hager as he saw her looking at it doubtfully. "We can get some better stuff. Claude's dead broke, that's why he drinks it. I mean, it's only about one cent a glass."

"Oh, I'm sure it's quite good," she replied, though she was sure it wasn't. She tasted it and smiled because Claude was watching.

"C'est bon, n'est-ce pas?" he demanded.

"Oh, yes, it's really awfully good," she replied, and took another sip to prove she meant it. Claude nodded approvingly. He was eating salad now. He paused, leaned forward, and pulled a limp, black, stringy object out of the bowl. Mrs. Bridge saw it was a spider. Evidently it had climbed into the salad, or had fallen in, and drowned. Claude indifferently dropped it into a shell half filled with ashes and cigarette stubs and continued eating. In a little while the spider recovered and crawled unsteadily out of the ash tray, across the table, and disappeared on the other side.

Presently the waiter arrived with the first course and stood around for a few moments to see if they would enjoy it. The spider had taken the edge from Mrs. Bridge's appetite, and as for salad, though she tried valiantly she could eat nothing more than a bit of tomato.

Back at the hotel that night Mr. Bridge observed that he had always heard so much about French cooking but if that was a fair sample he would rather eat in Kansas City.

"I thought it was very good," she said loyally.

"You didn't eat much," he said.

"Well, good heavens," she replied, "we didn't go there for the food."

73

Strangers in Paradise

Next day they went window-shopping along the boulevards near the Opéra, and in the course of this stroll Mrs. Bridge became slightly separated from her husband. They were walking slowly up the rue Auber, stopping at whatever interested them, and she had drifted ahead, musing on the difference between Paris and Kansas City, observing the French businessmen who seemed content to loiter for hours in sidewalk cafés, and whose attitude, she reflected, was certainly pleasure before business.

Finding herself alone, she looked back and saw him standing with his arms folded, staring into one of the shop windows. She waited a while, thinking he would be coming along, but whatever he saw had hypnotized him. Her curiosity aroused, she retraced her steps. He sensed her approach and looked around with a start. They wandered along as before, but she had seen the object of his attention: a black lace brassière with the tips cut off.

The more she mulled over this incident the more concerned she became. The French, after all, might do as they pleased; she need have nothing to do with the French, but she must live with her husband. She had lived with him for a long time now, and assumed she knew whatever was worth knowing about him. True, there were occasional surprises—once he had told her, and afterward seemed to regret having divulged the secret, that when he was a boy he used to dream of becoming a great composer—but the revelations of his nature had seemed meaningless, no matter how fascinating, and she was not apt to dwell on them, but now she did.

Why had he stood there looking? What had he been thinking? His expression had been so serious. Were there things he had never told her about himself? Who was he, really? From all the recesses of her being came the questions, questions which had never before occurred to her, and there on the foreign street she felt lost and forsaken, and with great longing she began to think of Kansas City.

78

Mirror

Mrs. Bridge slept later than she intended to the second morning in Monte Carlo; they had visited the casino the previous night, and while she had not gambled she had found it nonetheless a rather strenuous experience. Her husband was gone when she finally awoke, but this was not surprising because he had gotten so accustomed to rising early in order to put in a full day at the office that he was no longer able to lie in bed past seven o'clock. Probably he was walking briskly around town, and no doubt he would be waiting to check on the Italian reservations as soon as the travel agency opened its doors for the day. She often wondered where he found so much energy.

The clock on the night table told her it was almost noon. She felt a trifle guilty. And yet it was delicious to lie in bed and to feel on her cheek and on her arms the mild breezes drifting up the hillside from the Mediterranean. A few minutes more, she thought, then she really must get up. And so, with eyes half open, she lay motionless and knew how fortunate she was. And she inquired of herself what she had done to deserve all this. There was no answer. All at once she perceived something so obvious and vulgar that she could not imagine why it had failed to escape her attention. She could see herself in the mirror on the wall, the mirror faced the bed, and she had suddenly realized that in every one of their European hotel rooms a large mirror had faced the bed. At the significance of this her blue eyes opened wide and she quickly turned her head on the pillow. In Paris a beautiful ornate Louis Quatorze mirror had frankly revealed her intimacy with her husband, and in London, too, now that she thought about it, they had been mirrored.

Deeply troubled, puzzled, no longer thankful, Mrs. Bridge lay in bed with an expression of listless despair and gazed through the opened doors of the balcony, through the iron grillwork to the distant sea, to the purple clarity and the white sails.

101

Quo Vadis, Madame?

That evening, while preparing for bed, Mrs. Bridge suddenly paused with the fingertips of one hand just touching her cheek. She was seated before her dressing table in her robe and slippers and had begun spreading cold cream on her face. The touch of the cream, the unexpectedness of it—for she had been thinking deeply about how to occupy tomorrow—the swift cool touch demoralized her so completely that she almost screamed.

She continued spreading the cream over her features, steadily observing herself in the mirror, and wondered who she was, and how she happened to be at the dressing table, and who the man was who sat on the edge of the bed taking off his shoes. She considered her fingers, which dipped into the jar of their own accord. Rapidly, soundlessly, she was disappearing into white, sweetly scented anonymity. Gratified by this she smiled, and perceived a few seconds later that beneath the mask she was not smiling. All the same, being committed, there was nothing to do but proceed.

103

Psychotherapy

Mabel Ong was going to an analyst. Mrs. Bridge was surprised to learn this because Mabel in her tailored suits and with her authoritative masculine manner had always seemed the very picture of confidence. At luncheon club not long after Dr. Foster's eloquent sermon on church attendance she found herself sitting next to Mabel, and by the time luncheon was over Mrs. Bridge was convinced that she, too, needed analysis. She had, in fact, privately thought so long before her talk with Mabel. More and more it had occurred to her that she was no longer needed. Ruth was gone, so very gone—even her letters said so little— and Carolyn was almost gone, and Douglas, though still at home, was growing so independent, more like his father every year. Soon he too would be leaving home. What would she do then? It had been a long time, she felt, since her husband truly needed her. He accepted her, and he loved her, of this she had never had a doubt, but he was accustomed to and quite unconscious of love, whereas she wanted him to think about it and to tell her about it. The promise of the past had been fulfilled: she had three fine children and her husband was wonderfully successful. But Mrs. Bridge felt tired and ill. She wanted help.

She surmised her husband would not be sympathetic to her idea of being psychoanalyzed, so, for a number of weeks before mentioning it, she planned the conversation. She meant to open with the direct, positive, almost final statement that she was going downtown the first thing in the morning to arrange a series of appointments. That certainly ought to settle the matter—he ought to be able to understand the situation. Possibly he was going to inquire how much it would cost, and she was uneasy about this, suspecting it was going to be expensive, with the result that she avoided finding out what it would cost. After all, in spite of his complaints, she knew, and he was aware that she knew, that they had plenty of money.

She tried to imagine all his objections to her idea, but really there was nothing he could say. He would simply be forced to agree. It had been years since she had asked him for anything, no matter how slight; indeed, every once in a while he would inquire if there wasn't something she wanted—anything for the house, or for herself. No, there was nothing. It was difficult to find things to buy. She had the money, but she had already bought everything she could use, which was why she often spent an entire day shopping and came home without having bought anything except lunch, and perhaps some pastry during the afternoon.

Having solved whatever objection he might make in regard to the expense, she concluded that all she had to do was let him know her intention. She kept putting it off. She rehearsed the scene many times and it always came out satisfactorily. The difficulty lay in finding the opportunity to begin. So it was that several weeks slipped away, then one evening after supper, as they were settling themselves in the living room, she with a bag of knitting and he with the stock-market page of the newspaper, she knew the time had come. She pretended to be straightening her knitting, but she was greatly occupied with marshaling her thoughts. He always got to the heart of a matter at once, wasting no energy on preliminaries, and she had to be ready for this. Just then he lowered the paper and she was terrified that somehow he had been reading her mind. Quite often he could, and this more than anything else was the reason she found it exceedingly difficult to defend her ideas. He was glaring at the newspaper.

"Listen to this: The Central has asked the ICC to investigate the circumstances of the sale of eight hundred thousand shares of stock, owned by the Chesapeake and Ohio Railway, to Murchison and Richardson last week." He looked across the paper at her as if she were responsible.

"Well!" said Mrs. Bridge in what she thought an appropriate tone. It would be unwise to annoy him at this point, but until he made it clear whose side he was on she could not say anything specific. Her expression remained intent and neutrally expectant, as though she wanted to hear more.

"What in God's name do those people think they're doing?" he demanded sharply.

"It certainly doesn't seem right," she answered, still not certain whether the scoundrels were Central, or Chesapeake and Ohio, or Murchison and Richardson. Or, of course, he could be angry with the newspaper for having publicized it.

Mr. Bridge had taken off his glasses and was staring at her.

"I don't know a thing in the world about it, of course," she added hastily.

He resumed reading. A few minutes later he said, "Allied Chemical: up four! Great Lord! What's going on here?" After this he was quiet for a long time, coughing once, shaking the paper into shape. Mrs. Bridge, having noted it was almost time for bed, decided she must speak.

"Walter," she began in a tremulous voice, and went on rapidly, "I've been thinking it over and I don't see any way out except through analysis."

He did not look up. Minutes went by. Finally he muttered, "Australian wool is firm." And then, roused by the sound of his own voice, he glanced at her inquisitively. She gave him a stark, desperate look; it was unnecessary to repeat what she had said because he always heard everything even when he failed to reply.

"What?" he demanded. "Nonsense," he said absently, and he struck the paper into submission and continued reading.

104

Pineapple Bread

The following day being Thursday, Harriet's day off, Mrs. Bridge prepared supper for herself and her husband. Douglas had telephoned a few minutes after school let out to say he was at a fraternity meeting and that as soon as it was over he and a couple of friends were going to get a hamburger somewhere and then were going downtown to a track meet in the municipal auditorium.

"What about your homework?" she asked.

"Homework," he replied, giving a very final opinion of it.

"Well, I don't think you should stay out late," she answered. "After all, it's a week night."

He said he would be home early, but early could mean any hour.

"All right now, don't forget," she said. "Your grades haven't been worth boasting about."

"I'll get by," said Douglas. "Holy Cow!"

"Yes, well you just might Holy Cow yourself right out of graduating."

With that the conversation ended and she went into the kitchen to start preparing a casserole, as she had done many, many times before. She moved around the kitchen slowly. She had plenty of time. The house was so quiet that she began to think of how noisy it had been when all the children were there, how very much different everything had been, and presently, remembering the days when she used to cook the meals, she went to the cupboard where the old recipe books were stored. Harriet occasionally referred to them, but otherwise they had lain untouched for years. Mrs. Bridge began looking through them, seeing pencil notations in her own handwriting, scarcely legible any more. Her husband liked more pepper in this, no bay leaves in that—whatever he wanted and whatever he did not like was expertly registered in the margins, and as she turned through these recipes she thought how strangely intimate the faded penciled notes remained; they brought back many scenes, many sweet and private memories; they brought back youth.

Mrs. Bridge grew thoughtfully excited. A glance at the electric clock on the stove panel told her there might be time enough to alter her plans for supper. She was thinking of fixing spaghetti for him, with the special sauce he had so often said was the best in the world. She had not fixed it for years. Harriet could not sense just how long to let it simmer, and without that particular flavor to the sauce there was not much point in eating spaghetti. A quick search of the refrigerator and of the cupboards disclosed there were not the right ingredients. She found some canned sauce and thought about improvising from it, but it would not be the same. He would taste the difference. And so, regretfully, she admitted it was going to be the casserole again. Next week they would have spaghetti. A little sadly she turned on through the cookbooks, and once more she had an idea. She had come across the recipe for pineapple bread and there was time for that and she was certain they had the ingredients—not only the pineapple but the chipped pecans, the raisins—yes, yes, she could do it.

She carried the bread to the table wrapped in a towel because it was still hot from the oven, and Mr. Bridge, who, as he unfolded his napkin, had been looking at the casserole with resignation, now glanced with puzzled interest at what she was bringing him. His expression began to brighten. He smiled.

"Oh-ho!" said Mr. Bridge, rubbing his hands together, "What have we here?"

She placed it before him, too thrilled to speak, and hurried back to the kitchen for the bread knife.

"Well, well!" said he, accepting the knife, and he smacked his lips and shut his eyes for a moment to inhale the fragrance of the small plump loaf.

"Go ahead and cut it," she said to him intensely, and waited beside his chair.

The first slice fell down like a corpse and they saw bubbles of dank white dough around the pecans. After a moment of silence Mrs. Bridge covered it with the towel and carried it to the kitchen. Having disposed of the bread she untied her little ruffled apron and waited quietly until she regained control of herself.

A few minutes later she re-entered the dining room with a loaf of grocery-store bread on a silver tray. She smiled and said, "It's been a long time, I'm afraid."

"Never mind," said Mr. Bridge as he removed the lid of the casserole, and the next day he brought her a dozen roses.

111

Old Acquaintance

The country was now at war. Douglas had graduated from high school and wanted to join the Army. Ruth was gone; she seldom wrote. Carolyn, unable to get along with her husband, was coming home more frequently. And Mrs. Bridge, lost in confusion, often lay down to rest awhile, and thought back to happier times. She saw that it was inevitable these things had come to pass, and she could not escape a feeling of unreality. One day, while shopping on the Plaza, she had recognized someone who used to live next door to her when she was a child. The woman was now evidently verging on old age, and Mrs. Bridge, counting down the years as she observed, from a distance, the conclusion of the youth which was her own, felt a growing sense of despair and futility, and ever after that day she herself moved a little more slowly.

114

Letter from a Buddhist

Douglas, having exchanged telegrams with the commandant of his camp, remained in Kansas City till after the funeral. Ruth had flown home from New York and Carolyn had driven up from Parallel; both of them were struck by the change in Douglas. Ruth had no difficulty accepting him as the new head of the family, though he was nearly five years younger than she. Carolyn challenged him once or twice, half-heartedly. Neither of them expected their mother to make decisions. And to Mrs. Bridge herself it seemed natural that he should become the authority. Harriet, keenly attuned to every situation, asked Douglas if she could have a raise; he said no. From that moment on she stopped calling him by his first name and referred to him as Mr. Bridge, and his mother, hearing this for the first time, began to weep.

Soon, like birds abandoning a tree, they flew off in different directions. Ruth went back to New York, Carolyn to southern Kansas, and Douglas to the Army. The functions of the house were carried on by Harriet, and Mrs. Bridge was left alone. She often went to Auxiliary meetings, and she went shopping downtown, and to the Plaza for luncheon, and to a number of parties, but she could no longer lose herself in these activities; the past was too much with her, and so she was frequently content to stay at home, waiting for the mail, or waiting for someone to call, remotely conscious of the persistent roar of the vacuum cleaner, no longer caring if Harriet smoked in the kitchen.

When she received the first letter Douglas wrote after returning to camp she thought how intimately it resembled the letters her huband used to write when he was out of town on business. There had been something quaint about her husband, an old-fashioned inclination which had caused him to begin his letters to her with, "My dear wife . . ."

How strange that Douglas should write:

My dear Mother,
   My father loved you above all else, and if he was apt to be rude or tyrannical it was because he wanted to protect you. He wanted so much for us all. He did not ever realize that what we needed was himself instead of what he could give us. On more than one occasion he and I discussed the family and its problems and in these talks I felt his constant preoccupation with your welfare after he was gone. I guess he knew he was not going to live much longer. He said he had never told you about the trouble with his heart.
   There is nothing at all for you to worry about. You made him very happy during his life. I am quite certain that never once was he interested in another woman. My love to you, Mother, and to both my sisters. Tell Ruth when next you write her that I am anxious to hear from her.
   Well, we have to go out on maneuvers now, but I'll write you again pretty soon.

With love, as always,
Douglas

117

Hello?

One December morning near the end of the year when snow was falling moist and heavy for miles all around, so that the earth and the sky were indivisible, Mrs. Bridge emerged from her home and spread her umbrella. With small cautious steps she proceeded to the garage, where she pressed the button and waited impatiently for the door to lift. She was in a hurry to drive downtown to buy some Irish lace antimacassars that were advertised in the newspaper, and she was planning to spend the remainder of the day browsing through the stores because it was Harriet's day off and the house was empty—so empty.

She had backed just halfway out of the garage when the engine died. She touched the starter and listened without concern because, despite her difficulties with the Lincoln, she had grown to feel secure in it. The Lincoln was a number of years old and occasionally recalcitrant, but she could not bear the thought of parting with it, and in the past had resisted this suggestion of her husband, who, mildly puzzled by her attachment to the car, had allowed her to keep it.

Thinking she might have flooded the engine, which was often true, Mrs. Bridge decided to wait a minute or so.

Presently she tried again, and again, and then again. Deeply disappointed, she opened the door to get out and discovered she had stopped in such a position that the car doors were prevented from opening more than a few inches on one side by the garage partition, and on the other side by the wall. Having tried all four doors she began to understand that until she could attract someone's attention she was trapped. She pressed the horn, but there was not a sound. Half inside and half outside she remained.

For a long time she sat there with her gloved hands folded in her lap, not knowing what to do. Once she looked at herself in the mirror. Finally she took the keys from the ignition and began tapping on the window, and she called to anyone who might be listening, "Hello? Hello out there?"

But no one answered, unless it was the falling snow.

QUESTIONS

1. What use does Connell make of his chapter titles? Give some examples of ironic titles. Where else does he make use of irony?
2. What were Mrs. Bridge's motives for her marriage? Were other choices available to her? Why does she never demand more love from her husband?
3. What values does Mrs. Bridge try to inculcate in her children? What other values does she inculcate unconsciously? Why does her naked child, Ruth, scream hysterically when she sees the expression on her mother's face? How could this incident influence the child in later life?
4. Why is Mrs. Bridge upset by Miss Bloch's strange habit in the classroom? Why could it be said that such an incident is a particularly good example of Connell's literary strategy?
5. How does Countess Mariska comment on all that is lacking in Mrs. Bridge's life?
6. What kind of unconscious feelings might Doug be expressing by

building his tower? What effect might Mrs. Bridge's destruction of it have on him later?

7. What feelings of anxiety are aroused in Mrs. Bridge by her children's growing sexual awareness?

8. What perceptions force their way into Mrs. Bridge's consciousness when she and Mr. Bridge visit Europe?

9. What is Connell's tone in the final chapter? Is he merely objective or is there a sense of compassion? Why is Mrs. Bridge's fate at the end thematically appropriate?

QUESTIONS FOR STUDY AND WRITING (PART I)

1. Interpret one of Whitman's shorter poems. Analyze his use of language, rhythm, meter, and figures of speech. Do his literary devices help or hinder your enjoyment of the poem?

2. Contrast the prose style of Dos Passos in his biographies with that of Fitzgerald in "Winter Dreams." How do they differ in their choice of words and their use of irony and tone? What mood is each writer trying to evoke?

3. What elements of theme are common to Whitman's poems and Fitzgerald's "Winter Dreams"? Contrast how each writer makes use of symbols.

4. Compare the narrative techniques of Fitzgerald and Connell. How does each handle the problem of narrative point of view? Which author reveals more of his personal feelings towards his characters?

5. Examine the characterizations of Dexter Green and Mrs. Bridge. Which is the more believable character? Which is more likable and which evokes more compassion? Does your sex influence your opinion?

"The Imprisoned Self

HERMAN MELVILLE

HERMAN MELVILLE (1819–91), like Walt Whitman, was one of America's literary giants in the nineteenth century and, also like Whitman, was generally rejected by the American public. His best-known work, *Moby Dick* (1851), was preceded by five novels about his earlier voyages and adventures on the South Seas. In his next novel, *Pierre* (1852), he abandoned the sea story to write a somewhat self-revealing "tragedy" of a young writer; it failed badly. "Bartleby the Scrivener" was part of a collection of short stories called *The Piazza Tales*, published soon after *Pierre* in 1856. In this collection Melville tried to make up for the financial disaster of *Pierre* by returning to the more lucrative genre of the adventure story. There are some critics who see in Bartleby's reply—"I would prefer not to" —Melville's own reply to a commercial-minded American culture that would undermine his creativity by accepting from him only what was superficial and non-threatening to its values.

There are also some satirical elements in "Bartleby the Scrivener" that may or may not be related to Melville's personal life. Melville's brothers, Gansevourt and Allen, actually were Wall Street lawyers and his father-in-law was yet another successful lawyer who helped Melville's family out of financial difficulty. As an artist Melville certainly felt like an outsider in their world. Perhaps there were times when he had to act as if he fitted in, but the majority of his critics feel that he was a deeply-alienated non-conformist in American society and that he, like Bartleby, had said "no" to an American society that he felt had at its base a superficial conception of the possibilities of human life.

The personality of the lawyer who narrates the story seems to confirm this view. We know much more about him than we do about any other character, and what we know is not very appealing. At first glance he seems kind, kind in that he seems to care about Bartleby's welfare and refuses to abruptly throw him out onto the street. But despite his kindness and his momentary invocation of Christian charity, he really believes only in making money and preserving his tight little world of finance. When Bartleby enters this world, the lawyer becomes quite upset and loses control because he cannot deal with anything so irrational.

Although every reader must come to his own conclusions about Bartleby and his response, "I would prefer not to," it is clear from his refusal to do many of the onerous business tasks assigned him that he does not enjoy such work. (Nor do the other clerks find such labor rewarding.) Images of confinement and prisons, in fact, abound and accumulate as the story progresses. Bartleby's office, for example, has no windows. Furthermore, Bartleby himself seems cut off from any private life; he has no personal pleasures, no friends, no hobbies. Without a private self, it is perhaps inevitable that his only release from such a world is an unheroic, passive, self-annihilation.

Bartleby the Scrivener
A STORY OF WALL STREET

I am a rather elderly man. The nature of my avocations for the last thirty years has brought me into more than ordinary contact with what would seem an interesting and somewhat singular set of men, of whom as yet nothing that I know of has ever been written:—I mean the law-copyists or scriveners. I have known very many of them, professionally and privately, and if I pleased, could relate divers histories, at which good-natured gentlemen might smile, and sentimental souls might weep. But I waive the biographies of all other scriveners for a few passages in the life of Bartleby, who was a scrivener the strangest I ever saw or heard of. While of other law-copyists I might write the complete life, of Bartleby nothing of that sort can be done. I believe that no materials exist for a full and satisfactory biography of this man. It is an irreparable loss to literature. Bartleby was one of those beings of whom nothing is ascertainable, except from the original sources, and in his case those are very small. What my own astonished eyes saw of Bartleby, *that* is all I know of him, except, indeed, one vague report which will appear in the sequel.

Ere introducing the scrivener, as he first appeared to me, it is fit I make some mention of myself, my *employés*, my business, my chambers, and general surroundings; because some such description is indispensable to an adequate understanding of the chief character about to be presented.

Imprimis: I am a man who, from his youth upward, has been filled with a profound conviction that the easiest way of life is the best. Hence, though I belong to a profession proverbially energetic and nervous, even to turbulence, at times, yet nothing of that sort have I ever suffered to invade my peace. I am one of those unambitious lawyers who never addresses a jury, or in any way draws down public applause; but in the cool tranquillity of a snug retreat, do a snug business among rich men's bonds and mortgages and title-deeds. All who know me, consider me an eminently *safe* man. The late John Jacob Astor, a personage little given to poetic enthusiasm, had no hesitation in pronouncing my first grand point to be prudence; my next, method. I do not speak it in vanity, but simply record the fact, that I was not unemployed in my profession by the late John Jacob Astor; a name which, I admit, I love to repeat, for it hath a rounded and orbicular sound to it, and rings like unto bullion. I will freely add, that I was not insensible to the late John Jacob Astor's good opinion.

Some time prior to the period at which this little history begins, my

From THE PIAZZA TALES, 1856.

avocations had been largely increased. The good old office, now extinct in the State of New York, of a Master in Chancery, had been conferred upon me. It was not a very arduous office, but very pleasantly remunerative. I seldom lose my temper; much more seldom indulge in dangerous indignation at wrongs and outrages; but I must be permitted to be rash here and declare that I consider the sudden and violent abrogation of the office of Master in Chancery, by the new Constitution, as a —— premature act; inasmuch as I had counted upon a life-lease of the profits, whereas I only received those of a few short years. But this is by the way.

My chambers were upstairs at No. —— Wall Street. At one end they looked upon the white wall of the interior of a spacious sky-light shaft, penetrating the building from top to bottom. This view might have been considered rather tame than otherwise, deficient in what landscape painters call "life." But if so, the view from the other end of my chambers offered, at least, a contrast, if nothing more. In that direction my windows commanded an unobstructed view of a lofty brick wall, black by age and everlasting shade; which wall required no spy-glass to bring out its lurking beauties, but for the benefit of all near-sighted spectators, was pushed up to within ten feet of my window panes. Owing to the great height of the surrounding buildings, and my chambers being on the second floor, the interval between this wall and mine not a little resembled a huge square cistern.

At the period just preceding the advent of Bartleby, I had two persons as copyists in my employment, and a promising lad as an office-boy. First, Turkey; second, Nippers; third, Ginger Nut. These may seem names, the like of which are not usually found in the Directory. In truth they were nicknames, mutually conferred upon each other by my three clerks, and were deemed expressive of their respective persons or characters. Turkey was a short, pursy Englishman of about my own age, that is, somewhere not far from sixty. In the morning, one might say, his face was of a fine florid hue, but after twelve o'clock, meridian—his dinner hour—it blazed like a grate full of Christmas coals; and continued blazing—but, as it were, with a gradual wane—till 6 o'clock P.M. or thereabouts, after which I saw no more of the proprietor of the face, which, gaining its meridian with the sun, seemed to set with it, to rise, culminate, and decline the following day, with the like regularity and undiminished glory. There are many singular coincidences I have known in the course of my life, not the least among which was the fact, that exactly when Turkey displayed his fullest beams from his red and radiant countenance, just then, too, at that critical moment, began the daily period when I considered his business capacities as seriously disturbed for the remainder of the twenty-four hours. Not that he was absolutely idle, or averse to business then; far from it. The difficulty was, he was apt to be altogether too energetic. There was a strange, inflamed, flurried, flighty recklessness of activity about him. He would be incautious in dipping his pen into his inkstand. All his blots upon my documents, were dropped there after twelve o'clock, meridian. Indeed, not only would he be reckless and sadly given to making blots in the afternoon, but some days he went further, and was rather noisy. At such times, too, his face flamed with augmented blazonry, as if cannel coal had been heaped on anthracite. He made an unpleasant racket with his chair; spilled his sand-box; in mending his pens, impatiently split them all to pieces, and threw them on the floor in a sudden passion; stood up and leaned over his table, boxing his papers about in a most indecorous manner, very sad to behold in an elderly man like him. Nevertheless, as he was in many ways a most valuable person to me, and all the time before twelve o'clock, meridian, was the quickest, steadiest creature, too, accomplishing a great deal of work in a style not easy to be matched—for these reasons, I was willing to overlook his eccentricities, though indeed, occasionally, I remonstrated with him. I did this very gently, however, because, though the civilest, nay, the blandest and most reverential of men in the morning, yet in the afternoon he was disposed, upon provocation, to be slightly rash with his tongue, in fact, insolent. Now, valuing his morning services as I did, and resolving not to lose them—yet, at the same time, made uncomfortable by his inflamed ways after twelve o'clock; and being a man of peace, unwilling by my admonitions to call forth unseemly retorts from him—I took upon me, one Saturday noon (he was always worse on Saturdays), to hint to him, very kindly, that perhaps now that he was growing old, it might be well to abridge his labours; in short, he need not come to my chambers after twelve o'clock, but, dinner over, had best go home to his lodgings and rest himself till tea-time. But no; he insisted upon his afternoon devotions. His countenance became intolerably fervid, as he oratorically assured me—gesticulating, with a long ruler, at the other side of the room—that if his services in the morning were useful, how indispensable, then, in the afternoon?

"With submission, sir," said Turkey on this occasion, "I consider myself your right-hand man. In the morning I but marshal and deploy my columns; but in the afternoon I put myself at their head, and gallantly charge the foe, thus!"—and he made a violent thrust with the ruler.

"But the blots, Turkey," intimated I.

"True,—but, with submission, sir, behold these hairs! I am getting old. Surely, sir, a blot or two of a warm afternoon is not to be severely urged against grey hairs. Old age—even if it blot the page—is honourable. With submission, sir, we *both* are getting old."

This appeal to my fellow-feeling was hardly to be resisted. At all events, I saw that go he would not. So I made up my mind to let him stay, resolving, nevertheless, to see to it, that during the afternoon he had to do with my less important papers.

Nippers, the second on my list, was a whiskered, sallow, and, upon the whole, rather piratical-looking young man of about five and twenty. I always deemed him the victim of two evil powers—ambition and indigestion. The ambition was evinced by a certain impatience of the duties of a mere copyist—an unwarrantable usurpation of strictly professional affairs, such as the original drawing up of legal documents. The indigestion seemed betokened in an occasional nervous testiness and grinning irritability, causing the teeth to audibly grind together over mistakes committed in copying; unnecessary maledictions, hissed, rather than spoken, in the heat of business; and especially by a continual discontent with the height of the table where he worked. Though of a very ingenious mechanical turn, Nippers could never get this table to suit him. He put chips under it, blocks of various sorts, bits of pasteboard, and at last went so far as to attempt an exquisite adjustment by final pieces of folded blotting-paper. But no invention would answer. If, for the sake of easing his back, he brought the table lid at a sharp angle well up toward his chin, and wrote there like a man using the steep roof of a Dutch house for his desk—then he declared that it stopped the circulation in his arms. If now he lowered the table to his waistbands, and stooped over it in writing, then there was a sore aching in his back. In short, the truth of the matter was, Nippers knew not what he wanted. Or, if he wanted anything, it was to be rid of a scrivener's table altogether. Among the manifestations of his diseased ambition was a fondness he had for receiving visits from certain ambiguous-looking fellows in seedy coats, whom he called his clients. Indeed I was aware that not only was he, at times, considerable of a ward-politician, but he occasionally did a little business at the Justices' courts, and was not unknown on the steps of the Tombs. I have good reason to believe, however, that one individual who called upon him at my chambers, and who, with a grand air, he insisted was his client, was no other than a dun, and the alleged title-deed, a bill. But with all his failings, and the annoyances he caused me, Nippers, like his compatriot Turkey, was a very useful man to me; wrote a neat, swift hand; and, when he chose, was not deficient in a gentlemanly sort of deportment. Added to this, he always dressed in a gentlemanly sort of way; and so, incidentally, reflected credit upon my chambers. Whereas with respect to Turkey, I had much ado to keep him from being a reproach to me. His clothes were apt to look oily and smell of eating-houses. He wore his pantaloons very loose and baggy in summer. His coats were execrable; his hat not to be handled. But while the hat was a thing of indifference to me, inasmuch as his natural civility and deference, as a dependent Englishman, always led him to doff it the moment he entered the room, yet his coat was another matter. Concerning his coats, I reasoned with him; but with no effect. The truth was, I suppose, that a man with so small an income could not afford to sport such a lustrous face and a lustrous coat at one and the same time. As Nippers once observed, Turkey's money went chiefly for red ink. One winter day I presented Turkey with a highly respectable-looking coat of my own, a padded grey coat, of a most comfortable warmth, and which buttoned straight up from the knee to the neck. I thought Turkey would appreciate the favour, and abate his rashness and obstreperousness of afternoons. But no. I verily believe that buttoning himself up in so downy and blanket-like a coat had a pernicious effect upon him; upon the same principle that too much oats are bad for horses. In fact, precisely as a rash, restive horse is said to feel his oats, so Turkey felt his coat. It made him insolent. He was a man whom prosperity harmed.

Though concerning the self-indulgent habits of Turkey I had my own private surmises, yet touching Nippers I was well persuaded that whatever might be his faults in other respects, he was, at least, a temperate young man. But, indeed, nature herself seemed to have been his vintner, and at his birth charged him so thoroughly with an irritable, brandy-like disposition, that all subsequent potations were needless. When I consider how, amid the stillness of my chambers, Nippers would sometimes impatiently rise from his seat, and stooping over his table, spread his arms wide apart, seize the whole desk, and move it, and jerk it, with a grim, grinding motion on the floor, as if the table were a perverse voluntary agent, intent on thwarting and vexing him; I plainly perceive that for Nippers, brandy and water were altogether superfluous.

It was fortunate for me that, owing to its peculiar cause—indigestion—the irritability and consequent nervousness of Nippers were mainly observable in the morning, while in the afternoon he was comparatively mild. So that Turkey's paroxysms only coming on about twelve o'clock, I never had to do with their eccentricities at one time. Their fits relieved each other like guards. When Nippers's was on, Turkey's was off; and *vice versa*. This was a good natural arrangement under the circumstances.

Ginger Nut, the third on my list, was a lad some twelve years old. His father was a cartman, ambitious of seeing his son on the bench instead of a cart, before he died. So he sent him to my office as student at law, errand boy, and cleaner and sweeper, at the rate of one dollar a week. He had a little desk to himself, but he did not use it much. Upon inspection, the drawer exhibited a great array of the shells of various sorts of nuts. Indeed, to this quick-witted youth the whole noble science of the law was contained in a nut-shell. Not the least among the employments of Ginger Nut, as well as one which he discharged with the most alacrity, was his duty as cake and apple purveyor for Turkey and Nippers. Copying law papers being proverbially a dry, husky sort of business, my two scriveners were fain to moisten their mouths very often with Spitzenbergs to be had at the numerous stalls nigh the Custom House and Post Office. Also, they sent Ginger Nut very frequently for that peculiar cake

—small, flat, round, and very spicy—after which he had been named by them. Of a cold morning, when business was but dull, Turkey would gobble up scores of these cakes, as if they were mere wafers—indeed they sell them at the rate of six or eight for a penny—the scrape of his pen blending with the crunching of the crisp particles in his mouth. Of all the fiery afternoon blunders and flurried rashness of Turkey, was his once moistening a ginger-cake between his lips, and clapping it on to a mortgage for a seal. I came within an ace of dismissing him then. But he mollified me by making an oriental bow and saying—"With submission, sir, it was generous of me to find you in stationery on my own account."

Now my original business—that of a conveyancer and title hunter, and drawer-up of recondite documents of all sorts—was considerably increased by receiving the master's office. There was now great work for scriveners. Not only must I push the clerks already with me, but I must have additional help. In answer to my advertisement, a motionless young man one morning stood upon my office threshold, the door being open, for it was summer. I can see that figure now—pallidly neat, pitiably respectable, incurably forlorn! It was Bartleby.

After a few words touching his qualifications, I engaged him, glad to have among my corps of copyists a man of so singularly sedate an aspect, which I thought might operate beneficially upon the flighty temper of Turkey, and the fiery one of Nippers.

I should have stated before that ground glass folding-doors divided my premises into two parts, one of which was occupied by my scriveners, the other by myself. According to my humour I threw open these doors, or closed them. I resolved to assign Bartleby a corner by the folding-doors, but on my side of them, so as to have this quiet man within easy call, in case any trifling thing was to be done. I placed his desk close up to a small side-window in that part of the room, a window which originally had afforded a lateral view of certain grimy back-yards and bricks, but which, owing to subsequent erections, commanded at present no view at all, though it gave some light. Within three feet of the panes was a wall, and the light came down from far above, between two lofty buildings, as from a very small opening in a dome. Still further to a satisfactory arrangement, I procured a high green folding screen, which might entirely isolate Bartleby from my sight, though not remove him from my voice. And thus, in a manner, privacy and society were conjoined.

At first Bartleby did an extraordinary quantity of writing. As if long famishing for something to copy, he seemed to gorge himself on my documents. There was no pause for digestion. He ran a day and night line, copying by sun-light and by candle-light. I should have been quite delighted with his application, had he been cheerfully industrious. But he wrote on silently, palely, mechanically.

It is, of course, an indispensable part of a scrivener's business to verify the accuracy of his copy, word by word. Where there are two or more scriveners in an office, they assist each other in this examination, one reading from the copy, the other holding the original. It is a very dull, wearisome, and lethargic affair. I can readily imagine that to some sanguine temperaments it would be altogether intolerable. For example, I cannot credit that the mettlesome poet Byron would have contentedly sat down with Bartleby to examine a law document of, say five hundred pages, closely written in a crimpy hand.

Now and then, in the haste of business, it had been my habit to assist in comparing some brief document myself, calling Turkey or Nippers for this purpose. One object I had in placing Bartleby so handy to me behind the screen, was to avail myself of his services on such trivial occasions. It was on the third day, I think, of his being with me, and before any necessity had arisen for having his own writing examined, that, being much hurried to complete a small affair I had in hand, I abruptly called to Bartleby. In my haste and natural expectancy of instant compliance, I sat with my head bent over the original on my desk, and my right hand sideways, and somewhat nervously extended with the copy, so that immediately upon emerging from his retreat, Bartleby might snatch it and proceed to business without the least delay.

In this very attitude did I sit when I called to him, rapidly stating what it was I wanted him to do—namely, to examine a small paper with me. Imagine my surprise, nay, my consternation, when without moving from his privacy, Bartleby in a singularly mild, firm voice, replied, "I would prefer not to."

I sat awhile in perfect silence, rallying my stunned faculties. Immediately it occurred to me that my ears had deceived me, or Bartleby had entirely misunderstood my meaning. I repeated my request in the clearest tone I could assume. But in quite as clear a one came the previous reply, "I would prefer not to."

"Prefer not to," echoed I, rising in high excitement, and crossing the room with a stride. "What do you mean? Are you moon-struck? I want you to help me compare this sheet here—take it," and I thrust it toward him.

"I would prefer not to," said he.

I looked at him steadfastly. His face was leanly composed; his grey eye dimly calm. Not a wrinkle of agitation rippled him. Had there been the least uneasiness, anger, impatience or impertinence in his manner; in other words, had there been anything ordinarily human about him; doubtless I should have violently dismissed him from the premises. But as it was, I should have as soon thought of turning my pale plaster-of-paris bust of Cicero out of doors. I stood gazing at him awhile, as he went on with his own writing, and then reseated myself at my desk. This is very strange, thought I. What had one best do? But my business hurried me. I concluded to forget the matter for the present, reserving it for my future leisure. So calling Nippers from the other room, the paper was speedily examined.

A few days after this, Bartleby concluded four lengthy documents, being quadruplicates of a week's testimony taken before me in my High Court of Chancery. It became necessary to examine them. It was an important suit, and great accuracy was imperative. Having all things arranged, I called Turkey, Nippers and Ginger Nut from the next room, meaning to place the four copies in the hands of my four clerks, while I should read from the original. Accordingly Turkey, Nippers and Ginger Nut had taken their seats in a row, each with his document in hand, when I called to Bartleby to join this interesting group.

"Bartleby! quick, I am waiting."

I heard a slow scrape of his chair legs on the uncarpeted floor, and soon he appeared standing at the entrance of his hermitage.

"What is wanted?" said he mildly.

"The copies, the copies," said I hurriedly. "We are going to examine them. There"—and I held toward him the fourth quadruplicate.

"I would prefer not to," he said, and gently disappeared behind the screen.

For a few moments I was turned into a pillar of salt, standing at the head of my seated column of clerks. Recovering myself, I advanced toward the screen, and demanded the reason for such extraordinary conduct.

"*Why* do you refuse?"

"I would prefer not to."

With any other man I should have flown outright into a dreadful passion, scorned all further words, and thrust him ignominiously from my presence. But there was something about Bartleby that not only strangely disarmed me, but in a wonderful manner touched and disconcerted me. I began to reason with him.

"These are your own copies we are about to examine. It is labour saving to you, because one examination will answer for your four papers. It is common usage. Every copyist is bound to help examine his copy. Is it not so? Will you not speak? Answer!"

"I prefer not to," he replied in a flute-like tone. It seemed to me that while I had been addressing him, he carefully revolved every statement that I made; fully comprehended the meaning; could not gainsay the irresistible conclusion; but, at the same time, some paramount consideration prevailed with him to reply as he did.

"You are decided, then, not to comply with my request—a request made according to common usage and common sense?"

He briefly gave me to understand that on that point my judgment was sound. Yes: his decision was irreversible.

It is not seldom the case that when a man is browbeaten in some unprecedented and violently unreasonably way, he begins to stagger in his own plainest faith. He begins, as it were, vaguely to surmise that, wonderful as it may be, all the justice and all the reason are on the other side. Accordingly, if any disinterested persons are present, he turns to them for some reinforcement for his own faltering mind.

"Turkey," said I, "what do you think of this? Am I not right?"

"With submission, sir," said Turkey, with his blandest tone, "I think that you are."

"Nippers," said I, "what do *you* think of it?"

"I think I should kick him out of the office."

(The reader of nice perceptions will here perceive that, it being morning, Turkey's answer is couched in polite and tranquil terms but Nippers's reply in ill-tempered ones. Or, to repeat a previous sentence, Nippers's ugly mood was on duty, and Turkey's off.)

"Ginger Nut," said I, willing to enlist the smallest suffrage in my behalf, "what do *you* think of it?"

"I think, sir, he's a little *luny*," replied Ginger Nut, with a grin.

"You hear what they say," said I, turning towards the screen, "come forth and do your duty."

But he vouchsafed no reply. I pondered a moment in sore perplexity. But once more business hurried me. I determined again to postpone the consideration of this dilemma to my future leisure. With a little trouble we made out to examine the papers without Bartleby, though at every page or two, Turkey deferentially dropped his opinion that this proceeding was quite out of the common; while Nippers, twitching in his chair with a dyspeptic nervousness, ground out between his set teeth occasional hissing maledictions against the stubborn oaf behind the screen. And for his (Nippers's) part, this was the first and the last time he would do another man's business without pay.

Meanwhile Bartleby sat in his hermitage, oblivious to everything but his own peculiar business there.

Some days passed, the scrivener being employed upon another lengthy work. His late remarkable conduct led me to regard his ways narrowly. I observed that he never went to dinner; indeed that he never went anywhere. As yet I had never of my personal knowledge known him to be outside of my office. He was a perpetual sentry in the corner. At about eleven o'clock though, in the morning, I noticed that Ginger Nut would advance towards the opening in Bartleby's screen, as if silently beckoned thither by a gesture invisible to me where I sat. The boy would then leave the office jingling a few pence, and reappear with a handful of ginger-nuts which he delivered in the hermitage, receiving two of the cakes for his trouble.

He lives, then, on ginger-nuts, thought I; never eats a dinner, properly speaking; he must be a vegetarian then; but no; he never eats even vegetables, he eats nothing but ginger-nuts. My mind then ran on in reveries concerning the probable effects upon the human constitution of living entirely on ginger-nuts. Ginger-nuts are so called because they contain ginger as one of their peculiar constituents, and the final flavouring one. Now what was ginger? A hot, spicy thing. Was Bartleby hot and spicy? Not at all. Ginger, then, had no effect upon Bartleby. Probably he preferred it should have none.

Nothing so aggravates an earnest person as a passive resistance. If the individual so resisted be of a not inhumane temper, and the resisting one perfectly harmless in his passivity; then, in the better moods of the former, he will endeavour charitably to construe to his imagination what proves impossible to be solved by his judgment. Even so, for the most part, I regarded Bartleby and his ways. Poor fellow! thought I, he means no mischief; it is plain he intends no insolence; his aspect sufficiently evinces that his eccentricities are involuntary. He is useful to me. I can get along with him. If I turn him away, the chances are he will fall in with some less indulgent employer, and then he will be rudely treated, and perhaps driven forth miserably to starve. Yes. Here I can cheaply purchase a delicious self-approval. To befriend Bartleby; to humour him in his strange wilfulness, will cost me little or nothing, while I lay up in my soul what will eventually prove a sweet morsel for my conscience. But this mood was not invariable with me. The passiveness of Bartleby sometimes irritated me. I felt strangely goaded on to encounter him in new opposition, to elicit some angry spark from him answerable to my own. But indeed I might as well have essayed to strike fire with my knuckles against a bit of Windsor soap. But one afternoon the evil impulse in me mastered me, and the following little scene ensued:

"Bartleby," said I, "when those papers are all copied, I will compare them with you."

"I would prefer not to."

"How? Surely you do not mean to persist in that mulish vagary?"

No answer.

I threw open the folding-doors near by, and turning upon Turkey and Nippers, exclaimed in an excited manner:

"He says, a second time, he won't examine his papers. What do you think of it, Turkey?"

It was afternoon, be it remembered. Turkey sat glowing like a brass boiler, his bald head steaming, his hands reeling among his blotted papers.

"Think of it?" roared Turkey; "I think I'll just step behind his screen, and black his eyes for him!"

So saying, Turkey rose to his feet and threw his arms into a pugilistic position. He was hurrying away to make good his promise, when I detained him, alarmed at the effect of incautiously rousing Turkey's combativeness after dinner.

"Sit down, Turkey," said I, "and hear what Nippers has to say. What do you think of it, Nippers? Would I not be justified in immediately dismissing Bartleby?"

"Excuse me, that is for you to decide, sir. I think his conduct quite unusual, and indeed unjust, as regards Turkey and myself. But it may only be a passing whim."

"Ah," exclaimed I, "you have strangely changed your mind then—you speak very gently of him now."

"All beer," cried Turkey; "gentleness is effects of beer—Nippers and I dined together to-day. You see how gentle *I* am, sir. Shall I go and black his eyes?"

"You refer to Bartleby, I suppose. No, not to-day, Turkey," I replied; "pray, put up your fists."

I closed the doors, and again advanced towards Bartleby. I felt additional incentives tempting me to my fate. I burned to be rebelled against again. I remembered that Bartleby never left the office.

"Bartleby," said I, "Ginger Nut is away; just step round to the Post Office, won't you? (it was but a three minutes' walk), and see if there is anything for me."

"I would prefer not to."

"You *will* not?"

"I *prefer* not."

I staggered to my desk, and sat there in a deep study. My blind inveteracy returned. Was there any other thing in which I could procure myself to be ignominiously repulsed by this lean, penniless wight?—my hired clerk? What added thing is there, perfectly reasonable, that he will be sure to refuse to do?

"Bartleby!"

No answer.

"Bartleby," in a louder tone.

No answer.

"Bartleby," I roared.

Like a very ghost, agreeable to the laws of magical invocation, at the third summons, he appeared at the entrance of his hermitage.

"Go to the next room, and tell Nippers to come to me."

"I prefer not to," he respectfully and slowly said, and mildly disappeared.

"Very good, Bartleby," said I, in a quiet sort of serenely severe self-possessed tone, intimating the unalterable purpose of some terrible retribution very close at hand. At the moment I half intended something of the kind. But upon the whole, as it was drawing towards my dinner-hour, I thought it best to put on my hat and walk home for the day, suffering much from perplexity and distress of mind.

Shall I acknowledge it? The conclusion of this whole business was, that it soon became a fixed fact of my chambers, that a pale young scrivener, by the name of Bartleby, had a desk there; that he copied for me at the usual rate of four cents a folio (one hundred words); but he was permanently exempt from examining the work done by him, that duty being transferred to Turkey and Nippers, out of compliment doubtless to their superior acuteness; moreover, said Bartleby was never on any account to be despatched on the most trivial errand of any sort; and that even if entreated to take upon him such a matter, it was generally understood that he would prefer not to—in other words, that he would refuse point-blank.

As days passed on, I became considerably reconciled to Bartleby. His steadiness, his freedom from all dissipation, his incessant industry (except when he chose to throw himself into a standing revery behind his screen), his great stillness, his unalterableness of demeanour under all circumstances, made him a valuable acquisition. One prime thing was this, —*he was always there;*—first in the morning, continually through the day, and the last at night. I had a singular confidence in his honesty. I felt my most precious papers perfectly safe in his hands. Sometimes to be sure I could not, for the very soul of me, avoid falling into sudden spasmodic passions with him. For it was exceeding difficult to bear in mind all the time those strange peculiarities, privileges, and unheard of exemptions, forming the tacit stipulations on Bartleby's part under which he remained in my office. Now and then, in the eagerness of despatching pressing business, I would inadvertently summon Bartleby, in a short, rapid tone, to put his finger, say, on the incipient tie of a bit of red tape with which I was about compressing some papers. Of course, from behind the screen the usual answer, "I prefer not to," was sure to come; and then, how could a human creature with the common infirmities of our nature, refrain from bitterly exclaiming upon such perverseness— such unreasonableness. However, every added repulse of this sort which I received only tended to lessen the probability of my repeating the inadvertence.

Here it must be said, that according to the custom of most legal gentlemen occupying chambers in densely-populated law buildings, there were several keys to my door. One was kept by a woman residing in the attic, which person weekly scrubbed and daily swept and dusted my apartments. Another was kept by Turkey for convenience sake. The third I sometimes carried in my own pocket. The fourth I knew not who had.

Now, one Sunday morning I happened to go to Trinity Church, to hear a celebrated preacher, and finding myself rather early on the ground, I thought I would walk round to my chambers for awhile. Luckily I had my key with me; but upon applying it to the lock, I found it resisted by something inserted from the inside. Quite surprised, I called out; when to my consternation a key was turned from within; and thrusting his lean visage at me, and holding the door ajar, the apparition of Bartleby appeared, in his shirt sleeves, and otherwise in a strangely tattered *dishabille*, saying quietly that he was sorry, but he was deeply engaged just then, and—preferred not admitting me at present. In a brief word or two, he moreover added, that perhaps I had better walk round the block two or three times, and by that time he would probably have concluded his affairs.

Now, the utterly unsurmised appearance of Bartleby, tenanting my law-chambers of a Sunday morning, with his cadaverously gentlemanly *nonchalance*, yet withal firm and self-possessed, had such a strange effect upon me, that incontinently I slunk away from my own door, and did as desired. But not without sundry twinges of impotent rebellion against the mild effrontery of this unaccountable scrivener. Indeed, it was his wonderful mildness chiefly, which not only disarmed me, but unmanned me, as it were. For I consider that one, for the time, is in a way unmanned when he tranquilly permits his hired clerk to dictate to him, and order him away from his own premises. Furthermore, I was full of uneasiness as to what Bartleby could possibly be doing in my office in his shirt sleeves, and in an otherwise dismantled condition of a Sunday morning. Was anything amiss going on? Nay, that was out of the question. It was not to be thought of for a moment that Bartleby was an immoral person. But what could he be doing there—copying? Nay again, whatever might be his eccentricities, Bartleby was an eminently decorous person. He would be the last man to sit down to his desk in any state approaching to nudity. Besides, it was Sunday; and there was something about Bartleby that forbade the supposition that he would by any secular occupation violate the proprieties of the day.

Nevertheless, my mind was not pacified; and full of a restless curiosity, at last I returned to the door. Without hindrance I inserted my key, opened it, and entered. Bartleby was not to be seen. I looked round anxiously, peeped behind his screen; but it was very plain that he was gone. Upon more closely examining the place, I surmised that for an indefinite period Bartleby must have ate, dressed, and slept in my office, and that too without plate, mirror, or bed. The cushioned seat of a ricketty old sofa in one corner bore the faint impress of a lean, reclining form. Rolled away under his desk, I found a blanket; under the empty grate, a blacking box and brush; on a chair, a tin basin, with soap and a ragged towel; in a newspaper a few crumbs of ginger-nuts and a morsel of cheese. Yes, thought I, it is evident enough that Bartleby has been making his home here, keeping bachelor's hall all by himself. Immediately then the thought came sweeping across me, What miserable friendlessness and loneliness are here revealed! His poverty is great; but his solitude, how horrible! Think of it. Of a Sunday, Wall Street is deserted as Petra; and every night of every day it is an emptiness. This building too, which of week-days hums with industry and life, at nightfall echoes with sheer vacancy, and all through Sunday is forlorn. And here Bartleby makes his home; sole spectator of a solitude which he has seen all populous—a sort of innocent and transformed Marius brooding among the ruins of Carthage!

For the first time in my life a feeling of overpowering stinging melancholy seized me. Before, I had never experienced aught but a not-unpleasing sadness. The bond of a common humanity now drew me irresistibly to gloom. A fraternal melancholy! For both I and Bartleby were sons of Adam. I remembered the bright silks and sparkling faces I had seen that day, in gala trim, swan-like sailing down the Mississippi of Broadway; and I contrasted them with the pallid copyist, and thought to myself, Ah, happiness courts the light, so we deem the world is gay; but misery hides aloof, so we deem that misery there is none. These sad fancyings—chimeras, doubtless, of a sick and silly brain—led on to other and more special thoughts, concerning the eccentricities of Bartleby. Presentiments of strange discoveries hovered round me. The scrivener's pale form appeared to me laid out, among uncaring strangers, in its shivering winding sheet.

Suddenly I was attracted by Bartleby's closed desk, the key in open sight left in the lock.

I mean no mischief, seek the gratification of no heartless curiosity, thought I; besides, the desk is mine, and its contents, too, so I will make bold to look within. Everything was methodically arranged, the papers smoothly placed. The pigeon holes were deep, and, removing the files of documents, I groped into their recesses. Presently I felt something there, and dragged it out. It was an old bandana handkerchief, heavy and knotted. I opened it, and saw it was a savings' bank.

I now recalled all the quiet mysteries which I had noted in the man. I remembered that he never spoke but to answer; that though at intervals he had considerable time to himself, yet I had never seen him reading—no, not even a newspaper; that for long periods he would stand looking out, at his pale window behind the screen, upon the dead brick wall; I was quite sure he never visited any refectory or eating-house; while his pale face clearly indicated that he never drank beer like Turkey, or tea and coffee even, like other men; that he never went anywhere in particular that I could learn; never went out for a walk, unless indeed that was the case at present; that he had declined telling who he was, or whence he came, or whether he had any relatives in the world; that though so thin and pale, he never complained of ill health. And more than all, I remembered a certain unconscious air of pallid—how shall I call it?—of pallid haughtiness, say, or rather an austere reserve about him, which had positively awed me into my tame compliance with his eccentricities, when I had feared to ask him to do the slightest incidental thing for me, even though I might know, from his long-continued motionlessness, that behind his screen he must be standing in one of those dead-wall reveries of his.

Revolving all these things, and coupling them with the recently discovered fact that he made my office his constant abiding place and home, and not forgetful of his morbid moodiness; revolving all these things, a prudential feeling began to steal over me. My first emotions had been those of pure melancholy and sincerest pity; but just in proportion as the forlornness of Bartleby grew and grew to my imagination, did that same melancholy merge into fear, that pity into repulsion. So true it is, and so terrible, too, that up to a certain point the thought or sight of misery enlists our best affections; but, in certain special cases, beyond that point it does not. They err who would assert that invariably this is owing to the inherent selfishness of the human heart. It rather proceeds from a certain hopelessness of remedying excessive and organic ill. To a sensitive being, pity is not seldom pain. And when at last it is perceived that such pity cannot lead to effectual succour, common sense bids the soul be rid of it. What I saw that morning persuaded me that the scrivener was the victim of innate and incurable disorder. I might give alms to his body; but his body did not pain him; it was his soul that suffered, and his soul I could not reach.

I did not accomplish the purpose of going to Trinity Church that morning. Somehow, the things I had seen disqualified me for the time from church-going. I walked homeward, thinking what I would do with Bartleby. Finally, I resolved upon this:—I would put certain calm questions to him the next morning, touching his history, &c., and if he declined to answer them openly and unreservedly (and I supposed he would prefer not), then to give him a twenty dollar bill over and above whatever I might owe him, and tell him his services were no longer required; but that if in any other way I could assist him, I would be happy to do so, especially if he desired to return to his native place, wherever that might be, I would willingly help to defray the expenses. Moreover, if, after reaching home, he found himself at any time in want of aid, a letter from him would be sure of a reply.

The next morning came.

"Bartleby," said I, gently calling to him behind his screen.

No reply.

"Bartleby," said I, in a still gentler tone, "come here; I am not going to ask you to do anything you would prefer not to do—I simply wish to speak to you."

Upon this he noiselessly slid into view.

"Will you tell me, Bartleby, where you were born?"

"I would prefer not to."

"Will you tell me *anything* about yourself?"

"I would prefer not to."

"But what reasonable objection can you have to speak to me? I feel friendly towards you."

He did not look at me while I spoke, but kept his glance fixed upon my bust of Cicero, which, as I then sat, was directly behind me, some six inches above my head.

"What is your answer, Bartleby?" said I, after waiting a considerable time for a reply, during which his countenance remained immovable, only there was the faintest conceivable tremor of the white attenuated mouth.

"At present I prefer to give no answer," he said, and retired into his hermitage.

It was rather weak in me I confess, but his manner on this occasion nettled me. Not only did there seem to lurk in it a certain calm disdain, but his perverseness seemed ungrateful, considering the undeniable good usage and indulgence he had received from me.

Again I sat ruminating what I should do. Mortified as I was at his behaviour, and resolved as I had been to dismiss him when I entered my office, nevertheless I strangely felt something superstitious knocking at my heart, and forbidding me to carry out my purpose, and denouncing me for a villain if I dared to breathe one bitter word against this forlornest of mankind. At last, familiarly drawing my chair behind his screen, I sat down and said: "Bartleby, never mind then about revealing your history; but let me entreat you, as a friend, to comply as far as may be with the usages of this office. Say now you will help to examine papers to-morrow or next day: in short, say now that in a day or two you will begin to be a little reasonable:—say so, Bartleby."

"At present I would prefer not to be a little reasonable," was his mildly cadaverous reply.

Just then the folding-doors opened, and Nippers approached. He seemed suffering from an unusually bad night's rest, induced by severer indigestion than common. He overheard those final words of Bartleby.

"*Prefer not*, eh?" gritted Nippers—"I'd *prefer* him, if I were you, sir," addressing me—"I'd *prefer* him; I'd give him preferences, the stubborn mule! What is it, sir, pray, that he *prefers* not to do now?"

Bartleby moved not a limb.

"Mr. Nippers," said I, "I'd prefer that you would withdraw for the present."

Somehow, of late I had got into the way of involuntarily using this word "prefer" upon all sorts of not exactly suitable occasions. And I trembled to think that my contact with the scrivener had already and seriously affected me in a mental way. And what further and deeper aberration might it not yet produce? This apprehension had not been without efficacy in determining me to summary means.

As Nippers, looking very sour and sulky, was departing, Turkey blandly and deferentially approached.

"With submission, sir," said he, "yesterday I was thinking about Bartleby here, and I think that if he would but prefer to take a quart of good ale every day, it would do much towards mending him, and enabling him to assist in examining his papers."

"So you have got the word, too," said I, slightly excited.

"With submission, what word, sir," asked Turkey, respectfully crowding himself into the contracted space behind the screen, and by so doing, making me jostle the scrivener. "What word, sir?"

"I would prefer to be left alone here," said Bartleby, as if offended at being mobbed in his privacy.

"*That's* the word, Turkey," said I—"*that's* it."

"Oh, *prefer?* oh, yes—queer word. I never use it myself. But, sir, as I was saying, if he would but prefer—"

"Turkey," interrupted I, "you will please withdraw."

"Oh certainly, sir, if you prefer that I should."

As he opened the folding-door to retire, Nippers at his desk caught a glimpse of me, and asked whether I would prefer to have a certain paper copied on blue paper or white. He did not in the least roguishly accent the word prefer. It was plain that it involuntarily rolled from his tongue. I thought to myself, surely I must get rid of a demented man, who already has in some degree turned the tongues, if not the heads, of myself and clerks. But I thought it prudent not to break the dismission at once.

The next day I noticed that Bartleby did nothing but stand at his window in his dead-wall revery. Upon asking him why he did not write, he said that he had decided upon doing no more writing.

"Why, how now? what next?" exclaimed I, "do no more writing?"

"No more."

"And what is the reason?"

"Do you not see the reason for yourself?" he indifferently replied.

I looked steadfastly at him, and perceived that his eyes looked dull and glazed. Instantly it occurred to me, that his unexampled diligence in copying by his dim window for the first few weeks of his stay with me might have temporarily impaired his vision.

I was touched. I said something in condolence with him. I hinted that, of course, he did wisely in abstaining from writing for a while, and urged him to embrace that opportunity of taking wholesome exercise in the open air. This, however, he did not do. A few days after this, my other clerks being absent, and being in a great hurry to despatch certain letters by the mail, I thought that, having nothing else earthly to do, Bartleby would surely be less inflexible than usual, and carry these letters to the Post Office. But he blankly declined. So, much to my inconvenience, I went myself.

Still added days went by. Whether Bartleby's eyes improved or not, I could not say. To all appearance, I thought they did. But when I asked him if they did, he vouchsafed no answer. At all events, he would do no copying. At last, in reply to my urgings, he informed me that he had permanently given up copying.

"What!" exclaimed I; "suppose your eyes should get entirely well— better than ever before—would you not copy then?"

"I have given up copying," he answered and slid aside.

He remained, as ever, a fixture in my chamber. Nay—if that were possible—he became still more of a fixture than before. What was to be done? He would do nothing in the office: why should he stay there? In plain fact, he had now become a millstone to me, not only useless as a necklace, but afflictive to bear. Yet I was sorry for him. I speak less than truth when I say that, on his own account, he occasioned me uneasiness. If he would but have named a single relative or friend, I would instantly have written, and urged their taking the poor fellow away to some convenient retreat. But he seemed alone, absolutely alone in the universe. A bit of wreckage in the mid-Atlantic. At length, necessities connected with my business tyrannized over all other considerations. Decently as I could, I told Bartleby that in six days' time he must unconditionally leave the office. I warned him to take measures, in the interval, for procuring some other abode. I offered to assist him in this endeavour, if he himself would but take the first step towards a removal. "And when you finally quit me, Bartleby," added I, "I shall see that you go away not entirely unprovided. Six days from this hour, remember."

At the expiration of that period, I peeped behind the screen, and lo! Bartleby was there.

I buttoned up my coat, balanced myself; advanced slowly towards him, touched his shoulder, and said, "The time has come; you must quit this place; I am sorry for you; here is money; but you must go."

"I would prefer not," he replied, with his back still towards me.

"You *must*."

He remained silent.

Now I had an unbounded confidence in this man's common honesty. He had frequently restored to me sixpences and shillings carelessly dropped upon the floor, for I am apt to be very reckless in such shirt-button affairs. The proceeding then which followed will not be deemed extraordinary.

"Bartleby," said I, "I owe you twelve dollars on account; here are thirty-two; the odd twenty are yours.—Will you take it?" and I handed the bills towards him.

But he made no motion.

"I will leave them here then," putting them under a weight on the table. Then taking my hat and cane and going to the door, I tranquilly turned and added—"After you have removed your things from these offices, Bartleby, you will of course lock the door—since every one is now gone for the day but you—and if you please, slip your key underneath the mat, so that I may have it in the morning. I shall not see you again; so good-bye to you. If hereafter in your new place of abode I can be of any service to you, do not fail to advise me by letter. Good-bye, Bartleby, and fare you well."

But he answered not a word; like the last column of some ruined temple, he remained standing mute and solitary in the middle of the otherwise deserted room.

As I walked home in a pensive mood, my vanity got the better of my pity. I could not but highly plume myself on my masterly management in getting rid of Bartleby. Masterly I call it, and such it must appear to any dispassionate thinker. The beauty of my procedure seemed to consist in its perfect quietness. There was no vulgar bullying, no bravado of any sort, no choleric hectoring, no striding to and fro across the apartment, jerking out vehement commands for Bartleby to bundle himself off with his beggarly traps. Nothing of the kind. Without loudly bidding Bartleby depart—as an inferior genius might have done—I *assumed* the ground that depart he must; and upon that assumption built all I had to say. The more I thought over my procedure, the more I was charmed with it. Nevertheless, next morning, upon awakening, I had my doubts,—I had somehow slept off the fumes of vanity. One of the coolest and wisest hours a man has, is just after he awakes in the morning. My procedure seemed as sagacious as ever,—but only in theory. How it would prove in practice—there was the rub. It was truly a beautiful thought to have assumed Bartleby's departure; but, after all, that assumption was simply my own, and none of Bartleby's. The great point was, not whether I had assumed that he would quit me, but whether he would prefer so to do. He was more a man of preferences than assumptions.

After breakfast, I walked down town, arguing the probabilities *pro* and *con*. One moment I thought it would prove a miserable failure, and Bartleby would be found all alive at my office as usual; the next moment it seemed certain that I should see his chair empty. And so I kept veering about. At the corner of Broadway and Canal Street, I saw quite an excited group of people standing in earnest conversation.

"I'll take odds he doesn't," said a voice as I passed.

"Doesn't go?—done!" said I, "put up your money."

I was instinctively putting my hand in my pocket to produce my own, when I remembered that this was an election day. The words I had overheard bore no reference to Bartleby, but to the success or non-success of some candidate for the mayoralty. In my intent frame of mind, I had, as it were, imagined that all Broadway shared in my excitement, and were debating the same question with me. I passed on, very thankful that the uproar of the street screened my momentary absent-mindedness.

As I had intended, I was earlier than usual at my office door. I stood listening for a moment. All was still. He must be gone. I tried the knob. The door was locked. Yes, my procedure had worked to a charm; he indeed must be vanished. Yet a certain melancholy mixed with this: I was almost sorry for my brilliant success. I was fumbling under the door mat for the key, which Bartleby was to have left there for me, when accidentally my knee knocked against a panel, producing a summoning sound, and in response a voice came to me from within—"Not yet; I am occupied."

It was Bartleby.

I was thunderstruck. For an instant I stood like the man who, pipe in mouth, was killed one cloudless afternoon long ago in Virginia, by summer lightning; at his own warm open window he was killed, and remained leaning out there upon the dreamy afternoon, till some one touched him, and he fell.

"Not gone!" I murmured at last. But again obeying that wondrous ascendency which the inscrutable scrivener had over me—and from which ascendency, for all my chafing, I could not completely escape—I slowly went down-stairs and out into the street, and while walking round the block, considered what I should next do in this unheard-of perplexity. Turn the man out by an actual thrusting I could not; to drive him away by calling him hard names would not do; calling in the police was an unpleasant idea; and yet, permit him to enjoy his cadaverous triumph over me,—this too I could not think of. What was to be done? or, if nothing could be done, was there anything further that I could *assume* in the matter? Yes, as before I had prospectively assumed that Bartleby would depart, so now I might retrospectively assume that departed he was. In the legitimate carrying out of this assumption, I might enter my office in a great hurry, and pretending not to see Bartleby at all, walk straight against him as if he were air. Such a proceeding would in a singular degree have the appearance of a home-thrust. It was hardly possible that Bartleby could withstand such an application of the doctrine of assumptions. But, upon second thought, the success of the plan seemed rather dubious. I resolved to argue the matter over with him again.

"Bartleby," said I, entering the office, with a quietly severe expression, "I am seriously displeased. I am pained, Bartleby. I had thought better of you. I had imagined you of such a gentlemanly organization, that in any delicate dilemma a slight hint would suffice—in short, an assumption;

but it appears I am deceived. Why," I added, unaffectedly starting, "you have not even touched that money yet," pointing to it, just where I had left it the evening previous.

He answered nothing.

"Will you, or will you not, quit me?" I now demanded in a sudden passion, advancing close to him.

"I would prefer *not* to quit you," he replied, gently emphasizing the *not*.

"What earthly right have you to stay here? Do you pay any rent? Do you pay my taxes? Or is this property yours?"

He answered nothing.

"Are you ready to go on and write now? Are your eyes recovered? Could you copy a small paper for me this morning? or help examine a few lines? or step round to the Post Office? In a word, will you do any thing at all, to give a colouring to your refusal to depart the premises?"

He silently retired into his hermitage.

I was now in such a state of nervous resentment that I thought it but prudent to check myself, at present, from further demonstrations. Bartleby and I were alone. I remembered the tragedy of the unfortunate Adams and the still more unfortunate Colt in the solitary office of the latter; and how poor Colt, being dreadfully incensed by Adams, and imprudently permitting himself to get wildly excited, was at unawares hurried into his fatal act—an act which certainly no man could possibly deplore more than the actor himself. Often it had occurred to me in my ponderings upon the subject, that had that altercation taken place in the public street, or at a private residence, it would not have terminated as it did. It was the circumstance of being alone in a solitary office, upstairs, of a building entirely unhallowed by humanizing domestic associations—an uncarpeted office, doubtless, of a dusty, haggard sort of appearance;—this it must have been, which greatly helped to enhance the irritable desperation of the hapless Colt.

But when this old Adam of resentment rose in me and tempted me concerning Bartleby, I grappled him and threw him. How? Why, simply by recalling the divine injunction: "A new commandment give I unto you, that ye love one another." Yes, this it was that saved me. Aside from higher considerations, charity often operates as a vastly wise and prudent principle—a great safeguard to its possessor. Men have committed murder for jealousy's sake, and anger's sake, and hatred's sake, and selfishness' sake, and spiritual pride's sake; but no man that ever I heard of, ever committed a diabolical murder for sweet charity's sake. Mere self-interest, then, if no better motive can be enlisted, should, especially with high-tempered men, prompt all beings to charity and philanthropy. At any rate, upon the occasion in question, I strove to drown my exasperated feelings toward the scrivener by benevolently construing his conduct. Poor fellow, poor fellow! thought I, he doesn't mean any thing; and besides, he has seen hard times, and ought to be indulged.

I endeavoured also immediately to occupy myself, and at the same time to comfort my despondency. I tried to fancy that in the course of the morning, at such time as might prove agreeable to him, Bartleby, of his own free accord, would emerge from his hermitage, and take up some decided line of march in the direction of the door. But no. Half-past twelve o'clock came; Turkey began to glow in the face, overturn his ink-stand, and become generally obstreperous; Nippers abated down into quietude and courtesy; Ginger Nut munched his noon apple; and Bartleby remained standing at his window in one of his profoundest dead-wall reveries. Will it be credited? Ought I to acknowledge it? That afternoon I left the office without saying one further word to him.

Some days now passed, during which at leisure intervals I looked a little into "Edwards on the Will," and "Priestley on Necessity." Under the circumstances, those books induced a salutary feeling. Gradually I slid into the persuasion that these troubles of mine, touching the scrivener, had been all predestinated from eternity, and Bartleby was billeted upon me for some mysterious purpose of an all-wise Providence, which it was not for a mere mortal like me to fathom. Yes, Bartleby, stay there behind your screen, thought I; I shall persecute you no more; you are harmless and noiseless as any of these old chairs; in short, I never feel so private as when I know you are here. At least I see it, I feel it; I penetrate to the predestinated purpose of my life. I am content. Others may have loftier parts to enact; but my mission in this world, Bartleby, is to furnish you with office room for such period as you may see fit to remain.

I believe that this wise and blessed frame of mind would have continued with me had it not been for the unsolicited and uncharitable remarks obtruded upon me by my professional friends who visited the rooms. But thus it often is, that the constant friction of illiberal minds wears out at last the best resolves of the more generous. Though to be sure, when I reflected upon it, it was not strange that people entering my office should be struck by the peculiar aspect of the unaccountable Bartleby, and so be tempted to throw out some sinister observations concerning him. Sometimes an attorney having business with me, and calling at my office, and finding no one but the scrivener there, would undertake to obtain some sort of precise information from him touching my whereabouts; but without heeding his idle talk, Bartleby would remain standing immovable in the middle of the room. So, after contemplating him in that position for a time, the attorney would depart, no wiser than he came.

Also, when a Reference was going on, and the room full of lawyers and witnesses and business was driving fast, some deeply occupied legal gentleman present, seeing Bartleby wholly unemployed, would request him to run round to his (the legal gentleman's) office and fetch some papers for him. Thereupon, Bartleby would tranquilly decline, and yet remain idle as before. Then the lawyer would give a great stare, and turn to me. And what could I say? At last I was made aware that all through the circle of my professional acquaintance, a whisper of wonder was running round, having reference to the strange creature I kept at my office. This worried me very much. And as the idea came upon me of his possibly turning out a long-lived man, and keep occupying my chambers, and denying my authority; and perplexing my visitors; and scandalizing my professional reputation; and casting a general gloom over the premises; keeping soul and body together to the last upon his savings (for doubtless he spent but half a dime a day), and in the end perhaps outlive me, and claim possession of my office by right of his perpetual occupancy: as all these dark anticipations crowded upon me more and more, and my friends continually intruded their relentless remarks upon the apparition in my room, a great change was wrought in me. I resolved to gather all my faculties together, and for ever rid me of this intolerable incubus.

Ere revolving any complicated project, however, adapted to this end, I first simply suggested to Bartleby the propriety of his permanent departure. In a calm and serious tone, I commended the idea to his careful and mature consideration. But having taken three days to meditate upon it, he apprised me that his original determination remained the same; in short, that he still preferred to abide with me.

What shall I do? I now said to myself, buttoning up my coat to the last button. What shall I do? what ought I to do? what does conscience say I *should* do with this man, or rather ghost? Rid myself of him, I must; go, he shall. But how? You will not thrust him, the poor, pale, passive mortal,—you will not thrust such a helpless creature out of your door? you will not dishonour yourself by such cruelty? No, I will not, I cannot do that. Rather would I let him live and die here, and then mason up his remains in the wall. What then will you do? For all your coaxing, he will not budge. Bribes he leaves under your own paperweight on your table; in short, it is quite plain that he prefers to cling to you.

Then something severe, something unusual must be done. What! surely you will not have him collared by a constable, and commit his innocent pallor to the common jail? And upon what ground could you procure such a thing to be done?—a vagrant, is he? What! he a vagrant, a wanderer, who refuses to budge? It is because he will *not* be a vagrant, then, that you seek to count him *as* a vagrant. That is too absurd. No visible means of support: there I have him. Wrong again: for indubitably he *does* support himself, and that is the only unanswerable proof that any man can show of his possessing the means so to do. No more then. Since he will not quit me, I must quit him. I will change my offices; I will move elsewhere; and give him fair notice, that if I find him on my new premises I will then proceed against him as a common trespasser.

Acting accordingly, next day I thus addressed him: "I find these chambers too far from the City Hall; the air is unwholesome. In a word, I propose to remove my offices next week, and shall no longer require your services. I tell you this now, in order that you may seek another place."

He made no reply, and nothing more was said.

On the appointed day I engaged carts and men, proceeded to my chambers, and having but little furniture, everything was removed in a few hours. Throughout all, the scrivener remained standing behind the screen, which I directed to be removed the last thing. It was withdrawn; and being folded up like a huge folio, left him the motionless occupant of a naked room. I stood in the entry watching him a moment, while something from within me upbraided me.

I re-entered, with my hand in my pocket—and—and my heart in my mouth.

"Good-bye, Bartleby; I am going—good-bye, and God some way bless you; and take that," slipping something in his hand. But it dropped upon the floor and then—strange to say—I tore myself from him whom I had so longed to be rid of.

Established in my new quarters, for a day or two I kept the door locked, and started at every footfall in the passages. When I returned to my rooms after any little absence, I would pause at the threshold for an instant, and attentively listen, ere applying my key. But these fears were needless. Bartleby never came nigh me.

I thought all was going well, when a perturbed looking stranger visited me, inquiring whether I was the person who had recently occupied rooms at No. —— Wall Street.

Full of forebodings, I replied that I was.

"Then sir," said the stranger, who proved a lawyer, "you are responsible for the man you left there. He refuses to do any copying, he refuses to do anything; and he says he prefers not to; and he refuses to quit the premises."

"I am very sorry, sir," said I, with assumed tranquillity, but an inward tremor, "but, really, the man you allude to is nothing to me—he is no relation or apprentice of mine, that you should hold me responsible for him."

"In mercy's name, who is he?"

"I certainly cannot inform you. I know nothing about him. Formerly I employed him as a copyist; but he has done nothing for me now for some time past."

"I shall settle him then,—good morning, sir."

Several days passed, and I heard nothing more; and though I often felt a charitable prompting to call at the place and see poor Bartleby, yet a certain squeamishness of I know not what withheld me.

All is over with him, by this time, thought I at last, when through another week no further intelligence reached me. But coming to my room the day after, I found several persons waiting at my door in a high state of nervous excitement.

"That's the man—here he comes," cried the foremost one, whom I recognized as the lawyer who had previously called upon me alone.

"You must take him away, sir, at once," cried a portly person among them, advancing upon me, and whom I knew to be the landlord of No. —— Wall Street. "These gentlemen, my tenants, cannot stand it any longer; Mr. B——," pointing to the lawyer, "has turned him out of his room, and he now persists in haunting the building generally, sitting upon the banisters of the stairs by day, and sleeping in the entry by night. Everybody here is concerned; clients are leaving the offices; some fears are entertained of a mob; something you must do, and that without delay."

Aghast at this torrent, I fell back before it, and would fain have locked myself in my new quarters. In vain I persisted that Bartleby was nothing to me—no more than to any one else there. In vain:—I was the last person known to have anything to do with him, and they held me to the terrible account. Fearful then of being exposed in the papers (as one person present obscurely threatened) I considered the matter, and at length said, that if the lawyer would give me a confidential interview with the scrivener, in his (the lawyer's) own room, I would that afternoon strive my best to rid them of the nuisance they complained of.

Going up stairs to my old haunt, there was Bartleby silently sitting upon the banister at the landing.

"What are you doing here, Bartleby?" said I.

"Sitting upon the banister," he mildly replied.

I motioned him into the lawyer's room, who then left us.

"Bartleby," said I, "are you aware that you are the cause of great tribulation to me, by persisting in occupying the entry after being dismissed from the office?"

No answer.

"Now one of two things must take place. Either you must do something, or something must be done to you. Now what sort of business would you like to engage in? Would you like to re-engage in copying for some one?"

"No; I would prefer not to make any change."

"Would you like a clerkship in a dry-goods store?"

"There is too much confinement about that. No, I would not like a clerkship; but I am not particular."

"Too much confinement," I cried, "why you keep yourself confined all the time!"

"I would prefer not to take a clerkship," he rejoined, as if to settle that little item at once.

"How would a bartender's business suit you? There is no trying of the eyesight in that."

"I would not like it at all; though, as I said before, I am not particular."

His unwonted wordiness inspirited me. I returned to the charge.

"Well then, would you like to travel through the country collecting bills for the merchants? That would improve your health."

"No, I would prefer to be doing something else."

"How then would going as a companion to Europe to entertain some young gentleman with your conversation,—how would that suit you?"

"Not at all. It does not strike me that there is anything definite about that. I like to be stationary. But I am not particular."

"Stationary you shall be then," I cried, now losing all patience, and for the first time in all my exasperating connection with him fairly flying into a passion. "If you do not go away from these premises before night, I shall feel bound—indeed I *am* bound—to—to—to quit the premises myself!" I rather absurdly concluded, knowing not with what possible threat to try to frighten his immobility into compliance. Despairing of all further efforts, I was precipitately leaving him, when a final thought occurred to me—one which had not been wholly unindulged before.

"Bartleby," said I, in the kindest tone I could assume under such exciting circumstances, "will you go home with me now—not to my office, but my dwelling—and remain there till we can conclude upon some convenient arrangement for you at our leisure? Come, let us start now, right away."

"No: at present I would prefer not to make any change at all."

I answered nothing; but effectually dodging every one by the suddenness and rapidity of my flight, rushed from the building, ran up Wall Street toward Broadway, and then jumping into the first omnibus was soon removed from pursuit. As soon as tranquillity returned I distinctly perceived that I had now done all that I possibly could, both in respect to the demands of the landlord and his tenants, and with regard to my own desire and sense of duty, to benefit Bartleby, and shield him from rude persecution. I now strove to be entirely care-free and quiescent; and my conscience justified me in the attempt; though indeed it was not so successful as I could have wished. So fearful was I of being again hunted out by the incensed landlord and his exasperated tenants, that, surrendering my business to Nippers, for a few days I drove about the upper part of the town and through the suburbs, in my rockaway; crossed over to Jersey City and Hoboken, and paid fugitive visits to Manhattanville and Astoria. In fact I almost lived in my rockaway for the time.

When again I entered my office, lo, a note from the landlord lay upon the desk. I opened it with trembling hands. It informed me that the writer had sent to the police, and had Bartleby removed to the Tombs as a vagrant. Moreover, since I knew more about him than any one else, he wished me to appear at that place, and make a suitable statement of the facts. These tidings had a conflicting effect upon me. At first I was indignant; but at last almost approved. The landlord's energetic, summary disposition had led him to adopt a procedure which I do not think I would have decided upon myself; and yet as a last resort, under such peculiar circumstances, it seemed the only plan.

As I afterwards learned, the poor scrivener, when told that he must be conducted to the Tombs, offered not the slightest obstacle, but in his own pale, unmoving way silently acquiesced.

Some of the compassionate and curious bystanders joined the party; and headed by one of the constables, arm-in-arm with Bartleby the silent procession filed its way through all the noise, and heat, and joy of the roaring thoroughfares at noon.

The same day I received the note I went to the Tombs, or, to speak more properly, the Halls of Justice. Seeking the right officer, I stated the purpose of my call, and was informed that the individual I described was indeed within. I then assured the functionary that Bartleby was a perfectly honest man, and a greatly to be compassionated (however unaccountable) eccentric. I narrated all I knew, and closed by suggesting the idea of letting him remain in as indulgent confinement as possible till something less harsh might be done—though indeed I hardly knew what. At all events, if nothing else could be decided upon, the alms-house must receive him. I then begged to have an interview.

Being under no disgraceful charge, and quite serene and harmless in all his ways, they had permitted him freely to wander about the prison, and especially in the inclosed grass-platted yards thereof. And so I found him there, standing all alone in the quietest of the yards, his face toward a high wall—while all around, from the narrow slits of the jail windows, I thought I saw peering out upon him the eyes of murderers and thieves.

"Bartleby!"

"I know you," he said, without looking round,—"and I want nothing to say to you."

"It was not I that brought you here, Bartleby," said I, keenly pained at his implied suspicion. "And to you, this should not be so vile a place. Nothing reproachful attaches to you by being here. And see, it is not so sad a place as one might think. Look, there is the sky and here is the grass."

"I know where I am," he replied, but would say nothing more, and so I left him.

As I entered the corridor again a broad, meat-like man in an apron accosted me, and jerking his thumb over his shoulder said—"Is that your friend?"

"Yes."

"Does he want to starve? If he does, let him live on the prison fare, that's all."

"Who are you?" asked I, not knowing what to make of such an unofficially speaking person in such a place.

"I am the grub-man. Such gentlemen as have friends here, hire me to provide them with something good to eat."

"Is this so?" said I, turning to the turnkey.

He said it was.

"Well then," said I, slipping some silver into the grub-man's hands (for so they called him), "I want you to give particular attention to my friend there; let him have the best dinner you can get. And you must be as polite to him as possible."

"Introduce me, will you?" said the grub-man, looking at me with an expression which seemed to say he was all impatience for an opportunity to give a specimen of his breeding.

Thinking it would prove of benefit to the scrivener, I acquiesced; and asking the grub-man his name, went up with him to Bartleby.

"Bartleby, this is Mr. Cutlets; you will find him very useful to you."

"Your sarvant, sir, your sarvant," said the grub-man, making a low salutation behind his apron. "Hope you find it pleasant here, sir;—spacious grounds—cool apartments, sir—hope you'll stay with us some time—try to make it agreeable. May Mrs. Cutlets and I have the pleasure of your company to dinner, sir, in Mrs. Cutlets' private room?"

"I prefer not to dine to-day," said Bartleby, turning away. "It would disagree with me; I am unused to dinners." So saying, he slowly moved to the other side of the inclosure and took up a position fronting the dead-wall.

"How's this?" said the grub-man, addressing me with a stare of astonishment. "He's odd, ain't he?"

"I think he is a little deranged," said I, sadly.

"Deranged? deranged is it? Well now, upon my word, I thought that friend of yours was a gentleman forger; they are always pale and genteel-like, them forgers. I can't help pity 'em—can't help it, sir. Did you know Monroe Edwards?" he added touchingly, and paused. Then, laying his hand pityingly on my shoulder, sighed, "he died of the consumption at Sing-Sing. So you weren't acquainted with Monroe?"

"No, I was never socially acquainted with any forgers. But I cannot stop longer. Look to my friend yonder. You will not lose by it. I will see you again."

Some few days after this, I again obtained admission to the Tombs, and went through the corridors in quest of Bartleby; but without finding him.

"I saw him coming from his cell not long ago," said a turnkey, "maybe he's gone to loiter in the yards."

So I went in that direction.

"Are you looking for the silent man?" said another turnkey passing me. "Yonder he lies—sleeping in the yard there. 'Tis not twenty minutes since I saw him lie down."

The yard was entirely quiet. It was not accessible to the common prisoners. The surrounding walls, of amazing thickness, kept off all sounds behind them. The Egyptian character of the masonry weighed upon me with its gloom. But a soft imprisoned turf grew under foot. The heart of the eternal pyramids, it seemed, wherein by some strange magic, through the clefts grass-seed, dropped by birds, had sprung.

Strangely huddled at the base of the wall—his knees drawn up, and lying on his side, his head touching the cold stones—I saw the wasted Bartleby. But nothing stirred. I paused; then went close up to him; stooped over, and saw that his dim eyes were open; otherwise he seemed profoundly sleeping. Something prompted me to touch him. I felt his hand, when a tingling shiver ran up my arm and down my spine to my feet.

The round face of the grub-man peered upon me now. "His dinner is ready. Won't he dine to-day, either? Or does he live without dining?"

"Lives without dining," said I, and closed the eyes.

"Eh!—He's asleep, ain't he?"

"With kings and counsellors," murmured I.

*   *   *

There would seem little need for proceeding further in this history. Imagination will readily supply the meagre recital of poor Bartleby's interment. But ere parting with the reader, let me say, that if this little narrative has sufficiently interested him, to awaken curiosity as to who Bartleby was, and what manner of life he led prior to the present narrator's making his acquaintance, I can only reply, that in such curiosity I fully share—but am wholly unable to gratify it. Yet here I hardly know whether I should divulge one little item of rumour, which came to my ear a few months after the scrivener's decease. Upon what basis it rested, I could never ascertain; and hence, how true it is I cannot now tell. But inasmuch as this vague report has not been without a certain strange suggestive interest to me, however sad, it may prove the same with some others; and so I will briefly mention it. The report was this: that Bartleby had been a subordinate clerk in the Dead Letter Office at Washington, from which he had been suddenly removed by a change in the administration. When I think over this rumour I cannot adequately express the emotions which seize me. Dead letters! does it not sound like dead men? Conceive a man by nature and misfortune prone to a pallid hopelessness:

can any business seem more fitted to heighten it than that of continually handling these dead letters, and assorting them for the flames? For by the cartload they are annually burned. Sometimes from out the folded paper the pale clerk takes a ring:—the finger it was meant for, perhaps, moulders in the grave; a bank-note sent in swiftest charity:—he whom it would relieve, nor eats nor hungers any more; pardon for those who died despairing; hope for those who died unhoping; good tidings for those who died stifled by unrelieved calamities. On errands of life, these letters speed to death.

Ah Bartleby! Ah humanity!

QUESTIONS

1. What kind of environment existed in the office before Bartleby's arrival? How does the nature of the job and the way in which the three other clerks do their work define the conditions of Bartleby's life?

2. What is the significance of the narrator's use of John Jacob Astor as a personal model? In what ways doesn't he live up to his model?

3. What are some of the possible resonances of Bartleby's reply, "I would prefer not to?" How would the meaning change without the word "would"? Why does the narrator later find himself using the word *prefer* "upon all sorts of not exactly suitable occasions"?

4. How are you affected by Bartleby's enigmatic manner? Is he capable of any human feeling, any pain or depression? Does he deserve our compassion?

5. What is the effect of Melville's continued use of walls or other images of confinement?

6. Does Bartleby represent some internal conflict or doubt for the narrator? What does the narrator's method of dealing with Bartleby reveal about the former? How do his religious views reveal him?

7. Is the revelation concerning the Dead Letter Office a kind of joke or is it the key to the mystery of Bartleby?

8. What, if anything, is the realization expressed by the final comment: "Ah Bartleby! Ah humanity"?

HAMLIN GARLAND

IN "A Branch Road" Hamlin Garland (1860–1940) reveals that nineteenth-century Midwestern farm life could be every bit as rigid as the most routinized Wall Street office. Garland himself was born in Wisconsin to parents who moved on several times during his youth when their farm failed. He soon became tired of the relentless drudgery of farm life and, after graduating from a seminary in Iowa, ran off to Boston where he first became a school teacher and then, encouraged by William Dean Howells, a writer. He returned to the Midwest several times, but each time found it more distasteful. Like Fitzgerald, however, he was always haunted by poignant feelings about his past.

Garland was more than a regional writer even though all his best fiction is set in the Midwest. On the basis of his own theory of fiction, which he called "veritism," he advocated that American fiction divorce itself from tradition and imitation and explore meanings below the surface; that it deal with the unpleasant as well as the pleasant aspects of life; and that it try to capture the exact feeling of particular moments of experience. At his best he does all these things by concentrating on simple, sharp impressions of life as he had lived it. He writes of common people and their real problems—unadorned hardships lightened by only occasional small pleasures.

"A Branch Road" appears in a volume of Garland's stories called *Main-Travelled Roads* (1891). He describes the typical "main-travelled" road in the Midwest as one which "is long and wearyful, and has a dull little town at one end, and a home of toil at the other. Like the main-travelled road of life, it is traversed by many classes of people, but the poor and the weary predominate." "A Branch Road" seems somewhat modern because of Garland's psychological insights into his characters' emotions and sexual feelings. Even though these people are both poor and oppressed by narrow social conventions, they possess, besides a necessary resignation to the routine and drudgery of their lives, some power of individual action to control their fate. Certainly Will Hannan is granted a wide range of actions throughout "A Branch Road," even though, as one might expect, it is the women's lot to toil and suffer at home. One of Garland's themes is the irrelevance of romantic love in such a setting. In some of his stories we see how daughters of Norwegian and German immigrants are forced to work in the fields like the men. These girls dream that some "Yankee" will come along and marry them so that they can live the life of comparative ease in the kitchen and nursery.

Garland does focus on romantic love in "A Branch Road"; Agnes and Will really do love each other. Their problems in communicating with each other are the result of courtship standards that conflict in Will and balk the expression of his feelings. He will not be affectionate to Agnes in front of others and he shames her when she tries to be affectionate to him in the same circumstance; but the lovers are not allowed to be alone. Because this system allows them so little human communication, Will doubts both himself and Agnes and is plagued by feelings of jealousy and possessiveness. An extremely narrow code prescribes how he is to act as a "man," and he cannot allow himself the "feminine" indulgence of being forgiven by Agnes. Yet he is so sensitive that he is incensed by his friends' "vulgarizing tone," which he feels will sully his "holy" and "exquisite" relationship. At the end of the first section, unable to apologize to her and to confront his shame, he flees his love—and himself as well.

After seven years he returns. Whether he has been sexually frustrated or a victim of degrading experiences one does not know, but when he sees Agnes (no longer physically attractive to him) a prisoner in her own home, he decides to "save" her and take her away. According to William Dean Howells, Will "tempts the broken-hearted drudge away from her loveless home. It is all morally wrong, but the author leaves you to say that for yourself." Today most of us would not question the morality, but would wonder instead at their chances for happiness. But Garland does allow this desperate gesture to be made—and that is what surprises and satisfies us.

A Branch Road

In the windless September dawn a voice went ringing clear and sweet, a man's voice, singing a cheap and common air. Yet something in the sound of it told he was young, jubilant, and a happy lover.

Above the level belt of timber to the east a vast dome of pale un-dazzling gold was rising, silently and swiftly. Jays called in the thickets where the maples flamed amid the green oaks, with irregular splashes of red and orange. The grass was crisp with frost under the feet, the road smooth and gray-white in color, the air was indescribably pure, resonant, and stimulating. No wonder the man sang!

He came into view around the curve in the lane. He had a fork on his shoulder, a graceful and polished tool. His straw hat was tilted on the back of his head; his rough, faded coat was buttoned close to the chin, and he wore thin buckskin gloves on his hands. He looked muscular and intelligent, and was evidently about twenty-two years of age.

As he walked on, and the sunrise came nearer to him, he stopped his song. The broadening heavens had a majesty and sweetness that made him forget the physical joy of happy youth. He grew almost sad with the vague thoughts and great emotions which rolled in his brain as the wonder of the morning grew.

He walked more slowly, mechanically following the road, his eyes on the ever-shifting streaming banners of rose and pale green, which made the east too glorious for any words to tell. The air was so still it seemed to await expectantly the coming of the sun.

Then his mind went forward to Agnes. Would she see it? She was at work, getting breakfast, but he hoped she had time to see it. He was in that mood, so common to him now, wherein he could not fully enjoy any sight or sound unless sharing it with her. Far down the road he heard the sharp clatter of a wagon. The roosters were calling near and far, in many keys and tunes. The dogs were barking, cattle-bells were jangling in the wooded pastures, and as the youth passed farmhouses, lights in the kitchen windows showed that the women were astir about breakfast, and the sound of voices and the tapping of curry-combs at the barn told that the men were at their morning chores.

And the east bloomed broader! The dome of gold grew brighter, the faint clouds here and there flamed with a flush of red. The frost began to glisten with a reflected color. The youth dreamed as he walked; his broad face and deep earnest eyes caught and retained some part of the beauty and majesty of the sky.

But his brow darkened as he passed a farm gate and a young man of

From MAIN-TRAVELLED ROADS, 1891.

about his own age joined him. The other man was equipped for work like himself.

"Hello, Will!"

"Hello, Ed!"

"Going down to help Dingman thrash!"

"Yes," replied Will, shortly. It was easy to see he did not welcome company.

"So'm I. Who's goin' to do your thrashin'—Dave McTurg?"

"Yes, I guess so. Haven't spoken to anybody yet."

They walked on side by side. Will hardly felt like being rudely broken in on in this way. The two men were rivals, but Will, being the victor, would have been magnanimous, only he wanted to be alone with his lover's dream.

"When do you go back to the Sem?" Ed asked after a little.

"Term begins next week. I'll make a break about second week."

"Le's see: you graduate next year, don't yeh?"

"I expect to, if I don't slip up on it."

They walked on side by side, both handsome fellows; Ed a little more showy in his face, which had a certain clear-cut precision of line, and a peculiar clear pallor that never browned under the sun. He chewed vigorously on a quid of tobacco, one of his most noticeable bad habits.

Teams could be heard clattering along on several roads now, and jovial voices singing. One team coming along rapidly behind the two men, the driver sung out in good-natured warning, "Get out o' the way, there." And with a laugh and a chirp spurred his horses to pass them.

Ed, with a swift understanding of the driver's trick, flung out his left hand and caught the end-gate, threw his fork in and leaped after it. Will walked on, disdaining attempt to catch the wagon. On all sides now the wagons of the ploughmen or threshers were getting out into the fields, with a pounding, rumbling sound.

The pale-red sun was shooting light through the leaves, and warming the boles of the great oaks that stood in the yard, and melting the frost off the great gaudy, red and gold striped threshing machine standing between the stacks. The interest, picturesqueness, of it all got hold of Will Hannan, accustomed to it as he was. The horses stood about in a circle, hitched to the ends of the six sweeps, every rod shining with frost.

The driver was oiling the great tarry cog-wheels underneath. Laughing fellows were wrestling about the yard. Ed Kinney had sealed the highest stack, and stood ready to throw the first sheaf. The sun, lighting him where he stood, made his fork-handle gleam like dull gold. Cheery words, jests, and snatches of song rose everywhere. Dingman bustled about giving his orders and placing his men, and the voice of big David McTurg

was heard calling to the men as they raised the long stacker into place:
"Heave ho, there! *Up* she rises!"

And, best of all, Will caught a glimpse of a smiling girl-face at the kitchen window that made the blood beat in his throat.

"Hello, Will!" was the general greeting, given with some constraint by most of the young fellows, for Will had been going to Rock River to school for some years, and there was a little feeling of jealousy on the part of those who pretended to sneer at the "seminary chaps like Will Hannan and Milton Jennings."

Dingman came up. "Will, I guess you'd better go on the stack with Ed."

"All ready. Hurrah, there!" said David in his soft but resonant bass voice that always had a laugh in it. "Come, come, every sucker of yeh git hold o' something. All ready!" He waved his hand at the driver, who climbed upon his platform. Everybody scrambled into place.

The driver began to talk:

"*Chk, chk!* All ready, boys! Stiddy there, Dan! *Chk, chk! All* ready, boys! *Stiddy* there, boys! *All* ready now!" The horses began to strain at the sweeps. The cylinder began to hum.

"Grab a root there! Where's my band-cutter? Here, you, climb on here!" And David reached down and pulled Shep Watson up by the shoulder with his gigantic hand.

Boo-oo-oo-oom, Boo-woo-woo-oom-oom-ow-owm, yarr, yarr! The whirling cylinder boomed, roared, and snarled as it rose in speed. At last, when its tone became a rattling yell, David nodded to the pitchers and rasped his hands together. The sheaves began to fall from the stack; the band cutter, knife in hand, slashed the bands in twain, and the feeder with easy majestic movement gathered them under his arm, rolled them out into an even belt of entering wheat, on which the cylinder tore with its smothered, ferocious snarl.

Will was very happy in a quiet way. He enjoyed the smooth roll of his great muscles, and the sense of power in his hands as he lifted, turned, and swung the heavy sheaves two by two upon the table, where the band-cutter madly slashed away. His frame, sturdy rather than tall, was nevertheless lithe, and he made a fine figure to look at, so Agnes thought, as she came out a moment and bowed and smiled.

This scene, one of the jolliest and most sociable of the Western farm, had a charm quite aside from human companionship. The beautiful yellow straw entering the cylinder; the clear yellow-brown wheat pulsing out at the side; the broken straw, chaff, and dust puffing out on the great stacker; the cheery whistling and calling of the driver; the keen, crisp air, and the bright sun somehow weirdly suggestive of the passage of time.

Will and Agnes had arrived at a tacit understanding of mutual love only the night before, and Will was powerfully moved to glance often toward the house, but feared as never before the jokes of his companions. He worked on, therefore, methodically, eagerly; but his thoughts were on the future—the rustle of the oak-tree near by, the noise of whose sere leaves he could distinguish sifting beneath the booming snarl of the machine, was like the sound of a woman's dress: on the sky were great fleets of clouds sailing on the rising wind, like merchantmen bound to some land of love and plenty.

When the Dingmans first came in, only a couple of years before, Agnes had been at once surrounded by a swarm of suitors. Her pleasant face and her abounding good-nature made her an instant favorite with all. Will, however, had disdained to become one of the crowd, and held himself aloof, as he could easily do, being away at school most of the time.

The second winter, however, Agnes also attended the seminary, and Will saw her daily, and grew to love her. He had been just a bit jealous of Ed Kinney all the time, for Ed had a certain rakish grace in dancing and a dashing skill in handling a team, which made him a dangerous rival.

But, as Will worked beside him all the Monday, he felt so secure in his knowledge of the caress Agnes had given him at parting the night before that he was perfectly happy—so happy that he didn't care to talk, only to work on and dream as he worked.

Shrewd David McTurg had his joke when the machine stopped for a few minutes. "Well, you fellers do better 'n I expected yeh to, after bein' out so late last night. The first feller I see gappin' has got to treat to the apples."

"Keep your eye on me," said Shep Watson.

"You?" laughed one of the others. "Anybody knows if a girl so much as looked crossways at you, you'd fall in a fit."

"Another thing," said David. "I can't have you fellers carryin' grain goin' to the house every minute for fried cakes or cookies."

"Now you git out," said Bill Young from the straw pile. "You ain't goin' to have all the fun to yerself."

Will's blood began to grow hot in his face. If Bill had said much more, or mentioned Agnes by name, he would have silenced him. To have this rough joking come to a close upon the holiest and most exquisite evening of his life was horrible. It was not the words they said, but the tones they used, that vulgarized it all. He breathed a sigh of relief when the sound of the machine began again.

This jesting made him more wary, and when the call for dinner sounded and he knew he was going to see her, he shrank from it. He took no part in the race of the dust-blackened, half-famished men to get at the washing-place first. He took no part in the scurry to get seats at the first table.

Threshing-time was always a season of great trial to the housewife. To have a dozen men with the appetites of dragons to cook for, in addition to their other everyday duties, was no small task for a couple of women. Preparations usually began the night before with a raid on a hen-roost, for "biled chickun" formed the *pièce de resistance* of the dinner. The table, enlarged by boards, filled the sitting room. Extra seats were made out of planks placed on chairs, and dishes were borrowed from neighbors, who came for such aid in their turn.

Sometimes the neighboring women came in to help; but Agnes and her mother were determined to manage the job alone this year, and so the girl, in neat dark dress, her eyes shining, her cheeks flushed with the work, received the men as they came in, dusty, coatless, with grime behind their ears, but a jolly good smile on every face.

Most of them were farmers of the neighborhood, and her schoolmates. The only one she shrank from was Bill Young, with his hard, glittering eyes and red, sordid face. She received their jokes, their noise, with a silent smile which showed her even teeth and dimpled her round cheek. "She was good for sore eyes," as one of the fellows said to Shep. She seemed deliciously sweet and dainty to these roughly dressed fellows.

They ranged along the table with a great deal of noise, boots thumping, squeaking, knives and forks rattling, voices bellowing out.

"Now hold on, Steve! Can't hev yeh so near that chickun!"

"Move along, Shep! I want to be next to the kitchen door! I won't get nothin' with *you* on that side o' me."

"Oh, that's too thin! I see what you're—"

"No, I won't need any sugar, if you just smile into it." This from gallant David, greeted with roars of laughter.

"Now, Dave, s'pose your wife 'ud hear o' that?"

"She'd snatch 'im bald-headed, that's what she'd do."

"Say, somebody drive that chow down this way," said Bill.

"Don't get off that drive! It's too old," criticised Shep, passing the milk-jug.

Potatoes were seized, cut in halves, sopped in gravy, and taken *one, two!* Corn cakes went into great jaws like coal into a steam-engine. Knives in the right hand cut meat and scooped gravy up. Great, muscular, grimy, but wholesome fellows they were, feeding like ancient Norse, and capable of working like demons. They were deep in the process, half-hidden by steam from the potatoes and stew, in less than sixty seconds after their entrance.

With a shrinking from the comments of the others upon his regard for Agnes, Will assumed a reserved and almost haughty air toward his fellow-workmen, and a curious coldness toward her. As he went in, she came forward smiling brightly.

"There's one more place, Will." A tender, involuntary droop in her voice betrayed her, and Will felt a wave of hot blood surge over him as the rest roared.

"Ha, ha! Oh, there'd be a place for *him!*"

"Don't worry, Will! Always room for *you* here!"

Will took his seat with a sudden, angry flame.

"Why can't she keep it from these fools?" was his thought. He didn't even thank her for showing him the chair.

She flushed vividly, but smiled back. She was so proud and happy she didn't care very much if they *did* know it. But as Will looked at her with that quick, angry glance, she was hurt and puzzled. She redoubled her exertions to please him, and by so doing added to the amusement of the crowd that gnawed chicken-bones, rattled cups, knives, and forks, and joked as they ate with small grace and no material loss of time.

Will remained silent through it all, eating his potato, in marked contrast to the others, with his fork instead of his knife, and drinking his tea from his cup rather than from his saucer—"finnickies" which did not escape the notice of the girl nor the sharp eyes of the workmen.

"See that? That's the way we do down to the Sem! See? Fork for pie in yer right hand! Hey? *I* can't do it? Watch me!"

When Agnes leaned over to say, "Won't you have some more tea, Will?" they nudged each other and grinned. "Aha! What did I tell you?"

Agnes saw at last that for some reason Will didn't want her to show her regard for him—that he was ashamed of it in some way, and she was wounded. To cover it up, she resorted to the natural device of smiling and chatting with the others. She asked Ed if he wouldn't have another piece of pie.

"I will—with a fork, please."

"This is 'bout the only place *you* can use a fork," said Bill Young, anticipating a laugh by his own broad grin.

"Oh, that's too old," said Shep Watson. "Don't drag that out agin. A man that'll eat seven taters—"

"Shows who does the work."

"Yes, with his jaws," put in Jim Wheelock, the driver.

"If you'd put in a little more work with soap 'n water before comin' in to dinner, it 'ud be a religious idee," said David.

"It ain't healthy to wash."

"Well, you'll live forever, then."

"He ain't washed his face sence I knew 'im."

"Oh, that's a little too tough! He washes once a week," said Ed Kinney.

"Back of his ears?" inquired David, who was munching a doughnut, his black eyes twinkling with fun.

"Yep."

"What's the cause of it?"

"Dade says she won't kiss 'im if he don't."

Everybody roared.

"Good fer Dade! I wouldn't if I was in her place."

Wheelock gripped a chicken-leg imperturbably, and left it bare as a toothpick with one or two bites at it. His face shone in two clean sections around his nose and mouth. Behind his ears the dirt lay undisturbed. The grease on his hands could not be washed off.

Will began to suffer now because Agnes treated the other fellows too well. With a lover's exacting jealousy, he wanted her in some way to hide their tenderness from the rest, and also to show her indifference to men like Young and Kinney. He didn't stop to inquire of himself the justice of such a demand, nor just how it was to be done. He only insisted she ought to do it.

He rose and left the table at the end of his dinner without having spoken to her, without even a tender, significant glance, and he knew, too, that she was troubled and hurt. But he was suffering. It seemed as if he had lost something sweet, lost it irrecoverably.

He noticed Ed Kinney and Bill Young were the last to come out, just before the machine started up again after dinner, and he saw them pause outside the threshold and laugh back at Agnes standing in the doorway. Why couldn't she keep those fellows at a distance, not go out of her way to bandy jokes with them?

In some way the elation of the morning was gone. He worked on doggedly now, without looking up, without listening to the leaves, without seeing the sunlighted clouds. Of course he didn't think that she meant anything by it, but it irritated him and made him unhappy. She gave herself too freely.

Toward the middle of the afternoon the machine stopped for some repairing; and while Will lay on his stack in the bright yellow sunshine, shelling wheat in his hands and listening to the wind in the oaks, he heard his name and her name mentioned on the other side of the machine, where the measuring-box stood. He listened.

"She's pretty sweet on him, ain't she? Did yeh notus how she stood around over him?"

"Yes; an' did yeh see him when she passed the cup o' tea down over his shoulder?"

Will got up, white with wrath, as they laughed.

"Someway he didn't seem to enjoy it as I would. I wish she'd reach her arm over my neck that way."

Will walked around the machine, and came on the group lying on the chaff near the straw-pile.

"Say, I want you fellers to understand that I won't have any more of this talk. I won't have it."

There was a dead silence. Then Bill Young got up.

"What yeh goin' to do about ut?" he sneered.

"I'm going to stop it."

The wolf rose in Young. He moved forward, his ferocious soul flaming from his eyes.

"W'y, you damned seminary dude, I can break you in two!"

An answering glare came into Will's eyes. He grasped and slightly shook his fork, which he had brought with him unconsciously.

"If you make one motion at me, I'll smash your head like an egg-shell!" His voice was low but terrific. There was a tone in it that made his own blood stop in his veins. "If you think I'm going to roll around on this ground with a hyena like you, you've mistaken your man. I'll *kill* you, but I won't *fight* with such men as you are."

Bill quailed and slunk away, muttering some epithet like "coward."

"I don't care what you call *me*, but just remember what I say: you keep your tongue off that girl's affairs."

"That's the talk," said David. "Stand up for your girl always, but don't use a fork. You can handle him without that."

"I don't propose to try," said Will, as he turned away. As he did so, he caught a glimpse of Ed Kinney at the well, pumping a pail of water for Agnes, who stood beside him, the sun on her beautiful yellow hair. She was laughing at something Ed was saying as he slowly moved the handle up and down.

Instantly, like a foaming, turbid flood, his rage swept out toward her. "It's all *her* fault," he thought, grinding his teeth. "She's a fool. If she'd hold herself in, like other girls! But no; she must smile and smile at everybody." It was a beautiful picture, but it sent a shiver through him.

He worked on with teeth set, white with rage. He had an impulse that would have made him assault her with words as with a knife. He was possessed of a terrible passion which was hitherto latent in him, and which he now felt to be his worst self. But he was powerless to exorcise it. His set teeth ached with the stress of his muscular tension, and his eyes smarted with the strain.

He had always prided himself on being cool, calm, above these absurd quarrels which his companions had indulged in. He didn't suppose he could be so moved. As he worked on, his rage settled into a sort of stubborn bitterness—stubborn bitterness of conflict between this evil nature and his usual self. It was the instinct of possession, the organic feeling of proprietorship of a woman, which rose to the surface and mastered him. He was not a self-analyst, of course, being young, though he was more introspective than the ordinary farmer.

He had a great deal of time to think it over as he worked on there, pitching the heavy bundles, but still he did not get rid of the miserable desire to punish Agnes; and when she came out, looking very pretty in her straw hat, and came around near his stack, he knew she came to see him, to have an explanation, a smile; and yet he worked away with his hat pulled over his eyes, hardly noticing her.

Ed went over to the edge of the stack and chatted with her; and she—poor girl!—feeling Will's neglect, could only put a good face on the matter, and show that she didn't mind it, by laughing back at Ed.

All this Will saw, though he didn't appear to be looking. And when Jim Wheelock—Dirty Jim—with his whip in his hand, came up and playfully pretended to pour oil on her hair, and she laughingly struck at him with a handful of straw, Will wouldn't have looked at her if she had called him by name.

She looked so bright and charming in her snowy apron and her boy's straw hat tipped jauntily over one pink ear, that David and Steve and Bill, and even Shep, found a way to get a word with her, and the poor fellows in the high straw-pile looked their disappointment and shook their forks in mock rage at the lucky dogs on the ground. But Will worked on like a fiend, while the dapples of light and shade fell on the bright face of the merry girl.

To save his soul from hell-flames he couldn't have gone over there and smiled at her. It was impossible. A wall of bronze seemed to have arisen between them. Yesterday—last night—seemed a dream. The clasp of her hands at his neck, the touch of her lips, were like the caresses of an ideal in some revery long ago.

As night drew on the men worked with a steadier, more mechanical action. No one spoke now. Each man was intent on his work. No one had any strength or breath to waste. The driver on his power changed his weight on weary feet and whistled and sang at the tired horses. The feeder, his face gray with dust, rolled the grain into the cylinder so evenly, so steadily, so swiftly that it ran on with a sullen, booming roar. Far up on the straw-pile the stackers worked with the steady, rhythmic action of men rowing a boat, their figures looming vague and dim in the flying dust and chaff, outlined against the glorious yellow and orange-tinted clouds.

"Phe-e-eew-*ee*," whistled the driver with the sweet, cheery, rising notes of a bird. "*Chk, chk, chk!* Phe-e-eew-e! Go on there, boys! *Chk, chk, chk!* Step up there, Dan, step up! (*Snap!*) Phe-e-eew-ee! G'-wan—g'-wan, g'-wan! *Chk, chk, chk!* Wheest, wheest, wheest! *Chk, chk!*"

In the house the women were setting the table for supper. The sun had gone down behind the oaks, flinging glorious rose-color and orange shadows along the edges of the slate-blue clouds. Agnes stopped her work at the kitchen window to look up at the sky, and cry silently. "What was the matter with Will?" She felt a sort of distrust of him now. She thought she knew him so well, but now he was so strange.

"Come, Aggie," said Mrs. Dingman, "they're gettin' 'most down to the bottom of the stack. They'll be pilin' in here soon."

"Phe-e-eew-ee! G'-wan, Doll! G'-wan, boys! *Chk, chk, chk!* Phe-e-eew-ee!" called the driver out in the dusk, cheerily swinging the whip over the horses' backs. *Boom-oo-oo-oom!* roared the machine, with a muffled, monotonous, solemn tone. "G'-wan, boys! G'-wan, g'-wan!"

Will had worked unceasingly all day. His muscles ached with fatigue. His hands trembled. He clenched his teeth, however, and worked on, determined not to yield. He wanted them to understand that he could do as much pitching as any of them, and read Caesar's Commentaries beside. It seemed as if each bundle were the last he could raise. The sinews of his wrist pained him so; they seemed swollen to twice their natural size. But still he worked on grimly, while the dusk fell and the air grew chill.

At last the bottom bundle was pitched up, and he got down on his knees to help scrape the loose wheat into baskets. What a sweet relief it was to kneel down, to release the fork, and let the worn and cramping muscles settle into rest! A new note came into the driver's voice, a soothing tone, full of kindness and admiration for the work his teams had done.

"Wo-o-o, lads! Stiddy-y-y, boys! Wo-o-o, there, Dan. Stiddy, stiddy, old man! *Ho*, there!" The cylinder took on a lower key, with short, rising yells, as it ran empty for a moment. The horses had been going so long that they came to a stop reluctantly. At last David called, "Turn out!" The men seized the ends of the sweep, David uncoupled the tumbling-rods, and Shep slowly shoved a sheaf of grain into the cylinder, choking it into silence.

The stillness and the dusk were very impressive. So long had the bell-metal cog-wheel sung its deafening song into his ear that, as he walked away into the dusk, Will had a weird feeling of being suddenly deaf, and his legs were so numb that he could hardly feel the earth. He stumbled away like a man paralyzed.

He took out his handkerchief, wiped the dust from his face as best he could, shook his coat, dusted his shoulders with a grain-sack, and was starting away, when Mr. Dingman, a rather feeble, elderly man, came up.

"Come, Will, supper's all ready. Go in and eat."

"I guess I'll go home to supper."

"Oh, no; that won't do. The women'll be expecting you to stay."

The men were laughing at the well, the warm yellow light shone from the kitchen, the chill air making it seem very inviting, and she was there —waiting! But the demon rose in him. He knew Agnes would expect him, and she would cry that night with disappointment, but his face hardened. "I guess I'll go home," he said, and his tone was relentless. He turned and walked away, hungry, tired—so tired he stumbled, and so unhappy he could have wept.

2

On Thursday the county fair was to be held. The fair is one of the gala-days of the year in the country districts of the West, and one of the times when the country lover rises above expense to the extravagance of hiring a top-buggy, in which to take his sweetheart to the neighboring town.

It was customary to prepare for this long beforehand, for the demand for top-buggies was so great the liverymen grew dictatorial, and took no chances. Slowly but surely the country beaux began to compete with the clerks, and in many cases actually outbid them, as they furnished their own horses and could bid higher, in consequence, on the carriages.

Will had secured his brother's "rig," and early on Thursday morning he was at work, busily washing the mud from the carriage, dusting the cushions, and polishing up the buckles and rosettes on his horses' harnesses. It was a beautiful, crisp, clear dawn—the ideal day for a ride; and Will was singing as he worked. He had regained his real self, and, having passed through a bitter period of shame, was now joyous with anticipation of forgiveness. He looked forward to the day, with its chances of doing a thousand little things to show his regret and his love.

He had not seen Agnes since Monday; Tuesday he did not go back to help thresh, and Wednesday he had been obliged to go to town to see about board for the coming term; but he felt sure of her. It had all been arranged the Sunday before; she'd expect him, and he was to call at eight o'clock.

He polished up the colts with merry tick-tack of the brush and comb, and after the last stroke on their shining limbs, threw his tools in the box and went to the house.

"Pretty sharp last night," said his brother John, who was scrubbing his face at the cistern."

"Should say so by that rim of ice," Will replied, dipping his hands into the icy water.

"I ought 'o stay home to-day and dig 'tates," continued the older man, thoughtfully, as they went into the woodshed and wiped consecutively on the long roller-towel. "Some o' them Early Rose lay right on top o' the ground. They'll get nipped, sure."

"Oh, I guess not. You'd better go, Jack; you don't get away very often. And then it would disappoint Nettie and the children so. Their little hearts are overflowing," he ended, as the door opened and two sturdy little boys rushed out.

"B'ekfuss, poppa; all yeady!"

The kitchen table was set near the stove; the window let in the sun, and the smell of sizzling sausages and the aroma of coffee filled the room.

The kettle was doing its duty cheerily, and the wife, with flushed face and smiling eyes, was hurrying to and fro, her heart full of anticipation of the day's outing.

There was a hilarity almost like some strange intoxication on the part of the two children. They danced and chattered and clapped their chubby brown hands and ran to the windows ceaselessly.

"Is yuncle Will goin' yide nour buggy?"

"Yus; the buggy and the colts."

"Is he goin' to take his girl?"

Will blushed a little and John roared.

"Yes, I'm goin'—"

"Is Aggie your girl?"

"H'yer! h'yer! young man," called John, "you're gettin' personal."

"Well, set up!" said Nettie, and with a good deal of clatter they drew around the cheerful table.

Will had already begun to see the pathos, the pitiful significance of his great joy over a day's outing, and he took himself a little to task at his own selfish freedom. He resolved to stay at home some time and let Nettie go in his place. A few hours in the middle of the day on Sunday, three or four holidays in summer; the rest of the year, for this cheerful little wife and her patient husband, was made up of work—work which accomplished little and brought them almost nothing that was beautiful.

While they were eating breakfast, teams began to clatter by, huge lumber-wagons with three seats across, and a boy or two jouncing up and down with the dinner baskets near the end-gate. The children rushed to the window each time to announce who it was and how many there were in.

But as Johnny said "firteen" each time, and Ned wavered between "seven" and "sixteen," it was doubtful if they could be relied upon. They had very little appetite, so keen was their anticipation of the ride and the wonderful sights before them. Their little hearts shuddered with joy at every fresh token of preparation—a joy that made Will say, "Poor little men!"

They vibrated between the house and the barn while the chores were being finished, and their happy cries started the young roosters into a renewed season of crowing. And when at last the wagon was brought out and the horses hitched to it, they danced like mad sprites.

After they had driven away, Will brought out the colts, hitched them in, and drove them to the hitching-post. Then he leisurely dressed himself in his best suit, blacked his boots with considerable exertion, and at about 7.30 o'clock climbed into his carriage and gathered up the reins.

He was quite happy again. The crisp, bracing air, the strong pull of the spirited young team, put all thought of sorrow behind him. He had planned it all out. He would first put his arm round her and kiss her— there would not need to be any words to tell her how sorry and ashamed he was. She would know!

Now, when he was alone and going toward her on a beautiful morning, the anger and bitterness of Monday fled away, became unreal, and the sweet dream of the Sunday parting grew the reality. She was waiting for him now. She had on her pretty blue dress, and the wide hat that always made her look so arch. He had said about eight o'clock.

The swift team was carrying him along the crossroad, which was little travelled, and he was alone with his thoughts. He fell again upon his plans. Another year at school for them both, and then he'd go into a law office. Judge Brown had told him he'd give him—

"Whoa! *Ho!*"

There was a swift lurch that sent him flying over the dasher. A confused vision of a roadside ditch full of weeds and bushes, and then he felt the reins in his hands and heard the snorting horses trample on the hard road.

He rose dizzy, bruised, and covered with dust. The team he held securely and soon quieted. The cause of the accident was plain; the right fore-wheel had come off, letting the front of the buggy drop. He unhitched the excited team from the carriage, drove them to the fence and tied them securely, then went back to find the wheel, and the *burr* whose failure to hold its place had done all the mischief. He soon had the wheel on, but to find the *burr* was a harder task. Back and forth he ranged, looking, scraping in the dust, searching the weeds.

He knew that sometimes a wheel will run without the burr for many rods before coming off, and so each time he extended his search. He traversed the entire half mile several times, each time his rage and disappointment getting more bitter. He ground his teeth in a fever of vexation and dismay.

He had a vision of Agnes waiting, wondering why he did not come. It was this vision that kept him from seeing the burr in the wheel-track, partly covered by a clod. Once he passed it looking wildly at his watch, which was showing nine o'clock. Another time he passed it with eyes dimmed with a mist that was almost tears of anger.

There is no contrivance that will replace an axle-burr, and farm-yards have no unused axle-burrs, and so Will searched. Each moment he said: "I'll give it up, get onto one of the horses, and go down and tell her." But searching for a lost axle-burr is like fishing; the searcher expects each moment to find it. And so he groped, and ran breathlessly, furiously, back and forth, and at last kicked away the clod that covered it, and hurried, hot and dusty, cursing his stupidity, back to the team.

It was ten o'clock as he climbed again into the buggy, and started his team on a swift trot down the road. What *would* she think? He saw her now with tearful eyes and pouting lips. She was sitting at the window, with hat and gloves on; the rest had gone, and she was waiting for him.

But she'd *know* something had happened, because he had promised to be there at eight. He had told her what team he'd have. (He had forgotten at this moment the doubt and distrust he had given her on Monday.) She'd know he'd surely come.

But there was no smiling or tearful face watching at the window as he came down the lane at a tearing pace, and turned into the yard. The house was silent, and the curtains down. The silence sent a chill to his heart. Something rose up in his throat to choke him.

"Agnes!" he called. "Hello! I'm here at last!"

There was no reply. As he sat there the part he had played on Monday came back to him. She may be sick! he thought, with a cold thrill of fear.

An old man came round the corner of the house with a potato fork in his hands, his teeth displayed in a grin.

"She ain't here. She's gone."

"Gone!"

"Yes—more'n an hour ago."

"Who'd she go with?"

"Ed Kinney," said the old fellow, with a malicious grin. "I guess your goose is cooked."

Will lashed the horses into a run, and swung round the yard and out of the gate. His face was white as a dead man's, and his teeth were set like a vice. He glared straight ahead. The team ran wildly, steadily homeward, while their driver guided them unconsciously without seeing them. His mind was filled with a tempest of rages, despairs, and shames.

That ride he will never forget. In it he threw away all his plans. He gave up his year's schooling. He gave up his law aspirations. He deserted his brother and his friends. In the dizzying whirl of passions he had only one clear idea—to get away, to go West, to escape from the sneers and laughter of his neighbors, and to make her suffer by it all.

He drove into the yard, did not stop to unharness the team, but rushed into the house, and began packing his trunk. His plan was formed.

He would drive to Cedarville, and hire someone to bring the team back. He had no thought of anything but the shame, the insult, she had put upon him. Her action on Monday took on the same levity it wore then, and excited him in the same way. He saw her laughing with Ed over his dismay. He sat down and wrote a letter to her at last—a letter that came from the ferocity of the mediæval savage in him:

"If you want to go to hell with Ed Kinney, you can. I won't say a word. That's where he'll take you. You won't see me again."

This he signed and sealed, and then he bowed his head and wept like a girl. But his tears did not soften the effect of the letter. It went as straight to its mark as he meant it should. It tore a seared and ragged path to an innocent, happy heart, and he took a savage pleasure in the thought of it as he rode away in the cars toward the South.

3

The seven years lying between 1880 and 1887 made a great change in Rock River and in the adjacent farming land. Signs changed and firms went out of business with characteristic Western ease of shift. The trees grew rapidly, dwarfing the houses beneath them, and contrasts of newness and decay thickened.

Will found the country changed, as he walked along the dusty road from Rock River toward "The Corners." The landscape was at its fairest and liberalest, with its seas of corn, deep-green and moving with a mournful rustle, in sharp contrast to its flashing blades; its gleaming fields of barley, and its wheat already mottled with soft gold in the midst of its pea-green.

The changes were in the hedges, grown higher, in the greater predominance of cornfields and cattle pastures, and especially in the destruction of homes. As he passed on, Will saw the grass growing and cattle feeding on a dozen places where homes had once stood. They had given place to the large farm and the stock-raiser. Still the whole scene was bountiful and beautiful to the eye.

It was especially grateful to Will, for he had spent nearly all his years of absence among the rocks, treeless swells, and bleak cliffs of the Southwest. The crickets rising before his dusty feet appeared to him something sweet and suggestive, and the cattle feeding in the clover moved him to deep thought—they were so peaceful and slow motioned.

As he reached a little popple tree by the roadside, he stopped, removed his broad-brimmed hat, put his elbows on the fence, and looked hungrily upon the scene. The sky was deeply blue, with only here and there a huge, heavy, slow-moving, massive, sharply outlined cloud sailing like a berg of ice in a shoreless sea of azure.

In the fields the men were harvesting the ripened oats and barley, and the sound of their machines clattering, now low, now loud, came to his ears. Flies buzzed near him, and a kingbird clattered overhead. He noticed again, as he had many a time when a boy, that the softened sound of the far-off reaper was at times exactly like the hum of a blue-bottle fly buzzing heedlessly about his ears.

A slender and very handsome young man was shocking grain near the fence, working so desperately he did not see Will until greeted by him. He looked up, replied to the greeting, but kept on until he had finished his last stook; then he came to the shade of the tree and took off his hat.

"Nice day to sit under a tree and fish."

Will smiled. "I ought to know you, I suppose; I used to live here years ago."

"Guess not; we came in three years ago."

The young man was quick-spoken and pleasant to look at. Will felt freer with him.

"Are the Kinneys still living over there?" He nodded at a group of large buildings.

"Tom lives there. Old man lives with Ed. Tom ousted the old man some way, nobody seems to know how, and so he lives with Ed."

Will wanted to ask after Agnes, but hardly felt able. "I s'pose John Hannan is on his old farm?"

"Yes. Got a good crop this year."

Will looked again at the fields of rustling wheat over which the clouds rippled, and said with an air of conviction: "This lays over Arizony, dead sure."

"You're from Arizony, then?"

"Yes—a good ways from it," Will replied, in a way that stopped further question. "Good luck!" he added, as he walked on down the road toward the creek, musing.

"And the spring—I wonder if that's there yet. I'd like a drink." The sun seemed hotter than at noon, and he walked slowly. At the bridge that spanned the meadow brook, just where it widened over a sandy ford, he paused again. He hung over the rail and looked at the minnows swimming there.

"I wonder if they're the same identical chaps that used to boil and glitter there when I was a boy—looks so. Men change from one generation to another, but the fish remain the same. The same eternal procession of types. I suppose Darwin 'ud say their environment remains the same."

He hung for a long time over the railing, thinking of a vast number of things, mostly vague, flitting things, looking into the clear depths of the brook, and listening to the delicious liquid note of a blackbird swinging on the willow. Red lilies starred the grass with fire, and golden-rod and chicory grew everywhere; purple and orange and yellow-green the prevailing tints.

Suddenly a water-snake wriggled across the dark pool above the ford and the minnows disappeared under the shadow of the bridge. Then Will sighed, lifted his head and walked on. There seemed to be something prophetic in it, and he drew a long breath. That's the way his plans broke and faded away.

Human life does not move with the regularity of a clock. In living there are gaps and silences when the soul stands still in its flight through abysses—and there come times of trial and times of struggle when we grow old without knowing it. Body and soul change appallingly.

Seven years of hard, busy life had made changes in Will.

His face had grown bold, resolute, and rugged; some of its delicacy and all of its boyish quality was gone. His figure was stouter, erect as of old, but less graceful. He bore himself like a man accustomed to look out for himself in all kinds of places. It was only at times that there came into his deep eyes a preoccupied, almost sad, look which showed kinship with his old self.

This look was on his face as he walked toward the clump of trees on the right of the road.

He reached the grove of popple trees and made his way at once to the spring. When he saw it, he was again shocked. They had allowed it to fill with leaves and dirt!

Overcome by the memories of the past, he flung himself down on the cool and shadowy bank, and gave himself up to the bitter-sweet reveries of a man returning to his boyhood's home. He was filled somehow with a strange and powerful feeling of the passage of time; with a vague feeling of the mystery and elusiveness of human life. The leaves whispered it overhead, the birds sang it in chorus with the insects, and far above, in the measureless spaces of sky, the hawk told it in the silence and majesty of his flight from cloud to cloud.

It was a feeling hardly to be expressed in words—one of those emotions whose springs lie far back in the brain. He lay so still the chipmunks came curiously up to his very feet, only to scurry away when he stirred like a sleeper in pain.

He had cut himself off entirely from the life at The Corners. He had sent money home to John, but had concealed his own address carefully. The enormity of his folly now came back to him, racking him till he groaned.

He heard the patter of feet and half-mumbled monologue of a running child. He roused up and faced a small boy, who started back in terror like a wild fawn. He was deeply surprised to find a man there, where only boys and squirrels now came. He stuck his fist in his eye, and was backing away when Will spoke.

"Hold on, sonny! Nobody's hit you. Come, I ain't goin' to eat yeh." He took a bit of money from his pocket. "Come here and tell me your name. I want to talk with you."

The boy crept upon the dime.

Will smiled. "You ought to be a Kinney. What is your name?"

"Tomath Dickinthon Kinney. I'm thix and a half. I've got a colt," lisped the youngster, breathlessly, as he crept toward the money.

"Oh, you are, eh? Well, now, are you Tom's boy, or Ed's?"

"Tomth's boy. Uncle Ed heth got a little—"

"Ed got a boy?"

"Yeth, thir—a lil baby. Aunt Agg letth me hold 'im."

"Agg! Is that her name?"

"Tha'th what Uncle Ed callth her."

The man's head fell, and it was a long time before he asked his next question.

"How *is* she anyhow?"

"Purty well," piped the boy, with a prolongation of the last words into a kind of chirp. "She'th been thick, though," he added.

"Been sick? How long?"

"Oh, a long time. But she ain't thick abed; she'th awful poor, though. Gran'pa thayth she'th poor ath a rake."

"Oh, he does, eh?"

"Yeth, thir. Uncle Ed he jawth her, then she crieth."

Will's anger and remorse broke out in a groaning curse. "O my God! I see it all. That great lunkin' houn' has made life a hell for her." Then that letter came back to his mind—he had never been able to put it out of his mind—he never would till he saw her and asked her pardon.

"Here, my boy, I want you to tell me some more. Where does your Aunt Agnes live?"

"At gran'pa'th. You know where my gran'pa livth?"

"Well, *you* do. Now I want you to take this letter to her. Give it to *her*." He wrote a little note and folded it. "Now dust out o' here."

The boy slipped away through the trees like a rabbit; his little brown feet hardly rustled. He was like some little wood-animal. Left alone, the man fell back into a revery which lasted till the shadows fell on the thick little grove around the spring. He rose at last, and taking his stick in hand, walked out to the wood again and stood there gazing at the sky. He seemed loath to go farther. The sky was full of flame-colored clouds floating in a yellow-green sea, where bars of faint pink streamed broadly away.

As he stood there, feeling the wind lift his hair, listening to the crickets' ever-present crying, and facing the majesty of space, a strange sadness and despair came into his eyes.

Drawing a quick breath, he leaped the fence and was about going on up the road, when he heard, at a little distance, the sound of a drove of cattle approaching, and he stood aside to allow them to pass. They snuffed and shied at the silent figure by the fence, and hurried by with snapping heels—a peculiar sound that made Will smile with pleasure.

An old man was driving the cows, crying out:

"St—*boy*, there! Go on there! Whay, boss!"

Will knew that hard-featured, wiry old man, now entering his second childhood and beginning to limp painfully. He had his hands full of hard clods which he threw impatiently at the lumbering animals.

"Good-evening, uncle!"

"I ain't y'r uncle, young man."

His dim eyes did not recognize the boy he had chased out of his plum patch years before.

"I don't know yeh, neither," he added.

"Oh, you will, later on. I'm from the East. I'm a sort of a relative to John Hannan."

"I want 'o know if y' be!" the old man exclaimed, peering closer.

"Yes. I'm just up from Rock River. John's harvesting, I s'pose?"

"Yus."

"Where's the youngest one—Will?"

"William? Oh! he's a bad aig—he lit out f'r the West somewhere. He was a hard boy. He stole a hatful o' my plums once. He left home kind o' sudden. He! he! I s'pose he was purty well cut up jest about them days."

"How's that?"

The old man chuckled.

"Well, y' see, they was both courtin' Agnes then, an' my son cut William out. Then William he lit out f'r the West, Arizony, 'r California, 'r somewhere out West. Never been back sence."

"Ain't, heh?"

"No. But they say he's makin' a *terrible* lot o' money," the old man said in a hushed voice. "But the *way* he makes it is awful scaly. I tell my wife if I had a son like that an' he'd send me home a bushel-basket o' money, earnt like that, I wouldn't touch a finger to it—no sir!"

"You wouldn't? Why?"

"Cause it ain't right. It ain't made right noway, you—"

"But *how* is it made? What's the feller's trade?"

"He's a gambler—that's his trade! He plays cards, and every cent is bloody. I wouldn't touch such money nohow you could fix it."

"Wouldn't, heh?" The young man straightened up. "Well, look-a-here, old man: did you ever hear of a man foreclosing a mortgage on a widow and two boys, getting a farm f'r one quarter what it was really worth? You damned old hypocrite! I know all about you and your whole tribe—you old blood-sucker!"

The old man's jaw fell; he began to back away.

"Your neighbors tell some good stories about you. Now skip along after those cows, or I'll tickle your old legs for you!"

The old man, appalled and dazed at this sudden change of manner, backed away, and at last turned and racked off up the road, looking back with a wild face, at which the young man laughed remorselessly.

"The doggoned old skeesucks!" Will soliloquized as he walked up the road. "So that's the kind of a character he's been givin' me!"

"Hullo! A whippoorwill. Takes a man back into childhood— No, *don't 'whip poor Will'*; he's got all he can bear now."

He came at last to the little farm Dingman had owned, and he stopped in sorrowful surprise. The barn had been moved away, the garden ploughed up, and the house, turned into a granary, stood with boards nailed across its dusty, cobwebbed windows. The tears started into the man's eyes; he stood staring at it silently.

In the face of this house the seven years that he had last lived stretched away into a wild waste of time. It stood as a symbol of his wasted, ruined life. It was personal, intimately personal, this decay of her home.

All that last scene came back to him; the booming roar of the threshing-machine, the cheery whistle of the driver, the loud, merry shouts of the men. He remembered how warmly the lamp-light streamed out of that door as he turned away tired, hungry, sullen with rage and jealousy. Oh, if he had only had the courage of a man!

Then he thought of the boy's words. She was sick, Ed abused her. She had met her punishment. A hundred times he had been over the whole scene. A thousand times he had seen her at the pump smiling at Ed Kinney, the sun lighting her hair; and he never thought of that without hardening.

At this very gate he had driven up that last forenoon; to find that she had gone with Ed. He had lived that sickening, depressing moment over many times, but not times enough to keep down the bitter passion he had felt then, and felt now as he went over it in detail.

He was so happy and confident that morning, so perfectly certain that all would be made right by a kiss and a cheery jest. And now! Here he stood sick with despair and doubt of all the world. He turned away from the desolate homestead and walked on.

"But I'll see her—just once more. And then—"

And again the mighty significance, responsibility of life, fell upon him. He felt, as young people seldom do, the irrevocableness of living, the determinate, unalterable character of living. He determined to begin to live in some new way—just how he could not say.

4

Old man Kinney and his wife were getting their Sunday-school lessons with much bickering, when Will drove up the next day to the dilapidated gate and hitched his team to a leaning-post under the oaks. Will saw the old man's head at the open window, but no one else, though he looked eagerly for Agnes as he walked up the familiar path. There stood the great oak under whose shade he had grown to be a man. How close the great tree seemed to stand to his heart, someway! As the wind stirred in the leaves, it was like a rustle of greeting.

In that old house they had all lived, and his mother had toiled for thirty years. A sort of prison after all. There they were all born, and there his father and his little sister had died. And then it passed into old Kinney's hands.

Walking along up the path he felt a serious weakness in his limbs, and he made a pretence of stopping to look at a flower-bed containing nothing but weeds. After seven years of separation he was about to face once more the woman whose life came so near being a part of his— Agnes, now a wife and a mother.

How would she look? Would her face have that old-time peachy bloom, her mouth that peculiar beautiful curve? She was large and fair, he recalled, hair yellow and shining, eyes blue—

He roused himself. This was nonsense! He was trembling. He composed himself by looking around again.

"The old scoundrel has let the weeds choke out the flowers and surround the bee-hives. Old man Kinney never believed in anything but a petty utility."

Will set his teeth, and marched up to the door and struck it like a man delivering a challenge. Kinney opened the door, and started back in fear when he saw who it was.

"How de do? How de do?" said Will, walking in, his eyes fixed on a woman seated beyond, a child in her lap.

Agnes rose, without a word; a fawn-like, startled widening of the eyes, her breath coming quick, and her face flushing. They couldn't speak; they only looked at each other an instant, then Will shivered, passed his hand over his eyes and sat down.

There was no one there but the old people, who were looking at him in bewilderment. They did not notice any confusion in Agnes's face. She recovered first.

"I'm glad to see you back, Will," she said, rising and putting the sleeping child down in a neighboring room. As she gave him her hand, he said:

"I'm glad to get back, Agnes. I hadn't ought to have gone." Then he turned to the old people:

"I'm Will Hannan. You needn't be scared, Daddy; I was jokin' last night."

"Dew tell! I want 'o know!" exclaimed Granny. "Wal, I never! An' you're my little Willy boy who ust 'o be in my class? Well! Well! W'y, pa, ain't he growed tall! Grew handsome tew. I ust 'o think he was a *dretful* humly boy; but my sakes, that mustache—"

"Wal, he gave me a *turrible* scare last night. My land! scared me out of a year's growth," cackled the old man.

This gave them all a chance to laugh, and the air was cleared. It gave Agnes time to recover herself, and to be able to meet Will's eyes. Will himself was powerfully moved; his throat swelled and tears came to his eyes every time he looked at her.

She was worn and wasted incredibly. The blue of her eyes seemed dimmed and faded by weeping, and the old-time scarlet of her lips had been washed away. The sinews of her neck showed painfully when she turned her head, and her trembling hands were worn, discolored, and lumpy at the joints.

Poor girl! She knew she was under scrutiny, and her eyes felt hot and restless. She wished to run away and cry, but she dared not. She stayed, while Will began to tell her of his life and to ask questions about old friends.

The old people took it up and relieved her of any share in it; and Will, seeing that she was suffering, told some funny stories which made the old people cackle in spite of themselves.

But it was forced merriment on Will's part. Once or twice Agnes smiled, with just a little flash of the old-time sunny temper. But there was no dimple in the cheek now, and the smile had more suggestion of an invalid—or even a skeleton. He was almost ready to take her in his arms and weep, her face appealed so pitifully to him.

"It's most time f'r Ed to be gittin' back, ain't it, pa?"

"Sh'd say 't was! He jest went over to Hobkirk's to trade horses. It's dretful tryin' to me to have him go off tradin' horses on Sunday. Seems if he might wait till a rainy day, 'r do it evenin's. I never *did* believe in horse-tradin' anyhow."

"Have y' come back to stay, Willie?" asked the old lady.

"Well—it's hard tellin'," answered Will, looking at Agnes.

"Well, Agnes, ain't you goin' to git no dinner? I'm 'bout ready f'r dinner. We must git to church early today. Elder Wheat is goin' to preach, an' they'll be a crowd. He's goin' to hold communion."

"You'll stay to dinner, Will?" asked Agnes.

"Yes—if you wish it."

"I *do* wish it."

"Thank you; I want to have a good visit with you. I don't know when I'll see you again."

As she moved about, getting dinner on the table, Will sat with gloomy face, listening to the "clack" of the old man. The room was a poor little sitting room, with furniture worn and shapeless; hardly a touch of pleasant color, save here and there a little bit of Agnes's handiwork. The lounge, covered with calico, was rickety; the rocking-chair matched it, and the carpet of rags was patched and darned with twine in twenty places. Everywhere was the influence of the Kinneys. The furniture looked like them, in fact.

Agnes was outwardly calm, but her real distraction did not escape Mrs. Kinney's hawk-like eyes.

"Well, I declare if you hain't put the butter on in one o' my blue chainy saucers? Now you *know* I don't allow that saucer to be took down by nobody. I don't see what's got into yeh! Anybody'd s'pose you never see any comp'ny b'fore—wouldn't they, pa?"

"Sh'd say th' would," said pa, stopping short in a long story about Ed. "Seems if we couldn't keep anything in this house sep'rit from the rest. Ed he uses my curry-comb—"

He launched out a long list of grievances, to which Will shut his ears as completely as possible, and was thinking how to stop him, when there came a sudden crash. Agnes had dropped a plate.

"*Good* land o' Goshen!" screamed Granny. "If you ain't the worst I *ever* see. I'll bet that's my grapevine plate. If it is— Well, of all the mercies, it ain't. But it might 'a' ben. I never see your beat—never! That's the third plate since I came to live here."

"Oh, look-a-here, Granny," said Will, desperately, "don't make so much fuss about the plate. What's it worth, anyway? Here's a dollar."

Agnes cried quickly:

"Oh, don't do that, Will! It ain't *her* plate. It's *my* plate, and I can break every plate in the house if I want to," she cried defiantly.

"Course you can," Will agreed.

"Wal, she *can't*! Not while *I'm* around," put in Daddy. "I've helped to pay f'r them plates, if she does call 'em her'n—"

"What the devul is all this row about? Agg, can't you get along without stirring up the old folks every time I'm out o' the house?"

The speaker was Ed, now a tall and slouchily dressed man of thirty-two or three; his face still handsome in a certain dark, cleanly-cut style, but he wore a surly look as he lounged in with insolent swagger, clothed in greasy overalls and a hickory shirt.

"Hello, Will! I heard you'd got home. John told me as I came along."

They shook hands, and Ed slouched down on the lounge. Will could have kicked him for laying the blame of the dispute upon Agnes; it showed him in a flash just how he treated her. He disdained to quarrel; he simply silenced and dominated her.

Will asked a few questions about crops, with such grace as he could show, and Ed, with keen eyes fixed on Will's face, talked easily and stridently.

"Dinner ready?" he asked of Agnes. "Where's Pete?"

"He's asleep."

"All right. Let 'im sleep. Well, let's go out an' set up. Come, Dad, sling away that Bible and come to grub. Mother, what the devul are you snifflin' at? Say, now, look here! If I hear any more about this row, I'll simply let you walk down to meetin'. Come, Will, set up."

He led the way into the little kitchen where the dinner was set.

"What was the row about? Hain't been breakin' some dish, Agg?"

"Yes, she has," broke in the old lady.

"One o' the blue ones?" winked Ed.

"No, thank goodness, it was a white one."

"Well, now, I'll git into that dod-gasted cubberd some day an' break the whole eternal outfit. I ain't goin' to have this damned jawin' goin' on," he ended, brutally unconscious of his own "jawin'."

After this the dinner proceeded in comparative silence, Agnes sobbing under breath. The room was small and very hot; the table was warped so badly that the dishes had a tendency to slide to the centre; the walls were bare plaster, grayed with time; the food was poor and scant, and the flies absolutely swarmed upon everything, like bees. Otherwise the room was clean and orderly.

"They say you've made a pile o' money out West, Bill. I'm glad of it. We fellers back here don't make anything. It's a dam tight squeeze. Agg, it seems to me the flies are devilish thick to-day. Can't you drive 'em out?"

Agnes felt that she must vindicate herself a little.

"I do drive 'em out, but they come right in again. The screen-door is broken and they come right in."

"I told Dad to *fix* that door."

"But he won't do it for me."

Ed rested his elbows on the table and fixed his bright black eyes on his father.

"Say, what d' you mean by actin' like a mule? I swear I'll trade you off f'r a yaller dog. What do *I* keep you round here for anyway—to look purty?"

"I guess I've as good a right here as you have, Ed Kinney."

"Oh, go soak y'r head, old man. If you don't 'tend out here a little better, down goes your meat-house! I won't drive you down to meetin' till you promise to fix that door. Hear me!"

Daddy began to snivel. Agnes could not look up for shame. Will felt sick. Ed laughed.

"I c'n bring the old man to terms that way; he can't walk very well late years, an' he can't drive my colt. You know what a cuss I used to be about fast nags? Well, I'm just the same. Hobkirk's got a colt I want. Say, that reminds me: your team's out there by the fence. I forgot. I'll go out and put 'em up."

"No, never mind; I can't stay but a few minutes."

"Goin' to be round the country long?"

"A week—maybe."

Agnes looked up a moment, and then let her eyes fall.

"Goin' back West, I s'pose?"

"No. May go East, to Europe, mebbe."

"The devul y' say! You must 'a' made a ten-strike out West."

"They say it didn't come lawful," piped Daddy, over his blackberries and milk.

"Oh, you shet up, who wants your put-in? Don't work in any o' your Bible on us."

Daddy rose to go into the other room.

"Hold on, old man. You goin' to fix that door?"

"Course I be," quavered he.

"Well see 't y' do, that's all. Now get on y'r duds, an' I'll go an' hitch up." He rose from the table. "Don't keep me waiting."

He went out unceremoniously, and Agnes was alone with Will.

"Do you go to church?" he asked. She shook her head. "No, I don't go anywhere now. I have too much to do; I haven't strength left. And I'm not fit anyway."

"Agnes, I want to say something to you; not now—after they're gone."

He went into the other room, leaving her to wash the dinner-things. She worked on in a curious, almost dazed way, a dream of something sweet and irrevocable in her eyes. Will represented so much to her. His voice brought up times and places that thrilled her like song. He was associated with all that was sweetest and most care-free and most girlish in her life.

Ever since the boy had handed her that note she had been re-living those days. In the midst of her drudgery she stopped to dream—to let some picture come back into her mind. She was a student again at the Seminary, and stood in the recitation-room with suffocating beat of the heart; Will was waiting outside—waiting in a tremor like her own, to walk home with her under the maples.

Then she remembered the painfully sweet mixture of pride and fear with which she walked up the aisle of the little church behind him. Her pretty new gown rustled, the dim light of the church had something like romance in it, and he was so strong and handsome. Her heart went out in a great silent cry to God—

"Oh, let me be a girl again!"

She did not look forward to happiness. She hadn't power to look forward at all.

As she worked, she heard the high, shrill voices of the old people as they bustled about and nagged at each other.

"Ma, where's my specticles?"

"I ain't seen y'r specticles."

"You have, too."

"I ain't neither."

"You had 'em this forenoon."

"Didn't no such thing. Them was my own brass-bowed ones. You had your'n jest 'fore goin' to dinner. If you'd put 'em into a proper place you'd find 'em again."

"I want 'o know if I would," the old man snorted.

"Wal, you'd orter know."

"Oh, you're awful smart, ain't yeh? *You* never have no trouble, and use mine—do yeh?—an' lose 'em so 't I can't—"

"And if this is the thing that goes on when I'm here it must be hell when visitors are gone," thought Will.

"Willy, ain't you goin' to meetin'?"

"No, not to-day. I want to visit a little with Agnes, then I've got to drive back to John's."

"Wal, we must be goin'. Don't you leave them dishes f'r me to wash," she screamed at Agnes as she went out the door. "An' if we don't git home by five, them caaves orter be fed."

As Agnes stood at the door to watch them drive away, Will studied her, a smothering ache in his heart as he saw how thin and bent and weary she was. In his soul he felt that she was a dying woman unless she had rest and tender care.

As she turned, she saw something in his face—a pity and an agony of self-accusation—that made her weak and white. She sank into a chair, putting her hand on her chest, as if she felt a failing of breath. Then the blood came back to her face and her eyes filled with tears.

"Don't—don't look at me like that," she said in a whisper. His pity hurt her.

At sight of her sitting there pathetic, abashed, bewildered, like some gentle animal, Will's throat contracted so that he could not speak. His voice came at last in one terrific cry—

"Oh, Agnes, for God's sake forgive me!" He knelt by her side and put his arm about her shoulders and kissed her bowed head. A curious numbness involved his whole body; his voice was husky, the tears burned in his eyes. His whole soul and body ached with his pity and his remorseful, self-accusing wrath.

"It was all my fault. Lay it all to me. . . . I am the one to bear it. . . . Oh, I've dreamed a thousand times of sayin' this to you, Aggie! I thought if I could only see you again and ask your forgiveness, I'd—"

He ground his teeth together in his assault upon himself. "I threw my life away an' killed you—that's what I did!"

He rose, and raged up and down the room till he had mastered himself.

"What did you think I meant that day of the thrashing?" he said, turning suddenly. He spoke of it as if it were but a month or two past.

She lifted her head and looked at him in a slow way. She seemed to be remembering. The tears lay on her hollow cheeks.

"I thought you was ashamed of me. I didn't know—why—"

He uttered a snarl of self-disgust.

"You couldn't know. Nobody could tell what I meant. But why didn't you write? I was ready to come back. I only wanted an excuse—only a line."

"How could I, Will—after your letter?"

He groaned, and turned away.

"And Will, I—I got mad too. I *couldn't* write."

"Oh, that letter—I can see every line of it! F'r God's sake, don't think of it again! But I didn't think, even when I wrote that letter, that I'd find you where you are. I didn't think. I hoped, anyhow, Ed Kinney wouldn't—"

She stopped him with a startled look in her great eyes.

"Don't talk about him—it ain't right. I mean it don't do any good. What could I do, after father died? Mother and I. Besides, I waited three years to hear from you, Will."

He gave a strange, choking cry. It burst from his throat—that terrible thing, a man's sob of agony. She went on, curiously calm now.

"Ed was good to me; and he offered a home, anyway, for mother—"

"And all the time I was waiting for some line to break down my cussed pride, so I could write to you and explain. But you *did* go with Ed to the fair," he ended suddenly, seeking a morsel of justification for himself.

"Yes. But I waited an' waited; and I thought you was mad at me, so when they came I—no, I didn't really go with Ed. There was a wagon load of them."

"But I started," he explained, "but the wheel came off. I didn't send word because I thought you'd feel sure I'd come. If you'd only trusted me a little more— No! It was all my fault. I acted like a crazy fool. I didn't stop to reason about anything."

They sat in silence after these explanations. The sound of the snapping wings of the grasshoppers came through the windows, and a locust high in a poplar sent down his ringing whir.

"It can't be helped now, Will," Agnes said at last, her voice full of the woman's resignation. "We've got to bear it."

Will straightened up. "Bear it?" He paused. "Yes, I s'pose so. If you hadn't married Ed Kinney! Anybody but him. How did you do it?"

"Oh, I don't know," she answered, wearily brushing her hair back from her eyes. "It seemed best when I did it—and it can't be helped now." There was infinite, dull despair and resignation in her voice.

Will went over to the window. He thought how bright and handsome Ed used to be. "After all, it's no wonder you married him. Life pushes us into such things." Suddenly he turned, something resolute and imperious in his eyes and voice.

"It can be helped, Aggie," he said. "Now just listen to me. We've made an awful mistake. We've lost seven years o' life, but that's no reason why we should waste the rest of it. Now hold on; don't interrupt me just yet. I come back thinking just as much of you as ever. I'm not going to say a word more about Ed; let the past stay past. I'm going to talk about the future."

She looked at him in a daze of wonder as he went on.

"Now I've got some money, I've got a third interest in a ranch, and I've got a standing offer to go back on the Santa Fee road as conductor. There is a team standing out there. I'd like to make another trip to Cedarville—with you—"

"Oh, Will, don't!" she cried; "for pity's sake don't talk—"

"Wait!" he exclaimed, imperiously. "Now look at it. Here you are in hell! Caged up with two old crows picking the life out of you. They'll kill you—I can see it; your being killed by inches. You can't go anywhere, you can't have anything. Life is just torture for you—"

She gave a little moan of anguish and despair, and turned her face to her chair-back. Her shoulders shook with weeping, but she listened. He went to her and stood with his hand on the chair-back.

His voice trembled and broke. "There's just one way to get out of this, Agnes. Come with me. He don't care for you; his whole idea of women is that they are created for his pleasure and to keep house. Your whole life is agony. Come! Don't cry. There's a chance for life yet."

She didn't speak, but her sobs were less violent; his voice growing stronger reassured her.

"I'm going East, maybe to Europe; and the woman who goes with me will have nothing to do but get strong and well again. I've made you suffer so, I ought to spend the rest of my life making you happy. Come! My wife will sit with me on the deck of the steamer and see the moon rise, and walk with me by the sea, till she gets strong and happy again —till the dimples get back into her cheeks. I never will rest till I see her eyes laugh again."

She rose flushed, wild-eyed, breathing hard with the emotion his vibrant voice called up, but she could not speak. He put his hand gently upon her shoulder, and she sank down again. And he went on with his appeal. There was something hypnotic, dominating, in his voice and eyes.

On his part there was no passion of an ignoble sort, only a passion of pity and remorse, and a sweet, tender, reminiscent love. He did not love the woman before him so much as the girl whose ghost she was—the woman whose promise she was. He held himself responsible for it all, and he throbbed with desire to repair the ravage he had indirectly caused. There was nothing equivocal in his position—nothing to disown. How others might look at it, he did not consider, and did not care. His impetuous soul was carried to a point where nothing came in to mar or divert.

"And then after you're well, after our trip, we'll come back—to Houston, or somewhere in Texas, and I'll build my wife a house that will make her eyes shine. My cattle will give us a good living, and she can have a piano and books, and go to the theatre and concerts. Come, what do you think of that?"

Then she heard his words beneath his voice somehow, and they produced pictures that dazzled her. Luminous shadows moved before her eyes, drifting across the gray background of her poor, starved, work-weary life.

As his voice ceased the rosy cloud faded, and she realized again the faded, musty little room, the calico-covered furniture, and looking down at her own cheap and ill-fitting dress, she saw her ugly hands lying there. Then she cried out with a gush of tears:

"Oh, Will, I'm so old and homely now, I ain't fit to go with you now! Oh, why couldn't we have married *then?*"

She was seeing herself as she was then, and so was he; but it deepened his resolution. How beautiful she used to be! He seemed to see her there as if she stood in perpetual sunlight, with a warm sheen in her hair and dimples in her cheeks.

She saw her thin red wrists, her gaunt and knotted hands. There was a pitiful droop in the thin, pale lips, and the tears fell slowly from her drooping lashes. He went on:

"Well, it's no use to cry over what was. We must think of what we're going to do. Don't worry about your looks; you'll be the prettiest woman in the country when we get back. Don't wait, Aggie; make up your mind."

She hesitated, and was lost.

"What will people say?"

"I don't care what they say," he flamed out. "They'd say, stay here and be killed by inches. I say you've had your share of suffering. They'd say—the liberal ones—stay and get a divorce; but how do you know we can get one after you've been dragged through the mud of a trial? We can get one as well in some other state. Why should you be worn out at thirty? What right or justice is there in making you bear all your life the consequences of our—my schoolboy folly?"

As he went on his argument rose to the level of Browning's philosophy.

"We can make this experience count for us yet. But we mustn't let a mistake ruin us—it should teach us. What right has any one to keep you in a hole? God don't expect a toad to stay in a stump and starve if it can get out. He don't ask the snakes to suffer as you do."

She had lost the threads of right and wrong out of her hands. She was lost in a maze, but she was not moved by passion. Flesh had ceased to stir her; but there was vast power in the new and thrilling words her deliverer spoke. He seemed to open a door for her, and through it turrets shone and great ships crossed on dim blue seas.

"You can't live here, Aggie. You'll die in less than five years. It would kill me to see you die here. Come! It's suicide."

She did not move, save the convulsive motion of her breath and the nervous action of her fingers. She stared down at a spot in the carpet. She could not face him.

He grew insistent, a sterner note creeping into his voice.

"If I leave this time of course you know I'll never come back."

Her hoarse breathing, growing quicker each moment, was her only reply.

"I'm done," he said with a note of angry disappointment. He did not give her up, however. "I've told you what I'd do for you. Now, if you think—"

"Oh, give me time to think, Will!" she cried out, lifting her face.

He shook his head. "No. You might as well decide now. It won't be any easier to-morrow. Come, one minute more and I go out o' that door —unless—" He crossed the room slowly, doubtful himself of his desperate last measure. "My hand is on the knob. Shall I open it?"

She stopped breathing; her fingers closed convulsively on the chair. As he opened the door she sprang up.

"Don't go, Will! Don't go, please don't! I need you here—I—"

"That ain't the question. Are you going with me, Agnes?"

"Yes, yes! I tried to speak before. I trust you, Will; you're—"

He flung the door open wide. "See the sunlight out there shining on that field o' wheat? That's where I'll take you—out into the sunshine. You shall see it shining on the Bay of Naples. Come, get on your hat; don't take anything more'n you actually need. Leave the past behind you—"

The woman turned wildly and darted into the little bedroom. The man listened. He whistled in surprise almost comical. He had forgotten the baby. He could hear the mother talking, cooing.

"Mommie's 'ittle pet! *She* wasn't goin' to leave her 'ittle man—no, she wasn't! There, there, don't 'e cry. Mommie ain't goin' away and leave him—wicked mommie ain't—'ittle treasure!"

She was confused again; and when she reappeared at the door, with the child in her arms, there was a wandering look on her face pitiful to see. She tried to speak, tried to say, "Please go, Will."

He designedly failed to understand her whisper. He stepped forward. "The baby! Sure enough. Why, certainly! to the mother belongs the child. Blue eyes, thank heaven!"

He put his arm about them both. She obeyed silently. There was something irresistible in his frank, clear eyes, his sunny smile, his strong brown hand. He slammed the door behind them.

"That closes the door on your sufferings," he said, smiling down at her. "Good-by to it all."

The baby laughed and stretched out its hands toward the light.

"Boo, boo!" he cried.

"What's he talking about?"

She smiled in perfect trust and fearlessness, seeing her child's face beside his own. "He says it's beautiful."

"Oh, he does! I can't follow his French accent."

She smiled again, in spite of herself. Will shuddered with a thrill of fear, she was so weak and worn. But the sun shone on the dazzling, rustling wheat, the fathomless sky, blue as a sea, bent above them—and the world lay before them.

QUESTIONS

1. How does Garland dramatize Will's love for Agnes? How does Agnes know that Will loves her?
2. Why has Will developed an "instinct of possession" for Agnes? Why is he so ashamed of revealing his relationship in front of the other men? What is his definition of "masculine" behavior?
3. Is the incident involving the broken wheel a bad plot device? What does it contribute to the story?
4. When Will decides to punish Agnes by leaving, in what ways is he really punishing himself?
5. When Will returns after seven years, what is the difference between his "old self" and his "new self"?
6. In what ways has Agnes been in prison during the time Will has been away?
7. Is Garland's bleak account of Midwestern farm life exaggerated?

What are some of the realistic details he uses to argue his case? Do they tend to reinforce or undermine his earlier descriptions of Will enjoying the natural beauty of the area?

8. What are some of the internal forces that motivate Will to persuade Agnes to take her child and run away with him? Would he ask her if she were still sexually attractive? What kind of life could they lead after running away?

NORMAN MAILER

ALTHOUGH *The Naked and the Dead* is generally regarded as the best American novel about World War II, for many, this section of that book will disclose a "new" Norman Mailer (b. 1923). Since 1960, twelve years after the publishing of *The Naked and the Dead*, his books and essays have become more overtly political, and he has developed what has come to be called the "new journalism"—a genre in which the reporter makes no attempt to be objective, but deliberately pursues and even revels in a highly personalized interpretation of external events. Mailer tries to present himself as a version of the American self in the tradition of Whitman. While it is true that he is vulnerable to the same charges of "egotism," Mailer combines three fine qualities it is difficult not to admire: (1) actual involvement in what he writes about, whether drugs, sex, or radical politics (He recently ran a vigorous, if somewhat absurd and unsuccessful campaign for mayor of New York.); (2) a very honest, compelling self-awareness; and (3) an essentially intellectual, ironic detachment towards himself and the events he reports.

In *The Naked and the Dead* Mailer tries to give us objective, realistic portraits of a group of American men. At this point in his career he is, like Dos Passos, a somewhat "naturalistic" writer. Most of the soldiers on Anopopei, a Pacific island the Americans are trying to capture from the Japanese, seem somewhat psychologically "determined" by forces of which they are ignorant. But Mailer is aware of this: "I tried to explore the outrageous propositions of cause and effect, of efforts and recompense, in a sick society." In the novel the institution of the American army becomes a metaphor for American society. The vast, impersonal military system, like American society, greatly controls the private destinies of its enlisted men and officers.

Included here are three portraits that appear in the novel in sections that Mailer calls "The Time Machine," a technical device similar to some of those employed by Dos Passos in *U.S.A.* Altogether there are actually ten such sections which give biographical background about the ten major characters who represent an ethnic and geo-graphical cross-section of America. (Indeed, the "melting pot" platoon became a cliché of American war movies.) All of the men portrayed are, in some sense, imprisoned by the forms, values, and pressures of American society. Of those dealt with here, each has some kind of sexual problem traceable to his family or other en-vironmental situation. And yet Mailer gives us a sense that each man does have some power of decision concerning his fate. What they lack is self-awareness; they stumble into marriage, choose careers haphazardly, and accept mechanically the fact that they must go to war. (Perhaps awareness would only have made their problems more difficult to endure.) Many will find a greater understanding of their parents, of the generation that has preceded theirs, for practically everyone will find some revelation about his family in at least one of the portraits. The hang-ups are not unique—they are "cultural": we find them popping up again and again in novels, plays, and movies about this period.

Of the three men, one is pretty much a victim of the draft (Gallagher), and two (Cummings and Croft) are power-hungry men who find that war fits naturally into the pattern of their life. Although Gallagher's domestic life is generally drab and wretched, he would have been immensely better off could he have stayed home. Cum-mings, completely unable to adjust to domestic society, is clearly at home in the jungle-ethic world of World War II. Sgt. Croft is a hunter and sadist who likes to kill for the thrill of killing. (For the ultimate on the relation of hunting, power, and American capitalism, see Mailer's *Why We Are in Vietnam.*)

The story of General Cummings, although lengthier than the other portraits, should be read with great attention. It is a classic account of the "weak" American male who seeks reassurance through power and domination. (Combat is one way a man can assure himself that he is a man. To be masculine is to be violent, crude, and insensitive.) Mailer also understands the process by which Cummings has become an "intellectual" who represses his feelings to such an extent that he can function almost totally on cold rationality.

It is clear from the account of General Cummings's marriage and his encounter in a Roman alley that he is a latent homosexual whose urges are not loving, but compulsively destructive. Thus, he decides the way to deal with this fear is to repress it at all costs. After the in-cident in the alley, he centers all his energy on his career in the service. He becomes a brilliant, calculating strategist who is totally cynical about the value of human life. (In the novel itself Mailer has revenge on Cummings by making a bumbling major the strategic hero.)

[FROM The Naked and the Dead]

The Time Machine
SAM CROFT: THE HUNTER

*A lean man of medium height but he held himself so erectly he ap-
peared tall. His narrow triangular face was utterly without expression.
There seemed nothing wasted in his hard small jaw, gaunt firm cheeks
and straight short nose. His gelid eyes were very blue . . . he was efficient
and strong and usually empty and his main cast of mind was a superior
contempt toward nearly all other men. He hated weakness and he loved
practically nothing. There was a crude unformed vision in his soul but he
was rarely conscious of it.*

No, but why *is* Croft that way?

Oh, there are answers. He is that way because of the corruption-of-the-
society. He is that way because the devil has claimed him for one of his
own. It is because he is a Texan; it is because he has renounced God.

He is that kind of man because the only woman he ever loved cheated
on him, or he was born that way, or he was having problems of adjustment.

Croft's father, Jesse Croft, liked to say, "Well, now, my Sam is a mean
boy. I reckon he was whelped mean." And then Jesse Croft, thinking of
his wife who was ailing, a weak woman sweet and mild, might add,
" 'Course Sam got mother's milk if ever a one did, but Ah figger it turned
sour for him 'cause that was the only way his stomach would take it."
Then he would cackle and blow his nose into his hand and wipe it on
the back of his pale-blue dungarees. (Standing before his dirty wood
barn, the red dry soil of western Texas under his feet.) "Why, Ah 'member once Ah took Sam huntin', he was only an itty-bitty runt, not big
enough to hold up the gun hardly . . . but he was a mean shot from the
beginning. And Ah'll tell ya, he just didn't like to have a man interfere
with him. That was one thing could always rile him, even when he was
an itty-bitty bastard.

"Couldn't stand to have anyone beat him in anythin'.

"Never could lick him. Ah'd beat the piss out o' him, and he'd never
make a sound. Jus' stand there lookin' at me as if he was fixin' to
wallop me back, or maybe put a bullet in mah head."

Croft hunted early. In the winter, in the chill Texas desert, it used to be a cold numbing ride across twenty miles of rutted hard-baked road with the dust blowing like emery into the open battered Ford. The two big men in the front would say little, and the one who was not driving would blow on his fingers. When they reached the forest, the sun would still be straining to rise above the brown-red line of ridge.

Now, look, boy, see that trail, that's a deer run. They ain't hardly a man is smart enough to track down a deer. You set an' wait for 'em, and you set where the wind is blowin' down from the deer to you. You got to wait a long time.

The boy sits shivering in the wood. Ah'm fugged if Ah'll wait for any ole deer. Ah'm gonna track 'em.

He stalks through the forest with the wind on his face. It's dark, and the trees are silver-brown, and the ground is a deep-olive velvet. Where is that ole deer? He kicks a twig out of his way, and stiffens as a buck goes clattering through the brush. Goddam! Ole deer is fast.

Next time he is more cautious. He finds a deer track, kneels down and traces the hoofprint tenderly, feeling a thrill. Ah'm gonna track this old deer.

For two hours he creeps through the forest, watching where he places his feet, putting his heel down first, then his toes before he shifts his weight. When the dried thorny branches catch in his clothing, he pulls them free quietly, one by one.

In a little clearing he sees a deer and freezes. The wind is blowing gently against his face, and he thinks he can smell the animal. Goddam, he whispers to himself. What a big ole bastard. The stag turns slowly, looks past him from a hundred yards. Sonofabitch cain't see me.

The boy raises his gun, and trembles so badly the sights waver. He lowers it, and curses himself. Jus' a little ole woman. He brings it up again, holding it steadily, moving the front sight over until it points a few inches below the muscle of the foreleg. Ah'm goin' to git him through the heart.

BAA-WOWWW!

It is someone else's gun, and the deer drops. The boy runs forward almost weeping. Who shot him? That was mah deer. I'll kill the sonofabitch who shot him.

Jesse Croft is laughing at him. Ah tole you, boy, to set where Ah put you.

Ah tracked that deer.

You scared that deer into me. Ah heard ya footing it from a mile away.

You're a liar. You're a goddam liar. The boy throws himself at his father, and tries to strike him.

Jesse Croft gives him a blow across the mouth, and he sits down. You ole sonofabitch, he screams, and flings himself at his father again.

Jesse holds him off, laughing. Little ole wildcat, ain't ya? Well, you got to wait ten years 'fore you can whop your pa.

That deer were mine.

One that wins is the one that gits it.

The tears freeze in the boy's eyes and wither. He is thinking that if he hadn't trembled he would have shot the deer first.

"Yes, sir," Jesse Croft said, "they wa'n' a thing my Sam could stand to have ya beat him in. When he was 'bout twelve, they was a fool kid down at Harper who used to give Sam a lickin'." (Scratching the back of his gray scraggly hair, his hat in his hand.) "That kid would lick Sam every day, and Sam would go back and pick a fight the next day. Ah'll tell ya, he ended up by whoppin' the piss out of that kid.

"And then when he was older, about seventeen maybe, he used to be bustin' horses down to the fair in August, and he was known to be 'bout the best rider in the county. Then one time a fella all the way from Denison came down and beat him in a reg'lar competition with judges and all. I 'member Sam was so mad he wouldn't talk to no one for two days.

"He got good stock in him," Jesse Croft declared to his neighbors. "We was one of the first folks to push in here, must be sixty years ago, and they was Crofts in Texas over a hunnerd years ago. Ah'd guess some of them had that same meanness that Sam's got. Maybe it was what made 'em push down here."

Deer hunting and fighting and busting horses at the fair make up in hours a total of perhaps ten days a year. There are the other things, the long flat sweeps of the terrain, the hills in the distance, the endless meals in the big kitchen with his parents and brothers and the ranch foremen.

There are the conversations in the bunkhouse. The soft reflective voices.

Ah tell ya that little gal is gonna remember me unless she was too goddam drunk.

Ah jus' looked at that nigger after that, an' Ah said, Boy, you no-good black bastard, an' Ah jus' picked up that hatchet an' let him have it right across the head. But the sonofabitch didn't even bleed much. You can kill an elephant about as fast as you can kill a nigger in the head.

A whoor is no damn good for a man, Ah gotta have it at least five six times 'fore Ah'm satisfied, and that ole business of stickin' it in once an' then reachin' for your hat jus' leaves me more fussed than it's worth.

Ah been keepin' an eye on that south herd leader, the red one with the spot 'hind his ear, an' he's gonna be gittin' mean when the hot weather comes.

The Education of Samuel Croft.

And always, day after day, the dust of cattle through the long shimmering afternoons in the sun. A man gets bored and it's uncomfortable falling asleep in a saddle. Thinking of town maybe. (Bar and a whorehouse, dry goods.)

Sam, you gittin' itchy?

A lazy somnolent pulsing in his loins. The sun refracts from the hide of his horse, bathes his thighs in a lazy heat. Yeah, some.

They're fixin' to start a National Guard outfit in Harper.

Yeah?

Ah figger they'll be some women hangin' round the uniforms, an' ya git to do a lot of shootin'.

Maybe I'll go down with ya. He wheels his horse to the left and rides out to turn back a straggler.

The first time Croft ever killed a man he was in a National Guard uniform. There was a strike on at Lilliput in the oil fields, and some scabs had been hurt.

They called the Guard. (The sonsofbitches started this strike come from up north, New York. They's some good boys in the oil fields but they got they heads turned by Reds, an' next thing they'll have ya kissin' niggers' asses.) The guardsmen made a line against the gate to the plant and stood sweating in a muggy summer sun. The pickets yelled and jeered at them.

Hey, drillers, they called out the Boy Scouts.

Let's rush 'em. They're jus' company scabs too.

Croft stands in line with his mouth tightening.

They're gonna rush us, the soldier next to him says.

The Guard lieutenant is a haberdashery salesman. If there're rocks being thrown you better lie down, men. If it should git real bad, fire a couple of rounds over their heads.

A stone lofts through the air. The crowd is sullen outside the gate, and every now and then one of them shouts some curses at the soldiers.

No sonofabitch'll talk to me that way, Croft says.

A rock strikes one of the soldiers, and they lie down on the ground and point their rifles above the heads of the advancing crowd.

Let's rip the place apart.

About ten men start to walk toward the gate. Some stones fly over their heads and scatter among the soldiers.

All right, men, the lieutenant pipes, fire over them.

Croft sights down his barrel. He has pointed his gun at the chest of the nearest man, and he feels a curious temptation.

I'll just squeeze the trigger a little bit.

BAA-WOWWW! The shot is lost in the volley, but the striker drops. Croft feels a hollow excitement.

The lieutenant is cursing. Goddam, who shot him, men?

Guess they's no way to find out, Lieutenant, Croft says. He watches the mob retreating in a panic. Bunch o' dogs, he tells himself. His heart is beating, and his hands feel very dry.

" 'Member that gal, Janey, he married. Ah'll say one thing for her, she was a reg'lar ole tomcat," Jesse Croft said. (He spewed an oyster of phlegm, and ground it reflectively with his boot.) "Jus' the meanest little ole girl, Ah'll tell ya she was a mate for him till they busted up. They ain't one of the gals my boys've married that I woulda taken up against her. Ah'm an old man, but Ah'll tell ya, mah balls would git to itchin' when Ah'd look at her and jus' think of lovin' up to her." (Scratching his pants vigorously.) "Trouble with Sam he shouldn'ta married her. When a man can knock off a piece with a woman without slippin' her a weddin' ring, it don' pay to git any ideas about settlin' down with her. A woman that likes her nookie ain't gonna be satisfied with one man after she gits used to him." (Pointing his finger at the man he is talking to.) "Reckon that's a law of life."

Oh, give it to me, you sonofabitch, give it to me, I'LL KILL YOU IF YOU STOP.

Who's your man?

You're my man, you give it to me, give it to me, give it to me.

They ain't nobody can make love to you like me.

They ain't anybody, anybody, oh, you're just a goddam fuggin machine.

The long sliding of a belly against a belly.

I love ya better than any man ever could.

You do, baby, you do.

Ah'm jus' an old fuggin machine. (Crack . . . that . . . whip! Crack . . . that . . . WHIP!)

After they married, Croft rented a little house on the ranch from his father. He and Janey petered out for each other through a slow taciturn year, through a thousand incidents which they forgot while the effects still remained. At night they would sit by themselves in the parlor, listen to the radio and seldom talk. In a dumb instinctive way, Croft would search for an approach.

Want to go to bed?

It's early, Sam.

Yeah. And an anger would work in him. They had torn at each other once, had felt sick when they were close together and other people were with them. Now, in sleep their bodies intruded; there was always a heavy limb in the way. And the nights together working on them, this new change, this living together between them like a heavy dull weight, washing dishes and mouthing familiar kisses.

The buddy system.

But he wanted no buddy. In the quiet nights in the cheap parlor of this house set on the Texas plains, an undefined rage increased and increased. There were the things he did not know how to utter (the great space of the night), the fury between them balked almost completely now. There were the trips to town, the drinking bouts between them, the occasional kindling of their bodies in a facsimile of their earlier passion, only confusing and protracting the irreversible reaction.

It ended with him going to town alone, and taking a whore when he was drunk, beating her sometimes with a wordless choler. And for Janey it resulted in other men, ranch hands, once one of his brothers.

"It jus' don' pay to marry a woman with hot pants," Jesse Croft said later.

Croft found out in a quarrel.

And another thing, you go tomcattin' to town, and jus' hellin' around, well, don' be thinkin' Ah'm jus' sittin' around. They's things Ah can tell you too.

What things?

You want to know, don't ya? You got yore water hot. Jus' don' push me around.

What things?

She laughs. Jus' a way of talkin'.

Croft slaps her across the face, catches her wrists and shakes her.

WHAT THINGS?

You sonofabitch. (Her eyes glaring.) You know what kind of things.

He strikes her so heavily that she falls.

That's one thing you ain't best in, she screams.

Croft stands there trembling and then wrenches out of the room. (Goddam whore.) He feels nothing and then anger and shame and then nothing again. At this moment his initial love, his initial need of her is full-throated again. (Jus' an ole fuggin machine.)

"If Sam coulda found any of the boys who was scooting up her pants, he'da killed 'em," Jesse Croft said. "He tore around like he was gonna choke us all with his hands and then he took off for town and threw himself about as good a drunk as Ah've seen him indulge. And when he got back he'd enlisted himself in the Army."

After that there were always other men's wives.

You must think I'm a pretty cheap woman going out with you like this.

Wouldn't say that. Everybody likes to have a good time.

That's it. (Drinking her beer.) That's my philosophy. Need to have a good time. You don't think a bit cheap of me, do you, soldier?

Hell, you're too good-lookin' a woman for me to think cheap. (Have another beer.)

And later. Jack don't treat me right. You understand me.

That's right, honey, I understand you. They roll together in bed.

Ain't nothing wrong with that philosophy, she says.

Not a damn thing wrong. (And . . . crack . . . that . . . WHIP!)

You're all fuggin whores, he thinks.

His ancestors pushed and labored and strained, drove their oxen, sweated their women, and moved a thousand miles.

He pushed and labored inside himself and smoldered with an endless hatred.

(You're all a bunch of fuggin whores)

(You're all a bunch of dogs)

(You're all deer to track)

I HATE EVERYTHING WHICH IS NOT IN MYSELF

The Time Machine
GALLAGHER: THE REVOLUTIONARY REVERSED

A short man with a bunched wiry body that gave the impression of being gnarled and sour. His face was small and ugly, pocked with the scars of a severe acne which had left his skin lumpy, spotted with swatches of purple-red. Perhaps it was the color of his face, or it might have been the shape of his long Irish nose, which slanted resentfully to one side, but he always looked wroth. Yet he was only twenty four.

In South Boston and Dorchester and Roxbury the gray wooden houses parade for miles in a file of drabness and desolation and waste. The streetcars jangle through a wilderness of cobblestone and sapless wood; the brick is old and powders under your fingertips if you rub it vigorously. All colors are lost in the predominating gray; the face of the people have assumed it at last. There are no Jews or Italians or Irish—their features have blurred in an anonymous mortar which has rendered them homogeneous and dusty. It is in their speech. They all talk with the same depressing harsh arid tongue. "If I had a caah, I'd show it some caaer, I mean some caaer, I wouldn't paaark it just anywhaah."

It was founded by burghers and is ruled by bourgeois; everything flows on glabrous surfaces, everything is fine in Boston to read the newspapers, which are all the same, everything is okay in politics because the political parties are the same. Everybody belongs to the middle class, everybody down to the bums who drowse and retch on the subway that goes to Maverick Square in East Boston at two A.M. on Saturday night. Somewhere they must have protested against going into the mortar but it is all lost now.

There is a deadening regularity and a sullen vicious temper that rides underneath the surface, the glabrous surface of the Boston *Herald* and *Post* and *Traveler* and *Daily Record* and *Boston-American,* it erupts in the drunks who splatter the subways more completely than the drunks of any other city, it skitters around Scollay Square, where lust is always sordid and Sodom copulates in garbage. It even moves in the traffic, which is snarled and sullen and frenetic, and it rides the brow when the kids are beaten up in the alleyways, and the synagogues and cemeteries are fouled with language and symbol, "The fuggin kikes" and the cross or swastika. "I am distressed to hear of it," says Governor Curley, Saltonstall, Tobin.

The kids have gang fights with stones and sticks and knucklebands; in the winter the snowballs are packed with rocks. It is of course harmless, a mere tapping of the healthycompetitiveinstinct.

Hey, Gallagheh, Lefty Finkelstein's gang is gonna fight us.

Sonsofbitches, let's get them. (Fear is something alien to the gang, stored far down in his stomach.) I been layin' for him.

Get Packy and Al and Fingers, we're gonna clean up the Yids.

What time we start?

What the fug you caaeh? Ya yella?

Who's yella. I'm gonna get me my bat.

(On the way he passes a synagogue. "Ya yella?" He spits on it.) Hey, Whitey, I'm givin' it one for good luck.

Hey, Gallagheh, the kids yell . . .

Watch out for your old man when he's got a bag on.

In the house his mother winces at sounds and walks on tiptoe. His old man sits at the round table in the living-dining room, and grabs the yellow lace cover and crushes it in his big mitts. Then he spreads it out on the table again.

Goddam, sure a man has . . . Sonofabitch. Hey, PEG!

What is it, Will?

His father massages his nose and chin. Cut out the goddam mousing around, walk like a woman goddammit.

Yes, Will?

That's all goddammit, get away.

When your old man's as big a sonofabitch as Will Gallagher, you leave him alone when he's got a bag on. But you watch him so one of his mitts don't catch you on the side of the mouth.

He sits stolidly at the round table, and beats his fist down once or twice. He looks at the walls. (The brown pictures which once were green of shepherd girls in a wooded valley. They came off a calendar.) GOD-DAM PLACE.

The triptych on the whatnot shudders as he bangs the table.

Will, don't drink so much.

SHUT UP! Shut your stupid mouth. He lumbers to his feet and staggers to the wall. The glass over the shepherd girl splatters as he throws it to the floor. He sprawls on the shabby gray-brown sofa, looks at the gray shiny nap of the carpet where it has worn through. Work your ass off, FOR WHAT?

His wife tries to slip the bottle off the table. LEAVE IT THERE!

Will, maybe you can get something else.

Yeah . . . yeah. Have you whining I need a little this, a little that. Grocers butchers. Just let me break me back wrestling that truck around. Something ELSE. I'm stuck, I'm in a hole. GET THAT BOTTLE DOWN.

He stands up, lurches toward her, and strikes her. She slips to the floor and lies there without moving, uttering a dull passionless whimpering. (A slim woman, drab now.)

CUT OUT THE GODDAM NOISE! He looks at her dumbly, mops his nose again and rumbles toward the door. Get out of the way, Roy. At the door he stumbles, sighs, and then goes pitching down the street into the night.

Gallagher looks at his mother. He is empty, close to weeping. Here, Ma. He helps her up. She begins to cry loudly, and numbly he supports her.

Ya keep your mouth shut when the old man's got a bag on, he thinks.

Later, he goes up to his room, and reads a book he drew from the library. King Arthur and His Knights of the Round Table. Boy-wise, he dreams of women in . . . lavender dresses he picks.

I ain't gonna be like the old man. (He shall defend his wife with his sword.)

The bright glorious passage of youth.

His teachers never remember him in high school, a sullen morose student without enthusiasm. He quits a year before graduation, out into the tag end of the depression and a job as an elevator boy. His old man is without work that year, and his mother goes out by day, cleans stucco, Spanish tile, and Colonial houses in Brookline, in Newton. At night she goes to sleep after supper, and his old man is down at the corner bar, waiting for someone to offer him an argument or a drink.

Roy starts hanging around the Democratic Club in his ward. In the small rooms at the back there are the poker games, crap games, the con talk. The big room at the entrance where the kids come in and mingle with the cigar smoke, the serge suits, the attendants.

Ladies in waiting.

And the recruiting talks. Steve Macnamara who is getting up in the party:

Sure, you guys, take a look, just take a look. A man can split a gut tryin' to go it the hard way. What's in it for ya? The only thing is politics, politics, that's what gets ya somewheah, you put in a couple of yeaahs, you show 'em you're a right guy, an' you're made, the organization'll take caah of ya. I remembeh when I was a punk like you kids, I showed 'em I was a willin' workeh, and now I'm set, you know this ain't a bad waard, it's easy to pull in the vote heah.

Yeah, Gallagher admits, yeah.

Listen, I've had my eye on you, Roy, you're okay, I can see wheah you'd have a future heah, you just got to show the boys you're a willin' workeh. I know y'are but you got to prove it to them. I'll tell ya what, the primary's comin' up in another month, and theah's a lot of leg work got to be done, givin' out the pamphlets, and havin' a couple of boys in the crowd to do a little yellin' when one of our candidates is makin' a speech, we'll tell you when.

Yeah, that's okay.

Sure, listen, theah's money to be made in this, you know you stick with the boys theah's always a lot of jobs, a lot of easy gelt, you'll be a big guy someday, I'll say I knew you when, I can see right off and I'm a student of human nature, you got to be in this racket, that you got the stuff for politics, you know, chaaarm.

I'll be puttin' in my nights here.

That's it, how old are ya now? Close to eighteen, by the time you're twenty you'll be making ten times what you are now . . .

On the way home, he meets a girl he has talked to once or twice, and he stops to banter with her.

I'm tired of my job, I'm gettin' a better one, he bursts out.

What?

Something big. (Suddenly he is shy.) Big, something big.

You're mysterious, Roy, cut the kiddin'. (She giggles.)

Yeah. (He can think of nothing to say.) Yeah, I'm on my way, I'm going places.

You're a caard.

Yeah. (He looks at her, lights a cigarette with elaborate nonchalance, swaggers self-consciously.) Yeah. (He looks at her again, and feels panicky.) I'll be seein' ya.

When he is twenty, he has a new job, he works in a warehouse. (Roy, you done a lotta work, Steve Macnamara has said to him, don't let anyone tell ya different, and the boys appreciate it, you're goin' places. He makes himself say, Yeah, but Whitey's on the payroll, I done as much work as him . . . Now, listen, Roy, listen, don't let anyone hear ya talkin' like that, Jesus, they'll be thinkin' you're a sorehead, you built up a name heah for yourself, you don't want to be takin' chances with it.)

One night he goes out to Cambridge to see a girl, but she has stood him up. He ends by walking through the streets, and wandering along the banks of the Charles. The goddam bitch, none of them can fool me, they all put out for the right guy, but they just don' gimme a chance, the caards are stacked against me, it's the goddam breaks I just never get them. I work my ass off at the club, and what does it get me?

He sits down on a bench, and looks at the water languidly flowing. The lights from the Harvard Houses arc reflecting in it. Work your ass off, work, work, work, and who the hell gives a damn, you're just stuck, if I'd had some big dough she'da been waitin' around for me, and with her legs ready to spread too, I bet she ran off with some Jewboy who's got the dough. I don't know, they always grab all the money, grab, grab, grab, you'd think that was all there was in life. Disgusting.

Two Harvard undergraduates pass, and he stiffens in momentary panic. I wonder if I can sit here. Jesus. I shouldn'ta sat down.

I just held my breath, I tell you, that extension of Markova's was the most superbly terrifying thing I have ever seen, it was, oh, simple and subtle and just tremendous, terriFYING, absolutely terrifying.

Coupla fairies, what kind of crap was that, talkin' like a bunch of women. He turns around and looks at the lights in the Harvard buildings. Somebody ought to wipe out all those mother-fuggers. He watches the automobiles speeding past on Memorial Drive. Go ahead, hit the gas, hit it, hit it, go as fast as you goddam please, and break your goddam necks. That Harvard, goddam lefty outfit, somebody ought to blow up the fuggin place, work your ass off so some of those goddam fairies can sit around and act like women, life of Riley, how do they rate it, aah, the caards are never shuffled right, I'd like to kill every one of the mother-fuggers, there ought to be a man to take care of them, somebody ought to drop a bomb.

He sits on the bench for over an hour, calms at last. The river languishes by, stippled and quivering like the play of light on a metallic cloth. Across from him, the dormitories of the business school lance their reflections into the water, and the automobiles in the distance seem tiny and alive. He feels the earth under him germinating in the spring night, the sweet assuasive air. In the sky the stars are studded in the warm intimate velvet of the night.

Jeez, it's beautiful out. A play of yearnings, lost and never articulate. Makes ya think. He sighs. Real beautiful, makes ya think. The woman with whom he could share this. I'm gonna be something.

Awe. Night like this makes you know there's a God, dumb atheists. Jeez, it's beautiful, really beautiful, it makes ya think things are gonna be okay.

He sits there, absorbed in the night. I ain't like the other guys, theah's somethin' special in me. He sighs again. Boy, to . . . to . . . He fumbles for his thought as though his hand were groping for a fish in the water. Jeez to . . .

Roy, you're okay with us, I don't have to tell ya that, you know that we're gonna be givin' ya somethin' special real soon, and to show what the boys think of ya, we got a little outfit you're gonna be working with for a while, it ain't tied up to us exactly [Macnamara moves his hand deprecatingly] but mentioning no names theah's a couple of the big boys kinda like the way they work against the international plot, you know the one the rich kikes got all figured out to bring us communism.

On the payroll at ten dollars a week even though he is only working nights. The office is on the top of a two-story loft, a desk and a room filled with pamphlets and magazines tied in bundles. Behind the desk there is a large banner with a cross and an interlocking C and U.

Christians United, that's the name of this here outfit, Gallagheh, CHRISTIANS . . . UNITED, you get it, we're out to break the goddam conspiracy, what this country needs is some blood, y'afraid of blood? the big guy behind the desk asks. He has pale-brown eyes like panes of dull glass. We gotta start mobilizing and get ready, the International Jews is tryin' to get us to war, an' we gotta get them first, ya see the way they take away all the jobs, we let it go an' we won't have a fuggin chance, they're high up but we got our friends too.

He sells magazines on street corners (READ ABOUT THE BIG FOREIGN PLOT! GET FATHER KILIAN'S MAGAZINE AND LEARN THE TRUTH!), he goes to secret meetings, drills for an hour a week in a sporting club which uses old Springfields.

What I wanta know is when we gonna staart, I wanta see some action.

Y' got to take it easy, Gallagheh, it takes time, we gotta get everything set up and then we can come out in the open, we're gonna get this country run right, you come in with us at the bottom and you're in.

Yeah. (At night sometimes he cannot sleep, the thick lusting dreams, the quick ache in his chest.) I swear I'm gonna bust up if we don't . . . we don't get goin'.

But . . .

The girl friend at last, the hormones no longer distilled into vinegar.

You know, Gallagher says to Mary, you're really a swell kid, I . . . I get a bang outa talkin' to ya.

This is a swell night, Roy. (Looking off across the beach, searching the lights of Boston Harbor, which flicker like star formations in an uncertain clouded sky. She picks up a handful of sand, and pours it on her shoe, the glare from the bonfire making her hair seem golden. Her slim long face, freckled and sad, seems pleasant, almost lovely.)

Ya want me to toast a hot dog?

Let's just talk, Roy.

Around them, the couples with whom they have come have deserted the fire and are giggling in the shadowed hollows of the beach. A girl screams in mock fright, and he strains at the noise; uncomfortable, he thinks he hears the liquid slapping sounds of love.

Yeah, it's been a swell night, he repeats. He wonders if he can make love to her, and becomes suddenly shy. (She ain't like that, she's the pure kind, a good religious girl.) He feels guilty with his desire.

There's lots of things I'd like to talk to you about.

Sure, Roy.

Well, you know, we been goin' out for a coupla months, you know, what do ya think of me? He flushes at the crudeness of it, at the part of his mind that hopes for a physical issue. (The giggles become louder on the beach.) I mean do ya like me?

I think you're really swell, Roy, you know you are a gentleman, you're not fresh like all the other fellows.

Oh, yeah. He is disappointed, vaguely humiliated, and yet he generates some pride. I got other things on my mind.

I know, you always seem to be thinking, you know, Roy, I never know what's going on in your head, and I'd like to know because I think you're different.

How?

Well, you're shy, I don't mean shy but you're nice.

You should heah me talkin' to the guys. (They laugh.)

Oh, I believe you're just the same with them, you wouldn't be any different. (Her hand drops abstractedly on his knee, and she jerks it away with embarrassment.) I wish you'd go to church more often.

I go pretty regularly.

Yes, but there's something bothering you, I wonder about it, you're a mystery.

Yeah? He is pleased.

Roy, you always seem so angry about something, it worries me. My father was talking about you, and he said you're in Christians United, I don't know anything about politics, but I know one of them, Jackie Evans, was a nasty kid.

Aw, he's all right, it's just something with the club, you know they were tryin' me out, but it's nothin' much.

I wouldn't want you to get in trouble.

Why?

(She looks at him, her eyes passive and calm. This time she puts her hand on his arm.) You know why, Roy.

His throat is tense and his chest aches with warmth and hunger. He shivers as he hears the girl giggling again. This is swell out here at City Point, he says. (The thick lusting dreams at night for he knows not what.) I'll tell ya, Mary, if I was goin' steady—his voice is strong with his sense of renunciation—I wouldn' be hangin' around with them so much, 'cause you know I'd be wantin' to see more of you.

You would?

He listens to the lapping of the surf. I love ya, Mary, he says suddenly, holding himself stiff and cold, troubled delicately by a passing uncertainty.

I think I do too, Roy.

Yeah. After a while he kisses her gently, then hungrily, but a corner of his mind has retreated and become cold. Oh, I love ya, kid, he says huskily, trying to cauterize the doubt. His eyes stare away.

City Point is so beautiful, she says.

In the night they cannot see the garbage that litters the beach, the seaweed and driftwood, the condoms that wallow sluggishly on the foam's edge, discarded on the shore like the minuscule loathsome animals of the sea.

Yeah, it's something, he says slowly.

Hey, theah, Roy, how's the old married man, how's it feel gettin' it steady, what do ya say?

Aw, it's okay. (He shivers in the September dawn that lifts bleakly over the gray-stone pavement and the slatternly wooden houses.) Jesus, it's cold out, I wish the goddam polls'd open.

I'm glad you're with me today, Roy, you know we think you're all right, but we ain't seen much of ya.

Aaah, well, I quit the CU, he mumbles, and I thought maybe the boys were you know not so glad to see me.

Well, ya shoulda told 'em, but between you an' me, the club is gonna lay off 'em for a while, started gettin' pressure from on top, clear out of the state I heard. It always pays to stick with the club, you don't go wrong that way, I bet if you hadn't been with the CU you woulda been the election captain here today, I hope there's no hahd feelin's, Roy.

Naw. (He feels a dull resentment. Back wheah I staarted.) I bet some of those rich kikes in the party are the ones that creamed the CU.

Might have been.

The wife wanted me to quit 'em.

How is she?

Okay. (He thinks of her sleeping now, hears the rough surprisingly male heartiness of her snoring.)

Married life gone okay with ya? What're ya doin' now?

Yeah, it's fine. I'm drivin' a truck . . . like my old man. (Mary has bought a lace cover for the table.)

Listen, these Reds who are runnin' M'Gillis, aw, M'Gillis a Black Irishman if there ever was one, imagine a guy givin' up his religion, well, anyway the big boys ain't worryin' about him for the primaries, but theah's a bunch of union men in this district and Mac says we got to make a good showing right here so they won't be buildin' up.

We bringin' over any repeatehs? Gallagher asks.

Yeah, but I got me own little idea. (He removes several bottles of ketchup from a paper bag, and begins to pour them on the sidewalk.)

What are ya doin'?

Oh, this is neat, this is gonna take the cake. That's good, get it. You stand here and give out the pamphlets for Haney, and give 'em a spiel with it, we can't miss.

Yeah, that's a good one. (Why didn't I think of it?) Your idea?

All mine, Mac was really tickled when I told him, he called up Nolan who's the saargeant for the two bulls in this poll, and they ain't gonna cause us no trouble.

Gallagher stands by the ketchup, and begins to talk as the first voters get in line for the polls. TAKE A LOOK, SEE WHAT HAPPENS. THIS IS BLOOD, THIS IS WHAT HAPPENS TO DECENT AMERICANS WHEN THEY TRY TO VOTE AGAINST A RED. THEY GET BEAT UP BY THE FOREIGNERS THAT ARE BE-HIND M'GILLIS. THIS IS M'GILLIS'S WORK, BLOOD, HUMAN BLOOD.

During a lull he examines the ketchup, which seems too red. He sprinkles a little dirt on it. (Work and work and then some smart guy gets a bright idea and gets all the credit, those goddam Reds, they're causin' me all the trouble.)

HERE Y'ARE, TAKE A LOOK, he shouts as some voters approach.

Where you goin', Roy? Mary asks. Her voice has a whining nagging quality and he turns in the door, and shakes his head. I'm just goin' out. She cuts her boiled potato in half, and puts a big portion in her mouth. A few flakes of potato stick to her lip, which angers him. Don't ya ever eat anythin' but potatoes? he asks.

Roy, we have meat.

Yeah, I know. Questions tug at his mind. He wants to ask her why she never eats with him at night, but always serves him first; he wants to tell her that he doesn't like to be asked where he is going.

You're not going to be at a CU meeting, are ya? she asks.

What do you care? (Why don't you ever put a dress over that slip?)

Roy, you're going to get in trouble there, I don't like those men, you're only going to hurt yourself at the club, you know now the war's on they have nothing to do with them.

There's nothing wrong with the CU. Leave me alone, goddammit.

Roy, don't swear.

He slams the door, and walks into the night. It is snowing a little, and at the street corners his shoes crunch icily through the slush. He sneezes once or twice. A man's gotta get out and have some . . . some relaxation. Y' get some ideals to fight for in the organization and a woman wants to stop ya. I'm gonna be up there someday.

In the meeting hall, the air is hot and metallic from the heaters, and the smell of wet clothing is sour. He grits a cigarette butt into powder with his foot.

All right, we're in a war, men, the speaker says, we gotta fight for the country, but we don't want to be forgettin' our private enemies. He pounds the speaker's table over which a flag with a cross is spread. There's the foreign element we got to get rid of, that are conspiring to take over the country. There are cheers from the hundred men seated in camp chairs. We gotta stick together, or we'll be havin' our women raped, and the Red Hammer of Red Jew Fascist Russia WILL BE SMASHING YOUR DOOR DOWN.

That's tellin' him, the man next to Gallagher says.

Yeah, Wat's okay. Gallagher feels a pleasurable fury forming in him.

Who takes away your jobs, who tries to sneak up on your wives and your daughters and even your mothers 'cause they wouldn't stop at nothing, who's out to get YOU and YOU 'cause you ain't a Red and a Jew, and you don' wanta bow down before a filthy goddam no-good Communist who don't respect the Lord's name, and would stop at nothing.

Let's kill them! Gallagher shrieks. He is shaking with excitement.

That's it, men, we're gonna clean up on 'em, after the war we're really gonna have an organization, I got telegrams here from our com-*pat*-riots, patriots as well as friends, and they're all stickin' with us. You're all in on the ground floor, men, and those of ya that are goin' into the Army gotta learn to use your weapons so that afterward . . . afterward . . . You get the idea, men. We ain't licked, we're gettin' bigger all the time.

When the meeting is over, Gallagher drifts into a bar. The dry throat, the painful tension in his chest. As he drinks, his rage diffuses and he grows sullen and bitter.

They're always cheatin' ya at the last minute, he says to the man beside him. They had come out of the meeting together.

It's a plot.

That's all it is, it's a goddam mother-fuggin plot, and they ain't gonna break me, I'm gonna get out on top.

On the way home he slips in a puddle, and wets his pant leg up to his hip. Fug you, he roars at the pavement. Plot, always fuggin a guy, well, you ain't gonna get me.

He lurches into his flat, and pitches off his overcoat. His nose is bitter. He sneezes raspingly, and swears to himself.

Mary wakes up in her chair, and looks at him. You're all wet.

That all you got to say? I'm . . . I'm . . . what the hell do you know about it?

Roy, every time you come back you're like this.

Trying to keep a man down, all you're interested in is the goddam dough I bring back, well I'LL GIVE YOU ALL THE DOUGH YOU WANT.

Roy, don't talk to me like that. Her lip wavers.

Staaart crying, go ahead, staaart crying, I'm on to you.

I'm going to bed.

C'mere.

Roy, I'm not going to hold it against you, I don't know what's the matter with you, but there's something in you I just don't understand, what do you want of me?

Lea' me alone.

Oh, Roy, you're wet, take off your pants, honey, why do you drink, it always makes you so bitter, I've been praying for you, honest I have.

Oh, lea' me alone. He sits by himself for a few minutes staring at the lace doily on the table. Aaah, I don' know, I don' know.

What's in it for a guy?

Work tomorrow.

(He would defend the lady in the lavender dress with his sword.)

He fell asleep in the chair, and in the morning he had a cold.

The Time Machine
GENERAL CUMMINGS: A PECULIARLY AMERICAN STATEMENT

At first glance he did not look unlike other general officers. A little over medium height, well fleshed, with a rather handsome sun-tanned face and graying hair, but there were differences. His expression when he smiled was very close to the ruddy complacent and hard appearance of any number of American senators and businessmen, but the tough good-guy aura never quite remained. There was a certain vacancy in his face . . . there was the appearance and yet it was not there. Hearn always felt as if the smiling face were numb.

The town has existed for a long time in this part of the Midwest, more than seventy years by 1910, but it has not been a city very long. "Why, not so long ago," they will say, "I can remember when this here town was nothin' much more than a post office and the school house, the Old Presbyterian church and the Main Hotel. Old Ike Cummings had the general store then, and for a while we had a feller barbered hair, but he didn't last long, moved on some'er else. And then," with a slow evaluating wink, "they was a town whoor used to do business in the county."

And of course when Cyrus Cummings (named after the older Mc-Cormick) went to New York on those banking trips, he didn't waste his time. "I tell you," the people will say, "they had to bring that factory here. Cy Cummings didn't give his help to McKinley for nothing back in 'ninety-six; he's a Yankee trader. He might not a had much of a bank in those days but when he called in all the farmer debts the week before election this here became a McKinley county. Cy is even smarter than old Ike, an' you remember when Ike had the general store nobody traded him a horse with a canker." And the old man on the vanishing cracker barrel fluffs some spittle into his corded stale handkerchief. "Course," with a grin, "I ain't sayin' that anyone in town loves Cy more than is proper, but the town . . ." (with another grin) "I mean, the city, sure as hell owes him a lot, be it in gratitude or hard dollar bills."

The town is set in the middle of the great American plain. There are a few knolls or rills bordering it, one of the insignificant accidents of land in the long flat face of the Midwest, and you can find quite a few trees on the lee side of the railroad tracks. The streets are broad and the elm and oak bloom in summer, soften the harsh crabbed outlines of the Queen Anne houses, throw interesting shadows into the angles of the gable windows and truncated dormer roofs. Center Street has only a few buildings left with false façades, and there are lots of stores now, so many farmers in town on Saturday afternoons that they are beginning to pave it with cobblestones so the horses won't bog in the mud.

For the richest man in town, Cy Cummings's house is not too different. The Cummingses built it thirty years ago at a time when it stood all alone on the edge of town and you walked to your thighs in mud to reach it in early fall and spring. But the town has encompassed it now and there is not much Cy Cummings can do in the way of improvements.

The worst of the changes you can blame on his wife. The folks who know them say it's her fault, a fancy eastern woman with Culture. Cy's a hard man, but he isn't a fancy one, and that new front door with all the windowpanes on the bias is something French. She's mentioned the name at church meeting, Newvelle something. And Cy Cummings has even turned High Episcopal for her, was instrumental in getting the 'Piscopal church built.

Odd family, people will tell you, funny kids.

In the parlor with the portraits on the wall, the brown murky land-scapes in golden scalloped frames, the dark draperies, the brown furni-ture, the fireplace—in the parlor the family is sitting around.

That feller Debs is making trouble again, Cy Cummings says. (A sharp-featured face with a partially bald head, silver-rimmed glasses.)

Yes, dear? The wife turns to her sewing, embroiders another golden stitch on the buttocks of the Cupid in the center of the doily. (A pretty woman, flutters a little, with the long dress, the impressive bosom of the period.) Well, why does he make trouble?

Aaahr, Cy snorts, the basic disgust for a woman's remark.

Hang 'em, Ike Cummings says, with the old man's quaver. In the war (the Civil War) we used to take 'em up, set 'em on a mare, and spank her rump, and watch them kick their heels a little.

Cy rustles his paper. Don't need to hang 'em. He looks at his hands, laughs dourly. Edward go to sleep yet?

She looks up, answers quickly, nervously, I think so, that is he said he was. He and Matthew said they were going to sleep. (Matthew Arnold Cummings is the younger one.)

I'll take a look.

In the boys' bedroom, Matthew is asleep, and Edward, age seven, is sitting in a corner, sewing snips of thread into a scrap of cloth.

The father steps toward him, throws his shadow across the boy's face. What are you doing, boy?

The child looks up petrified. Sewin'. Ma said it was okay.

Give it to me. And the scraps, the thread, are hurled into the waste-basket. Come up, 'Lizabeth.

He hears the argument raging about him, conducted in hoarse pas-sionate whispers as a sop to his sleeping brother. I won't have him actin' like a goddam woman, you're to stop feedin' him all these books, all this womanish . . . claptrap. (The baseball bat and glove are gathering dust in the attic.)

But I didn't . . . I didn't tell him a thing.

You didn't tell him to sew?

Please, Cyrus, let him alone. The slap reddens his cheek from the ear to the mouth. The boy sits on the floor, the tears dropping in his lap.

And you're to act like a man from now on, do you understand?

Only when they have gone, too many things twist in his comprehen-sion. The mother had given him the thread, told him to do it quietly.

The sermon ends in church. We are all children of the Lord Jesus and God, instruments of His compassion, committed unto earth to enact the instruments of His goodness, to sow the seeds of brotherhood and good works.

A fine sermon, the mother says.

Yeahp.

Was he right? Edward asks.

Certainly, Cyrus says, only you got to take it with a grain of caution. Life's a hard thing and nobody gives you nothing. You do it alone. Every man's hand is against you, that's what you also find out.

Then he was wrong, Father.

I didn't say that. He's right and I'm right, and it's just in religion you act one way, and in business, which is a lesser thing, well, you go about things in another way. It's still Christian.

The mother caresses his shoulder. It was a wonderful sermon, Edward.

Nearly everybody in this town hates me, Cyrus says. They hate you too, Edward, you might as well learn it early, ain't nothing they hate like a success, and you're sure gonna be one, if they don't like you they can still lick your boots.

The mother and the son pack up the paints and easel, start back in the chilly spring afternoon from their jaunt outside the town, sketching the meager hills on the plain.

Have a good time, Eddie dear? Her voice has a new trill in it now, a new warmth when they are alone.

Loved it, Ma.

When I was a little girl, I always used to dream I'd have a little boy and I'd go out with him and paint, just like this. Come on, I'll teach you a funny song while we go back.

What is Boston like? he asks.

Oh, it's a big city, it's dirty, coooold, everybody's always dressed up.

Like Pa?

She laughs doubtfully. Yes, like Pa. Now, don't you say anything to him about what we did this afternoon. . . . Was it wrong?

No, now you just march right on home with me, and don't say a word to him, it's a secret.

He hates her suddenly, and is quiet, moody, as they walk back to the town. That night he tells his father, listens with a kind of delicious glee and fright to the quarrel that follows.

I'm going to tell you that that boy is all your fault, you indulge him, you bring out the worst in him, you never could get over leaving Boston, now, could you, we're really not fine enough out here for you.

Cyrus, please.

I'll be damned, I'm going to send him to military school, he's old enough to shift for himself, at nine years old a boy has to start thinking how to act like a man.

Ike Cummings nods. Military school's all right, that boy likes to listen to things about the war.

What is partially behind it all is the conversation Cyrus has had with the town doctor. The fabulous beard, the hard shrewd eyes have twinkled at him, got a little of their own back. Well, now, Mr. Cummings, there ain't a damn thing can be done now, it's over my head, if he were a little older I'd say take the boy over to Sally's and let him git some jism in his system.

The basic good-bye at the age of ten, the railroad train, the farewell to the muddy roads at the periphery of town, the gaunt family houses, the smell of his father's bank, and the laundry on the lines.

Good-bye, Son, and do all right for yourself, do you hear?

He has accepted the father's decision without any feeling, but now he shudders almost imperceptibly at the hand on his shoulder.

Good-bye, Ma. She is weeping, and he feels a mild contempt, an almost lost compassion.

Good-bye, and he goes, plummets into the monastery and becomes lost in the routine of the school, in polishing his buttons and making his bed.

There are changes in him. He has never been friendly with other boys, but now he is cold rather than shy. The water colors, the books like *Little Lord Fauntleroy* and *Ivanhoe* and *Oliver Twist* are far less important; he never misses them. Through the years there he gets the best marks in his class, becomes a minor athlete, No. 3 man on the tennis team. Like his father, he is respected if he is not loved.

And the crushes of course: he stands by his bunk at Saturday morning inspection, rigidly upright, clicking his heels as the colonel headmaster comes by. The suite of officer-teachers pass, and he waits numbly for the cadet colonel, a tall dark-haired youth.

Cummings, the cadet colonel says.

Yes, sir.

Your web belt has verdigris in the eyelets.

Yes, sir. And he watches him go, shuttling between anguish and a troubled excitement because he has been noticed. A subterranean phenomenon, for he takes no part in the special activities pertinent to a boys' private school, is almost conspicuous by his avoidance.

Nine years of it, the ascetic barracks, and the communal sleeping, the uniform-fears, the equipment-fears, the marching-tensions, and the meaningless vacations. He sees his parents for six weeks each summer, finds them strange, feels distant toward his brother. Mrs. Cyrus Cummings bores him now with her nostalgia.

Remember, Eddie, when we went out to the hill and painted?

Yes, Mother.

He graduates as cadet colonel.

At home he makes a little stir in his uniform. The people know he is going to West Point, and he is pointed out to the young girls, to whom he is polite and indifferent. He is handsome now, not too tall, but his build is respectable, and his face has an intelligent scrubbed look.

Cyrus talks to him. Well, Son, you're ready for West Point, eh?

Yes, sir, I expect so.

Mmm. Glad you went to military school?

Tried to do the best I could, sir.

Cyrus nods. West Point pleases him. He has decided long ago that little Matthew Arnold can carry on the bank, and this strange stiff son in the uniform is best away from home. Good idea sending you there, Cyrus says.

Why . . . His mind is blank, but a powerful anxiety stirs along his spine. His palms are always wet when he talks to his father. Why, yes, sir (knowing somehow that this is what Cyrus wants to hear). Yes, sir. I hope to do well at the Point, sir.

You will if you're a son of mine. (Laughing heartily in the consummation-of-business-deal heartiness, he claps him on the back.)

Again . . . Yes, sir. And he withdraws, the basic reaction.

He meets the girl he is to marry in the summer after his second year at West Point. He has not been home in two years because there have been no vacations long enough for him to make the trip, but he has not missed the town. When this vacation comes he goes to Boston to visit his mother's relatives.

The city delights him; the manners of his relatives come as a revelation after the crude probing speech of the town. He is very polite at first, very reticent, aware that until he learns the blunders he must not make he cannot talk freely. But there are stirrings. He walks the streets of Beacon Hill, ascending eagerly along the narrow sidewalks to the State House where he stands motionless, watching the light-play on the Charles, a half mile below him. The brass knockers, the dull black knockers intrigue him; he stares at all the narrow doors, touches his hat to the old ladies in black who smile pleasantly, a trifle doubtfully, at his cadet's uniform. *This is what I like.*

I'm very fond of Boston, he says a few weeks later to his cousin Margaret. They have become confidants.

Are you? she says. It's getting a little seedy. Father said there are always less and less places where one may go. (Her face is delicately long, pleasantly cold. Despite the length of her nose it turns up at the tip.)

Oh, well, the Irish, he miffs, but he is vaguely uncomfortable in saying it, conscious that his answer is trite.

Uncle Andrew is always complaining that they've taken the government away from us. I heard him say the other night that it's like France now, he was there, you know, the only careers left are in the service (State department) or in uniform, and even there the elements are undependable. (Conscious of an error, she adds quickly) He's very fond of you.

I'm glad.

You know, it's odd, Margaret says, only a few years ago Uncle Andrew was very intolerant about the whole thing. I'll tell you a secret. (She laughs, puts her arm through his.) He always preferred the Navy. He says they have better manners.

Oh. (For a moment he feels lost. All their politeness, their acceptance of him as a relative is seen from the other side of the door. There is the brief moment when he tries to reverse all the things he remembers their saying, examines them from the new approach.)

That doesn't mean anything, Margaret says, we're all such frauds. It's a terrible thing to say, but you know whatever we have in the family is what we accept. I was terribly shocked when I first realized that.

Then I'm all right, he says lightly.

Oh, no, you won't do at all. (She laughs first, and he joins in a little hesitantly.) You're just our second cousin from the West. That isn't done. (Her long face seems merry for a moment.) Seriously, it's just that we've known only Navy up till now. Tom Hopkinson and Thatcher Lloyd, I think you met him at Dennis, well, they're all Navy, and Uncle Andrew knows their fathers so well. But he likes you. I think he had a crush on your mother.

Well, that makes it better. (They laugh again, sit down on a bench and throw pebbles into the Charles River basin.)

You're awfully vivacious, Margaret.

Oh, I'm a fraud too. If you knew me you'd say I was awfully moody.

I bet I wouldn't.

Oh, I wept, you know I completely wept when Minot and I lost our boat class race two years ago. It was just silly. Father wanted us to win it, and I was terrified what he would say. You can't move around here at all, nothing one can do, there's always a reason why it isn't *advisable*. (For an instant her voice is almost bitter.) You're not like us at all, you're serious, you're important. (Her voice lilts again.) Father told me you were second from the top in your class. That's bad manners.

Would the middle third be respectable?

Not for you. You're going to be a general.

I don't believe it. (His voice in these weeks in Boston has assumed the proper tone, become a little higher, a little more lazy. He cannot express the excitement, perhaps the exaltation Boston gives him. Everyone is so perfect here.)

You're just doodling me, he says. (A leprous phrase of the Midwest, he realizes too late, and is unbalanced for a moment.)

Oh, no, I'm convinced you're going to be a great man.

I like you, Margaret.

You should after I praised you like that. (She giggles once more, says ingenuously) I suppose I want you to like me.

At the end of summer when he is leaving she hugs him, whispers in his ear, I wish we were definitely engaged so you could kiss me.

So do I. But it is the first time he has thought of her as a woman to be loved, and he is a little shocked, a little empty. On the train going back, she has lost her disturbing individuality already, remains as the pleasant focus of her family and Boston behind them. He feels an unfamiliar, a satisfying identity with his classmates when he talks about his girl. It's important to have one, he decides.

He is always learning things, understanding already that his mind must work on many levels. There is the thing he thinks of as the truth, the objective situation which his mind must unravel; there is the "deep layer," as he calls it, the mattress resting on the cloud, and he does not care to plumb for the legs; there is, and it is very important, the level where he must do and say things for their effect upon the men with whom he lives and works.

He learns the last dramatically in the hour on Military History and Tactics. (The brown scrubbed room, the blackboards at the front, the benches where the cadets sit in the unquestioned symmetry of ancient patterns, the squares of a chessboard.)

Sir (he gets permission to speak), is it fair to say that Lee was the better general than Grant? I know that their tactics don't compare, but Grant had the knowledge of strategy. What good are tactics, sir, if the . . . the larger mechanics of men and supplies are not developed properly, because the tactics are just the part of the whole? In this conception wasn't Grant the greater man because he tried to take into account the intangibles. He wasn't much good at the buck-and-wing but he could think up the rest of the show. (The classroom roars.)

It has been a triple error. He has been contradictory, rebellious and facetious.

Cummings, you'll make your points in the future more concisely.

Yes, sir.

You happen to be wrong. You men will find out that experience is worth a great deal more than theory. It is impossible to account for all your strategy, those things have a way of balancing out as happened at Richmond, as is happening now in the trench warfare in Europe. Tactics is always the determinant. (He writes it on the blackboard.)

And, Cummings . . .

Sir?

Since you will be fortunate if you command a battalion by the end of twenty years, you'll do a sight better to concern yourself with the strategic problems of a platoon (there is muffled laughter at his sarcasm) than with those of an Army. (Seeing the approval in his eyes, the class releases its laughter, singeing Cummings's flesh.)

He hears about it for weeks. Hey, Cummings, how many hours will you need to take Richmond?

They're sending you over, Ed, I hear, as adviser to the French. With the proper concepts the Hindenburg Line may be breached.

He learns so many things from this, understands, besides all else, that he is not liked, will not be liked, and he can't make mistakes, cannot expose himself to the pack. He will have to wait. But he is hurt, cannot restrain himself from writing about it to Margaret. And his contempt thrives in recompense; there is a world of manners about which these men know nothing.

In *The Howitzer*, when he graduates, they have printed "The Strategist" under his record, and then to soften it, for it jars with the mellow sentimental glow of yearbooks, they have added a little ambiguously, "Handsome Is as Handsome Does."

He goes out to an abridged furlough with Margaret, the announcement of their engagement, and the rapid shuttle on the transport to the war in Europe.

In the planning section of GHQ he lives in the remaining wing of a château, occupies the bare whitewashed room that had once belonged to a chambermaid, but he does not know this. The war has caught him up agreeably, altered the deadening routine of forms, the detail work of outlining troop movements. The sound of the artillery is always an enrichment to his work, the bare gnashed ground outside speaks of the importance of his figures.

There is even one night when the entire war stands out for him on the edge of a knife blade, a time when everything balances in his mind.

He goes out with his colonel, an enlisted chauffeur, and two other officers on an inspection of the front. It is picnic style with sandwiches packed away and a hot thermos of coffee. The canned rations are brought along, but there is not likely to be an opportunity of using them. They motor along the back roads to the front, jouncing slowly over the potholes and shellholes, splashing ponderously through the mud. For an hour they move along a vast desolated plain, the drab afternoon sky lighted only by the bursts of artillery, the crude evil flickering of the flares like heat lightning on a sultry evening in summer. A mile from the trenches they come to a low ridge-line barely obscuring the horizon and they halt, march slowly along a communication trench which is filled with a half foot of water from the morning's rain. As they approach the secondary trenches the communication ditch begins to zigzag and becomes deeper. Every hundred yards Cummings steps up on the parapet, and peers cautiously into the gloom of No Man's Land.

In the reserve trenches they halt, and take up their position in a concrete dugout, listening respectfully to the conversation between their colonel and the Regimental Commander of that sector of the line. He too has come up for the attack. An hour before dark the artillery begins a creeping barrage which moves closer and closer to the enemy trenches, finally centers on them for a bombardment which lasts fifteen minutes. German artillery is answering, and every few minutes a misdirected shell swooshes down near their observation post. The trench mortars have begun to fire and the volume of sound increases, floods everything, until they are shouting at each other.

It's time, there they go, someone bellows.

Cummings puts up his field glasses, looks out the slit in the concrete wall. In the twilight, covered with mud, the men look like silver shadows on a wan silver plain. It is raining again, and they waver forward between a walk and a run, falling on their faces, tottering backward, sliding on their bellies in the leaden-colored muck. The German lines are aroused and furious, return the fire cruelly. Light and sound erupt from them viciously, become so immense that his senses are overwhelmed, finally perceive them only as a background for the advance of the infantry across the plain.

The men move slowly now, leaning forward as if striding into the wind. He is fascinated by the sluggishness of it all, the lethargy with which they advance and fall. There seems no pattern to the attack, no volition to the men; they advance in every direction like floating leaves in a pool disturbed by a stone, and yet there is a cumulative movement forward. The ants in the final sense all go in one direction.

Through the field glasses he watches one soldier run forward, plunge his head toward the mud, stand up and run again. It is like watching a crowd from a high window or separating a puppy from the rest of the wriggling brood in a pet-store window. There is an oddness, an unreality, in realizing that the group is made up of units.

The soldier falls, quivers in the mud, and he switches his glasses to another.

They're at the German trenches, someone shouts.

He looks up hastily, sees a few men jumping over the parapet, their bayonets forward like pole vaulters approaching the bar. They seem to move so leisurely, so few men follow them that he is puzzled. Where are the rest he is about to say when there is a shout from the Regimental Commander. They took it, they're good boys, they took it. He is holding the phone in his hand, shouting orders quickly.

The German artillery is beginning to fall on the newly taken trenches, and columns of men advance slowly through the dusk over the quiet field, circling around the dead men, and filing into the German trenches. It is almost dark, and the sky has assumed a rosy wash in the east where a house is burning. He cannot see through his field glasses any longer, and he puts them down, stares across the field with a silent wonder. It looks primal, unfamiliar, the way he has imagined the surface of the moon might look. In the craters the water glistens, slides away in long rippling shadows from the bodies of the men who have fallen.

What'd you think of it? The Colonel nudges him.

Oh, it was . . . But he cannot find the words. It has been too immense, too shattering. The long dry battles of the textbooks come alive for him, mass themselves in his mind. He can only think of the man who has ordered the attack, and he pictures him with wonder. What . . . courage. The responsibility. (For want of a richer word he picks up the military expression.)

There were all those men, and there had been someone above them, ordering them, changing perhaps forever the fiber of their lives. In the darkness he looks blankly at the field, tantalized by the largest vision that has ever entered his soul.

There were things one could do.

To command all that. He is choked with the intensity of his emotion, the rage, the exaltation, the undefined and mighty hunger.

He returns a captain (temporary), is promoted and demoted in the same order, made first lieutenant (permanent). There is his marriage with Margaret against the subtle opposition of her parents, the brief honeymoon, and they settle down at an Army post, drift in the pleasantly vacant circle of parties and Saturday night dances at the officers' club.

Their lovemaking is fantastic for a time:

He must subdue her, absorb her, rip her apart and consume her.

This motif is concealed for a month or two, clouded over by their mutual inexperience, by the strangeness, the unfamiliarity, but it must come out eventually. And for a half year, almost a year, they have love passages of intense fury, enraged and powerful, which leave him sobbing from exhaustion and frustration on her breast.

Do you love me, are you mine, love me.

Yes yes.

I'll take you apart, I'll eat you, oh, I'll make you mine, I'll make you mine, you bitch.

And surprising profanity, words he is startled to hear himself speak.

Margaret is kindled by it, exalted for a time, sees it as passion, glows and becomes rounded, but only for a time. After a year it is completely naked, apparent to her, that he is alone, that he fights out battles with himself upon her body, and something withers in her. There is all the authority she has left, the family and the Boston streets and the history hanging upon them, and she has left it, to be caught in a more terrifying authority, a greater demand.

This is all of course beneath words, would be unbearable if it were ever said, but their marriage re-forms, assumes a light and hypocritical companionship with a void at the center, and very little lovemaking now, painfully isolated when it occurs. He retreats from her, licks his wounds, and twists in the circle beyond which he cannot break. Their social life becomes far more important.

She busies herself with running her house, keeping a list of the delicate debits and credits of entertainment and visiting. It always takes them two hours to figure out the list for their monthly party.

Once they spend a week wondering if they can invite the General to their house, discuss the elaborate arguments on either side. They conclude it would be in bad taste, might hurt them even if he came, but a few nights later Captain Cummings wrestles with the problem again, wakes up at dawn and knows it is a chance he must take.

They plan it very carefully, picking a weekend when the General has no obligations and it seems as if none will develop. From the General's house orderly, Margaret finds out which foods he likes; at a post dance she talks to the General's wife for twenty minutes, discovers an acquaintance of her father's whom the General knows.

They send out the invitations and the General accepts. There is the nervous preceding week, the tension at the party. The General walks in, stands about at the buffet table, picking not without zeal at the smoked turkey, the shrimp for which she has sent to Boston.

It is finally a success and the General smiles at Cummings mistily, pleased with his eighth Scotch, the puffed and tufted furniture (he had been expecting maple), the sharp sweet bite of the shrimp sauce through the fur of drinking. When he says good-bye he pats Cummings on the shoulder, pinches Margaret's cheek. The tension collapses, the junior officers and their wives begin to sing. But they are too exhausted and the party ends early.

That night when they congratulate each other Cummings is satisfied.

But Margaret ruins it; she has a facility for ruining things now. You know, honestly, Edward, I wonder what the point to it all was, you can't get promoted any faster, and the old fart (she has taken to swearing mildly) will be dead by the time it's a question of recommending you for general's rank.

You have to start your reputation early, he says quickly. He has accepted all these mores, forced himself dutifully into them, but he does not like them to be questioned.

Oh, what a perfectly vague thing to say. You know I'm feeling now as if we were silly to have invited him. It would have been much more fun without him.

Fun? (This hits at the core of him, leaves him actually weak with anger.) *There are more important things than fun.* He feels as if he has closed a door behind him.

You're in danger of becoming a bore.

Let it go, he almost shouts, and she subsides before his rage. But there it is between them, stated again.

I don't know what gets into you, he mutters.

There are other movements, other directions. For a time he moves through the drinking circles of the officers' club, plays poker, and indulges in a few side affairs. But it is a repetition of Margaret with humiliating endings, and in another year or two he keeps to himself, devotes himself to running his outfits.

In that he has talent. He absorbs the problem completely, thinks at night in bed of how best to treat the different men, how to command them most effectively. In the daytime he spends nearly all his time with the company, supervising labor details, conducting continual inspections. His companies are always the best managed on the post; his company street is easily the cleanest and neatest.

On Saturday mornings a squad from each platoon is put to work cutting the weeds from under the barracks.

He has all the patent brass polishers tested, selects the best, and has an order posted that the men can use only that brand.

In the daily latrine inspections he is always one step ahead of the men; one morning he gets down on his hands and knees, lifts the drain plate, and gigs the platoon because there is grease in the pipe.

When he inspects he brings a needle, probes the cracks on the stairs for dust.

In the gymkhana which the post holds every summer his company teams always win. He has them practicing from the first of February.

The company mess floor is scrubbed with boiling water after every meal.

He is always ahead of the men. One big Saturday inspection when a visiting general is expected, he instructs his first sergeant to have the men grease the soles of their extra shoes, which are exhibited at the foot of their bed.

He has been known to strip a rifle on the parade ground and examine the rear of the hammer spring for dirt.

There is always a standing gag in his company that the Old Man is thinking of having the men take off their shoes before they enter the barracks.

The field officers are agreed that Captain Cummings is the best junior officer on the post.

On a visit to her family in Boston, Margaret is questioned.

You're not planning any children yet?

No, I don't think so, she laughs. I'm afraid to. Edward would probably have him scrubbing the bassinette.

Don't you think seven years now is a long time?

Oh, it is, I suppose. I really don't know.

It's not a good idea to wait too long.

Margaret sighs. Men are very odd, positively odd. You always think they're one thing and they turn out to be another.

Her aunt purses her thin mouth. I've always felt, Margaret, that you'd have done better to have married someone we know.

That's an awfully stuffy idea. Edward is going to be a great general. All we need is a war, and I'll feel just like Josephine.

(The shrewd look.) There's no need to be flippant, Margaret. I had expected that marriage in all this time might have made you more . . . womanly. It isn't wise to marry someone about whom you know nothing, and I've always suspected that you married Edward for precisely that reason. (The significant pause.) Ruth, Thatcher's wife, is carrying a third child.

(Margaret is angry.) I wonder if I shall be as dirty as you when I'm as old.

I'm afraid you'll always be *pungent*, my dear.

At the officers' dance on Saturday night, Margaret gets drunk a little more frequently. There are times when an indiscretion is not too far away.

Captain, I see you're all alone, one of the officers' ladies remarks.

Yes, I'm afraid I'm a little too old-fashioned. The war and . . . (Her husband has been commissioned after 1918.) One of my more recurrent regrets is that I never learned to dance well. (His manner, which is to set him off from other professional officers, is beginning in these years.)

Your wife does.

Yes. (At the other end of the officers' club, Margaret is the center of a circle of men. She is laughing loudly now, her hand on the sleeve of a second lieutenant's blouse.) He stares across at her with loathing and disgust.

From Webster's: *hatred*, n., strong aversion or detestation; settled ill will or malevolence.

A thread in most marriages, growing dominant in Cummings's.

The cold form of it. No quarrels. No invective.

He is all application now, all study. At night, in the parlor of the succession of post houses in which they live, he reads five or six nights a week. There is all the education he has missed, and he takes giant strides in recouping it. There is philosophy first, and then political science, sociology, psychology, history, even literature and art. He absorbs it all with the fantastic powers of memory and assimilation he can exhibit at times, absorbs it and immediately transmutes it into something else, satisfies the dominant warp of his mind.

It comes out a little in the infrequent intellectual discussions he can find on an Army post. I find Freud rather stimulating, he says. The idea is that man is a worthless bastard, and the only problem is how best to control him.

In 1931 Spengler is particularly congenial. To his company he makes short cautious talks.

I don't have to tell you men how bad things are. Some of you are in the Army for just that reason. But I want to point out that we may have an important function. If you read the papers you see where troops are being called out everywhere. There may be a great many changes, and your duty in such a case will be to obey the orders of the government as they come down through me.

The plans, not quite defined, never put to paper, dissolve at last. By 1934 Major Cummings is far more interested in foreign news.

I tell you that Hitler is not a flash in the pan, he will argue. He has the germ of an idea, and moreover you've got to give him political credit. He plays on the German people with consummate skill. That Siegfried business is fundamental to them.

In 1935 Cummings is remembered for making some innovations at the Infantry School in Fort Benning.

In '36 he is considered the most promising field officer of the year at the War College in Washington. And he makes a little ripple in Washington society, becomes friendly with a few congressmen, meets the most important hostess in town. For a while he is in danger of becoming Military Adviser to Washington Society.

But always he is branching out. The confusions, the cross-impulses are concealed now, buried under the concentration with which he works. On a thirty-day leave in the summer of '37 he pays a visit to his brother-in-law, who is vacationing in Maine. They have become very friendly during Cummings's tour of duty in Washington.

On one of the afternoons in a sailboat:

You know, I've always disagreed with the family, Edward. Through no fault of your own they've never entirely approved of you. I think their backward attitude is a little distressing, but of course you understand it.

I think I do, Minot. (There is this other network of emotions and ambitions which recurs now and then. The ineffable perfection of Boston, which had beckoned him, leaves him always curiously satisfied yet troubled. He has traded on Boston in Washington, he knows cynically, aware of himself, but there is still the attraction and the uncertainty.)

His speech sounds florid in his ears. Margaret has been mighty fine about it all.

Wonderful woman, that sister of mine.

Yes.

I think it a shame I didn't know you very well years ago. You really would have fitted into the department. I've watched you develop, Edward; I think, when the occasion demands, you have as much perception and tact, you grasp the core of a situation as quickly as any man I know. It's a pity it's too late now.

I think sometimes I might have been good at it, Cummings agrees. But you know I'll be lieutenant colonel in a year or two, and after that I'm free of seniority. It might be a little impolitic to brag, but I should make colonel within a year after.

Mmm. You don't speak French, do you?

A fair amount. I learned some over there in '17, and I've kept up with it since.

The brother-in-law fingers his chin. You know, Edward, I suppose it's one of the laws of government, but there are always many points of view in a department. I'll tell you, I've been wondering if you couldn't be sent on a little joust to France, in your capacity as an officer of course. Nothing official.

What about, Minot?

Oh, it's nebulous. A few talks here and there. An element in the department is attempting to change our Spain policy. I don't think they're going to succeed but it would be disastrous if they should, be tantamount to handing Gibraltar to the Russians. What worries me is France. So long as they stay on the fence I don't think there's a chance of our trying anything by ourselves.

I'm to keep them on the fence?

Nothing so big as that. I've got some assurances, some financial contracts which might put a little pressure in the proper places. The thing to remember is that everyone in France can be bought, none of them has clean hands.

I wonder if I could get away.

We're sending a military mission to France and Italy. I can work it through the War Department. I'll have quite a briefing to give you, but that should give you no trouble.

I'm very interested, Cummings says. The problems of manipulation . . . He trails off, not finishing the sentence.

The water slaps past, resolves itself again behind the stern, quietly, softly, like a cat grooming its fur. Beyond the catboat the sunlight is scattered over the bay, tinkling upon the water.

We might as well put back, the brother-in-law says.

The shore line is wooded, olive-green, a pristine cove.

I never get over this, he says to Cummings. I still expect to see Indians in the forest. Pure country, Maine.

The office is smaller than he has expected, more leathery, somehow more greasy. The map of France is covered with pencil smudges, and a corner is folded over like a dog-eared book.

I must apologize for this place, the man says. (His accent is negligible, a certain preciseness of speech perhaps.) When you first suggested the nature of our business I thought it perhaps best to meet here, not that there should be anything clandestine, but you would attract attention at the Bourse. There are spies everywhere.

I understand. It's been difficult to see you. The party we know suggested Monsieur de Vernay, but I think he is a little too far away to judge.

You state there are credits?

More than enough. I must emphasize that this is not official. There is a tacit agreement . . .

Tacit? Tacit?

An understanding with Leeway Chemical that they will invest in such French firms as *he* thinks advisable. There is no *chou* involved. (He wonders if the slang is correct.) A legitimate business arrangement, but the profits I think are large enough to benefit Sallevoisseux Frères, and enable you to conduct any *adjustments* which might be necessary.

On s'arrangera.

I would have to know some further details of course on the processes you will employ.

Ah, Major Cummings, I can assure you of the vote of twenty-five members of the Chamber of Deputies.

I think it would be best if it didn't come to a vote. There are other ways.

I do not believe I may disclose my routes of access.

(The core of the situation.) Monsieur Sallevoisseux, a man of your . . . vision can see certainly that an enterprise of the magnitude which Leeway Chemical is proposing would demand something more concrete on your part. The decision to set up a subsidiary in France has been taken for some years; it is a question of who will get it. I have with me, subject to the necessary financial guarantees on your part, the power to consolidate with Sallevoisseux Frères. If you cannot give me more definite assurances I will be obliged unfortunately to deal in other channels which I am investigating at present.

I should regret that, Major Cummings.

I should regret it myself.

Sallevoisseux twists in the chair, stares out the high narrow window at the cobblestones in the street below. The horns of the French automobiles sound high-pitched to Cummings.

There are routes. For example—I will give the assurances, the documents, the introductions afterward—for example, I have friends in Les Cagoulards who can influence certain firms, not Chemical, by virtue of some tasks they have performed for them in the past. These firms in turn could if necessary control the decision of a bloc of seventy-five deputies. (He raises his hand.) I know you prefer it does not come to a vote, but no man may control that for you. I can free the vote of any uncertainty. Many of these deputies can influence members of the Ministry.

He pauses. These politics are complicated.

I understand them.

There are several Radical Socialists high-placed in the Foreign Department whom I may influence. I know from a service that there is information to be bought about them. They will be amiable. There are journalists by the dozen, several men in the Bank of France whose *dossiers intimes* I possess. A block of Socialists is controlled by a labor leader with whom I have an understanding. These routes, all indirect, mount up, create a necessary dispersion. You must realize I am not working alone. I can assure you that nothing will be done for eighteen months; beyond that history is involved, and no man may divert it indefinitely.

They talk for several hours, work out the first terms of the agreement.

As he leaves, Cummings smiles. What we're doing is really in the long run what is best for France and America.

Sallevoisseux smiles also. Of course, Major Cummings. A peculiarly American statement, do you know?

You'll show me the dossiers you possess at hand. Tomorrow, is that right?

D'accord!

A month later, his part in the assignment completed, Cummings moves down to Rome. A telegram reaches him from his brother-in-law.

Preliminary dispositions satisfactory. Very well done. Congratulations.

He talks to an Italian colonel as part of the military mission.

I would like you to see, Signor Maggiore, our work on the problems of dysentery in the successful African campaign. We have discovered a new series of sanitary measures 73% more effective in avoiding the dreadful, the malign propensities of such a disease.

The summer heat is stifling. Despite the lecture by the Italian Colonel he suffers from diarrhea, and is plagued by a severe cold. He spends a miserable week in bed, abysmally tired. A letter follows from his brother-in-law.

I think it's a shame to ruin the understandable elation you must be feeling now after such a neat job in Paris, but there's something I really ought to tell you. Margaret, you know, has been down in Washington with me for the past two weeks, and to put it as kindly as possible, she has been acting very odd. There's a certain abandonment about her which is not proper to her age; I must confess I find it hard to believe she is my sister at times. If it were not for you, I would have told her to leave my house. I'm really awfully disturbed to ruin what must be a vacation in Rome, but I think if you can it might not be a bad idea to be thinking of coming back. Do see Monsignor Truffenio and give him my regards.

This time it is a tired hatred. I just hope she keeps it quiet he swears to himself. He has a nightmare that evening, waking up on a fever-ridden bed. He thinks of his father for the first time in a year or two, remembers his death a few years ago and relives a little of the anxiety it had caused him. After midnight he gets up on an impulse and walks the streets, ending up in an alley where he becomes drunk in a bar.

There is a little man pawing him. Signor Maggiore you come home with me now?

He staggers along dimly aware of what he wants, but he does not find it. In another alley the little man and a confederate jump him, strip his pockets, and leave him to awaken in the harsh glare, the quick stench of the sun on a garbage-filled alley in Rome. He makes it back to his hotel without too many people seeing him, changes his clothes, takes a bath, and goes to bed for over a day. He feels as if he is breaking apart.

I must confess, your Reverence, that I have admired the Church for many years. In the immensity of your conception lies your greatness.

The Cardinal bows his head. I am pleased to give you an audience, my son. You have done good work already. I have heard of your labors in Paris against the Antichrist.

I labored for my country. (In this setting the words cause him no embarrassment.)

There is a nobler labor.

I am aware of it, your Reverence . . . There are times when I feel a great weariness.

You may be preparing for an important change.

Sometimes I think so. I've always looked upon your Church with admiration.

He walks through the great courtyard of the Vatican, stares for a long time at the dome of St. Peter's. The ceremony he has just heard has moved him, sent music lapping through his brain.

Maybe I should turn.

But on the boat going back he thinks of other things, reads with quiet satisfaction in the newspaper he has brought on board that Leeway Chemical is opening negotiations with Sallevoisseux Frères.

Man, I'll be glad to get back from frog-land and the wops, one of the officers who has been on the mission says to him.

Yes.

That Italy's a backward country even if they say Musso did a lot for it. You can still keep it. The Catholic countries are the ones who are always backward.

I suppose so.

He thinks clearly for a few minutes. The thing that happened in the Rome alley is a danger sign, and he will have to be very careful from now on. It must never come out again. The Church business is understandable in its light, a highly impractical move at this juncture. *I'll be a colonel soon. I can't risk it turning.*

Cummings sighs. I've learned a lot.

Yeah, me too.

Cummings looks at the water. Slowly his eyes raise, include the horizon. Lieutenant colonel . . . colonel . . . brigadier . . . major general . . . lieutenant general . . . general?

If there's a war soon it'll help.

But afterward. The politicos were even more important. After the war . . .

He must not commit himself politically yet. There would be too many turns. It might be Stalin, it might be Hitler. But the eventual line to power in America would always be anticommunism.

He must keep his eyes open, Cummings decided.

QUESTIONS

1. What are the components of the "Education of Sam Croft"?
2. Why did Sam shoot a man during the oil strike? What prejudices, if any, does he have against the union men?
3. What goes wrong with Sam's marriage to Janey?
4. What is the influence of his father's drinking on Gallagher? How does this help to foster a kind of unrealistic idealism? How does Gallagher try to play out idealistic roles in his courtship of Mary?
5. Why is Gallagher so hostile to Harvard students? Why does he think they are all "fairies"? What social class would you put him in?
6. What is it that originally attracts Gallagher to the city's Democratic Party organization? What is even more appealing about the CU?

7. Why did Mailer subtitle his portrait of General Cummings "A Peculiarly American Statement"? Near the end of the portrait Cummings says to a Frenchman, "What we're doing is really in the long run what is best for France and America." Why does the Frenchman reply, "A peculiarly American statement"?

8. Can Cummings's obsessive need of power be explained at all by his relationship with his parents? How is his relationship with his mother left unresolved?

9. How is Margaret a different type of woman from Cummings's mother? What typical problems does Mailer suggest exist in the sexual relationship between Cummings and Margaret? What does each substitute for their failed sexual relationship?

10. What does Cummings really think of the Army? His fellow-officers? Hitler?

11. Compare the childhood of Croft, Cummings, and Gallagher. Who was the most deprived? Who had the most advantages?

DAN WAKEFIELD

GOING ALL THE WAY (1970) is Dan Wakefield's (b. 1932) first novel, although he has written many essays, articles, and reviews. The book is about two young men, Sonny Burns and Gunner Casselman, who have returned home from the Korean War to their families in Indianapolis. They have completed college, but have not yet decided on their occupations. Before meeting Gunner, Sonny, through whose perspective we see the action, thought he would become a newspaper photographer, settle down in Indianapolis, and marry his old girlfriend, Buddie Porter. On the train home Sonny wonders when his "real life" will begin. Then he meets Gunner, who is everything Sonny has always wanted to be—football hero, fraternity president, successful lover. But Gunner rejects all these accomplishments. Because of his exposure to Japanese culture while in the service, he has become a strange animal, a Midwesterner in the Age of Eisenhower who is dissatisfied with his "life style." Sonny and Gunner become friends and see each other continually over the hot, humid, Indiana summer.

The entire novel, especially this episode, is permeated with a feeling of the '50's. It may be hard to believe how structured social institutions were just a decade or so ago—dating patterns, political opinions, even ways of having fun. For every situation there is a prescribed way to act, and Sonny feels that he is constantly falling below these standards of behavior. Wakefield documents hundreds of Sonny's insecurities—and we identify with many of them.

But the overriding insecurity, of course, is sex. In this episode Gunner sets Sonny up with Gail, a blind date. The kinds of dancing they do, the talk they make, even Sonny's sexual fantasies are all of a bygone era. Yet the psychological bind Sonny finds himself in is an age-old problem. To understand it we have to know something about Sonny's parents. His father is a dull businessman who has completely surrendered all domestic power to Sonny's mother: "Somewhere along the line, some years back, Mr. Burns seemed to have turned his emotions down to low, like the barest flame you could get on a gas burner before it went out altogether. That way you didn't feel much, one way or the other; the decrease of joy was maybe compensated by the decrease of pain." Not surprisingly, Mrs. Burns, a woman with great resources of hysterical energy, turns her attention to Sonny. When Sonny returns from Korea, he finds himself idling, accepting money from his mother, getting fat on her cooking, and generally increasing his emotional dependence on her. Clearly Sonny's insipid relationship with Buddie Porter (the name is almost asexual) does not challenge the primacy of his bond with his mother.

Sonny is now bored with Buddie; he has always wanted—and never had—sexual intercourse with a girl he greatly desires. Gail fits this description, but, even though it is only a first date and probably would ultimately result in no more than a superficial encounter, he cannot help but wonder whether he has found the Great Girl. He suddenly decides that he loves her. But, unfortunately, because he has an Oedipal fixation with his mother, he is impotent. Explained in the language of today, Sonny's inability to "get it up" is caused by his inability to "get it together"—that is, to combine his sexual desire with his feelings of affection. He can allow himself only very little sexual pleasure—as with a girl like Buddie—or he must degrade his erotic object (something he has not yet tried). Otherwise, sex would be too much like "going all the way" with his mother. It is all revealed in his comment to Gail: "I love you, but I want to go to bed with you."

Sonny's reflection about the constitutional right of every American to engage in the "pursuit of happiness" takes on great poignancy. The cards are stacked against him; he cannot advance towards his conception of happiness without stirring up great conflicts in himself. Most people don't discover their problems quite so dramatically as Sonny. Perhaps Sonny's father remained in exactly the same prison all his life without being aware of it. Sonny, however, has begun to learn who he really is.

[FROM Going All the Way]

On the way home Gunner mentioned casually that Marty had a girl friend from college coming in for the weekend, and wondered if Sonny'd like to be fixed up with her. Marty said the girl was pretty sexy-looking and wasn't short on brains, either. Sonny said sure, very casual, just as if such opportunities came along all the time. Gunner said the date would be for Saturday night, and then if Sonny liked the girl, they could all do something on Sunday, too. If *he* liked the girl. Sonny could only think about whether the girl would like *him*. He didn't even know her but he was already worried.

Sonny tried to work himself into a casual mood as he got dressed for the date on Saturday night. In the shower he sang "Bye, Bye, Blackbird" at the top of his voice, and after he got out and dried he slapped Old Spice After Shave Lotion all over himself with stinky abandon. Casual him. Devil may care. But beneath the loud, jaunty singing and the smell of Old Spice, he was terrified by the thought that his date might really be a great sexy girl and he would ruin everything. He tried to comfort himself with the thought that she wouldn't really be smart or sexy at all and there wouldn't be anything to be nervous about. But it wasn't usual for a girl to describe another girl as "sexy-looking" to a guy she was fixing her up with. Marty, of course, was sophisticated, and there was the possibility she really meant it and the girl was really sexy-looking. There was always that possibility. You knew there was no possibility at all when a girl tried to fix you up with a friend and described her by saying she had "real personality" or, even worse, was "loads of fun." It there was one thing Sonny couldn't stand, it was a girl who was "loads of fun." That meant she was homely and plain and hated sex and tried to make up for it by talking a blue streak and faking a lot of laughs and suggesting "fun" things to do like why don't we all go to the zoo and feed peanuts to the polar bears. Girls who were loads of fun always loved to go to the zoo. You couldn't lay a hand on them in the fucking zoo.

The deal for the evening was that they all were going to have dinner at the Italian Village Restaurant, and then go dancing out at Westlake. That was a very sexy plan if you had a good date; it showed you could have a real sophisticated evening in Indianapolis. Sonny put on a new sport coat his mother had bought him at Medallion Men's Wear—a plaid number—and a pair of white-linen slacks that were tight in the waist but

From GOING ALL THE WAY by Dan Wakefield. Copyright © 1970 by Dan Wakefield. A Seymour Lawrence Book/Delacorte Press. Reprinted by permission of the publisher.

looked debonair as hell, a sharp, thin black knit tie, and his old white bucks. He looked himself over in the mirror and judged the whole outfit to be pretty damned sharp, but goddam if he didn't have a pimple on the end of his nose. It seemed like whenever anything important was going to happen he sprouted a big ugly pimple on the end of his nose. He squeezed it, but instead of breaking, it just became redder and more clownish-looking. He put some of his mother's pancake makeup on it, and that helped a little. It wasn't so red then, it just looked flaky and cruddy.

The pimple really depressed Sonny, because that was one thing he thought would stop happening when his real life began—getting a goddam pimple on the end of his nose at a crucial time. But there it was again, blooming right on the end of his nose, even though he was a college graduate and a veteran of the U.S. Army. He guessed he would probably have a fucking pimple on the end of his nose the day he died, and they would have to spread pancake makeup over it when they fixed him up for the casket display. People would pass by and say, "My, he looks natural—he even has a pimple on the end of his nose." Sonny suspected he'd be able to hear them say it, too, even though he wouldn't be able to talk back. They probably had it rigged up that way for you in hell, so you could hear the last shitty comments and not be able to reply.

Sonny was getting himself in a terrible state, and he was thankful that Gunner picked him up early so they had time to stop at the Key for a drink. Sonny had two seven-and-sevens while Gunner drank a beer, and he wished he had even more when Gunner told him the unexpected good news.

"We got the house to ourselves," Gunner revealed. "Marty's folks are gone for the weekend."

Sonny had to take his hand off the drink to keep the glass from rattling. "Terrific," he said.

"Here's the plan. When we get back from Westlake, we'll hit the den and shoot the shit there for a while. Then Marty 'n I'll slip upstairs to the bedroom. You and the babe'll have the den. You know—I mean, if you want to make out with her."

Gunner said it as if it would be Sonny's decision to make, according to his own whim. He said it so matter-of-factly that Sonny actually felt a little cocky, like he was a regular make-out artist.

"Great," he said, nodding at Gunner. "That couch in the den looks real nice and cushiony."

Gunner slapped him on the back and said, "I recommend it highly, ole buddy," and both of them broke up laughing, just like a couple of cocksmen planning to knock off their piece for the night. The movie in Sonny's mind showed a couple of hooded, desert marauders riding down on the tents of the frightened, waiting women. He even forgot about the pimple on the end of his nose.

Marty's college girl friend was Gail Thayer, from Cincinnati. To Sonny's astonishment and terror, she was a goddam dream. Maybe not everybody's dream, but Sonny's. She was tiny and dark, with glossy black hair and big greenish-gray eyes and perfect white teeth circled by a lush little mouth with lipstick that was deep dark red. She had on a plain gold sleeveless dress with an emerald pin that looked like a bug, crawling up her tit. She wore white heels and sleek, seamless nylons. Sonny loved to see women in stockings, but it depressed the hell out of him when they had the seams crooked or were loose and all wrinkled up around the ankles. That ruined everything. But Gail's were just right, glistening tight against her legs, like a shiny second skin that could be peeled off.

Marty proposed they all have a drink before taking off for dinner, and Sonny silently blessed her. The carefree, cocksman feeling he had worked up before over drinks with Gunner had completely crumbled when he got a load of Gail. His date. Oh, God, *his* date. Holy shit. He couldn't speak or think, but luckily Gunner had sparked a nice casual conversation as he mixed a batch of martinis. Sonny was only vaguely aware of Gunner smiling and handing him a glass, but after a couple of deep slugs he was able to tune in to the story his buddy was telling. Evidently when Gunner heard Gail was from Cincy he had launched into a hilarious account of how Shortley had played Withers High of Cincinnati in his junior year and got their ass racked.

"We were undefeated going into that ball game," Gunner was explaining. "But we knew Withers had been the state champs of Ohio the year before and had fourteen returning lettermen. We were scared shitless, but tried not to let on. The coach could tell we were shaking in our goddam cleats, though, and he gave us this fiery pep talk, you know, like in the movie of the Big Game. Our coach was this guy Herman E. 'Nails' Nedrick, and he talked like Pat O'Brien playing Knute Rockne, you know, and he finished up the talk saying 'Men—'" Gunner stood up and pointed a menacing finger, imitating Herman E. "Nails" Nedrick, making his voice deep and bellowing just like "Nails" used to do it, and said, " 'Men, you may have heard a lot about how tough these Withers guys are, but *Men*, I'll tell you something right now and I want you to remember it. . . .' "

"Well," Gunner said in his regular voice, "we're all holding our breath and waiting for the big scoop, and 'Nails' says"—now Gunner made the deep imitation voice again—" 'Those Withers guys put their pants on the same as you do—*one leg at a time!*' "

Everybody broke up, Gunner included, and he sat back down, holding his stomach. He was great at telling those old high-school stories and making them sound funny as hell, like they were funny kid stuff that everyone had grown out of years ago, so everyone liked to laugh not just because Gunner told it funny but because it made you feel more mature and sophisticated to see how funny all that kid stuff had been. The girls laughed beautifully, throwing their heads back, and Gail asked in a tinkly, light voice, "What happened? What happened *then?*"

"We got slaughtered," Gunner said, smiling, "fifty-two to nothing."

Everyone laughed again, and Marty rubbed her hand on the back of Gunner's neck, scruffing up his hair a little.

"My hero," she said, making a fake sigh of awe. She was sort of pulling Gunner down to her, but he straightened up, pointed to Sonny, and said with great interest, "Hey, man, did you go to that one, the Withers game?"

"Not that one," Sonny said.

"Sonny was our ace photographer," Gunner said, turning to Gail, making it sound like a very big deal.

"Oh?" she asked, raising her eyebrows and looking fascinated as hell.

"Hell, yes, he shot all the action stuff of the games. Great stuff."

"Well, I made some trips," Sonny said modestly, "with the team." Catching Gunner's conversational lead, tossed like a perfectly pinpointed pass, Sonny grinned and said, "Hey, Gunner, you remember the trip to South Bend, senior year, to play South Bend Central, when the bus broke down and Herman E. 'Nails' Nedrick had everybody change into their uniforms on the bus and gave his pep talk about how 'The Game Must Go On,' and guys were getting their gear all mixed up and climbing all over each other like a Laurel and Hardy movie?"

Gunner gave a great guffaw and said, "Hey, that was fabulous, but I can't remember it all. You tell it."

"What happened?" asked Gail, as if she were totally enthralled.

Sonny told the story, making it as good as he could and throwing in some stuff that didn't even happen to make it funnier. Everybody laughed—led by Gunner—at the right places, and when Sonny finished telling it, he felt like a million. He wasn't clutched up at all, even with that sexy little babe fixing her misty, greenish-gray eyes on him like he was someone terrific. He hadn't even got tongue-tied or showed he was nervous, and it gave him the light, floating sensation that maybe now, maybe at last, his real life was actually beginning. The way it was supposed to be.

When they all piled into Gunner's car to go to the Italian Village to eat, Gail sat sort of in the middle of the back seat so that when Sonny got in he was right next to her, and it made him feel tremendous. He really hated it when a girl hugged the door. The loads-of-fun girls always did it, and the sexy ones did it if they didn't like you. It was a way of telling you without using words, "O.K., Buster, you stay on your side and I'll stay on my side, just keep your distance." When they did that it really depressed the shit out of Sonny. It made him feel like a fucking leper. But here was this great little sexy Gail, so close that her bare, sun-tanned shoulder was touching him, and he could smell the sharp tang of her perfume.

At the Italian Village, where they had red-checked tablecloths and drippy candles, Sonny drank a lot of wine and talked with great ease, but he only picked at his food. Whenever he was sexed up he didn't feel hungry; it was like the two things didn't go together. He just ate enough to make it look as if he were eating like a normal person, but he didn't actually taste anything.

It was a fresh, starry night and the roof was rolled back at the Westlake dance pavilion, which made for a great make-out atmosphere. There was a roof that they could roll over the dance pavilion if the weather was bad, and there were imitation clouds and stars set up in the roof, but it wasn't as good as the real job. Everyone ordered drinks, and the first time Sonny went out on the dance floor he put his right arm around Gail's tiny waist and she melted right into him. None of that stiff, plenty-of-space-between business that the loads-of-fun girls gave you. This was the real thing, the thing that made it worthwhile for a guy to go through all the crap of taking a girl to a dance. There was a good band that played a lot of slow, sexy stuff, and they even had a vocalist, a guy named Harry Henneman who used to play a little ball at Shortley but never made the team at Butler University and dropped out of school to become a crooner. He would never replace Frank Sinatra, but he sang the good, sexy ones like "The night is like a lovely tuuuuuuuuuuuuuune, Beware, my foolish heart. . . ."

He threw in a lot of warbly effects and did the whispery numbers with his eyes closed and his head bent back like he either was shooting his wad or had wrenched his spine. Sonny had a hell of a hard-on and Gail was moving her thighs against it so blatantly and beautifully that Sonny was afraid he might come right there on the dance floor, spoiling his debonair white-linen slacks. Once in high school that actually happened to him—his wad had blasted off right when he was dancing that way with Penny Sampleton, who was crawling all over him and secretly licking him in the ear. After the dance they parked and Penny cried and said she felt dirty for having such dirty feelings, and Sonny took her home. Later he heard she became a nurse and married a guy from Manual-Tech who drove stock cars and played the vibes.

Luckily the band broke into a mambo just when Sonny was afraid he was about to shoot it, and he said they'd better sit down. He confessed to not knowing the mambo and Gail said she didn't mind, but while it was playing, she snapped her fingers and wiggled her head to the rhythm, like she really wanted to be doing it, and that got Sonny a little depressed, but he tried not to let on and ordered another drink. Gunner said he didn't know the mambo either, but he and Marty got out on the dance floor and tilted around, looking to Sonny like a couple of experts. Around midnight Gunner said he thought they ought to shag the place, which was fine with Sonny, not only because he was tired of dancing but also because he'd about run through the last of the money his mother had given him buying seven-and-sevens for himself and Tom Collinses for Gail.

In the car going back Gail leaned her head against Sonny's shoulder and he put his arm around her with firm manliness but didn't try to kiss her. That was kid stuff, just kissing, when you had a house to go to where no one was home and there was plenty to drink. Sonny felt as confident as Roger the Lodger, the guy in the limerick who did it with the Old Lady from Cape Cod. By God.

Everyone went to the den when they got back to Marty's, and Gunner made drinks while Marty put on one of those hot Spanish gypsy records —the kind where they're all stamping their feet and it sounds like everybody's getting their rocks off about every two minutes. Sonny figured maybe that's why the Spanish were known as a "hot-blooded" people, the way they sang and danced like they all were shooting their wads.

Sonny sat down on the couch and Gail settled beside him, pulling off her shoes and tucking her feet in underneath herself. She leaned back, not touching Sonny, but making herself touchable. He casually slung his arm up on the back of the couch, not actually touching her but getting himself in position. After Gunner passed the drinks around, he flopped in one of the easy chairs and Marty curled up on his lap. Gunner told a couple good stories, a nice mix of high-school football and Japanese religion, and then Marty nestled down closer to him, pressing her mouth on his ear, and Gunner cleared his throat and said he and Marty were going upstairs for a while and everyone should make themselves at home. He gave a little look to Sonny, a look that said, "O.K., man, do your stuff," but wasn't too obvious or embarrassing. A lot of guys would go out of the room with some cornball wink or terrible joke like telling the girl, "Be careful, that guy's horny!" or something that would ruin everything for you, but Gunner wasn't like that, he made Sonny feel like he really did hope he made out.

Sonny was alone in the dimly lit room with Gail, and the passionate gypsy music was building to another climax. He got up and poured more whiskey in his glass, then sat back down and tried to think of something to talk about for a while. He wanted to talk some more before trying anything, so he would feel more sure of her wanting him to do it. They had already, at dinner and at the dance, got through the usual crap about what did you major in and what are you going to do (she majored in English and wanted to get an Interesting Job), plus the kind of extras you throw in like Do you remember what you were doing when you were a kid and Franklin D. Roosevelt died, and how older people didn't understand *The Catcher in The Rye* either because things had changed so much since they were kids or else they didn't remember, and how Adlai Stevenson was a brilliant man but seemed too wishy-washy for most people to trust him being a great leader; all the preliminary shit.

Sonny had really enjoyed the preliminary shit with Gail, though, because she seemed so feminine and sexy and impressed by his opinions, and looked him right in the eyes, and ran her tongue over her lips a lot, and laughed whenever he said something he meant to be funny. He gulped the hot solace of his new drink, thinking, Oh, God, oh, Jesus, maybe this is It, The Answer, the Great Girl who will make everything O.K., the perfect combination of sex and intelligence that every man is supposed to find, that is his rightful due, as stated by the United States Constitution itself, which promised Life, Liberty, and the Pursuit of Happiness, making it an actual law that was right on the books! Sonny sometimes wondered if the catch was in the word "pursuit" of happiness; suspected that the acquisition of it wasn't really promised, just the chase, and that you might have to keep pursuing it until you keeled over and couldn't even sue the government for your rightful share.

"Do you really think you might go to New York?" Gail asked. Sonny had been talking big about the GI Bill and him and Gunner maybe going to Columbia and getting interesting jobs in New York. Gail had said she was going there herself in the fall, maybe to look for a job in a publishing house, which her background in English qualified her for, and so Sonny had been more positive about the possibility of New York than he actually felt; but with the saying it he began to believe it. A whole life had bloomed in his mind, with him and Gunner and Marty and Gail having a youthful, sexy, fascinating life in New York, skipping hand in hand as a foursome down the Great White Way, like in those color musical movies about backstage life on Broadway, where people from little towns lived on spaghetti and wine in the basements of the big city until they were discovered and became great stars with their name in lights.

"New York is really the only place, when you get right down to it," Sonny said. "Don't you think?"

"Well, there's San Francisco, they say."

"I guess. But it's not New York."

"No," she sighed, "it's not," nestling closer against Sonny. He guzzled down the rest of his new drink and got up to pour some more.

"You like some more?" he asked.

Gail shook her head and got out a cigarette. When Sonny sat back down, she put her hand on his knee and whispered, "You won't drink too much, will you?"

"Oh, no," he said and laughed. "I got a large capacity."

"I'm having such a wonderful time," she said.

Sonny gulped so much from his glass that he almost choked.

He rubbed at his eyes and said, "Jesus, me too."

"I'm glad."

Sonny took another burning swig of the whiskey and said, "You know, really, I'd like to tell you something."

"Yes?"

She looked up into his eyes, and he inhaled her dizzy perfume.

"Well, what I want to say is, you're—" He took another fiery gulp, then set down his glass. "Fantastic," he said. "I mean, Jesus, you're everything, you're incredible, I never knew anyone. I'd do anything for you. I'd—"

She drew her head back off his shoulder and said, "You don't even know me."

"Yes I do! No kidding, I mean, I know what I feel, I feel—I don't know how to explain it. Everything."

"Shhh," she said and put a finger very gently on Sonny's mouth. She moved her own mouth up to about a hair's distance of his, and he leaned down just a little and tasted her lipstick, like some wonderfully sour jam, and then he put both his arms around her and they were kissing, really kissing, her sharp little tongue flicking at his teeth and in between them, and he started mashing his left hand all over her firm little tits and then reached down and felt her ass and she cuddled into him, biting at his lips, digging her nails in the back of his neck, and he suddenly pulled away.

"What's the matter?" she asked, her eyes searching.

"I have to go to the bathroom," he said.

He had been scared shitless he was going to come, and he felt if he could only take a piss he could get a new start. Gail moved back and primped some of the hair into place that was falling in her eyes.

"Oh," she said coolly.

"I didn't mean—"

"Go ahead, for God sake!"

Sonny got up and went to the downstairs bathroom. After he pissed he looked at himself in the mirror and brushed his hand through his messed-up hair. Most of the pancake stuff was rubbed off his nose, leaving the pimple red and sore-looking, with awful brown flakes from the makeup around it. He figured anything he did would only make it worse, and he just washed his hands and tried not to think about his nose. When he went back to the den he poured more booze in his glass and sat down. Gail had turned the gypsy record over and the fucking Spaniards were stamping and yelping again.

"I'm sorry," Sonny said.

"About what?"

"That I had to go to the bathroom."

"Don't be *sorry*," she said, kind of disgusted.

Sonny felt panicky, like he was in a bad dream where he did and said all the wrong things and couldn't stop. He had done all this before with girls he liked, practically slobbered over them until they demanded to be taken home, and he couldn't understand what had happened, why they didn't accept his trembling declarations of love, but now it was worse because he knew he was doing the wrong thing, saying the wrong thing, but he couldn't stop, couldn't break out of the nightmare he was making for himself on the spot. He wanted to explain but it was too complicated, and he reached out and took Gail's hands in his own.

"Listen," he said, "I wish I could make you understand. I love you, I am hopelessly and madly in love with you."

She closed her eyes and said, "Get me a drink."

Sonny jumped up and fixed the drink, and when he placed it in her hands, he said, "Here, darling."

He sat down and lit a cigarette, trying to steady himself. He knew he should be like Richard Widmark, or at least like Gunner, and say he wanted to screw her whether she liked it or not and hump her like a goddam maddened stallion, fucking her senseless.

"I'm sorry I said that stuff," he whispered. "I shouldn't have said it. About being in love with you and everything. But it's true. I'm sorry, but it's true."

She took a healthy swallow of her own drink, which Sonny had made strong as hell, and said in a very even, quiet tone, "If you don't stop being sorry, I'm going to scream."

"I'm—" He stopped himself and wavered up to slosh some more booze in his glass. He spilled some, and it dripped down his debonair white-linen slacks.

"You're drunk," she said.

"I'm not!" Sonny shouted, and he felt that was true, or partly true. The part that made his hands shake and made the room waver and her face go fuzzy right before his eyes was drunk, but somewhere, below all that, some part of himself saw everything soberly clear.

"Listen," he said, trying desperately to talk from that sober clear center of himself, "I love you, but I want to go to bed with you."

As soon as he said it, he realized the two things sounded contradictory, which maybe in awful fact they were, in his own body and mind.

"To bed?" she asked, with a mocking wide-eyed imitation of innocence. Her hand that was holding the drink dipped and some of the whiskey dripped in her lap.

Sonny wanted to say yes, to fuck, but what he said was "So we can have sexual intercourse."

She giggled, and he stared down into the warm brown hell of his drink.

Gail finished off her own drink and stood up, wobbling a little.

"All right," she said, and reached her hand in back of her neck. There was the sound of the zipper being glided down, and she pulled the dress up over her head and dropped it in a lump to the floor. She stood there looking at Sonny in her bra and panties and seamless stockings, just like the sexy babes in the jack-off magazines, but she was there, real, in the flesh, reachable and—oh, Holy God—fuckable. She burped, giggled, and then unhooked the stockings from the garters and rolled them down and off, teetering and swaying, flinging each stocking away with an ironic, stagy flair. They fell slowly, like punctured, long balloons.

"Well," she asked with a sour smile, "Sexu-all Intercourse?"

Sonny started ripping at his shirt, like he was blind and crazy, tearing at himself as well as the cloth, trembling and yanking down his pants, wrenching off his shoes, pulling the socks off his feet, and in only his light-blue jockey shorts lunged at her, wrestling her down to the plush carpet. They rolled and grabbed and bit, clawed and scratched, tearing off what flimsy stuff still hid them until, panting, Gail reached between his legs and said, "Oh, God."

His cock was limp and useless.

"Listen, it'll be all right," he promised in a panting desperation. "You'll see, it will be, just wait—"

"Oh, God," she said again.

Sonny rolled away from her, mashing his face in the carpet and cursing Buddie Porter, who could make him get hard when he didn't even care, and cursing himself for not being able to get hard when he cared so much he felt it would kill him. He shut off a scream that was rising from his chest, rolled over, grabbed the girl, and pressed himself on her, biting and fumbling in a messy mixture of fear and desire, and he felt down to his unresponsive cock that was growing just a little, tauntingly halfway there, and tried to work it inside her, but it shrank back, receding inside him, and she rolled away, muffling herself face down on the carpet, her creamy little ass heaving up and down in spasms against the floor. Sonny reached out and tentatively touched the back of her neck and she jerked away in a scooting motion across the floor, lying still, and then after a while, in a flat, dry final-sounding voice, said, "Leave me alone."

Sonny thrust his right hand inside his mouth and bit down as hard as he could. He wanted to kill himself, he wanted to die.

"Please," she murmured, "go away."

Sonny jumped up in a furious, gripping panic and wrestled his clothes on, relentlessly, tearing and pulling, shoved his ridiculous feet in his shoes without any socks and blindly started for the stairway, looking for Gunner, but after he grabbed the banister he heard the steady rhythmic thump thump thump of real sex, flesh pounding on flesh, and the place where the terrible movies ran through his head lit up with a neon sign that said *Don't ruin it for everyone else,* and he turned away and fled, out of the house, into the crickety night.

He never really knew how he got the mile or so back home; only remembered falling and starting again and clutching at fences and light-posts and throwing up in somebody's yard and tossing his shoes with a dumb, quick clatter on the stone apron of a filling station, and running a barefoot, mindless, nothing-headed one-man race in which each step on anything sharp or hurting brought relief out of punishing pain, and falling, somehow, falling and finding his own single bunk of a hunk of an empty bed.

He hit the pillow and slept for a fragment of uneasy time, knocked out the way you would be if your head hit a stone. He woke with a start, wondering where he was, and much worse, who, and worse than that even, why. He reached for his cock to see if it still was there, and it was, but withdrawn, unfunctional, defeated, for all purposes dead, and Sonny came coldly awake, with a single-toned hum in his head like a note struck on a pitchfork.

He stepped quietly to the bathroom, switched on the light, and closed the door behind him. Despising the face he saw in the mirror, he yanked the mirror door open and surveyed the bottle-crammed jumbled insides of the medicine cabinet. He slipped out a packet of Gillette Blue Blades. Sponsors of sporting events. Well, there would be an event all right, he didn't know how sporting. Some said bullfighting wasn't a sport, but a ritual. A ritual of death. Kill the bull and spare yourself. Spare the rod and spoil the child. Here's the church and here's the steeple, open the doors and here's the people. Sonny unwrapped the blue-paper jacket with a picture of Mr. Gillette on it and pulled out the naked blade, flat and black. He held it in his right hand, admiring the efficient, cold beauty of it. Be razor-sharp, with Gillette. He brought his left hand toward his face, palm up, and stared with fascination at the faint tracks of the veins in his wrist. They were supposed to be blue, but they looked more like turquoise. He had never really examined them before. They seemed too delicate and small to carry the blood of a person's life. Maybe if they were severed, the rest of the blood in your body came rushing to the opening, like water flooding through a hole in the dike. Hans Brinker held his finger in the dike and saved a city. What city was it? Amsterdam, Rotterdam. Who gives a damn?

Sonny took the blade and made a slight, tentative scratch on his wrist. Enough to make blood come. Not a lot, but still real blood, surprisingly red and real. Sonny made a braver scratch, and then two or three in a row, quickly, so that little rivulets of blood began to flow together, forming a thick little puddle. It looked very beautiful, and Sonny started crying, not with any noise, just feeling the warm run of tears down his cheeks, and yet he was smiling at the same time. He started smearing the blood over his face and over the front of his torn shirt, like an Indian painting himself to prepare for a ceremony—a battle, a blessing, a death. Sonny sat down on the seat of the toilet, making a few more cuts and watching the new blood. He hadn't really hit any vein that he could tell, but the blood came sliding out, pooling, running down into his hand, and Sonny watched it with a growing sense of calm, a deepening, cleansing relief, such as he had never known. He felt it was easier to breathe, easier to live; a horrible pressure in his head had subsided.

When he understood that he was not killing himself, that he didn't intend to do that—right then, anyway—the first thing he thought of was that anyone who found out about it would think he was a chicken, a showboat searching for sympathy. He had always thought that himself about people who cut their wrists but didn't really kill themselves—they were objects of pity and contempt, poor bastards so botched that they couldn't even succeed at their own death, or so mulingly sick for attention and love they could think of no way to gain it except to fake a suicide attempt and have the scars to show it. Sonny knew a guy in college who cut his wrist a couple times and always went around afterward with a lot of Band-Aids so everyone could tell what happened, and everyone laughed at him and thought him a coward and a fraud. But now Sonny understood that cutting yourself might not have anything to do with suicide or even sympathy, that it was a very private act, a thing of its own; a self-treatment, perhaps, like the lancing of a wound—the lancing of the wound of living. And it really had helped. Maybe that's why they really did it in the Middle Ages, the bloodletting cure, administered when they didn't know what else to do. As Sonny had administered it to himself. He felt cleaner and freer than he had in a long time, but also very much afraid. He vaguely understood there were forces in him, powers and impulses he couldn't control, that might kill him yet.

He went to the sink and ran cold water on his wrist, then wrapped a lot of gauze around it and slapped big strips of adhesive tape over it, making a bulky, awkward bandage. He tiptoed to his room, closed the door, and had a cigarette. The windows were tinted with gray, the morning beginning to open and spread. Sonny was dog-tired but he didn't want to sleep. He crawled into bed and stuck his wounded arm way down under the blanket so if his mother looked in she wouldn't see. He wanted to get out of the house without running into his mother or father, but didn't want to arouse suspicion by sneaking out before they got up. They'd be going to church. He waited it out until they woke and took their turns in the bathroom and scurried off in the half-conscious, helter-skelter manner in which they drove themselves into another day. They didn't eat real breakfast; his mother would have Pepsi with ice, his father a cup of black coffee, each one standing as they poured down the individual fuel they required to begin.

When Sonny knew they were gone he quickly dressed, putting on some khakis and the satiny orange shirt with the sleeves that were too long— at last the baggy-sleeved shirt had a purpose; it would hide his bandage. He called Gunner at Marty's, waking them both from their long night of lovemaking, telling Gunner that he had to meet him somewhere, quick, somewhere they could talk alone. Gunner said his mother had gone to church and was going to a picnic afterward, so they could go to the Meadowlark.

Gunner honked outside about ten minutes later. He hadn't had time to shave and he looked gray and bleary. Sonny didn't say anything and Gunner didn't ask any questions. When they got to the apartment, Sonny said he needed a drink, and Gunner poured him a whiskey, straight.

"What is it, man?" Gunner asked gently. "What's up?"

Sonny set his drink down on the coffee table, unbuttoned his left sleeve, and rolled it back, exposing the bandage. Gunner saw what it was, and he reached out and held Sonny's hand, squeezing it hard. His eyes got that look of staring into an atom blast, and he started shaking his head and saying softly, "No, man, that's not it, that's not the way. It isn't, man, it really isn't. I tell you, no, it's not."

He stood up and started pacing back and forth, clutching his temple, saying, "We gotta do something, we gotta figure something out. We gotta get outa here."

Sonny just sat and watched him, unable to speak or think.

Gunner suddenly stopped and made the pop of his fingers. "We'll take off," he said. "We'll go on a trip. I gotta go to Chi sometime anyway, and we can stop at the lake. We'll hit the road, get some fresh air, a little sun and water."

"How?"

"I'll get the car. I told Nina I had to borrow it sometime to go to Chi, and I'll tell her I have to go now, the agency called me. We'll get the hell out of here."

"What'll I tell my folks?" Sonny asked.

"Nothing. Anything. Leave a note. Say you'll be back in a week, you went on a camping trip. They're at church now, aren't they?"

"Yes."

Gunner hustled Sonny back down to the car and roared off to the Burns' house. No one was there. Sonny sat down in the den, feeling dizzy, not sure what he was doing.

"Listen," he said, "no shit, Gunner, what'll I do?"

Gunner popped his fingers and pointed one at Sonny like a gun, and then, making it an order, he just said one emphatic, clear, irrefutable word, said it so there wasn't any question or confusion:

"*Pack!*"

QUESTIONS

1. How does Wakefield manage to evoke a feeling of the '50's? In what ways is the episode a satire of that time?
2. Does Sonny make the social forms more rigid than they are? What would be alternatives to such a first date?
3. Why does Gail Thayer fit Sonny's "dream?" What tone does the author take in regard to Sonny's attraction to her?
4. Does Gail perceive Sonny's insecurity? How does her behavior help precipitate Sonny's failure? Does she live up to Sonny's projection of her?
5. Explain Sonny's thought, "He vaguely understood there were forces in him, powers and impulses he couldn't control, that might kill him yet." Why does the tone change abruptly from comic to serious near the end of the chapter? What does the author try to do with respect to our feelings concerning Sonny's suicide attempt?

RANDALL JARRELL

RANDALL JARRELL (1914–64) grew up in California and Tennessee and attended Vanderbilt University. He was in the Army Air Force during World War II, and a considerable portion of his poetry deals with the war. He taught at various colleges, the last being the Women's College of the University of North Carolina. "The Woman at the Washington Zoo" was the title poem for a volume of his poetry that appeared in 1960 and won the National Book Award for Poetry in 1961. His works also include novels and criticism.

In "The Woman at the Washington Zoo," the speaker is, of course, the woman of the title, one of the many women in Jarrell's poems to whom growing old is a brutal and inexplicable mystery. The first stanza is but a single line, "The saris go by me from the embassies." In this simple, dramatic stroke, Jarrell evokes the colorful and cosmopolitan cross-section of people who visit the zoo in the nation's capital. But the world of the government clerk is not nearly so interesting. We move towards darkness, inside her thoughts. Her deepest self, as well as her body, is imprisoned in a way that is perhaps worse than the lot of the caged animals. Jarrell does nothing to shield us from the bleakness of her world. Her final cry comes out of a shameless agony that gives her despair a kind of transcendent power.

The Woman at the Washington Zoo

The saris go by me from the embassies.

Cloth from the moon. Cloth from another planet.
They look back at the leopard like the leopard.

And I. . . .
                    this print of mine, that has kept its color
Alive through so many cleanings; this dull null
Navy I wear to work, and wear from work, and so
To my bed, so to my grave, with no
Complaints, no comment: neither from my chief,
The Deputy Chief Assistant, nor his chief—
Only I complain. . . . this serviceable
Body that no sunlight dyes, no hand suffuses
But, dome-shadowed, withering among columns,
Wavy beneath fountains—small, far-off, shining
In the eyes of animals, these beings trapped
As I am trapped but not, themselves, the trap,
Aging, but without knowledge of their age,
Kept safe here, knowing not of death, for death—
Oh, bars of my own body, open, open!

The world goes by my cage and never sees me.
And there come not to me, as come to these,
The wild beasts, sparrows pecking the llamas' grain,
Pigeons settling on the bear's bread, buzzards
Tearing the meat the flies have clouded. . . .
                                        Vulture,
When you come for the white rat that the foxes left,
Take off the red helmet of your head, the black
Wings that have shadowed me, and step to me as man:
The wild brother at whose feet the white wolves fawn,
To whose hand of power the great lioness
Stalks, purring. . . .
                    You know what I was,
You see what I am: change me, change me!

QUESTIONS

1. What is the tone of the woman's voice in the first part of the poem? Is it different toward the end? How does the poem's syntax reflect her emotional condition?
2. What is the effect of invoking sparrows, pigeons, buzzards, flies, and vultures? What is the relation of the woman to the "great lioness"?
3. What does the woman really want when she cries out, "Change me, change me!"

QUESTIONS FOR STUDY AND WRITING (PART II)

1. How do Melville and Garland make use of local color in their stories? How do their descriptions of people and places reinforce their themes? Are their descriptions ever extraneous?
2. Compare Garland and Mailer as "realists." Does either tend to exaggerate details in order to make points more forcefully? What restraints are imposed on Garland but not on Mailer? Does Garland manage to overcome these restraints in any way?
3. Compare the methods by which Hamlin Garland and Randall Jarrell dramatize the oppression of women.
4. What similarities are there between what Mailer's soldiers and Wakefield's ex-soldiers feel is the proper way for a man to act? Trace the sociological influences responsible for their views.
5. How does Mailer dramatize how society acts as a depersonalizing force in his portraits of Croft and Cummings?
6. Analyze the function of social satire in the selections by Melville and Wakefield.

III

Assertions of the Outsider

JAMES BALDWIN

JAMES BALDWIN was born in Harlem in 1924. *Go Tell It On the Mountain* (1953) was his first novel, and he has since become one of America's most important novelists. *Go Tell It On the Mountain* focuses on John Grimes, a boy of fourteen, whose life resembles Baldwin's in many ways. The whole novel takes place on John's fourteenth birthday in 1935 in Harlem, where he lives with his mother, Elizabeth, and his stepfather, Gabriel, whom he believes to be his real father.

Baldwin concentrates on one aspect of life in the ghetto during the depression. We see how the Black man, in order to explain his miserable plight in America to himself, has adopted a puritanical form of Christianity that places a heavy burden of responsibility and guilt on the individual. In fact it is a religion, defined by the condition of slavery, in which the Black people identify with the biblical children of Israel in bondage in Egypt. Yet Gabriel Grimes, who is a preacher and a bitter, religious zealot, misuses his authority to evade his family and human responsibilities. During the day on which the novel is set, he strikes his wife after he discovers that John's half-brother, Roy, has been knifed in a gang fight. Both boys, especially John, empathize with their mother and vow revenge against him for his violent outburst.

This particular episode, "Elizabeth's Prayer," recounts her reflections later that evening during the religious services at which Elisha, a young novice preacher, is presiding. It is one of three major flashbacks Baldwin uses in the novel to tell of the past of a whole culture —how Blacks lived in the South and what prompted them to make their way to the squalid world of the big city ghetto. (The wildly emotional nature of the religious service itself is a release for an oppressed people.) The figure of John, Elizabeth's son (and the young writer, Baldwin), should be kept in mind in the background of this episode, for it is only Elizabeth's love and close attachment to John that give the sensitive adolescent any real sense of identity.

We discover that Elizabeth was once the lover of another sensitive young man, a proud Black man named Richard who, after being arrested on a false charge, commits suicide, unaware that Elizabeth is pregnant with John. What the figure of Richard lacks in believable motivation he gains as a symbol of all the pent-up rage of the Black man who has had to endure the White man's injustice. He is a romantic, almost poetic figure. It is understandable why Baldwin would want such an image as the true father of John—and therefore of himself. We can see where the young boy gets his talent and idealism—and we can feel Baldwin's own intensity in Richard's "highstrung" emotions.

The episode as a whole helps to explain the racial heritage that John must accept. Perhaps the young boy will be able to break through the pattern of sin, guilt, and repentance that his mother relives in her thoughts during the religious service.

Elizabeth's story projects powerfully a sense of a world in which the races are almost unaware of each other in any human sense, a world that drives Richard to despair especially when he is pointed out as a thief by a White man who cannot tell one "Black bastard" from another.

Richard's consciousness of being an outsider in American society is at least a generation ahead of its time. He confronts his race's tensions during a period when it was not possible to put such knowledge into action. And, despite Richard's justified despair and Elizabeth's unnecessary guilt, both take on a dignity that makes them fitting literary parents for a young, angry writer.

[FROM Go Tell It On the Mountain]

3

Elizabeth's Prayer
LORD, I WISH I HAD OF DIED IN EGYPT LAND!

While Elisha was speaking, Elizabeth felt that the Lord was speaking a message to her heart, that this fiery visitation was meant for her; and that if she humbled herself to listen, God would give her the interpretation. This certainty did not fill her with exultation, but with fear. She was afraid of what God might say—of what displeasure, what condemnation, what prophesies of trials yet to be endured might issue from His mouth.

Now Elisha ceased to speak, and rose; now he sat at the piano. There was muted singing all around her; yet she waited. Before her mind's eyes wavered, in a light like the light from a fire, the face of John, whom she had brought so unwillingly into the world. It was for his deliverance that she wept tonight: that he might be carried, past wrath unspeakable, into a state of grace.

They were singing:

> *"Must Jesus bear the cross alone,*
> *And all the world go free?"*

Elisha picked out the song on the piano, his fingers seeming to hesitate, almost to be unwilling. She, too, strained against her great unwillingness, but forced her heart to say Amen, as the voice of Praying Mother Washington picked up the response:

> *"No, there's a cross for everyone,*
> *And there's a cross for me."*

She heard weeping near her—was it Ella Mae? or Florence? or the echo, magnified, of her own tears? The weeping was buried beneath the song. She had been hearing this song all her life, she had grown up with it, but she had never understood it as well as she understood it now. It filled the church, as though the church had merely become a hollow or a void, echoing with the voices that had driven her to this dark place. Her aunt had sung it always, harshly, under her breath, in a bitter pride:

> "The consecrated cross I'll bear
> Till death shall set me free,
> And then go home, a crown to wear,
> For there's a crown for me."

She was probably an old, old woman now, still in the same harshness of spirit, singing this song in the tiny house down home which she and Elizabeth had shared so long. And she did not know of Elizabeth's shame—Elizabeth had not written about John until long after she was married to Gabriel; and the Lord had never allowed her aunt to come to New York City. Her aunt had always prophesied that Elizabeth would come to no good end, proud, and vain, and foolish as she was, and having been allowed to run wild all her childhood days.

Her aunt had come second in the series of disasters that had ended Elizabeth's childhood. First, when she was eight, going on nine, her mother had died, an event not immediately recognized by Elizabeth as a disaster, since she had scarcely known her mother and had certainly never loved her. Her mother had been very fair, and beautiful, and delicate of health, so that she stayed in bed most of the time, reading spiritualist pamphlets concerning the benefits of disease and complaining to Elizabeth's father of how she suffered. Elizabeth remembered of her only that she wept very easily and that she smelled like stale milk —it was, perhaps, her mother's disquieting color that, whenever she was held in her mother's arms, made Elizabeth think of milk. Her mother did not, however, hold Elizabeth in her arms very often. Elizabeth very quickly suspected that this was because she was so very much darker than her mother and not nearly, of course, so beautiful. When she faced her mother she was shy, downcast, sullen. She did not know how to answer her mother's shrill, meaningless questions, put with the furious affectation of maternal concern; she could not pretend, when she kissed her mother, or submitted to her mother's kiss, that she was moved by anything more than an unpleasant sense of duty. This, of course, bred in her mother a kind of baffled fury, and she never tired of telling Elizabeth that she was an "unnatural" child.

But it was very different with her father; he was—and so Elizabeth never failed to think of him—young, and handsome, and kind, and generous; and he loved his daughter. He told her that she was the apple of his eye, that she was wound around his heartstrings, that she was surely the finest little lady in the land. When she was with her father she pranced and postured like a very queen: and she was not afraid of anything, save the moment when he would say that it was her bedtime, or that he had to be "getting along." He was always buying her things, things to wear and things to play with, and taking her on Sundays for long walks through the country, or to the circus, when the circus was in town, or to Punch and Judy shows. And he was dark, like Elizabeth, and gentle, and proud; he had never been angry with her, but she had seen him angry a few times with other people—her mother, for example, and later, of course, her aunt. Her mother was always angry and Elizabeth paid no attention; and, later, her aunt was perpetually angry and Elizabeth learned to bear it: but if her father had ever been angry with her—in those days—she would have wanted to die.

Neither had he ever learned of her disgrace; when it happened, she could not think how to tell him, how to bring such pain to him who had had such pain already. Later, when she would have told him, he was long past caring, in the silent ground.

She thought of him now, while the singing and weeping went on around her—and she thought how he would have loved his grandson, who was like him in so many ways. Perhaps she dreamed it, but she did not believe she dreamed when at moments she thought she heard in John echoes, curiously distant and distorted, of her father's gentleness, and the trick of his laugh—how he threw his head back and the years that marked his face fled away, and the soft eyes softened and the mouth turned upward at the corners like a little boy's mouth—and that deadly pride of her father's behind which he retired when confronted by the nastiness of other people. It was he who had told her to weep, when she wept, alone; never to let the world see, never to ask for mercy; if one had to die, to go ahead and die, but never to let oneself be beaten. He had said this to her on one of the last times she had seen him, when she was being carried miles away, to Maryland, to live with her aunt. She had reason, in the years that followed, to remember his saying this; and time, at last, to discover in herself the depths of bitterness in her father from which these words had come.

For when her mother died, the world fell down; her aunt, her mother's older sister, arrived, and stood appalled at Elizabeth's vanity and uselessness; and decided, immediately, that her father was no fit person to raise a child, especially, as she darkly said, an innocent little girl. And it was this decision on the part of her aunt, for which Elizabeth did not forgive her for many years, that precipitated the third disaster, the separation of herself from her father—from all that she loved on earth.

For her father ran what her aunt called a "house"—not the house where they lived, but another house, to which, as Elizabeth gathered, wicked people often came. And he had also, to Elizabeth's rather horrified confusion, a "stable." Low, common niggers, the lowest of the low, came from all over (and sometimes brought their women and sometimes found them there) to eat, and drink cheap moonshine, and play music all night long—and to do worse things, her aunt's dreadful silence then suggested, which were far better left unsaid. And she would, she swore, move Heaven and earth before she would let her sister's daughter grow up with such a man. Without, however, so much as looking at Heaven, and without troubling any more of the earth than that part of it which held the courthouse, she won the day: Like a clap of thunder, or like a magic spell, like light one moment and darkness the next, Elizabeth's life had changed. Her mother was dead, her father banished, and she lived in the shadow of her aunt.

Or, more exactly, as she thought now, the shadow in which she had lived was fear—fear made more dense by hatred. Not for a moment had she judged her father; it would have made no difference to her love for him had she been told, and even seen it proved, that he was first cousin to the Devil. The proof would not have existed for her, and if it had she would not have regretted being his daughter, or have asked for anything better than to suffer at his side in Hell. And when she had been taken from him her imagination had been wholly unable to lend reality to the wickedness of which he stood accused—*she*, certainly, did not accuse him. She screamed in anguish when he put her from him and turned to go, and she had to be carried to the train. And later, when she understood perfectly all that had happened then, still in her heart she could not accuse him. Perhaps his life had been wicked, but he had been very good to her. His life had certainly cost him enough in pain to make the world's judgment a thing of no account. *They* had not known him as she had known him; *they* did not care as she had cared! It only made her sad that he never, as he had promised, came to take her away, and that while she was growing up she saw him so seldom. When she became a young woman she did not see him at all; but that was her own fault.

No, she did not accuse him; but she accused her aunt, and this from the moment she understood that her aunt had loved her mother, but did not love *him*. This could only mean that her aunt could not love *her*, either, and nothing in her life with her aunt ever proved Elizabeth wrong. It was true that her aunt was always talking of how much she loved her sister's daughter, and what great sacrifices she had made on her account, and what great care she took to see to it that Elizabeth should grow up a good, Christian girl. But Elizabeth was not for a moment fooled, and did not, for as long as she lived with her, fail to despise her aunt. She sensed that what her aunt spoke of as love was something else—a bribe, a threat, an indecent will to power. She knew that the kind of imprisonment that love might impose was also, mysteriously, a freedom for the soul and spirit, was water in the dry place, and had nothing to do with the prisons, churches, laws, rewards, and punishments, that so positively cluttered the landscape of her aunt's mind.

And yet, tonight, in her great confusion, she wondered if she had not been wrong; if there had not been something that she had overlooked, for which the Lord had made her suffer. "You little miss great-I-am," her aunt had said to her in those days, "you better watch your step, you hear me? You go walking around with your nose in the air, the Lord's going to let you fall right on down to the bottom of the ground. You mark my words. You'll *see*."

To this perpetual accusation Elizabeth had never replied; she merely regarded her aunt with a wide-eyed, insolent stare, meant at once to register her disdain and to thwart any pretext for punishment. And this trick, which she had, unconsciously, picked up from her father, rarely failed to work. As the years went on, her aunt seemed to gauge in a look the icy distances that Elizabeth had put between them, and that would certainly never be conquered now. And she would add, looking down, and under her breath: " 'Cause God don't like it."

"I sure don't care what God don't like, or you, either," Elizabeth's heart replied. "I'm going away from here. He's going to come and get me, and I'm going away from here."

"He" was her father, who never came. As the years passed, she replied only: "I'm going away from here." And it hung, this determination, like a heavy jewel between her breasts; it was written in fire on the dark sky of her mind.

But, yes—there was something she had overlooked. *Pride goeth before destruction; and a haughty spirit before a fall.* She had not known this: she had not imagined that she could fall. She wondered, tonight, how she could give this knowledge to her son; if she could help him to endure what could now no longer be changed; if while life ran, he would forgive her—for her pride, her folly, and her bargaining with God! For, tonight, those years before her fall, in her aunt's dark house—that house which smelled always of clothes kept too long in closets, and of old women; which was redolent of their gossip, and was pervaded, somehow, by the odor of the lemon her aunt took in her tea, and by the odor of frying fish, and of the still that someone kept in the basement—came before her, entire and overwhelming; and she remembered herself, entering any room in which her aunt might be sitting, responding to anything her aunt might say, standing before her, as rigid as metal and cancerous with hate and fear, in battle every hour of every day, a battle that she continued in her dreams. She knew now of what it was that she had so silently and so early accused her aunt: it was of tearing a bewildered child away from the arms of the father she loved. And she knew now why she had sometimes, so dimly and so unwillingly, felt that her father had betrayed her: it was because he had not overturned the earth to take his daughter away from a woman who did not love her, and whom she did not love. Yet she knew tonight how difficult it was to overturn the earth, for she had tried once, and she had failed. And she knew, too—and it made the tears that touched her mouth more bitter than the most bitter herb—that without the pride and bitterness she had so long carried in her heart against her aunt she could never have endured her life with her.

And she thought of Richard. It was Richard who had taken her out of that house, and out of the South, and into the city of destruction. He had suddenly arrived—and from the moment he arrived until the moment of his death he had filled her life. Not even tonight, in the heart's nearly impenetrable secret place, where the truth is hidden and where only the truth can live, could she wish that she had not known him; nor deny that, so long as he was there, the rejoicing of Heaven could have meant nothing to her—that, being forced to choose between Richard and God, she could only, even with weeping, have turned away from God.

And this was why God had taken him from her. It was for all of this that she was paying now, and it was this pride, hatred, bitterness, lust— this folly, this corruption—of which her son was heir.

Richard had not been born in Maryland, but he was working there, the summer that she met him, as a grocery clerk. It was 1919, and she was one year younger than the century. He was twenty-two, which seemed a great age to her in those days. She noticed him at once because he was so sullen and only barely polite. He waited on folks, her aunt said, furiously, as though he hoped the food they bought would poison them. Elizabeth liked to watch him move; his body was very thin, and beautiful, and nervous—*high strung*, thought Elizabeth, wisely. He moved exactly like a cat, perpetually on the balls of his feet, and with a cat's impressive, indifferent aloofness, his face closed, in his eyes no light at all. He smoked all the time, a cigarette between his lips as he added up the figures, and sometimes left burning on the counter while he went to look for stock. When, as someone entered, he said good morning, or good day, he said it barely looking up, and with an indifference that fell just short of insolence. When, having bought what he wanted and counted his change, the customer turned to leave and Richard said: "Thank you," it sounded so much like a curse that people sometimes turned in surprise to stare.

"He sure don't like working in that store," Elizabeth once observed to her aunt.

"He don't like working," said her aunt, scornfully. "He just like you."

On a bright, summer day, bright in her memory forever, she came into the store alone, wearing her best white summer dress and with her hair, newly straightened and curled at the ends, tied with a scarlet ribbon. She was going to a great church picnic with her aunt, and had come in to buy some lemons. She passed the owner of the store, who was a very fat man, sitting out on the sidewalk, fanning himself; he asked her, as she passed, if it was hot enough for her, and she said something and walked into the dark, heavy-smelling store, where flies buzzed, and where Richard sat on the counter reading a book.

She felt immediately guilty about having disturbed him, and muttered apologetically that she only wanted to buy some lemons. She expected him to get them for her in his sullen fashion and go back to his book, but he smiled, and said:

"Is that all you want? You better think now. You sure you ain't forgot nothing?"

She had never seen him smile before, nor had she really, for that matter, ever heard his voice. Her heart gave a dreadful leap and then, as dreadfully, seemed to have stopped forever. She could only stand there, staring at him. If he had asked her to repeat what she wanted she could not possibly have remembered what it was. And she found that she was looking into his eyes and where she had thought there was no light at all she found a light she had never seen before—and he was smiling still, but there was something curiously urgent in his smile. Then he said: "How many lemons, little girl?"

"Six," she said at last, and discovered to her vast relief that nothing had happened: the sun was still shining, the fat man still sat at the door, her heart was beating as though it had never stopped.

She was not, however, fooled; she remembered the instant at which her heart had stopped, and she knew that it beat now with a difference.

He put the lemons into a bag and, with a curious diffidence, she came closer to the counter to give him the money. She was in a terrible state, for she found that she could neither take her eyes off him nor look at him.

"Is that your mother you come in with all the time?" he asked.

"No," she said, "that's my aunt." She did not know why she said it, but she did: "My mother's dead."

"Oh," he said. Then: "Mine, too." They both looked thoughtfully at the money on the counter. He picked it up, but did not move. "I didn't think it was your mother," he said finally.

"Why?"

"I don't know. She don't look like you."

He started to light a cigarette, and then looked at her and put the pack in his pocket again.

"Don't mind me," she said quickly. "Anyway, I got to go. She's waiting—we going out."

He turned and banged the cash register. She picked up her lemons.

He gave her her change. She felt that she ought to say something else —it didn't seem right, somehow, just to walk out—but she could not think of anything. But he said:

"Then *that's* why you so dressed up today. Where you going to go?"

"We going to a picnic—a church picnic," she said, and suddenly, unaccountably, and for the first time, smiled.

And he smiled, too, and lit his cigarette, blowing the smoke carefully away from her. "You like picnics?"

"Sometimes," she said. She was not comfortable with him yet, and still she was beginning to feel that she would like to stand and talk to him all day. She wanted to ask him what he was reading, but she did not dare. Yet: "What's your name?" she abruptly brought out.

"Richard," he said.

"Oh," she said thoughtfully. Then: "Mine's Elizabeth."

"I know," he said. "I heard her call you one time."

"Well," she said helplessly, after a long pause, "good-bye."

" 'Good-*bye?*' You ain't going away, is you?"

"Oh, no," she said, in confusion.

"Well," he said, and smiled and bowed, "good *day*."

"Yes," she said, "good day."

And she turned and walked out into the streets; not the same streets from which she had entered a moment ago. These streets, the sky above, the sun, the drifting people, all had, in a moment, changed, and would never be the same again.

"You remember that day," he asked much later, "when you come into the store?"

"Yes?"

"Well, you was mighty pretty."

"I didn't think you never looked at me."

"Well, I didn't think you never looked at me."

"You was reading a book."

"Yes."

"What book was it, Richard?"

"Oh, I don't remember. Just a book."

"You smiled."

"You did, too."

"No, I didn't. I remember."

"Yes, you did."

"No, I *didn't*. Not till you did."

"Well, anyway—you was mighty pretty."

She did not like to think of with what hardness of heart, what calculated weeping, what deceit, what cruelty she now went into battle with her aunt for her freedom. And she won it, even though on certain not-to-be-dismissed conditions. The principal condition was that she should put herself under the protection of a distant, unspeakably respectable female relative of her aunt's, who lived in New York City—for when the summer ended, Richard said that he was going there and he wanted her to come with him. They would get married there. Richard said that he hated the South, and this was perhaps the reason it did not occur to either of them to begin their married life there. And Elizabeth was checked by the fear that if her aunt should discover how things stood between her and Richard she would find, as she had found so many years before in the case of her father, some means of bringing about their separation. This, as Elizabeth later considered it, was the first in the sordid series of mistakes which was to cause her to fall so low.

But to look back from the stony plain along the road which led one to that place is not at all the same thing as walking on the road; the perspective, to say the very least, changes only with the journey; only when the road has, all abruptly and treacherously, and with an absoluteness that permits no argument, turned or dropped or risen is one able to see all that one could not have seen from any other place. In those days, had the Lord Himself descended from Heaven with trumpets telling her to turn back, she could scarcely have heard Him, and could certainly not have heeded. She lived, in those days, in a fiery storm, of which Richard was the center and the heart. And she fought only to reach him—only that; she was afraid only of what might happen if they were kept from one another; for what might come after she had no thoughts or fears to spare.

Her pretext for coming to New York was to take advantage of the greater opportunities the North offered colored people; to study in a Northern school, and to find a better job than any she was likely to be offered in the South. Her aunt, who listened to this with no diminution of her habitual scorn, was yet unable to deny that from generation to generation, things, as she grudgingly put it, were bound to change— and neither could she quite take the position of seeming to stand in Elizabeth's way. In the winter of 1920, as the year began, Elizabeth found herself in an ugly back room in Harlem in the home of her aunt's relative, a woman whose respectability was immediately evident from the incense she burned in her rooms and the spiritualist séances she held every Saturday night.

The house was still standing, not very far away; often she was forced to pass it. Without looking up, she was able to see the windows of the apartment in which she had lived, and the woman's sign was in the window still: Madame Williams, Spiritualist.

She found a job as chambermaid in the same hotel in which Richard worked as elevator boy. Richard said that they would marry as soon as he had saved some money. But since he was going to school at night and made very little money, their marriage, which she had thought of as taking place almost as soon as she arrived, was planned for a future that grew ever more remote. And this presented her with a problem that she had refused, at home in Maryland, to think about, but from which, now, she could not escape: the problem of their life together. Reality, so to speak, burst in for the first time on her great dreaming, and she found occasion to wonder, ruefully, what had made her imagine that, once with Richard, she would have been able to withstand him. She had kept, precariously enough, what her aunt referred to as her pearl without price while she had been with Richard down home. This, which she had taken as witness to her own feminine moral strength, had been due to nothing more, it now developed, than her great fear of her aunt, and the lack, in that small town, of opportunity. Here, in this great city where no one cared, where people might live in the same building for years and never speak to one another, she found herself, when Richard took her in his arms, on the edge of a steep place: and down she rushed, on the descent uncaring, into the dreadful sea.

So it began. Had it been waiting for her since the day she had been taken from her father's arms? The world in which she now found herself was not unlike the world from which she had, so long ago, been rescued. Here were the women who had been the cause of her aunt's most passionate condemnation of her father—hard-drinking, hard-talking, with whisky- and cigarette-breath, and moving with the mystic authority of women who knew what sweet violence might be acted out under the moon and stars, or beneath the tigerish lights of the city, in the raucous hay or the singing bed. And was she, Elizabeth, so sweetly fallen, so tightly chained, one of these women now? And here were the men who had come day and night to visit her father's "stable"—with their sweet talk and their music, and their violence and their sex— black, brown, and beige, who looked on her with lewd, and lustful, and laughing eyes. And these were Richard's friends. Not one of them ever went to Church—one might scarcely have imagined that they knew that churches existed—they all, hourly, daily, in their speech, in their lives, and in their hearts, cursed God. They all seemed to be saying, as Richard, when she once timidly mentioned the love of Jesus, said: "You can tell that puking bastard to kiss my big black ass."

She, for very terror on hearing this, had wept; yet she could not deny that for such an abundance of bitterness there was a positive fountain of grief. There was not, after all, a great difference between the world of the North and that of the South which she had fled; there was only this difference: the North promised more. And this similarity: what it promised it did not give, and what it gave, at length and grudgingly with one hand, it took back with the other. Now she understood in this nervous, hollow, ringing city, that nervousness of Richard's which had so attracted her—a tension so total, and so without the hope, or possibility of release, or resolution, that she felt it in his muscles, and heard it in his breathing, even as on her breast he fell asleep.

And this was perhaps why she had never thought to leave him, frightened though she was during all that time, and in a world in which, had it not been for Richard, she could have found no place to put her feet. She did not leave him, because she was afraid of what might happen to him without her. She did not resist him, because he needed her. And she did not press about marriage because, upset as he was about everything, she was afraid of having him upset about her, too. She thought of herself as his strength; in a world of shadows, the indisputable reality to which he could always repair. And, again, for all that had come, she could not regret this. She had tried, but she had never been and was not now, even tonight, truly sorry. Where, then, was her repentance? And how could God hear her cry?

They had been very happy together, in the beginning; and until the very end he had been very good to her, had not ceased to love her, and tried always to make her know it. No more than she had been able to accuse her father had she ever been able to accuse him. His weakness she understood, and his terror, and even his bloody end. What life had made him bear, her lover, this wild, unhappy boy, many another stronger and more virtuous man might not have borne so well.

Saturday was their best day, for they only worked until one o'clock. They had all the afternoon to be together, and nearly all of the night, since Madame Williams had her séances on Saturday night and preferred that Elizabeth, before whose silent skepticism departed spirits might find themselves reluctant to speak, should not be in the house. They met at the service entrance. Richard was always there before her, looking, oddly, much younger and less anonymous without the ugly, tight-fitting, black uniform that he had to wear when working. He would be talking, or laughing with some of the other boys, or shooting craps, and when he heard her step down the long, stone hall he would look up, laughing; and wickedly nudging one of the other boys, he would half shout, half sing: "He-y! Look-a-there, ain't she pretty?"

She never failed, at this—which was why he never failed to do it—to blush, half-smiling, half-frowning, and nervously to touch the collar of her dress.

"*Sweet* Georgia Brown!" somebody might say.

"*Miss* Brown to you," said Richard, then, and took her arm.

"Yeah, that's right," somebody else would say, "you *better* hold on to little Miss Bright-eyes, don't somebody sure going to take her away from you."

"Yeah," said another voice, "and it might be me."

"*Oh*, no," said Richard, moving with her towards the street, "ain't nobody going to take *my* little Little-bit away from *me*."

Little-bit: it had been his name for her. And sometimes he called her Sandwich Mouth, or Funnyface, or Frog-eyes. She would not, of course, have endured these names from anyone else, nor, had she not found herself, with joy and helplessness (and a sleeping panic), living it out, would she ever have suffered herself so publicly to become a man's property—"concubine," her aunt would have said, and at night, alone, she rolled the word, tart like lemon rind, on her tongue.

She was descending with Richard to the sea. She would have to climb back up alone, but she did not know this then. Leaving the boys in the hall, they gained the midtown New York streets.

"And what we going to do today, Little-bit?" With that smile of his, and those depthless eyes, beneath the towers of the white city, with people, white, hurrying all around them.

"I don't know, honey. What you want to do?"

"Well, maybe, we go to a *mus*eum."

The first time he suggested this, she demanded, in panic, if they would be allowed to enter.

"Sure, they let niggers in," Richard said. "Ain't we got to be educated, too—to live with the motherfuckers?"

He never "watched" his language with her, which at first she took as evidence of his contempt because she had fallen so easily, and which later she took as evidence of his love.

And when he took her to the Museum of Natural History, or the Metropolitan Museum of Art, where they were almost certain to be the only black people, and he guided her through the halls, which never ceased in her imagination to be as cold as tombstones, it was then she saw another life in him. It never ceased to frighten her, this passion he brought to something she could not understand.

For she never grasped—not at any rate with her mind—what, with such incandescence, he tried to tell her on these Saturday afternoons. She could not find, between herself and the African statuette, or totem pole, on which he gazed with such melancholy wonder, any point of contact. She was only glad that she did not look that way. She preferred to look, in the other museum, at the paintings; but still she did not understand anything he said about them. She did not know why he so adored things that were so long dead; what sustenance they gave him, what secrets he hoped to wrest from them. But she understood, at least, that they *did* give him a kind of bitter nourishment, and that the secrets they held for him were a matter of his life and death. It frightened her because she felt that he was reaching for the moon and that he would, therefore, be dashed down against the rocks; but she did not say any of this. She only listened, and in her heart she prayed for him.

But on other Saturdays they went to see a movie; they went to see a play; they visited his friends; they walked through Central Park. She

liked the park because, however spuriously, it re-created something of
the landscape she had known. How many afternoons had they walked
there! She had always, since, avoided it. They bought peanuts and for
hours fed the animals at the zoo; they bought soda pop and drank it
on the grass; they walked along the reservoir and Richard explained how
a city like New York found water to drink. Mixed with her fear for him
was a total admiration: that he had learned so young, so much. People
stared at them but she did not mind; he noticed, but he did not seem to
notice. But sometimes he would ask, in the middle of a sentence—concerned, possibly, with ancient Rome:

"Little-bit—d'you love me?"

And she wondered how he could doubt it. She thought how infirm
she must be not to have been able to make him know it; and she raised
her eyes to his, and she said the only thing she could say:

"I wish to God I may die if I don't love you. There ain't no sky above
us if I don't love you."

Then he would look ironically up at the sky, and take her arm with
a firmer pressure, and they would walk on.

Once, she asked him:

"Richard, did you go to school much when you was little?"

And he looked at her a long moment. Then:

"Baby, I done told you, my mama died when I was born. And my
daddy, he weren't nowhere to be found. Ain't nobody never took care of
me. I just moved from one place to another. When one set of folks got
tired of me they sent me down the line. I didn't hardly go to school at
all."

"Then how come you got to be so smart? How come you got to know
so much?"

And he smiled, pleased, but he said: "Little-bit, I don't know so
much." Then he said, with a change in his face and voice which she
had grown to know: "I just decided me one day that I was going to
get to know everything them white bastards knew, and I was going to
get to know it better than them, so could no white son-of-a-bitch no-
where never talk *me* down, and never make me feel like *I* was dirt,
when I could read him the alphabet, back, front, and sideways. Shit—
he weren't going to beat my ass, then. And if he tried to kill me, I'd
take him with me, I swear to my mother I would." Then he looked at
her again, and smiled and kissed her, and he said: "That's how I got
to know so much, baby."

She asked: "And what you going to do, Richard? What you want
to be?"

And his face clouded. "I don't know. I got to find out. Looks like I
can't get my mind straight nohow."

She did not know *why* he couldn't—or she could only dimly face it —but she knew he spoke the truth.

She had made her great mistake with Richard in not telling him that she was going to have a child. Perhaps, she thought now, if she had told him, everything might have been very different, and he would be living yet. But the circumstances under which she had discovered herself to be pregnant had been such to make her decide, for his sake, to hold her peace awhile. Frightened as she was, she dared not add to the panic that overtook him on the last summer of his life.

And yet perhaps it was, after all, this—this failure to demand of his strength what it might then, most miraculously, have been found able to bear; by which—indeed, how could she know?—his strength might have been strengthened, for which she prayed tonight to be forgiven. Perhaps she had lost her love because she had not, in the end, believed in it enough.

She lived quite a long way from Richard—four subway stops; and when it was time for her to go home, he always took the subway uptown with her and walked her to her door. On a Saturday when they had forgotten the time and stayed together later than usual, he left her at her door at two o'clock in the morning. They said good night hurriedly, for she was afraid of trouble when she got upstairs—though, in fact, Madame Williams seemed astonishingly indifferent to the hours Elizabeth kept—and he wanted to hurry back home and go to bed. Yet, as he hurried off down the dark, murmuring street, she had a sudden impulse to call him back, to ask him to take her with him and never let her go again. She hurried up the steps, smiling a little at this fancy: it was because he looked so young and defenseless as he walked away, and yet so jaunty and strong.

He was to come the next evening at suppertime, to make at last, at Elizabeth's urging, the acquaintance of Madame Williams. But he did not come. She drove Madame Williams wild with her sudden sensitivity to footsteps on the stairs. Having told Madame Williams that a gentleman was coming to visit her, she did not dare, of course, to leave the house and go out looking for him, thus giving Madame Williams the impression that she dragged men in off the streets. At ten o'clock, having eaten no supper, a detail unnoticed by her hostess, she went to bed, her head aching and her heart sick with fear; fear over what had happened to Richard, who had never kept her waiting before; and fear involving all that was beginning to happen in her body.

And on Monday morning he was not at work. She left during the lunch hour to go to his room. He was not there. His landlady said that he had not been there all weekend. While Elizabeth stood trembling and indecisive in the hall, two white policemen entered.

She knew the moment she saw them, and before they mentioned his name, that something terrible had happened to Richard. Her heart, as on that bright summer day when he had first spoken to her, gave a terrible bound and then was still, with an awful, wounded stillness. She put out one hand to touch the wall in order to keep standing.

"This here young lady was just looking for him," she heard the land-lady say.

They all looked at her.

"You his girl?" one of the policemen asked.

She looked up at his sweating face, on which a lascivious smile had immediately appeared, and straightened, trying to control her trembling.

"Yes," she said. "Where is he?"

"He's in jail, honey," the other policeman said.

"What for?"

"For robbing a white man's store, black girl. That's what for."

She found, and thanked Heaven for it, that a cold, stony rage had entered her. She would, otherwise, certainly have fallen down, or begun to weep. She looked at the smiling policeman.

"Richard ain't robbed no store," she said. "Tell me where he is."

"And *I* tell you," he said, not smiling, "that your boyfriend robbed a store and he's in jail for it. He's going to stay there, too—now, what you got to say to that?"

"And he probably did it for you, too," the other policeman said. "You look like a girl a man could rob a store for."

She said nothing; she was thinking how to get to see him, how to get him out.

One of them, the smiler, turned now to the landlady and said: "Let's have the key to his room. How long's he been living here?"

"About a year," the landlady said. She looked unhappily at Elizabeth. "He seemed like a real nice boy."

"Ah, yes," he said, mounting the steps, "they all seem like real nice boys when they pay their rent."

"You going to take me to see him?" she asked of the remaining policeman. She found herself fascinated by the gun in his holster, the club at his side. She wanted to take that pistol and empty it into his round, red face; to take that club and strike with all her strength against the base of his skull where his cap ended, until the ugly, silky, white man's hair was matted with blood and brains.

"Sure, girl," he said, "you're coming right along with us. The man at the station house wants to ask you some questions."

The smiling policeman came down again. "Ain't nothing up there," he said. "Let's go."

She moved between them, out into the sun. She knew that there was nothing to be gained by talking to them any more. She was entirely in their power; she would have to think faster than they could think; she would have to contain her fear and her hatred, and find out what could be done. Not for anything short of Richard's life, and not, possibly, even for that, would she have wept before them, or asked of them a kindness.

A small crowd, children and curious passers-by, followed them as they walked the long, dusty, sunlit street. She hoped only that they would not pass anyone she knew; she kept her head high, looking straight ahead, and felt the skin settle over her bones as though she were wearing a mask.

And at the station she somehow got past their brutal laughter. (*What was he doing with you, girl, until two o'clock in the morning?—Next time you feel like that, girl, you come by here and talk to* me.) She felt that she was about to burst, or vomit, or die. Though the sweat stood out cruelly, like needles on her brow, and she felt herself, from every side, being covered with a stink and filth, she found out, in their own good time, what she wanted to know: He was being held in a prison downtown called the Tombs (the name made her heart turn over), and she could see him tomorrow. The state, or the prison, or someone, had already assigned him a lawyer; he would be brought to trial next week.

But the next day, when she saw him, she wept. He had been beaten, he whispered to her, and he could hardly walk. His body, she later discovered, bore almost no bruises, but was full of strange, painful swellings, and there was a welt above one eye.

He had not, of course, robbed the store, but, when he left her that Saturday night, had gone down into the subway station to wait for his train. It was late, and trains were slow; he was all alone on the platform, only half awake, thinking, he said, of her.

Then, from the far end of the platform, he heard a sound of running; and, looking up, he saw two colored boys come running down the steps. Their clothes were torn, and they were frightened; they came up the platform and stood near him, breathing hard. He was about to ask them what the trouble was when, running across the tracks towards them, and followed by a white man, he saw another colored boy; and at the same instant another white man came running down the subway steps.

Then he came full awake, in panic; he knew that whatever the trouble was, it was now his trouble also; for these white men would make no distinction between him and the three boys they were after: They were all colored, they were about the same age, and here they stood together on the subway platform. And they were all, with no questions asked, herded upstairs, and into the wagon and to the station house.

At the station Richard gave his name and address and age and occupation. Then for the first time he stated that he was not involved, and asked one of the other boys to corroborate his testimony. This they rather despairingly did. They might, Elizabeth felt, have done it sooner, but they probably also felt that it would be useless to speak. And they were not believed; the owner of the store was being brought there to make the identification. And Richard tried to relax: the man *could* not say that he had been there if he had never seen him before.

But when the owner came, a short man with a bloody shirt—for they had knifed him—in the company of yet another policeman, he looked at the four boys before him and said: "Yeah, that's them, all right."

Then Richard shouted: "But *I* wasn't there! Look at me, goddammit —I wasn't *there!*"

"You black bastards," the man said, looking at him, "you're all the same."

Then there was silence in the station, the eyes of the white men all watching. And Richard said, but quietly, knowing that he was lost: "But all the same, mister, I wasn't there." And he looked at the white man's bloody shirt and thought, he told Elizabeth, at the bottom of his heart: "I wish to God they'd killed you."

Then the questioning began. The three boys signed a confession at once, but Richard would not sign. He said at last that he would die before he signed a confession to something he hadn't done. "Well then," said one of them, hitting him suddenly across the head, "maybe you *will* die, you black son-of-a-bitch." And the beating began. He would not, then, talk to her about it; she found that, before the dread and the hatred that filled her mind, her imagination faltered and held its peace.

"What we going to do?" she asked at last.

He smiled a vicious smile—she had never seen such a smile on his face before. "Maybe you ought to pray to that Jesus of yours and get Him to come down and tell these white men something." He looked at her a long, dying moment. "Because I don't know nothing *else* to do," he said.

She suggested: "Richard, what about another lawyer?"

And he smiled again. "I declare," he said, "Little-bit's been holding out on me. She got a fortune tied up in a sock, and she ain't never told me nothing about it."

She had been trying to save money for a whole year, but she had only thirty dollars. She sat before him, going over in her mind all the things she might do to raise money, even to going on the streets. Then, for very helplessness, she began to shake with sobbing. At this, his face became Richard's face again. He said in a shaking voice: "Now, look here, Little-bit, don't you be like that. We going to work this out all right." But she could not stop sobbing. "Elizabeth," he whispered, "Elizabeth, Elizabeth." Then the man came and said that it was time for her to go. And she rose. She had brought two packs of cigarettes for him, and they were still in her bag. Wholly ignorant of prison regulations, she did not dare to give them to him under the man's eyes. And, somehow, her failure to remember to give him the cigarettes, when she knew how much he smoked, made her weep the harder. She tried—and failed—to smile at him, and she was slowly led to the door. The sun nearly blinded her, and she heard him whisper behind her: "So long, baby. Be good."

In the streets she did not know what to do. She stood awhile before the dreadful gates, and then she walked and walked until she came to a coffee shop where taxi drivers and the people who worked in near-by offices hurried in and out all day. Usually she was afraid to go into downtown establishments, where only white people were, but today she did not care. She felt that if anyone said anything to her she would turn and curse him like the lowest bitch on the streets. If anyone touched her, she would do her best to send his soul to Hell.

But no one touched her; no one spoke. She drank her coffee, sitting in the strong sun that fell through the window. Now it came to her how alone, how frightened she was; she had never been so frightened in her life before. She knew that she was pregnant—knew it, as the old folks said, in her bones; and if Richard should be sent away, what, under Heaven, could she do? Two years, three years—she had no idea how long he might be sent away for—what would she do? And how could she keep her aunt from knowing? And if her aunt should find out, then her father would know, too. The tears welled up, and she drank her cold, tasteless coffee. And what would they do with Richard? And if they sent him away, what would he be like, then, when he returned? She looked out into the quiet, sunny streets, and for the first time in her life, she hated it all—the white city, the white world. She could not, that day, think of one decent white person in the whole world. She sat there, and she hoped that one day God, with tortures inconceivable, would grind them utterly into humility, and make them know that black boys and black girls, whom they treated with such condescension, such disdain, and such good humor, had hearts like human beings, too, more human hearts than theirs.

But Richard was not sent away. Against the testimony of the three robbers, and her own testimony, and, under oath, the storekeeper's indecision, there was no evidence on which to convict him. The courtroom seemed to feel, with some complacency and some disappointment, that it was his great good luck to be let off so easily. They went immediately to his room. And there—she was never all her life long to forget it—he threw himself, face downward, on his bed and wept.

She had only seen one other man weep before—her father—and it had not been like this. She touched him, but he did not stop. Her own tears fell on his dirty, uncombed hair. She tried to hold him, but for a long while he would not be held. His body was like iron; she could find no softness in it. She sat curled like a frightened child on the edge of the bed, her hand on his back, waiting for the storm to pass over. It was then that she decided not to tell him yet about the child.

By and by he called her name. And then he turned, and she held him against her breast, while he sighed and shook. He fell asleep at last, clinging to her as though he were going down into the water for the last time.

And it was the last time. That night he cut his wrists with his razor and he was found in the morning by his landlady, his eyes staring upward with no light, dead among the scarlet sheets.

· · ·

And now they were singing:

> *"Somebody needs you, Lord,*
> *Come by here."*

At her back, above her, she heard Gabriel's voice. He had risen and was helping the others to pray through. She wondered if John were still on his knees, or had risen, with a child's impatience, and was staring around the church. There was a stiffness in him that would be hard to break, but that, nevertheless, would one day surely be broken. As hers had been, and Richard's—there was no escape for anyone. God was everywhere, terrible, the living God; and so high, the song said, you couldn't get over Him; so low you couldn't get under Him; so wide you couldn't get around Him; but must come in at the door.

And she, she knew today that door: a living, wrathful gate. She knew through what fires the soul must crawl, and with what weeping one passed over. Men spoke of how the heart broke up, but never spoke of how the soul hung speechless in the pause, the void, the terror between the living and the dead; how, all garments rent and cast aside, the naked soul passed over the very mouth of Hell. Once there, there was no turning back; once there, the soul remembered, though the heart sometimes forgot. For the world called to the heart, which stammered to reply; life, and love, and revelry, and, most falsely, hope, called the forgetful, the human heart. Only the soul, obsessed with the journey it had made, and had still to make, pursued its mysterious and dreadful end; and carried, heavy with weeping and bitterness, the heart along.

QUESTIONS

1. Why is Elizabeth so effective as a consciousness to convey Baldwin's criticism of America? In what ways does her sweetness heighten his satire?
2. What is the place of religion in Elizabeth's life? Does it serve any purpose for Elizabeth to condemn herself and take full responsibility for what has happened in her life? Why might Baldwin be bitter at the social function of religion in the ghetto?
3. What did Elizabeth like about her father? Why couldn't she stay with him? In what ways does Richard resemble her father?
4. Why does Elizabeth dislike her aunt? What are her aunt's values? Why does Elizabeth feel that "what her aunt spoke of as love was something else?" How do her aunt's values force her into the dilemma of choosing "between Richard and God?"
5. What kind of hopes do Richard and Elizabeth have when they leave the South for New York City? Are these hopes typical of other Blacks who emigrated from the rural South to the industrial North?
6. In what ways is Richard a "romantic" figure? What about his life makes his violent, early death almost inevitable?

LARRY NEAL

LARRY NEAL (b. 1937) was born in Atlanta, Georgia, and reared in Philadelphia. He received his B.A. from Lincoln University, did graduate work at the University of Pennsylvania, and taught at both Yale and Wesleyan Universities. He is currently an editor of *Cricket* and a contributing editor of the *Journal of Black Poetry*. His poems have appeared in many periodicals and anthologies of Black poetry, including *Black Fire,* a volume he edited with LeRoi Jones.

Both Baldwin and Neal search the painful past of Black Americans in an attempt to connect their deepest personal feelings with their racial heritage. Baldwin, in *Go Tell It On the Mountain,* uses the example of one young man and his family's history; in "The Narrative of the Black Magicians," Neal evokes his race's history in America through the suffering, nameless "faces" who gradually become more aware of who they are as the narrative moves forward in time. The first three stanzas might be called the period of unconsciousness—slave-ships, plantation cabins, and "strange cities." In the fourth stanza the poet's references suddenly become more specific as he moves on to assert his race's identity in the sixth stanza, where their faces "Turn inward eyes on themselves." In the final stanza there is an agonizing fusion of his "ancestor['s] faces" with the present-day faces, which are "tearing into the open" in this "prison of America," the land that "must be ours in the living." Obsessed by the question of identity, most young Black poets find it difficult to resist being propagandistic. Neal succeeds in communicating his message primarily through poetic images.

The Narrative of the Black Magicians

Fast fly the faces through our blood-years,
faces fly by the windows of the moon
and pass the sons of the slaves standing
on the shores of home.
time in their faces stops, and dances stilled
by the chained-sea whose sounds bring with
it memories out of our private and collective past.
The sea contains the tightness of our dreams;
contains conversations under the ships'
floor-prisons:
touchless hands, I lay beside you,
lips part in fever,
and the receding drums
telling of a new death.

Faces peer up into the rocking darkness:
this is the ocean that birthed us newly;
but the chained-sea is hostile,
as white madnesses clink in children's dreams.
roll on Jordan to no end.
These faces live to appear on the land that became
theirs by their blood,
made ours by our blood.
these faces appear in swampy places bundled
in motherless callings,
appear on the slave blocks, sold into ugliness,
shaped into ugliness by the white touch.
Their appearances flicker above the plotting fires—
they plan night-death to pale monsters.
faces mute. the fire-sun burns visions
into his eyes. in his black hands blood burns.

Eastward their faces turn, morning eyes strain
for the horizon.
these faces slither under cabin doors and see
themselves in strange cities.

they mouth that language awkwardly in an eastern
blueness.
faces under the timeless sky. their sky.
made by them. made for them.

These faces catch scottsboro freights north,
sing blues for the river gods,
turn up strange in memphis, dallas, chicago,
kansas city . . .
hammered steel out of those mountains,
laid their lives down in spite of themselves
as steel killed them in narrow tunnels.
they laughed with John Henry,
and played spy with Harriet Tubman,
and strong ones mostly.

These faces pour out of slavetime
into the subways of fear,
jockey for life between grey crushing mountains
and the 42nd street movies.
See these faces. they saw their best
killed in bleak winters, and their homes
upheaved by the progress-blood-drinking-machines.

Faces that flew pass the president's coffin,
who saw their own leaders busy at morning
betrayals. who, in spite, managed to love.
Child faces, blackly playing on those backstreet's
are children of gods and the Lion.
faces charged with change; these faces turn
from the west, turn inward eyes on themselves,
control the black cosmos, are gods.
dancing faces making the Earth live
in green blackness.
our bones are in this land.
It must be our's in the living.

Ancestor faces form on the film of our brains.
form our contours out of deep wails of saxes.
form in the voice of Malcolm.
form child. form in the rush of war.
form child. form in the taking of life.
form child. form in the sun's explosion
and in the avenging waves.

form child. form child. form child. form.
form in the prison of america.
form child. form your image of men
and women tearing into the open,
tearing out the wombed deadness;
and face the form of our love in the final
clasping and embrace;
form your face out of the Earth;
form your face with searing waves of sound,
as beyond the wall there is a painful calm.

Spring—1965
a painful season

QUESTIONS

1. Why might Neal have chosen the title, "The Narrative of the Black Magicians"?
2. How does Neal make use of images of the sea? What associations surround his use of "east" and "west" in the poem?
3. What specific people and events does Neal recall to evoke present-day America?
4. What is the effect of the repetition of the word "faces" throughout the poem? What is the effect of the repetition of the word "form" in the final stanza?

JACK KEROUAC

JACK KEROUAC (1922–69) was probably the most renowned prose writer of the Beat Generation. He was born in Lowell, Massachusetts, spent his youth in the East, and began traveling across America in the years of relatively good feeling following the end of World War II. He has written one novel about life in the Beat world of San Francisco (*The Subterraneans*, 1958), and other books about his explorations of Eastern philosophies, but his most important work is still *On the Road* (1955). In it he evokes the spirit of Whitman's self exploring America; it is a celebration of the splintered, beleaguered self of a man frantically racing from New York to San Francisco and back. In his frenzied activity, Kerouac, speaking through the voice of Sal Paradise, finds, momentarily at least, an America alive with energy and the spirit of rebellion, the kind of radical dissent that is in the tradition of Emerson and Whitman. As a document of the Beat Generation the book is crucial in its tracing of the process by which Americans began to see, through the façade of the American dream, the elements of nightmare in our culture.

In *On the Road* Sal Paradise deliberately avoids the conventional, established people of America. The only ones who interest him are "the mad ones, the ones who are mad to live, mad to talk, mad to be saved, desirous of everything at the same time, the ones who never yawn or say a commonplace thing, but burn, burn, burn like fabulous yellow roman candles." The figure who best personifies such madness is Dean Moriarty (in reality Neal Cassady), a natural "speed-freak" possessed of great energy who, in his own way, has a quality of innocence and vulnerability that seems not too distant from Whitman's unguarded outpourings of self. Speaking of Dean, Sal says, "He was BEAT—the root, the soul of Beatific," and "He was finally an Angel." Other characters referred to in this episode are Dean's girlfriend, Mary Lou, and Sal's poet friend, Carlo Marx (Allen Ginsberg).

This episode is a kind of pastoral retreat from Sal's incessant wanderings and endless encounters with women, farmboys, truck drivers, and such characters as the fellow he refers to as "my Montana cowboy." It is the story of his affair with a Mexican–American girl named Terry. He first meets her in Los Angeles, which we see from the point of view of a penniless outsider: "the loneliest and most brutal of American cities." But the real poignancy of this section comes when Sal and Terry visit her family in the San Joaquin Valley, where the Chicanos work in the fields and lead a precarious day-by-day existence. Sal can only be an outsider to their deepest feelings, but, for a while, he settles down and becomes a part of their culture. He realizes that *they* are the real outsiders in America and thus he wants to identify with them. When one day he is actually mistaken for one of them by some fellow whites, he replies, "They thought I was a Mexican, of course, and in a way, I am."

In the world of migrant workers, despite the transitoriness and precariousness of life, indeed *because* of it, we see people living with a zest, a quality of enjoyment impossible in the country-club world of Mrs. Bridge. In their own unthinking way Terry and Rickey and their family counter the myth of American materialism. At the same time Kerouac makes us confront our sense of social outrage at how these people are exploited and degraded by our society.

[FROM On the Road]

I had bought my ticket and was waiting for the LA bus when all of a sudden I saw the cutest little Mexican girl in slacks come cutting across my sight. She was in one of the buses that had just pulled in with a big sigh of airbrakes; it was discharging passengers for a rest stop. Her breasts stuck out straight and true; her little flanks looked delicious; her hair was long and lustrous black; and her eyes were great big blue things with timidities inside. I wished I was on her bus. A pain stabbed my heart, as it did every time I saw a girl I loved who was going the opposite direction in this too-big world. The announcer called the LA bus. I picked up my bag and got on, and who should be sitting there alone but the Mexican girl. I dropped right opposite her and began scheming right off. I was so lonely, so sad, so tired, so quivering, so broken, so beat, that I got up my courage, the courage necessary to approach a strange girl, and acted. Even then I spent five minutes beating my thighs in the dark as the bus rolled down the road.

You gotta, you gotta or you'll die! Damn fool, talk to her! What's wrong with you? Aren't you tired enough of yourself by now? And before I knew what I was doing I leaned across the aisle to her (she was trying to sleep on the seat) and said, "Miss, would you like to use my raincoat for a pillow?"

She looked up with a smile and said, "No, thank you very much."

I sat back, trembling; I lit a butt. I waited till she looked at me, with a sad little sidelook of love, and I got right up and leaned over her. "May I sit with you, miss?"

"If you wish."

And this I did. "Where going?"

"LA." I loved the way she said "LA;" I love the way everybody says "LA" on the Coast; it's their one and only golden town when all is said and done.

"That's where I'm going too!" I cried. "I'm very glad you let me sit with you, I was very lonely and I've been traveling a hell of a lot." And we settled down to telling our stories. Her story was this: She had a husband and child. The husband beat her, so she left him, back at Sabinal, south of Fresno, and was going to LA to live with her sister awhile. She left her little son with her family, who were grape-pickers and lived in a shack in the vineyards. She had nothing to do but brood and get mad. I felt like putting my arms around her right away. We talked and talked. She said she loved to talk with me. Pretty soon she was saying she wished she could go to New York too. "Maybe we could!" I laughed. The bus groaned up Grapevine Pass and then we were coming down into the great sprawls of light. Without coming to any particular agreement we began holding hands, and in the same way it was mutely and beautifully and purely decided that when I got my hotel room in LA she would be beside me. I ached all over for her; I leaned my head in her beautiful hair. Her little shoulders drove me mad; I hugged her and hugged her. And she loved it.

"I love love," she said, closing her eyes. I promised her beautiful love. I gloated over her. Our stories were told; we subsided into silence and sweet anticipatory thoughts. It was as simple as that. You could have all your Peaches and Bettys and Marylous and Ritas and Camilles and Inezes in this world; this was my girl and my kind of girlsoul, and I told her that. She confessed she saw me watching her in the bus station. "I thought you was a nice college boy."

"Oh. I'm a college boy!" I assured her. The bus arrived in Hollywood. In the gray, dirty dawn, like the dawn when Joel McCrea met Veronica Lake in a diner, in the picture *Sullivan's Travels,* she slept in my lap. I looked greedily out the window: stucco houses and palms and drive-ins, the whole mad thing, the ragged promised land, the fantastic end of America. We got off the bus at Main Street, which was no different from where you get off a bus in Kansas City or Chicago or Boston—red brick, dirty, characters drifting by, trolleys grating in the hopeless dawn, the whorey smell of a big city.

And here my mind went haywire, I don't know why. I began getting the foolish paranoiac visions that Teresa, or Terry—her name—was a common little hustler who worked the buses for a guy's bucks by making appointments like ours in LA where she brought the sucker first to a breakfast place, where her pimp waited, and then to a certain hotel to which he had access with his gun or his whatever. I never confessed this to her. We ate breakfast and a pimp kept watching us; I fancied Terry was making secret eyes at him. I was tired and felt strange and lost in a faraway, disgusting place. The goof of terror took over my thoughts and made me act petty and cheap. "Do you know that guy?" I said.

"What guy you mean, ho-ney?" I let it drop. She was slow and hung-up about everything she did; it took her a long time to eat; she chewed slowly and stared into space, and smoked a cigarette, and kept talking, and I was like a haggard ghost, suspicioning every move she made, thinking she was stalling for time. This was all a fit of sickness. I was sweating as we went down the street hand in hand. The first hotel we hit had a room, and before I knew it I was locking the door behind me and she was sitting on the bed taking off her shoes. I kissed her meekly. Better she'd never know. To relax our nerves I knew we needed whisky, especially me. I ran out and fiddled all over twelve blocks, hurrying till I found a pint of whisky for sale at a newsstand. I ran back, all energy. Terry was in the bathroom, fixing her face. I poured one big drink in a water glass, and we had slugs. Oh, it was sweet and delicious and worth my whole lugubrious voyage. I stood behind her at the mirror, and we danced in the bathroom that way. I began talking about my friends back East.

I said, "You ought to meet a great girl I know called Dorie. She's a six-foot redhead. If you came to New York she'd show you where to get work."

"Who is this six-foot redhead?" she demanded suspiciously. "Why do you tell me about her?" In her simple soul she couldn't fathom my kind of glad, nervous talk. I let it drop. She began to get drunk in the bathroom.

"Come on to bed!" I kept saying.

"Six-foot redhead, hey? And I thought you was a nice college boy, I saw you in your lovely sweater and I said to myself, Hmm, ain't he nice? No! And no! And no! You have to be a goddam pimp like all of them!"

"What on earth are you talking about?"

"Don't stand there and tell me that six-foot redhead ain't a madame, 'cause I know a madame when I hear about one, and you, you're just a pimp like all the rest I meet, everybody's a pimp."

"Listen, Terry, I am not a pimp. I swear to you on the Bible I am not a pimp. Why should I be a pimp? My only interest is you."

"All the time I thought I met a nice boy. I was so glad, I hugged myself and said, Hmm, a real nice boy instead of a pimp."

"Terry," I pleaded with all my soul. "Please listen to me and understand, I'm not a pimp." An hour ago I'd thought *she* was a hustler. How sad it was. Our minds, with their store of madness, had diverged. O gruesome life, how I moaned and pleaded, and then I got mad and realized I was pleading with a dumb little Mexican wench and I told her so; and before I knew it I picked up her red pumps and hurled them at the bathroom door and told her to get out. "Go on, beat it!'" I'd sleep and forget it; I had my own life, my own sad and ragged life forever. There was a dead silence in the bathroom. I took my clothes off and went to bed.

Terry came out with tears of sorriness in her eyes. In her simple and funny little mind had been decided the fact that a pimp does not throw a woman's shoes against the door and does not tell her to get out. In reverent and sweet little silence she took all her clothes off and slipped her tiny body into the sheets with me. It was brown as grapes. I saw her poor belly where there was a Caesarian scar; her hips were so narrow she couldn't bear a child without getting gashed open. Her legs were like little sticks. She was only four foot ten. I made love to her in the sweetness of the weary morning. Then, two tired angels of some kind, hung-up forlornly in an LA shelf, having found the closest and most delicious thing in life together, we fell asleep and slept till late afternoon.

For the next fifteen days we were together for better or for worse. When we woke up we decided to hitchhike to New York together; she was going to be my girl in town. I envisioned wild complexities with Dean and Marylou and everybody—a season, a new season. First we had to work to earn enough money for the trip. Terry was all for starting at once with the twenty dollars I had left. I didn't like it. And, like a damn fool, I considered the problem for two days, as we read the want ads of wild LA papers I'd never seen before in my life, in cafeterias and bars, until my twenty dwindled to just over ten. We were very happy in our little hotel room. In the middle of the night I got up because I couldn't sleep, pulled the cover over baby's bare brown shoulder, and examined the LA night. What brutal, hot, siren-whining nights they are! Right across the street there was trouble. An old rickety rundown rooming house was the scene of some kind of tragedy. The cruiser was pulled up below and the cops were questioning an old man with gray hair. Sobbings came from within. I could hear everything, together with the hum of my hotel neon. I never felt sadder in my life. LA is the loneliest and most brutal of American cities; New York gets god-awful cold in the winter but there's a feeling of wacky comradeship somewhere in some streets. LA is a jungle.

South Main Street, where Terry and I took strolls with hot dogs, was a fantastic carnival of lights and wildness. Booted cops frisked people on practically every corner. The beatest characters in the country swarmed on the sidewalks—all of it under those soft Southern California stars that are lost in the brown halo of the huge desert encampment LA really is. You could smell tea, weed, I mean marijuana, floating in the air, together with the chili beans and beer. That grand wild sound of bop floated from beer parlors; it mixed medleys with every kind of cowboy and boogie-woogie in the American night. Everybody looked like Hassel. Wild Negroes with bop caps and goatees came laughing by; then long-haired brokendown hipsters straight off Route 66 from New York; then old desert rats, carrying packs and heading for a park bench at the Plaza; then Methodist ministers with raveled sleeves, and an occasional Nature Boy saint in beard and sandals. I wanted to meet them all, talk to everybody, but Terry and I were too busy trying to get a buck together.

We went to Hollywood to try to work in the drugstore at Sunset and Vine. Now there was a corner! Great families off jalopies from the hinterlands stood around the sidewalk gaping for sight of some movie star, and the movie star never showed up. When a limousine passed they rushed eagerly to the curb and ducked to look: some character in dark glasses sat inside with a bejeweled blonde. "Don Ameche! Don Ameche!"

"No, George Murphy! George Murphy!" They milled around, looking at one another. Handsome queer boys who had come to Hollywood to be cowboys walked around, wetting their eyebrows with hincty fingertip. The most beautiful little gone gals in the world cut by in slacks; they came to be starlets; they ended up in drive-ins. Terry and I tried to find work at the drive-ins. It was no soap anywhere. Hollywood Boulevard was a great, screaming frenzy of cars; there were minor accidents at least once a minute; everybody was rushing off toward the farthest palm—and beyond that was the desert and nothingness. Hollywood Sams stood in front of swank restaurants, arguing exactly the same way Broadway Sams argue at Jacob's Beach, New York, only here they wore light-weight suits and their talk was cornier. Tall, cadaverous preachers shuddered by. Fat screaming women ran across the boulevard to get in line for the quiz shows. I saw Jerry Colonna buying a car at Buick Motors, he was inside the vast plate-glass window fingering his mustachio. Terry and I ate in a cafeteria downtown which was decorated to look like a grotto, with metal tits spurting everywhere and great impersonal stone buttockses belonging to deities and soapy Neptune. People ate lugubrious meals around the waterfalls, their faces green with marine sorrow. All the cops in LA looked like handsome gigolos; obviously they'd come to LA to make the movies. Everybody had come to make the movies, even me. Terry and I were finally reduced to trying to get jobs on South Main Street among the beat countermen and dishgirls who made no bones about their beatness, and even there it was no go. We still had ten dollars.

"Man, I'm going to get my clothes from Sis and we'll hitchhike to New York," said Terry. "Come on, man. Let's do it. 'If you can't boogie I know I'll show you how.' " That last part was a song of hers she kept singing. We hurried to her sister's house in the sliverous Mexican shacks somewhere beyond Alameda Avenue. I waited in a dark alley behind Mexican kitchens because her sister wasn't supposed to see me. Dogs ran by. There were little lamps illuminating the little rat alleys. I could hear Terry and her sister arguing in the soft, warm night. I was ready for anything.

Terry came out and led me by the hand to Central Avenue, which is the colored main drag of LA. And what a wild place it is, with chicken-shacks barely big enough to house a jukebox, and the jukebox blowing nothing but blues, bop, and jump. We went up dirty tenement stairs and came to the room of Terry's friend Margarina, who owed Terry a skirt and a pair of shoes. Margarina was a lovely mulatto; her husband was black as spades and kindly. He went right out and bought a pint of whisky to host me proper. I tried to pay part of it, but he said no. They had two little children. The kids bounced on the bed; it was their play-place. They put their arms around me and looked at me with wonder. The wild humming night of Central Avenue—the night of Hamp's "Central

Avenue Breakdown"—howled and boomed along outside. They were singing in the halls, singing from their windows, just hell be damned and look out. Terry got her clothes and we said good-by. We went down to a chickenshack and played records on the jukebox. A couple of Negro characters whispered in my ear about tea. One buck. I said okay, bring it. The connection came in and motioned me to the cellar toilet, where I stood around dumbly as he said, "Pick up, man, pick up."

"Pick up what?" I said.

He had my dollar already. He was afraid to point at the floor. It was no floor, just basement. There lay something that looked like a little brown turd. He was absurdly cautious. "Got to look out for myself, things ain't cool this past week." I picked up the turd, which was a brown-paper cigarette, and went back to Terry, and off we went to the hotel room to get high. Nothing happened. It was Bull Durham tobacco. I wished I was wiser with my money.

Terry and I had to decide absolutely and once and for all what to do. We decided to hitch to New York with our remaining money. She picked up five dollars from her sister that night. We had about thirteen or less. So before the daily room rent was due again we packed up and took off on a red car to Arcadia, California, where Santa Anita race-track is located under snow-capped mountains. It was night. We were pointed toward the American continent. Holding hands, we walked several miles down the road to get out of the populated district. It was a Saturday night. We stood under a roadlamp, thumbing, when suddenly cars full of young kids roared by with streamers flying. "Yaah! Yaah! we won! we won!" they all shouted. Then they yoohooed us and got great glee out of seeing a guy and a girl on the road. Dozens of such cars passed, full of young faces and "throaty young voices," as the saying goes. I hated every one of them. Who did they think they were, yaahing at somebody on the road just because they were little high-school punks and their parents carved the roast beef on Sunday afternoons? Who did they think they were, making fun of a girl reduced to poor circumstances with a man who wanted to belove? We were minding our own business. And we didn't get a blessed ride. We had to walk back to town, and worst of all we needed coffee and I had the misfortune of going into the only place open, which was a high-school soda fountain, and all the kids were there and remembered us. Now they saw that Terry was Mexican, a Pachuco wildcat; and that her boy was worse than that.

With her pretty nose in the air she cut out of there and we wandered together in the dark up along the ditches of the highways. I carried the bags. We were breathing fogs in the cold night air. I finally decided to hide from the world one more night with her, and the morning be damned. We went into a motel court and bought a comfortable little suite for about four dollars—shower, bathtowels, wall radio, and all. We held each other tight. We had long, serious talks and took baths and discussed things with the light on and then with the light out. Something was being proved, I was convincing her of something, which she accepted, and we concluded the pact in the dark, breathless, then pleased, like little lambs.

In the morning we boldly struck out on our new plan. We were going to take a bus to Bakersfield and work picking grapes. After a few weeks of that we were headed for New York in the proper way, by bus. It was a wonderful afternoon, riding up to Bakersfield with Terry: we sat back, relaxed, talked, saw the countryside roll by, and didn't worry about a thing. We arrived in Bakersfield in late afternoon. The plan was to hit every fruit wholesaler in town. Terry said we could live in tents on the job. The thought of living in a tent and picking grapes in the cool California mornings hit me right. But there were no jobs to be had, and much confusion, with everybody giving us innumerable tips, and no job materialized. Nevertheless we ate a Chinese dinner and set out with reinforced bodies. We went across the SP tracks to Mexican town. Terry jabbered with her brethren, asking for jobs. It was night now, and the little Mextown street was one blazing bulb of lights: movie marquees, fruit stands, penny arcades, five-and-tens, and hundreds of rickety trucks and mud-spattered jalopies, parked. Whole Mexican fruit-picking families wandered around eating popcorn. Terry talked to everybody. I was beginning to despair. What I needed—what Terry needed, too—was a drink, so we bought a quart of California port for thirty-five cents and went to the railroad yards to drink. We found a place where hobos had drawn up crates to sit over fires. We sat there and drank the wine. On our left were the freight cars, sad and sooty red beneath the moon; straight ahead the lights and airport pokers of Bakersfield proper; to our right a tremendous aluminum Quonset warehouse. Ah, it was a fine night, a warm night, a wine-drinking night, a moony night, and a night to hug your girl and talk and spit and be heavengoing. This we did. She was a drinking little fool and kept up with me and passed me and went right on talking till midnight. We never budged from those crates. Occasionally bums passed, Mexican mothers passed with children, and the prowl car came by and the cop got out to leak, but most of the time we were alone and mixing up our souls ever more and ever more till it would be terribly hard to say good-by. At midnight we got up and goofed toward the highway.

Terry had a new idea. We would hitchhike to Sabinal, her hometown, and live in her brother's garage. Anything was all right with me. On the road I made Terry sit down on my bag to make her look like a woman in distress, and right off a truck stopped and we ran for it, all glee-giggles. The man was a good man; his truck was poor. He roared and crawled on up the valley. We got to Sabinal in the wee hours before dawn. I had finished the wine while Terry slept, and I was proper stoned. We got out and roamed the quiet leafy square of the little California town—a whistle stop on the SP. We went to find her brother's buddy, who would tell us where he was. Nobody home. As dawn began to break I lay flat on my back in the lawn of the town square and kept saying over and over again, "You won't tell what he done up in Weed, will you? What'd he do up in Weed? You won't tell will you? What'd he do in Weed?" This was from the picture *Of Mice and Men,* with Burgess Meredith talking to the foreman of the ranch. Terry giggled. Anything I did was all right with her. I could lie there and go on doing that till the ladies came out for church and she wouldn't care. But finally I decided we'd be all set soon because of her brother, and I took her to an old hotel by the tracks and we went to bed comfortably.

In the bright, sunny morning Terry got up early and went to find her brother. I slept till noon, when I looked out the window I suddenly saw an SP freight going by with hundreds of hobos reclining on the flatcars and rolling merrily along with packs for pillows and funny papers before their noses, and some munching on good California grapes picked up by the siding. "Damn!" I yelled. "Hooee! It *is* the promised land." They were all coming from Frisco; in a week they'd all be going back in the same grand style.

Terry arrived with her brother, his buddy, and her child. Her brother was a wild-buck Mexican hotcat with a hunger for booze, a great good kid. His buddy was a big flabby Mexican who spoke English without much accent and was loud and overanxious to please. I could see he had eyes for Terry. Her little boy was Johnny, seven years old, dark-eyed and sweet. Well, there we were, and another wild day began.

Her brother's name was Rickey. He had a '38 Chevy. We piled into that and took off for parts unknown. "Where we going?" I asked. The buddy did the explaining—his name was Ponzo, that's what everybody called him. He stank. I found out why. His business was selling manure to farmers; he had a truck. Rickey always had three or four dollars in his pocket and was happy-go-lucky about things. He always said, "That's right, man, there you go—dah you go, dah you go!" And he went. He drove seventy miles an hour in the old heap, and we went to Madera beyond Fresno to see some farmers about manure.

Rickey had a bottle. "Today we drink, tomorrow we work. Dah you go, man—take a shot!" Terry sat in back with her baby; I looked back at her and saw the flush of homecoming joy on her face. The beautiful green countryside of October in California reeled by madly. I was guts and juice again and ready to go.

"Where do we go now, man?"

"We go find a farmer with some manure laying around. Tomorrow we drive back in the truck and pick it up. Man, we'll make a lot of money. Don't worry about nothing."

"We're all in this together!" yelled Ponzo. I saw that was so—everywhere I went, everybody was in it together. We raced through the crazy streets of Fresno and on up the valley to some farmers in back roads. Ponzo got out of the car and conducted confused conversations with old Mexican farmers; nothing, of course, came of it.

"What we need is a drink!" yelled Rickey, and off we went to a crossroads saloon. Americans are always drinking in crossroads saloons on Sunday afternoon; they bring their kids; they gabble and brawl over brews; everything's fine. Come nightfall the kids start crying and the parents are drunk. They go weaving back to the house. Everywhere in America I've been in crossroads saloons drinking with whole families. The kids eat popcorn and chips and play in back. This we did. Rickey and I and Ponzo and Terry sat drinking and shouting with the music; little baby Johnny goofed with other children around the jukebox. The sun began to get red. Nothing had been accomplished. What was there to accomplish? "*Mañana*," said Rickey. "*Mañana*, man, we make it; have another beer, man, dah you go, *dah you go!*"

We staggered out and got in the car; off we went to a highway bar. Ponzo was a big, loud, vociferous type who knew everybody in San Joaquin Valley. From the highway bar I went with him alone in the car to find a farmer; instead we wound up in Madera Mextown, digging the girls and trying to pick up a few for him and Rickey. And then, as purple dusk descended over the grape country, I found myself sitting dumbly in the car as he argued with some old Mexican at the kitchen door about the price of a watermelon the old man grew in the back yard. We got the watermelon; we ate it on the spot and threw the rinds on the old man's dirt sidewalk. All kinds of pretty little girls were cutting down the darkening street. I said, "Where in the hell are we?"

"Don't worry, man," said big Ponzo. "Tomorrow we make a lot of money; tonight we don't worry." We went back and picked up Terry and her brother and the kid and drove to Fresno in the highway lights of night. We were all raving hungry. We bounced over the railroad tracks in Fresno and hit the wild streets of Fresno Mextown. Strange Chinese hung out of windows, digging the Sunday night streets; groups of Mex chicks swaggered around in slacks; mambo blasted from jukeboxes; the lights were festooned around like Halloween. We went into a Mexican restaurant and had tacos and mashed pinto beans rolled in tortillas; it was delicious. I whipped out my last shining five-dollar bill which stood between me and the New Jersey shore and paid for Terry and me. Now I had four bucks. Terry and I looked at each other.

"Where we going to sleep tonight, baby?"

"I don't know."

Rickey was drunk; now all he was saying was, "Dah you go, man—dah you go, man," in a tender and tired voice. It had been a long day.

None of us knew what was going on, or what the Good Lord appointed. Poor little Johnny fell asleep on my arm. We drove back to Sabinal. On the way we pulled up sharp at a roadhouse on Highway 99. Rickey wanted one last beer. In back of the roadhouse were trailers and tents and a few rickety motel-style rooms. I inquired about the price and it was two bucks. I asked Terry how about it, and she said fine because we had the kid on our hands now and had to make him comfortable. So after a few beers in the saloon, where sullen Okies reeled to the music of a cowboy band, Terry and I and Johnny went into a motel room and got ready to hit the sack. Ponzo kept hanging around; he had no place to sleep. Rickey slept at his father's house in the vineyard shack.

"Where do you live, Ponzo?" I asked.

"Nowhere, man. I'm supposed to live with Big Rosey but she threw me out last night. I'm gonna get my truck and sleep in it tonight."

Guitars tinkled. Terry and I gazed at the stars together and kissed. "*Mañana*," she said. "Everything'll be all right tomorrow, don't you think, Sal-honey, man?"

"Sure, baby, *mañana*." It was always *mañana*. For the next week that was all I heard—*mañana*, a lovely word and one that probably means heaven.

Little Johnny jumped in bed, clothes and all, and went to sleep; sand spilled out of his shoes, Madera sand. Terry and I got up in the middle of the night and brushed the sand off the sheets. In the morning I got up, washed, and took a walk around the place. We were five miles out of Sabinal in the cotton fields and grape vineyards. I asked the big fat woman who owned the camp if any of the tents were vacant. The cheapest one, a dollar a day, was vacant. I fished up a dollar and moved into it. There were a bed, a stove, and a cracked mirror hanging from a pole; it was delightful. I had to stoop to get in, and when I did there was my baby and my baby boy. We waited for Rickey and Ponzo to arrive with the truck. They arrived with beer bottles and started to get drunk in the tent.

"How about the manure?"

"Too late today. Tomorrow, man, we make a lot of money; today we have a few beers. What do you say, beer?" I didn't have to be prodded. "Dah you go—*dah you go!*" yelled Rickey. I began to see that our plans for making money with the manure truck would never materialize. The truck was parked outside the tent. It smelled like Ponzo.

That night Terry and I went to bed in the sweet night air beneath our dewy tent. I was just getting ready to go to sleep when she said, "You want to love me now?"

I said, "What about Johnny?"

"He don't mind. He's asleep." But Johnny wasn't asleep and he said nothing.

The boys came back the next day with the manure truck and drove off to find whisky; they came back and had a big time in the tent. That night Ponzo said it was too cold and slept on the ground in our tent, wrapped in a big tarpaulin smelling of cowflaps. Terry hated him; she said he hung around with her brother in order to get close to her.

Nothing was going to happen except starvation for Terry and me, so in the morning I walked around the countryside asking for cotton-picking work. Everybody told me to go to the farm across the highway from the camp. I went, and the farmer was in the kitchen with his women. He came out, listened to my story, and warned me he was paying only three dollars per hundred pounds of picked cotton. I pictured myself picking at least three hundred pounds a day and took the job. He fished out some long canvas bags from the barn and told me the picking started at dawn. I rushed back to Terry, all glee. On the way a grape truck went over a bump in the road and threw off great bunches of grapes on the hot tar. I picked them up and took them home. Terry was glad. "Johnny and me'll come with you and help."

"Pshaw!" I said. "No such thing!"

"You see, you see, it's very hard picking cotton. I show you how."

We ate the grapes, and in the evening Rickey showed up with a loaf of bread and a pound of hamburg and we had a picnic. In a larger tent next to ours lived a whole family of Okie cotton-pickers; the grandfather sat in a chair all day long, he was too old to work; the son and daughter, and their children, filed every dawn across the highway to my farmer's field and went to work. At dawn the next day I went with them. They said the cotton was heavier at dawn because of the dew and you could make more money than in the afternoon. Nevertheless they worked all day from dawn to sundown. The grandfather had come from Nebraska during the great plague of the thirties—that selfsame dustcloud my Montana cowboy had told me about—with the entire family in a jalopy truck. They had been in California ever since. They loved to work. In the ten years the old man's son had increased his children to the number of four, some of whom were old enough now to pick cotton. And in that time they had progressed from ragged poverty in Simon Legree fields to a kind of smiling respectability in better tents, and that was all. They were extremely proud of their tent.

"Ever going back to Nebraska?"

"Pshaw, there's nothing back there. What we want to do is buy a trailer."

We bent down and began picking cotton. It was beautiful. Across the field were the tents, and beyond them the sere brown cotton fields that stretched out of sight to the brown arroyo foothills and then the snow-capped Sierras in the blue morning air. This was so much better than washing dishes on South Main Street. But I knew nothing about picking cotton. I spent too much time disengaging the white ball from its crackly bed; the others did it in one flick. Moreover, my fingertips began to bleed; I needed gloves, or more experience. There was an old Negro couple in the field with us. They picked cotton with the same God-blessed patience their grandfathers had practiced in ante-bellum Alabama; they moved right along their rows, bent and blue, and their bags increased. My back began to ache. But it was beautiful kneeling and hiding in that earth. If I felt like resting I did, with my face on the pillow of brown moist earth. Birds sang an accompaniment. I thought I had found my life's work. Johnny and Terry came waving at me across the field in the hot lullal noon and pitched in with me. Be damned if little Johnny wasn't faster than I was!—And of course Terry was twice as fast. They worked ahead of me and left me piles of clean cotton to add to my bag—Terry workmanlike piles, Johnny little childly piles. I stuck them in with sorrow. What kind of old man was I that couldn't support his own ass, let alone theirs? They spent all afternoon with me. When the sun got red we trudged back together. At the end of the field I unloaded my burden on a scale; it weighed fifty pounds, and I got a buck fifty. Then I borrowed a bicycle from one of the Okie boys and rode down 99 to a crossroads grocery store where I bought cans of cooked spaghetti and meatballs, bread, butter, coffee, and cake, and came back with the bag on the handlebars. LA-bound traffic zoomed by; Frisco-bound harassed my tail. I swore and swore. I looked up at the dark sky and prayed to God for a better break in life and a better chance to do something for the little people I loved. Nobody was paying any attention to me up there. I should have known better. It was Terry who brought my soul back; on the tent stove she warmed up the food, and it was one of the greatest meals of my life. I was so hungry and tired. Sighing like an old Negro cotton-picker, I reclined on the bed and smoked a cigarette. Dogs barked in the cool night. Rickey and Ponzo had given up calling in the evenings. I was satisfied with that. Terry curled up beside me, Johnny sat on my chest, and they drew pictures of animals in my notebook. The light of our tent burned on the frightful plain. The cowboy music twanged in the roadhouse and carried across the fields, all sadness. It was all right with me. I kissed my baby and we put out the lights.

In the morning the dew made the tent sag; I got up with my towel and toothbrush and went to the general motel toilet to wash; then I came back, put on my pants, which were all torn from kneeling in the earth and had been sewed by Terry in the evening, put on my ragged straw hat, which had originally served as Johnny's toy hat, and went across the highway with my canvas cotton-bag.

Every day I earned approximately a dollar and a half. It was just enough to buy groceries in the evening on the bicycle. The days rolled by. I forgot all about the East and all about Dean and Carlo and the bloody road. Johnny and I played all the time; he liked me to throw him up in the air and down in the bed. Terry sat mending clothes. I was a man of the earth, precisely as I had dreamed I would be, in Paterson. There was talk that Terry's husband was back in Sabinal and out for me; I was ready for him. One night the Okies went mad in the roadhouse and tied a man to a tree and beat him to a pulp with sticks. I was asleep at the time and only heard about it. From then on I carried a big stick with me in the tent in case they got the idea we Mexicans were fouling up their trailer camp. They thought I was a Mexican, of course; and in a way I am.

But now it was October and getting much colder in the nights. The Okie family had a woodstove and planned to stay for the winter. We had nothing, and besides the rent for the tent was due. Terry and I bitterly decided we'd have to leave. "Go back to your family," I said. "For God's sake, you can't be batting around tents with a baby like Johnny; the poor little tyke is cold." Terry cried because I was criticizing her motherly instincts; I meant no such thing. When Ponzo came in the truck one gray afternoon we decided to see her family about the situation. But I mustn't be seen and would have to hide in the vineyard. We started for Sabinal; the truck broke down, and simultaneously it started to rain wildly. We sat in the old truck, cursing. Ponzo got out and toiled in the rain. He was a good old guy after all. We promised each other one more big bat. Off we went to a rickety bar in Sabinal Mextown and spent an hour sopping up the brew. I was through with my chores in the cottonfield. I could feel the pull of my own life calling me back. I shot my aunt a penny postcard across the land and asked for another fifty.

We drove to Terry's family's shack. It was situated on the old road that ran between the vineyards. It was dark when we got there. They left me off a quarter-mile away and drove to the door. Light poured out of the door; Terry's six other brothers were playing their guitars and singing. The old man was drinking wine. I heard shouts and arguments above the singing. They called her a whore because she'd left her no-good husband and gone to LA and left Johnny with them. The old man was yelling. But the sad, fat brown mother prevailed, as she always does among the great fellahin peoples of the world, and Terry was allowed to come back home. The brothers began to sing gay songs, fast. I huddled in the cold, rainy wind and watched everything across the sad vineyards of October in the valley. My mind was filled with that great song "Lover Man" as Billie Holiday sings it; I had my own concert in the bushes. "Someday we'll meet, and you'll dry all my tears, and whisper sweet, little things in my ear, hugging and a-kissing, oh what we've been missing, Lover Man, oh where can you be . . ." It's not the words so much as the great harmonic tune and the way Billie sings it, like a woman stroking her man's hair in soft lamplight. The winds howled. I got cold.

Terry and Ponzo came back and we rattled off in the old truck to meet

Rickey. Rickey was now living with Ponzo's woman, Big Rosey; we tooted the horn for him in rickety alleys. Big Rosey threw him out. Everything was collapsing. That night we slept in the truck. Terry held me tight, of course, and told me not to leave. She said she'd work picking grapes and make enough money for both of us; meanwhile I could live in Farmer Heffelfinger's barn down the road from her family. I'd have nothing to do but sit in the grass all day and eat grapes. "You like that?"

In the morning her cousins came to get us in another truck. I suddenly realized thousands of Mexicans all over the countryside knew about Terry and me and that it must have been a juicy, romantic topic for them. The cousins were very polite and in fact charming. I stood on the truck, smiling pleasantries, talking about where we were in the war and what the pitch was. There were five cousins in all, and every one of them was nice. They seemed to belong to the side of Terry's family that didn't fuss off like her brother. But I loved that wild Rickey. He swore he was coming to New York to join me. I pictured him in New York, putting off everything till *mañana*. He was drunk in a field someplace that day.

I got off the truck at the crossroads, and the cousins drove Terry home. They gave me the high sign from the front of the house; the father and mother weren't home, they were off picking grapes. So I had the run of the house for the afternoon. It was a four-room shack; I couldn't imagine how the whole family managed to live in there. Flies flew over the sink. There were no screens, just like in the song, "The window she is broken and the rain she is coming in." Terry was at home now and puttering around pots. Her two sisters giggled at me. The little children screamed in the road.

When the sun came out red through the clouds of my last valley afternoon, Terry led me to Farmer Heffelfinger's barn. Farmer Heffelfinger had a prosperous farm up the road. We put crates together, she brought blankets from the house, and I was all set except for a great hairy tarantula that lurked at the pinpoint top of the barn room. Terry said it wouldn't harm me if I didn't bother it. I lay on my back and stared at it. I went out to the cemetery and climbed a tree. In the tree I sang "Blue Skies." Terry and Johnny sat in the grass; we had grapes. In California you chew the juice out of grapes and spit the skin away, a real luxury. Nightfall came. Terry went home for supper and came to the barn at nine o'clock with delicious tortillas and mashed beans. I lit a woodfire on the cement floor of the barn to make light. We made love on the crates. Terry got up and cut right back to the shack. Her father was yelling at her; I could hear him from the barn. She'd left me a cape to keep warm; I threw it over my shoulder and skulked through the moonlit vineyard to see what was going on. I crept to the end of a row and knelt in the warm dirt. Her five brothers were singing melodious songs in Spanish. The stars bent over the little roof; smoke poked from the stovepipe chimney. I smelled mashed beans and chili. The old man growled. The brothers kept right on yodeling. The mother was silent. Johnny and the kids were giggling in the bedroom. A California home; I hid in the grapevines, digging it all. I felt like a million dollars; I was adventuring in the crazy American night.

Terry came out, slamming the door behind her. I accosted her on the dark road. "What's the matter?"

"Oh, we fight all the time. He wants me to go to work tomorrow. He says he don't want me foolin around. Sallie, I want to go to New York with you."

"But how?"

"I don't know, honey. I'll miss you. I love you."

"But I have to leave."

"Yes, yes. We lay down one more time, then you leave." We went back to the barn; I made love to her under the tarantula. What was the tarantula doing? We slept awhile on the crates as the fire died. She went back at midnight; her father was drunk; I could hear him roaring; then there was silence as he fell asleep. The stars folded over the sleeping countryside.

In the morning Farmer Heffelfinger stuck his head through the horse gate and said, "How you doing, young fella?"

"Fine. I hope it's all right my staying here."

"Sure thing. You going with that little Mexican floozy?"

"She's a very nice girl."

"Very pretty too. I think the bull jumped the fence. She's got blue eyes." We talked about his farm.

Terry brought my breakfast. I had my canvas bag all packed and ready to go to New York, as soon as I picked up my money in Sabinal. I knew it was waiting there for me by now. I told Terry I was leaving. She had been thinking about it all night and was resigned to it. Emotionlessly she kissed me in the vineyard and walked off down the row. We turned at a dozen paces, for love is a duel, and looked at each other for the last time.

"See you in New York, Terry," I said. She was supposed to drive to New York in a month with her brother. But we both knew she wouldn't make it. At a hundred feet I turned to look at her. She just walked on back to the shack, carrying my breakfast plate in one hand. I bowed my head and watched her. Well, lackadaddy, I was on the road again.

I walked down the highway to Sabinal, eating black walnuts from the walnut tree. I went on the SP tracks and balanced along the rail. I passed a watertower and a factory. This was the end of something. I went to the telegraph office of the railroad for my money order from New York. It was closed. I swore and sat on the steps to wait. The ticket master got back and invited me in. The money was in; my aunt had saved my lazy butt again. "Who's going to win the World Series next year?" said the gaunt old ticket master. I suddenly realized it was fall and that I was going back to New York.

QUESTIONS

1. If Sal Paradise is supposed to be Jack Kerouac, what advantages does Kerouac gain by using a fictional narrator?
2. Why does Sal think that Terry is a hustler? Why does she think that he is a pimp? What do their suspicions reveal?
3. At first how do Sal and Terry fantasize about one another? What assumptions allow them to enjoy their affair with relatively few conflicts?
4. What sense of Los Angeles do we get from Sal's description of it? What literary techniques does he use to capture this sense of the city?
5. What enables people like big Ponzo and Rickey to enjoy the present, to live the *mañana* philosophy? Is Sal able to join them? What are the positive aspects of their culture?
6. Does Sal learn anything from this experience? Has he merely "used" these people for his own purposes or has he given them something in return?

CHRISTOPHER ISHERWOOD

CHRISTOPHER ISHERWOOD (b. 1904) is a native of England and was educated at Cambridge. From 1929 to 1933 he lived in Berlin where he found the materials for *The Berlin Stories*, two books of thematically related stories that describe conditions in Germany before the rise of Hitler (*The Last of Mr. Norris*, 1935, and *Goodbye to Berlin*, 1939). He has collaborated on several literary ventures with W. H. Auden and has written and translated several works on Indian philosophy. In 1946 he became an American citizen and now resides in Southern California.

A *Single Man* (1964) describes a single day in the life of a fifty-eight-year-old English expatriate, a professor of English at a California university. He is a homosexual who has recently been overwhelmed by the death of Jim, the man with whom he has lived. At times his daily routine is interrupted by his feelings of loss and nostalgia. While we share his day with him, we see life through a different perspective, an outsider's view of a world that is dominated by sexual prejudice. But despite the barriers he encounters and the necessity of playing roles, George tenaciously holds onto what is left of life for him. He lives with both heightened awareness and enjoyment. When good moments are available, he seizes on them. His suffering heightens his sense of what life has given him.

The two episodes here are from "recreational" periods in George's typical day as a college lecturer. The first is something of an escape from the pressures of his job. He visits a gym where he frankly confronts his middle-aged body and, although dismayed by certain inevitable signs of decay, he can assert that unlike many others his age he "hasn't given up." In the gym there is an honest celebration of the physical and George enjoys the beauty of the younger men as well as his feelings of camaraderie with everyone who is working out.

In both these episodes Isherwood is nostalgic about the Los Angeles world of twenty years past, which he sees being destroyed by tract homes and shopping centers. After his session at the gym,

George visits the hills where he used to feel the thrill of being a trespasser in a "primitive, alien nature." But now the hawks and coyotes are gone. The area is becoming suburban, and "he is oppressed by awareness of the city below." Similarly, at the start of the next section, he recalls the happy days of couples making love, including Jim and himself, on the beach immediately following the end of the war in the summer of 1946. But the "glorious Indian summer of lust" is over, replaced by scores of signs that list endless restrictions on what one can do and where it can be done. He returns to his favorite bar, The Starboard Side, to recall "the glory" that has "faded" both from Southern California and his own life. The innocence, beauty, and openness of Southern California seem to have gone forever.

His encounter with his student, Kenny, reopens some possibilities. Kenny is willing to relate to his teacher as a person, thus melting many of George's usual defenses against students. There is another aid to communication: As an "outlaw" in American society (and having had none of the joys and struggles of bringing up children of his own), George identifies with the young man's spirit of revolt and sense of alienation. Similarly he dares to swim later in the evening with Kenny because he has never repressed his boyish sense of adventure and romance.

Kenny is naïve about both George's sexual identity and relative happiness. "You've discovered the secret of the perfect life" he tells George when he sees his home. George, on the other hand, is caught between feelings of wanting to confess his homosexuality to Kenny and desiring to help Kenny by providing him a place where he can make love to his girl. The connections between the two may be somewhat tenuous, but some human contact is made. It brings out the best in George; he realizes that his secret, his hidden strength results from his unconventionality, his willingness to be "as crazy as a kid."

[FROM A Single Man]

As George drives down the boulevard, the big unwieldy Christmas decorations—reindeer and jingle bells slung across the street on cables secured to metal Christmas trees—are swinging in a chill wind. But they are merely advertisements for Christmas, paid for by the local merchants. Shoppers crowd the stores and the sidewalks, their faces somewhat bewildered, their eyes reflecting, like polished buttons, the cynical sparkle of the Yuletide. Hardly more than a month ago, before Khrushchev agreed to pull his rockets out of Cuba, they were cramming the markets, buying the shelves bare of beans, rice and other foodstuffs, utterly useless, most of them, for air-raid-shelter cookery, because they can't be prepared without pints of water. Well, the shoppers were spared—this time. Do they rejoice? They are too dull for that, poor dears; they never knew what didn't hit them. No doubt because of that panic buying, they have less money now for gifts. But they have enough. It will be quite a good Christmas, the merchants predict. Everyone can afford to spend at least something, except, maybe, some of the young hustlers (recognizable at once to experienced eyes like George's) who stand scowling on the street corners or staring into shops with the maximum of peripheral vision.

George is very far, right now, from sneering at any of these fellow creatures. They may be crude and mercenary and dull and low, but he is proud, is glad, is almost indecently gleeful to be able to stand up and be counted in their ranks—the ranks of that marvelous minority, The Living. They don't know their luck, these people on the sidewalk, but George knows his—for a little while at least—because he is freshly returned from the icy presence of The Majority, which Doris is about to join.

I am alive, he says to himself, *I am alive!* And life-energy surges hotly through him, and delight, and appetite. How good to be in a body—even this old beat-up carcass—that still has warm blood and live semen and rich marrow and wholesome flesh! The scowling youths on the corners see him as a dodderer, no doubt, or at best as a potential score. Yet he still claims a distant kinship with the strength of their young arms and shoulders and loins. For a few bucks he could get any one of them to climb into the car, ride back with him to his house, strip off butch leather jacket, skin-tight levis, shirt and cowboy boots and take part, a naked, sullen young athlete, in the wrestling bout of his pleasure. But George doesn't want the bought unwilling bodies of these boys. He wants to rejoice in his own body—the tough triumphant old body of a survivor. The body that has outlived Jim and is going to outlive Doris.

He decides to stop by the gym—although this isn't one of his regular days—on his way home.

In the locker room, George takes off his clothes, gets into his sweatsocks, jockstrap and shorts. Shall he put on a tee shirt? He looks at himself in the long mirror. Not too bad. The bulges of flesh over the belt of the shorts are not so noticeable today. The legs are quite good. The chest muscles, when properly flexed, don't sag. And, as long as he doesn't have his spectacles on, he can't see the little wrinkles inside the elbows, above the kneecaps and around the hollow of the sucked-in belly. The neck is loose and scraggy under all circumstances, in all lights, and would look gruesome even if he were half-blind. He has abandoned the neck altogether, like an untenable military position.

Yet he looks—and doesn't he know it!—better than nearly all of his age-mates at this gym. Not because they're in such bad shape—they are healthy enough specimens. What's wrong with them is their fatalistic acceptance of middle age, their ignoble resignation to grandfatherhood, impending retirement and golf. George is different from them because, in some sense which can't quite be defined but which is immediately apparent when you see him naked, *he hasn't given up*. He is still a contender, and they aren't. Maybe it's nothing more mysterious than vanity which gives him this air of a withered boy? Yes, despite his wrinkles, his slipped flesh, his graying hair, his grim-lipped, strutting spryness, you catch occasional glimpses of a ghostly someone else, soft-faced, boyish, pretty. The combination is bizarre, it is older than middle age itself, but it is there.

Looking grimly into the mirror, with distaste and humor, George says to himself, You old ass, who are you trying to seduce? And he puts on his tee shirt.

In the gym there are only three people. It's still too early for the office workers. A big heavy man named Buck—all that remains at fifty of a football player—is talking to a curly-haired young man named Rick, who aspires to television. Buck is nearly nude; his rolling belly bulges indecently over a kind of bikini, pushing it clear down to the bush line. He seems quite without shame. Whereas Rick, who has a very well-made muscular body, wears a gray wool sweatshirt and pants, covering all of it from the neck to the wrists and ankles. "Hi, George" they both say, nodding casually at him; and this, George feels, is the most genuinely friendly greeting he has received all day.

Buck knows all about the history of sport; he is an encyclopedia of batting averages, handicaps, records and scores. He is in the midst of telling how someone took someone else in the seventh round. He mimes the knockout: "*Pow! Pow!* And, boy, he'd *had* it!" Rick listens, seated astride a bench. There is always an atmosphere of leisureliness in this place. A boy like Rick will take three or four hours to work out, and spend most of the time just yakking about show biz, about sport cars, about football and boxing—very seldom, oddly enough, about sex. Perhaps this is partly out of consideration for the morals of the various young kids and early teen-agers who are usually around. When Rick talks to grownups, he is apt to be smart-alecky or actor-sincere; but with the kids he is as unaffected as a village idiot. He clowns for them and does magic tricks and tells them stories, deadpan, about a store in Long Beach (he gives its exact address) where once in a great while, suddenly and without any previous announcement, they declare a Bargain Day. On such days, every customer who spends more than a dollar gets a Jag or a Porsche or an MG for free. (The rest of the time, the place is an ordinary antique shop.) When Rick is challenged to show the car *he* got, he takes the kids outside and points to a suitable one on the street. When they look at its registration slip and find that it belongs to someone else, Rick swears that that's his real name; he changed it when he started acting. The kids don't absolutely disbelieve him, but they yell that he's a liar and crazy and they beat on him with their fists.While they do this, Rick capers grinning around the gym on all fours, like a dog.

George lies down on one of the inclined boards in order to do sit-ups. This is always something you have to think yourself into; the body dislikes them more than any other exercise. While he is getting into the mood, Webster comes over and lies down on the board next to his. Webster is maybe twelve or thirteen, slender and graceful and tall for his age, with long smooth golden boy-legs. He is gentle and shy, and he moves about the gym in a kind of dream; but he keeps steadily on with his workout. No doubt he thinks he looks scrawny and has vowed to become a huge wide awkward overloaded muscle man. George says, "Hi, Web," and Webster answers, "Hi, George," in a shy, secretive whisper.

Now Webster begins doing his sit-ups, and George, peeling off his tee shirt on a sudden impulse, follows his example. As they continue, George feels an empathy growing between them. They are not competing with each other; but Webster's youth and litheness seem to possess George, and this borrowed energy is terrific. Withdrawing his attention from his own protesting muscles and concentrating it upon Webster's flexing and relaxing body, George draws the strength from it to go on beyond his normal forty sit-ups, to fifty, to sixty, to seventy, to eighty. Shall he try for a hundred? Then, all at once, he is aware that Webster has stopped. The strength leaves him instantly. He stops too, panting hard —though not any harder than Webster himself. They lie there panting, side by side. Webster turns his head and looks at George, obviously rather impressed.

"How many do you do?" he asks.

"Oh—it depends."

"These things just kill me. Man!"

How delightful it is to be here. If only one could spend one's entire life in this state of easygoing physical democracy. Nobody is bitchy here, or ill-tempered, or inquisitive. Vanity, including the most outrageous posings in front of the mirrors, is taken for granted. The godlike young baseball player confides to all his anxiety about the smallness of his ankles. The plump banker, rubbing his face with skin cream, says simply, "I can't afford to get old." No one is perfect and no one pretends to be. Even the half-dozen quite well-known actors put on no airs. The youngest kids sit innocently naked beside sixty- and seventy-year-olds in the steam room, and they call each other by their first names. Nobody is too hideous or too handsome to be accepted as an equal. Surely everyone is nicer in this place than he is outside it?

Today George feels more than usually unwilling to leave the gym. He does his exercises twice as many times as he is supposed to; he spends a long while in the steam room; he washes his hair.

When he comes out onto the street again, it is already getting toward sunset. And now he makes another impulsive decision: instead of driving directly back to the beach, he will take a long detour through the hills.

Why? Partly because he wants to enjoy the uncomplicated relaxed happy mood which is nearly always produced by a workout at the gym. It is so good to feel the body's satisfaction and gratitude; no matter how much it may protest, it likes being forced to perform these tasks. Now, for a while at least, the vagus nerve won't twitch, the pylorus will be quiet, the arthritic thumbs and knee won't assert themselves. And how restful, now that there's no need for stimulants, not to have to hate anyone at all! George hopes to be able to stay in this mood as long as he keeps on driving.

Also, he wants to take a look at the hills again; he hasn't been up there in a long time. Years ago, before Jim even, when George first came to California, he used to go into the hills often. It was the wildness of this range, largely uninhabited yet rising right up out of the city, that fascinated him. He felt the thrill of being a foreigner, a trespasser there, of venturing into the midst of a primitive, alien nature. He would drive up at sunset or very early in the morning, park his car, and wander off along the firebreak trails, catching glimpses of deer moving deep in the chaparral of a canyon, stopping to watch a hawk circling overhead, stepping carefully among hairy tarantulas crawling across his path, following twisty tracks in the sand until he came upon a coiled dozing rattler. Sometimes, in the half-light of dawn, he would meet a pack of coyotes trotting toward him, tails down, in single file. The first time this happened he took them for dogs; and then, suddenly, without uttering a sound, they broke formation and went bounding away downhill, with great uncanny jumps.

But this afternoon George can feel nothing of that long-ago excitement and awe; something is wrong from the start. The steep, winding road, which used to seem romantic, is merely awkward now, and dangerous. He keeps meeting other cars on blind corners and having to swerve sharply. By the time he has reached the top, he has lost all sense of relaxation. Even up here they are building dozens of new houses. The area is getting suburban. True, there are still a few uninhabited canyons, but George can't rejoice in them; he is oppressed by awareness of the city below. On both sides of the hills, to the north and to the south, it has spawned and spread itself over the entire plain. It has eaten up the wide pastures and ranchlands and the last stretches of orange grove; it has sucked out the surrounding lakes and sapped the forests of the high mountains. Soon it will be drinking converted sea water. And yet it will die. No need for rockets to wreck it, or another ice age to freeze it, or a huge earthquake to crack it off and dump it in the Pacific. It will die of overextension. It will die because its taproots have dried up—the brashness and greed which have been its only strength. And the desert, which is the natural condition of this country, will return.

Alas, how sadly, how certainly George knows this! He stops the car and stands at the road's rough yellow dirt edge, beside a manzanita bush, and looks out over Los Angeles like a sad Jewish prophet of doom, as he takes a leak. *Babylon is fallen, is fallen, that great city.* But this city is not great, was never great, and has nearly no distance to fall.

Now he zips up his pants and gets into the car and drives on, thoroughly depressed. The clouds close in low upon the hills, making them seem northern and sad like Wales; and the day wanes, and the lights snap on in their sham jewel colors all over the plain, as the road winds down again on to Sunset Boulevard and he nears the ocean.

Well and good.

How to explain, then, that, with his foot actually on the bridge over the creek, George suddenly turns, chuckles to himself, and with the movement of a child wriggling free of a grownup—old guardian Cortex —runs off down the road, laughing, toward the ocean?

As he trots out of Camphor Tree Lane on to Las Ondas, he sees the round green porthole lights of The Starboard Side, down on the corner of the ocean highway across from the beach, shining to welcome him.

The Starboard Side has been here since the earliest days of the colony. Its bar, formerly a lunch counter, served the neighbors with their first post-prohibition beers, and the mirror behind it was sometimes honored by the reflection of Tom Mix. But its finest hours came later. That summer of 1945! The war as good as over. The blackout no more than an excuse for keeping the lights out at a gangbang. A sign over the bar said, "In case of a direct hit, we close immediately." Which was meant to be funny, of course. And yet, out across the bay, in deep water under the cliffs of Palos Verdes, lay a real Japanese submarine full of real dead Japanese, depth-bombed after they had sunk two or three ships in sight of the Californian coast.

You pushed aside the blackout curtain and elbowed your way through a jam-packed bar crowd, scarcely able to breathe or see for smoke. Here, in the complete privacy of the din and the crowd, you and your pickup yelled the preliminary sex advances at each other. You could flirt but you couldn't fight; there wasn't even room to smack someone's face. For that, you had to step outside. Oh, the bloody battles and the sidewalk vomitings! The punches flying wide, the heads crashing backwards against the fenders of parked cars! Huge diesel-dikes slugging it out, grimmer far than the men. The siren-wailing arrival of the police; the sudden swoopings of the shore patrol. Girls dashing down from their apartments to drag some gorgeous endangered young drunk upstairs to safety and breakfast served next morning in bed like a miracle of joy. Hitch-hiking servicemen delayed at this corner for hours, nights, days; proceeding at last on their journey with black eyes, crab-lice, clap, and only the dimmest memory of their hostess or host.

And then the war's end and the mad spree of driving up and down the highway on the instantly derationed gas, shedding great black chunks of your recaps all the way to Malibu. And then the beach-months of 1946. The magic squalor of those hot nights, when the whole shore was alive with tongues of flame, the watchfires of a vast naked barbarian tribe —each group or pair to itself and bothering no one, yet all a part of the life of the tribal encampment—swimming in the darkness, cooking fish, dancing to the radio, coupling without shame on the sand. George and Jim (who had just met) were out there among them evening after evening, yet not often enough to satisfy the sad fierce appetite of memory, as it looks back hungrily on that glorious Indian summer of lust.

The hitch-hiking servicemen are few now and mostly domesticated, going back and forth between the rocket base and their homes and wives. Beach fires are forbidden, except in designated picnic areas where you must eat sitting up on benches at communal tables, and mustn't screw at all. But, though so much of the glory has faded, nevertheless—thanks to the persecuted yet undying old gods of disorder—this last block of Las Ondas is still a bad neighborhood. Respectable people avoid it instinctively. Realtors deplore it. Property values are low here. The motels are new but cheaply stuck together and already slum-sordid; they cater

to one-night stands. And, though the charcoal remnants of those barbarian orgy-fires have long since been ground into the sand, this stretch
of the shore is still filthy with trash; high-school gangs still daub huge
scandalous words on its beach-wall; and seashells are still less easy to
find here than discarded rubbers.

The glory has faded, too, from The Starboard Side; only a true devotee
like George can still detect even a last faint gleam of it. The place has
been stripped of its dusty marine trophies and yellow group photo-
graphs. Right after the New Year it's to be what they dare to call re-
decorated: that's to say, desecrated, in readiness for next summer's mob
of blank-faced strangers. Already there is a new juke-box; and a new television fixed high up on the wall, so you can turn half right, rest your
elbow on the bar and go into a cowdaze, watching it. This is what most
of the customers are doing, as George enters.

He makes unsteadily but purposefully for his favorite little table in
the corner, from which the TV screen is invisible. At the table next to
him, two other unhypnotized nonconformists, an elderly couple who belong to the last handful of surviving colonists, are practicing their way of
love: a mild quarrelsome alcoholism which makes it possible for them to
live in a play-relationship, like children. *You old bag, you old prick, you
old bitch, you old bastard*: rage without resentment, abuse without
venom. This is how it will be for them till the end. Let's hope they will
never be parted, but die in the same hour of the same night, in their
beer-stained bed.

And now George's eyes move along the bar, stop on a figure seated
alone at the end nearest the door. The young man isn't watching the
TV; indeed, he is quite intent upon something he is writing on the back
of an envelope. As he writes, he smiles to himself and rubs the side of
his large nose with his forefinger. It is Kenny Potter.

At first, George doesn't move; seems hardly to react at all. But then
a slow intent smile parts his lips. He leans forward, watching Kenny
with the delight of a naturalist who has identified a rosy finch out of the
high sierras on a tree in a city park. After a minute he rises, crosses almost stealthily to the bar and slips onto the stool beside Kenny.

"Hello, there," he says.

Kenny turns quickly, sees who it is, laughs loudly, crumples the envelope and tosses it over the bar into a trash container. "Hello, sir."

"What did you do that for?"

"Oh. Nothing."

"I disturbed you. You were writing."

"It was nothing. Only a poem."

"And now it's lost to the world!"

"I'll remember it. Now I've written it down."

"Would you say it for me?"

This sends Kenny into convulsions of laughter. "It's crazy. It's—" he gulps down his giggles—"it's a—a *haiku!*"

"Well, what's so crazy about a haiku?"

"I'd have to count the syllables first."

But Kenny obviously isn't going to count them now. So George says, "I didn't expect to see you in this neck of the woods. Don't you live over on the other side of town, near campus?"

"That's right. Only sometimes I like to get way away from there."

"But imagine your happening to pick on this particular bar!"

"Oh, that was because one of the kids told me you're in here a lot."

"You mean, you came out here to see me?" Perhaps George says this a little too eagerly. Anyhow, Kenny shrugs it off with a teasing smile. "I thought I'd see what kind of a joint it was."

"It's nothing now. It used to be quite something, though. And I've gotten accustomed to coming here. You see, I live very close."

"Camphor Tree Lane?"

"How in the world did you know that?"

"Is it supposed to be a secret?"

"Why no—of course not! I have students come over to see me now and then. I mean, about their work—" George is immediately aware that this sounds defensive and guilty as hell. Has Kenny noticed? He is grinning; but then he has been grinning all the time. George adds, rather feebly, "You seem to know an awful lot about me and my habits. A lot more than I know about any of you—"

"There isn't much to know about us, I guess!" Kenny gives him a teasing, challenging look. "What would you like to know about us, sir?"

"Oh, I'll think of something. Give me time. Say, what are you drinking?"

"Nothing!" Kenny giggles. "He hasn't even noticed me yet." And, indeed, the bartender is absorbed in a TV wrestling match.

"Well, what'll you have?"

"What are you having, sir?"

"Scotch."

"Okay," Kenny says, in a tone which suggests that he would have agreed just as readily to buttermilk. George calls the bartender—very loudly, so he can't pretend not to have heard—and orders. The bartender, always a bit of a bitch, demands to see Kenny's I.D. So they go through all of that. George says stuffily to the bartender, "You ought to know me by this time. Do you really think I'd be such an idiot as to try to buy drinks for a minor?"

"We have to check," says the bartender, through a skin inches thick. He turns his back on them and moves away. George feels a brief spurt of powerless rage. He has been made to look like an ass—and in front of Kenny, too.

While they are waiting for the drinks, he asks, "How did you get here? In your car?"

"I don't have one. Lois drove me."

"Where is she now, then?"

"Gone home, I guess."

George senses something not quite in order. But, whatever it is, Kenny doesn't seem worried about it. He adds vaguely, "I thought I'd walk around for a while."

"But how'll you get back?"

"Oh, I'll manage."

(A voice inside George says, *You could invite him to stay the night at your place. Tell him you'll drive him back in the morning.* What in hell do you think I am? George asks it. *It was merely a suggestion,* says the voice.)

The drinks arrive. George says to Kenny, "Look, why don't we sit over there, at the table in the corner? That damned television keeps catching my eye."

"All right."

It *would* be fun, George thinks, if the young were just a little less passive. But that's too much to ask. You have to play it their way, or not at all. As they take their chairs, facing each other, George says, "I've still got my pencil sharpener," and, bringing it out of his pocket, he tosses it down on the table, as though shooting craps.

Kenny laughs. "I already lost mine!"

And now an hour, maybe, has passed. And they are both drunk: Kenny fairly, George very. But George is drunk in a good way, and one that he seldom achieves. He tries to describe to himself what this kind of drunkenness is like. Well—to put it very crudely—it's like Plato; it's a dialogue. A dialogue between two people. Yes, but not a Platonic dialogue in the hair-splitting, word-twisting, one-up-to-me sense; not a mock-humble bitching match; not a debate on some dreary set theme. You can talk about anything and change the subject as often as you like. In fact, what really matters is not what you talk about, but the being together in this particular relationship. George can't imagine having a dialogue of this kind with a woman, because women can only talk in terms of the personal. A man of his own age would do, if there was some sort of polarity; for instance, if he was a Negro. You and your dialogue-partner have to be somehow opposites. Why? Because you have to be symbolic figures—like, in this case, Youth and Age. Why do you have to be symbolic? Because the dialogue is by its nature impersonal.

It's a symbolic encounter. It doesn't involve either party personally. That's why, in a dialogue, you can say absolutely anything. Even the closest confidence, the deadliest secret, comes out objectively as a mere metaphor or illustration which could never be used against you.

George would like to explain all of this to Kenny. But it is so complicated, and he doesn't want to run the risk of finding that Kenny can't understand him. More than anything, he wants Kenny to understand, wants to be able to believe that Kenny knows what this dialogue is all about. And really, at this moment, it seems possible that Kenny *does* know. George can almost feel the electric field of the dialogue surrounding and irradiating them. *He* certainly feels irradiated. As for Kenny, he looks quite beautiful. *Radiant with rapport* is the phrase which George finds to describe him. For what shines out of Kenny isn't mere intelligence or any kind of switched-on charm. There the two of them sit, smiling at each other—oh, far more than that—fairly beaming with mutual insight.

"Say something," he commands Kenny.

"Do I have to?"

"Yes."

"What'll I say?"

"Anything. Anything that seems to be important, right now."

"That's the trouble. I don't know what is important and what isn't. I feel like my head is stopped up with stuff that doesn't matter—I mean, matter to me."

"Such as—"

"Look, I don't mean to be personal, sir—but—well, the stuff our classes are about—"

"That doesn't matter to you?"

"Jesus Christ, sir—I *said* I wasn't being personal! Yours are a whole lot better than most; we all think that. And you do try to make these books fit in with what's going on nowadays, only, it's not your fault, but —we always seem to end up getting bogged down in the past; like this morning, with Tithonus. Look, I don't want to pan the past; maybe it'll mean a whole lot to me when I'm older. All I'm saying is, the past doesn't really matter to most kids my age. When we talk like it does, we're just being polite. I guess that's because we don't have any pasts of our own—except stuff we want to forget, like things in high school, and times we acted like idiots—"

"Well, fine! I can understand that. You don't need the past, yet. You've got the present."

"Oh, but the present's a real drag! I just despise the present—I mean, the way it is right now—I mean, tonight's an exception, of course— What are you laughing at, sir?"

"Tonight—*sí!* The present—*no!*" George is getting noisy. Some people at the bar turn their heads. "Drink to tonight!" He drinks, with a flourish.

"Tonight—*sí!*" Kenny laughs and drinks.

"Okay," says George. "The past—no help. The present—no good. Granted. But there's one thing you can't deny; you're stuck with the future. You can't just sneeze that off."

"I guess we are. What's left of it. There may not be much, with all these rockets—"

"Death."

"Death?"

"That's what I said."

"Come again, sir. I don't get you."

"I said death. I said, do you think about death a lot?"

"Why, no. Hardly at all. Why?"

"The future—that's where death is."

"Oh—yeah. Yeah—maybe you've got a point there." Kenny grins. "You know something? Maybe the other generations before us used to think about death a lot more than we do. What I mean is, kids must have gotten mad, thinking how they'd be sent out to some corny war and killed, while their folks stayed home and acted patriotic. But it won't be like that any more. We'd all be in this thing together."

"You could still get mad at the older people. Because of all those extra years they'll have had before they get blown up."

"Yes, that's right, I could, couldn't I? Maybe I will. Maybe I'll get mad at you, sir."

"Kenneth—"

"Sir?"

"Just as a matter of the purest sociological interest, why do you persist in calling me sir?"

Kenny grins teasingly. "I'll stop if you want me to."

"I didn't ask you to stop. I asked you why."

"Why don't you like it? None of you do, though, I guess."

"You mean, none of us old folks?" George smiles a no-hard-feelings smile. Nevertheless, he feels that the symbolic relationship is starting to get out of hand. "Well, the usual explanation is that we don't like being reminded—"

Kenny shakes his head decisively. "No."

"What do you mean, 'No'?"

"You're not like that."

"Is that supposed to be a compliment?"

"Maybe. The point is, I *like* calling you sir."

"You do?"

"What's so phony nowadays is all this familiarity. Pretending there isn't any difference between people—well, like you were saying about minorities, this morning. If you and I are no different, what do we have to give each other? How can we ever be friends?"

He *does* understand, George thinks, delighted. "But two young people can be friends, surely?"

"That's something else again. They can, yes, after a fashion. But there's always this thing of competition, getting in the way. All young people are kind of competing with each other, do you know that?"

"Yes, I suppose so—unless they're in love."

"Maybe they are even then. Maybe that's what's wrong with—" Kenny breaks off abruptly. George watches him, expecting to hear some confidence about Lois. But it doesn't come. For Kenny is obviously following some quite different train of thought. He sits smiling in silence for a few moments and—yes, actually—he is blushing! "This sounds as corny as hell, but—"

"Never mind. Go ahead."

"I sometimes wish—I mean, when you read those Victorian novels— I'd have hated living in those days, all except for one thing—oh, hell— I can't say it!" He breaks off, blushing and laughing.

"Don't be silly!"

"When I say it, it's so corny, it's the end! But—I'd have liked living when you could call your father sir."

"Is your father alive?"

"Oh, sure."

"Why don't you call him sir, then? Some sons do, even nowadays."

"Not my father. He isn't the type. Besides, he isn't around. He ran out on us a couple of years ago. . . . Hell!"

"What's the matter?"

"Whatever made me tell you all that? Am I drunk or something?"

"No more drunk than I am."

"I must be stoned."

"Look—if it bothers you—let's forget you told me."

"I won't forget."

"Oh yes, you will. You'll forget if I tell you to forget."

"Will I?"

"You bet you will!"

"Well, if you say so—okay."

"Okay, *sir*."

"Okay, *sir!*" Kenny suddenly beams. He is really pleased—so pleased that his own pleasure embarrasses him. "Say, you know—when I came over here—I mean, when I thought I might just happen to run into you this evening—there was something I wanted to ask you. I just remembered what it was—" he downs the rest of his drink in one long swallow —"it's about experience. They keep telling you, when you're older, you'll have experience—and that's supposed to be so great. What would you say about that, sir? Is it really any use, would you say?"

"What kind of experience?"

"Well—places you've been to, people you've met. Situations you've been through already, so you know how to handle them when they come up again. All that stuff that's supposed to make you wise, in your later years."

"Let me tell you something, Kenny. For other people, I can't speak —but, personally, I haven't gotten wise on anything. Certainly, I've been through this and that; and when it happens again, I say to myself, Here it is again. But that doesn't seem to help me. In my opinion, I, personally, have gotten steadily sillier and sillier and sillier—and that's a fact."

"No kidding, sir? You can't mean that! You mean, sillier than when you were young?"

"Much, much sillier."

"I'll be darned. Then experience is no use at all? You're saying it might just as well not have happened?"

"No. I'm not saying that. I only mean, you can't *use* it. But if you don't try to—if you just realize it's there and you've got it—then it can be kind of marvelous."

"Let's go swimming," says Kenny abruptly, as if bored by the whole conversation.

"All right."

Kenny throws his head right back and laughs wildly. "Oh—that's terrific!"

"What's terrific?"

"It was a test. I thought you were bluffing, about being silly. So I said to myself, I'll suggest doing something wild, and if he objects—if he even hesitates—then I'll know it was all a bluff. You don't mind my telling you that, do you, sir?"

"Why should I?"

"Oh, that's terrific!"

"Well, I'm not bluffing—so what are we waiting for? You weren't bluffing, were you?"

"Hell, no!"

They jump up, pay, run out of the bar and across the highway, and Kenny vaults the railing and drops down, about eight feet, onto the beach. George, meanwhile, is clambering over the rail, a bit stiffly. Kenny looks up, his face still lit by the boardwalk lamps: "Put your feet on my shoulders, sir." George does so, drunk-trustful, and Kenny, with the deftness of a ballet dancer, supports him by ankles and calves, lowering him almost instantly to the sand. During the descent, their bodies rub against each other, briefly but roughly. The electric field of the dialogue is broken. Their relationship, whatever it now is, is no longer symbolic. They turn and begin to run toward the ocean.

Already the lights seem far, far behind. They are bright but they cast no beams; perhaps they are shining on a layer of high fog. The waves ahead are barely visible. Their blackness is immensely cold and wet. Kenny is tearing off his clothes with wild whooping cries. The last remaining minim of George's caution is aware of the lights and the possibility of cruise cars and cops, but he doesn't hesitate, he is no longer able to; this dash from the bar can only end in the water. He strips himself clumsily, tripping over his pants. Kenny, stark naked now, has plunged and is wading straight in, like a fearless native warrior, to attack the waves. The undertow is very strong. George flounders for a while in a surge of stones. As he finally struggles through and feels sand under his feet, Kenny comes body-surfing out of the night and shoots past him without a glance—a water-creature absorbed in its element.

As for George, these waves are much too big for him. They seem truly tremendous, towering up, blackness unrolling itself out of blackness, mysteriously and awfully sparkling, then curling over in a thundering slap of foam which is sparked with phosphorus. George has sparks of it all over his body, and he laughs with delight to find himself bejeweled. Laughing, gasping, choking, he is too drunk to be afraid; the salt water he swallows seems as intoxicating as whiskey. From time to time he catches tremendous glimpses of Kenny, arrowing down some toppling foam-precipice. Then, intent upon his own rites of purification, George staggers out once more, wide-open-armed, to receive the stunning baptism of the surf. Giving himself to it utterly, he washes away thought, speech, mood, desire, whole selves, entire lifetimes; again and again he returns, becoming always cleaner, freer, less. He is perfectly happy by himself; it's enough to know that Kenny and he are the sole sharers of the element. The waves and the night and the noise exist only for their play. Meanwhile, no more than two hundred yards distant, the lights shine from the shore and the cars flick past up and down the highway, flashing their long beams. On the dark hillsides you can see lamps in the windows of dry homes, where the dry are going dryly to their dry beds. But George and Kenny are refugees from dryness; they have escaped across the border into the water-world, leaving their clothes behind them for a customs fee.

And now, suddenly, here is a great, an apocalyptically great wave, and George is way out, almost out of his depth, standing naked and tiny before its presence, under the lip of its roaring upheaval and the towering menace of its fall. He tries to dive through it—even now he feels no real fear—but instead he is caught and picked up, turned over and over and over, flapping and kicking toward a surface which may be either up or down or sideways, he no longer knows.

And now Kenny is dragging him out, groggy-legged. Kenny's hands are under George's armpits and he is laughing and saying like a nanny, "That's enough for now!" And George, still water-drunk, gasps, "I'm all right," and wants to go straight back into the water. But Kenny says, "Well, *I'm* not—I'm cold," and nannylike he towels George, with his own shirt, not George's, until George stops him because his back is sore. The nanny-relationship is so convincing at this moment that George feels he could curl up and fall immediately asleep right here, shrunk to childsize within the safety of Kenny's bigness. Kenny's body seems to have grown gigantic since they left the water. Everything about him is larger than life: the white teeth of his grin, the wide dripping shoulders, the tall slim torso with its heavy-hung sex, and the long legs, now beginning to shiver.

"Can we go back to your place, sir?" he asks.

"Sure. Where else?"

"Where else?" Kenny repeats, seeming to find this very amusing. He picks up his clothes and turns, still naked, toward the highway and the lights.

"Are you crazy?" George shouts after him.

"What's the matter?" Kenny looks back, grinning.

"You're going to walk home like that? Are you crazy? They'd call the cops!"

Kenny shrugs his shoulders good-humoredly. "Nobody would have seen us. We're invisible—didn't you know?"

But he gets into his clothes now, and George does likewise. As they start up the beach again, Kenny puts his arm around George's shoulder. "You know something, sir? They ought not to let you out on your own, ever. You're liable to get into real trouble."

Their walk home sobers George quite a lot. By the time they reach the house, he no longer sees the two of them as wild water-creatures but as an elderly professor with wet hair bringing home an exceedingly wet student in the middle of the night. George becomes self-conscious and almost curt. "The bathroom's upstairs. I'll get you some towels."

Kenny reacts to the formality at once. "Aren't you taking a shower too, sir?" he asks, in a deferential, slightly disappointed tone.

"I can do that later. I wish I had some clothes your size to lend you. You'll have to wrap up in a blanket, while we dry your things on the heater. It's rather a slow process, I'm afraid, but that's the best we can do."

"Look, sir—I don't want to be a nuisance. Why don't I go now?"

"Don't be an idiot. You'd get pneumonia."

"My clothes'll dry on me. I'll be all right."

"Nonsense! Come on up and I'll show you where everything is."

George's refusal to let him leave appears to have pleased Kenny. At any rate, he makes a terrific noise in the shower, not so much singing as a series of shouts. He is probably waking up the neighbors, George thinks, but who cares? George's spirits are up again; he feels excited, amused, alive. In his bedroom, he undresses quickly, gets into his thick white terry-cloth bathrobe, hurries downstairs again, puts on the kettle and fixes some tuna fish and tomato sandwiches on rye. They are all ready, set out on a tray in the living room when Kenny comes down, wearing the blanket awkwardly, saved-from-shipwreck style.

Kenny doesn't want coffee or tea; he would rather have beer, he says. So George gets him a can from the icebox and unwisely pours himself a biggish Scotch. He returns to find Kenny looking around the room as though it fascinates him.

"You live here all by yourself, sir?"

"Yes," says George, and adds with a shade of irony, "Does that surprise you?"

"No. One of the kids said he thought you did."

"As a matter of fact, I used to share this place with a friend."

But Kenny shows no curiosity about the friend. "You don't even have a cat or a dog or anything?"

"You think I should?" George asks, a bit aggressive. The poor old guy doesn't have anything to love, he thinks Kenny is thinking.

"Hell, no! Didn't Baudelaire say they're liable to turn into demons and take over your life?"

"Something like that. This friend of mine had lots of animals, though, and they didn't seem to take *us* over. Of course, it's different when there's two of you. We often used to agree that neither one of us would want to keep on the animals if the other wasn't there. . . ."

No. Kenny is absolutely not curious about any of this. Indeed, he is concentrating on taking a huge bite out of his sandwich. So George asks him, "Is it all right?"

"I'll say!" He grins at George with his mouth full, then swallows and adds, "You know something, sir? I believe you've discovered the secret of the perfect life!"

"I have?" George has just gulped nearly a quarter of his Scotch to drown out a spasm which started when he talked about Jim and the animals. Now he feels the alcohol coming back on him with a rush. It is exhilarating, but it is coming much too fast.

"You don't realize how many kids my age just dream about the kind of setup you've got here. I mean, what more can you want? I mean, you don't have to take orders from anybody. You can do any crazy thing that comes into your head."

"And that's your idea of the perfect life?"

"Sure it is!"

"Honestly?"

"What's the matter, sir? Don't you believe me?"

"What I don't quite understand is, if you're so keen on living alone —how does Lois fit in?"

"Lois? What's she got to do with it?"

"Now, look, Kenny—I don't mean to be nosy—but, rightly or wrongly, I got the idea that you and she might be, well, considering—"

"Getting married? No. That's out."

"Oh?"

"She says she won't marry a Caucasian. She says she can't take people in this country seriously. She doesn't feel anything we do here *means* anything. She wants to go back to Japan and teach."

"She's an American citizen, isn't she?"

"Oh, sure. She's a Nisei. But, just the same, she and her whole family got shipped up to one of those internment camps in the Sierras, right after the war began. Her father had to sell his business for peanuts, give it away, practically, to some sharks who were grabbing all the Japanese property and talking big about avenging Pearl Harbor! Lois was only a small kid, then, but you can't expect anyone to forget a thing like that. She says they were all treated as enemy aliens; no one even gave a damn which side they were on. She says the Negroes were the only ones who acted decently to them. And a few pacifists. Christ, she certainly has the right to hate our guts! Not that she does, actually. She always seems to be able to see the funny side of things."

"And how do you feel about her?"

"Oh, I like her a lot."

"And she likes you, doesn't she?"

"I guess so. Yes, she does. A lot."

"But don't you *want* to marry her?"

"Oh sure. I guess so. If she were to change her attitude. But I doubt if she will. And, anyhow, I'm in no rush about marrying anyone. There's a lot of things I want to do, first—" Kenny pauses, regarding George with his most teasing, penetrating grin. "You know what I think, sir?"

"What do you think?"

"I don't believe you're that much interested whether I marry Lois or not. I think you want to ask me something different. Only you're not sure how I'll take it."

"What do I want to ask you?"

This is getting positively flirty, on both sides. Kenny's blanket, under the relaxing influence of the talk and beer, has slipped, baring an arm and a shoulder and turning itself into a classical Greek garment, the chlamys worn by a young disciple—the favorite, surely—of some philosopher. At this moment, he is utterly, dangerously charming.

"You want to know if Lois and I—if we make out together."

"Well, do you?"

Kenny laughs triumphantly. "So I was right!"

"Maybe. Maybe not. . . . Do you?"

"We did, once."

"Why only once?"

"It wasn't so long ago. We went to a motel. It's down the beach, as a matter of fact, quite near here."

"Is that why you drove out here tonight?"

"Yes—partly. I was trying to talk her into going there again."

"And that's what the argument was about?"

"Who says we had an argument?"

"You left her to drive home alone, didn't you?"

"Oh well, that was because. . . . No, you're right—she didn't want to. She hated that motel the first time, and I don't blame her. The office and the desk clerk and the register—all that stuff they put you through. And of course they know damn well what the score is. It all makes the thing much too important and corny, like some big sin or something. And the way they look at you! Girls mind all that much more than we do—"

"So now she's called the whole thing off?"

"Hell, no, it's not that bad! It's not that she's against it, you understand. Not on principle. In fact, she's definitely—well, anyhow, I guess we can work something out. We'll have to see. . . ."

"You mean, maybe you can find some place that isn't so public and embarrassing?"

"That'd be a big help, certainly." Kenny grins, yawns, stretches himself. The chlamys slips off his other shoulder. He pulls it back over both shoulders as he rises, turning it into a blanket again and himself into a gawky twentieth-century American boy comically stranded without his clothes. "Look, sir, it's getting as late as all hell. I have to be going."

"Where, may I ask?"

"Why, back across town."

"In what?"

"I can get a bus, can't I?"

"They won't start running for another two hours, at least."

"Just the same . . ."

"Why don't you stay here? Tomorrow I'll drive you."

"I don't think I . . ."

"If you start wandering around this neighborhood in the dark, now the bars are shut, the police will stop you and ask what you're doing. And you aren't exactly sober, if you don't mind my saying so. They might even take you in."

"Honestly, sir, I'll be all right."

"I think you're out of your mind. However, we'll discuss that in a minute. First—sit down. I've got something I want to tell you."

Kenny sits down obediently, without further protest. Perhaps he is curious to know what George's next move will be.

"Now listen to this very carefully. I am about to make a simple statement of fact. Or facts. No comment is required from you. If you like, you can decide that this doesn't concern you at all. Is that clear?"

"Yes, sir."

"There's a woman I know who lives near here—a very close friend of mine. We have supper together at least one day a week; often, more than that. Matter of fact, we had supper tonight. Now—it never makes any difference to her which day I pick. So what I've decided is this— and, mind, it has nothing whatsoever to do with you, *necessarily*— from now on, I shall go to her place for supper each week on the same night. *Invariably, on the same night.* Tonight, that is. Is that much clear? No, don't answer. Go right on listening, because I'm just coming to the point. These nights, when I have supper with my friend, *I shall never, under any circumstances*, return here before midnight. Is that clear? No—listen! This house is never locked, because anyone could get into it anyway just by breaking a panel in the glass door. Upstairs, in my study, you must have noticed that there's a couch bed? I keep it made up with clean sheets on it, just on the once-in-a-blue-moon chance that I'll get an unexpected guest—such as you are going to be tonight, for instance. . . . No—listen carefully! If that bed were ever used while I was out, and straightened up afterwards, I'd never be any the wiser. And if my cleaning woman were to notice anything, she'd merely put the sheets out to go to the laundry; she'd suppose I'd had a guest and forgotten to tell her. . . . All right! I've made a decision and now I've told you about it. Just as I might tell you I'd decided to water the garden on a certain day of the week. I have also told you a few facts about this house. You can make a note of them. Or you can forget them. That's all."

George looks straight at Kenny. Kenny smiles back at him faintly. But he is—yes, just a little bit—embarrassed.

"And now get me another drink."

"Okay, sir." Kenny rises from his chair with noticeable eagerness, as if glad of this breaking of tension. He picks up George's glass and goes into the kitchen. George calls after him, "And get yourself one, too!"

Kenny puts his head around the corner, grinning. "Is that an order, sir?"

"You're damn right it is!"

"I suppose you've decided I'm a dirty old man?"

While Kenny was getting the drinks from the kitchen, George felt himself entering a new phase. Now, as Kenny takes his seat again, he is, though he cannot have realized it yet, in the presence of a George transformed: a formidable George, who articulates thickly but clearly, with a menace behind his words. An inquisitorial George, seated in judgment and perhaps about to pronounce sentence. An oracular George, who may shortly begin to speak with tongues.

This isn't at all like their drunkenness at The Starboard Side. Kenny and he are no longer in the symbolic dialogue-relationship; this new phase of communication is very much person-to-person. Yet, paradoxically, Kenny seems farther away, not closer; he has receded far beyond the possible limits of an electric field. Indeed, it is only now and then that George can see him clearly, for the room has become dazzlingly bright, and Kenny's face keeps fading into the brightness. Also, there is a loud buzzing in George's ears, so loud that he can't be certain if Kenny answered his question or not.

"You needn't say anything," George tells Kenny (thus dealing with either possibility), "because I admit it—oh, hell, yes, of course I admit it—I *am* a dirty old man. Ninety-nine per cent of all old men are dirty. That is, if you want to talk that language; if you insist on that kind of dreariness. I'm not protesting against what you choose to call me or don't. I'm protesting against an attitude—and I'm only doing that for your sake, not mine. . . .

"Look—things are quite bad enough anyhow, nowadays—we're in quite enough of a mess, semantically and every other way—without getting ourselves entangled in these dreary categories. I mean, what is this life of ours supposed to be *for*? Are we to spend it identifying each other with catalogues, like tourists in an art gallery? Or are we to try to exchange *some* kind of a signal, however garbled, before it's too late? *You* answer *me* that!

"It's all very fine and easy for you young things to come to me on campus and tell me I'm cagey. Merciful Christ—*cagey!* Don't you even know better than that? Don't you have a glimmering of how I must feel—longing to *speak*?

"You asked me about experience. So I told you. Experience isn't any *use*. And yet, in quite another way, it *might* be. If only we weren't all such miserable fools and prudes and cowards. Yes, you too, my boy. And don't you dare deny it! What I said just now, about the bed in the study—that shocked you. Because you were determined to be shocked. You utterly refused to understand my motives. Oh God, don't you *see?* That bed—what that bed *means*—that's what experience *is!*

"Oh well, I'm not blaming you. It'd be a miracle if you *did* understand. Never mind. Forget it. Here am I. Here are you—in that damned blanket. Why don't you take it right off, for Christ's sake? What made me say that? I suppose you're going to misunderstand that, too? Well, if you do, I don't give a damn. The point is—here am I and here are you—and for once there's no one to disturb us. This may never happen again. I mean that literally! And the time is *desperately* short. All right, let's put the cards on the table. Why are you here in this room at this moment? *Because you want me to tell you something!* That's the true reason you came all the way across town tonight. You may have honestly believed it was to get Lois in bed with you. Mind you, I'm not saying one word against her. She's a truly beautiful angel. But you can't fool a dirty old man; he isn't sentimental about Young Love; he knows just how much it's worth—a great deal, but not everything. No, my dear Kenneth. You came here this evening to see *me*—whether you realize it or not. Some part of you knew quite well that Lois would refuse to go to that motel again; and that that would give you an excuse to send her home and get yourself stranded out here. I expect that poor girl is feeling terrible about it all, right now, and crying into her pillow. You must be very sweet to her when you see her again. . . .

"But I'm getting off the point. The point is, you came to ask me about something that really *is* important. So why be ashamed and deny it? You see, I know you through and through. I know *exactly* what you want. You want me to tell you *what I know.*

"Oh, Kenneth, Kenneth, believe me—there's nothing I'd rather do! I want *like hell* to tell you. But I can't. I quite literally can't. Because, don't you see, *what I know is what I am?* And I can't tell you that. You have to find it out for yourself. I'm like a book you have to read. A book can't read itself to you. It doesn't even know what it's about. I don't know what I'm about.

"You could know what I'm about. You could. But you can't be bothered to. Look—you're the only boy I ever met on that campus I really believe could. That's what makes it so tragically futile. Instead of trying to know, you commit the inexcusable triviality of saying 'he's a dirty old man,' and turning this evening, which might be the most precious and unforgettable of your young life, into a *flirtation!* You don't like that word, do you? But it's the word. It's the enormous tragedy of everything nowadays: flirtation. Flirtation instead of fucking, if you'll pardon my coarseness. All any of you ever do is flirt, and wear your blankets off one shoulder, and complain about motels. And miss the one thing that might really—and, Kenneth, I do not say this casually—*transform your entire life—*"

For a moment, Kenny's face is quite distinct. It grins, dazzlingly. Then his grin breaks up, is refracted, or whatever you call it, into rainbows of light. The rainbows blaze. George is blinded by them. He shuts his eyes. And now the buzzing in his ears is the roar of Niagara.

Half an hour, an hour, later—not long, anyway—George blinks and is awake.

Night, still. Dark. Warm. Bed. *Am in bed!* He jerks up, propped on his elbow. Clicks on the bedside lamp. His hand does this; arm in sleeve; pajama sleeve. *Am in pajamas!* Why? How?

Where is he?

George staggers out of bed, dizzy, a bit sickish, startled wide awake. Ready to lurch into the front room. No—wait. Here's paper propped against lamp:

Thought maybe I'd better split, after all. I like to wander around at night. If those cops pick me up, I won't tell them where I've been— I promise! Not even if they twist my arm!

That was great, this evening. Let's do it again, shall we? Or don't you believe in repeating things?

Couldn't find pajamas you already used, so took these clean ones from the drawer. Maybe you sleep raw? Didn't want to take a chance, though. Can't have you getting pneumonia, can we?

> Thanks for everything,
> KENNETH

George sits on the bed, reading this. Then, with slight impatience, like a general who has just glanced through an unimportant dispatch, he lets the paper slide to the floor, stands up, goes into the bathroom, empties his bladder, doesn't glance in the mirror, doesn't even turn on the light, returns to bed, gets in, switches off bed lamp.

Little teaser, his mind says, but without the least resentment. Just as well he didn't stay.

But, as he lies on his back in the dark, there is something that keeps him from sleep: a tickle in the blood and the nerves of the groin. The alcohol itches in him, down there.

Lying in the dark, he conjures up Kenny and Lois in their car, makes them drive into Camphor Tree Lane, park further down the street, in case a neighbor should be watching, hurry discreetly across the bridge, get the door open—it sticks, she giggles—bump against the living-room furniture—a tiny Japanese cry of alarm—tiptoe upstairs without turning on the lights. . . .

No—it won't work. George tries several times, but he just cannot make Lois go up those stairs. Each time he starts her up them, she dematerializes, as it were. (And now he knows, with absolute certainty, that Kenny will never be able to persuade her even to enter this house.)

But the play has begun, now, and George isn't about to stop it. Kenny must be provided with a partner. So George turns Lois into the sexy little gold cat, the Mexican tennis player. No trouble about getting *him* upstairs! He and Kenny are together in the front room, now. George hears a belt drop to the floor. They are stripping themselves naked.

The blood throbs deep down in George's groin. The flesh stirs and swells up, suddenly hard hot. The pajamas are pulled off, tossed out of bed.

George hears Kenny whisper to the Mexican, *Come on, kid!* Making himself invisible, he enters the front room. He finds the two of them just about to lie down together. . . .

No. That won't work, either. George doesn't like Kenny's attitude. He isn't taking his lust seriously; in fact, he seems to be on the verge of giggles. Quick—we need a substitute! George hastily turns Kenny into the big blond boy from the tennis court. Oh, much better! Perfect! Now they can embrace. Now the fierce hot animal play can begin. George hovers above them, watching; then he begins passing in and out of their writhing, panting bodies. He is either. He is both at once. Ah—it is so good! Ah—ah . . . !

You old idiot, George's mind says. But he is not ashamed of himself. He speaks to the now slack and sweating body with tolerant good humor, as if to an old greedy dog which has just gobbled down a chunk of meat far bigger than it really wanted. Well, maybe you'll let us sleep, now?

As sleep begins to wash lightly over him, he asks himself, Shall I mind meeting Kenny's eye in class on Monday?

No. Not a bit. Even if he has told Lois (which I doubt): I undressed him, I put him to bed, he was drunk as a skunk. For then he will have told her about the swimming, too: You should have seen him in that water—as crazy as a kid! They ought not to let you out on your own, I said to him.

George smiles to himself, with entire self-satisfaction. Yes, I *am* crazy, he thinks. That is my secret; my strength.

And I'm about to get much crazier, he announces. Just watch me, all of you! Do you know what? I'm flying to Mexico for Christmas! You dare me to? I'll make reservations first thing in the morning!

He falls asleep, still smiling.

QUESTIONS

1. What kind of assertions does George make about himself in the first episode? Is his trip to the gym dominated by thoughts of self-awareness or self-delusion? What kind of extra dimension does George's homosexuality give to his visits to the gym? What extra poignancy?
2. What sense of loss does George feel in the Los Angeles hills? How does Isherwood imply that in some ways Los Angeles might be a good deal more repressed in the 60's than in the 40's? What are the attractions of the past for George?
3. In what ways does Kenny treat George as a teacher and in what ways as a fellow human being? Why, according to George, does being "opposites" help his dialogue with Kenny?
4. Is George foolish or admirable for going swimming with Kenny? Explain.
5. What are George's motives in offering his house to Kenny and his girl, Lois? Is it important for the story to know whether Kenny suspects George of being homosexual? Does George feel it is important?
6. Why does George find it impossible to fantasize about Kenny? Why is it easier to substitute the tennis players?

ALLEN GINSBERG

LIKE Jack Kerouac, Allen Ginsberg (b. 1926) is a "wanderer" who is often identified as a leading member of the Beat Generation. Born in Paterson, New Jersey, Ginsberg became familiar with the New York City worlds of Columbia University, Harlem, and 42nd Street before he journeyed west to be part of the famous 50's "scenes" in Denver and San Francisco. He has also lived in many remote places in Mexico, Europe, and Asia. His poetry reflects these wanderings, but it is ultimately of the mind's internal adventures. Many of his poems demonstrate the way in which the Beat Movement really moved toward a kind of religious aspiration rather than a social revolt.

Ginsberg's poetry is deliberately rough and undisciplined; in his dedication to his famous poem, *Howl*, he acknowledges his debt to Kerouac's "spontaneous bop prosody." Through this improvisatory mode, he tries to recreate the "natural" man and recapture both the openness and outrageousness of his American experience. The stylistic and spiritual debt is again to Walt Whitman, whom he specifically invokes and whose all-inclusiveness and long, taut poetic lines he revives in "A Supermarket in California." In this poem, whose scene is the Berkeley Co-op, Ginsberg wanders the aisles, accompanied by Whitman's spirit, trying to make connections between America's past and present. He emphasizes the differences between his trip to the market and that of the ordinary shopper and, viewing the scene from many levels and perspectives, he makes his "trip" into a significant experience.

The general purpose of most of Ginsberg's poetry is an attempt to face up to all the suffering and nightmare horrors of the modern world in order to transcend them. Ginsberg is willing to take great risks and reveal himself in order to make us more aware. By abandoning any pretense at typical adult decorum or responsibility, he enables us to see our world in ways not usually possible for "adjusted" people.

In "America," the political and social criticism that was implicit in "Howl" becomes overt. The names and places to which Ginsberg refers, as well as the general spirit of outrage, recalls Don Passos. The poet mocks the repressive conformists of America who see only themselves as "patriots." Recoiling against the general repression of dissent in America after World War II—during a period now generally associated with "McCarthyism"—he reaffirms his physical defects and his "deviant" sexual leanings. This outsider, after all, believes in our ideals of hard work and "getting the job done." Whether we like it or not, he is an American who is committed to his country. In the final line, laden with both irony and sincerity, he declares, "America I'm putting my queer shoulder to the wheel."

[FROM Howl]

A Supermarket in California

What thoughts I have of you tonight, Walt Whitman, for I walked down the sidestreets under the trees with a headache self-conscious looking at the full moon.

In my hungry fatigue, and shopping for images, I went into the neon fruit supermarket, dreaming of your enumerations!

What peaches and what penumbras! Whole families shopping at night! Aisles full of husbands! Wives in the avocados, babies in the tomatoes!—and you, Garcia Lorca,[1] what were you doing down by the watermelons?

I saw you, Walt Whitman, childless, lonely old grubber, poking among the meats in the refrigerator and eyeing the grocery boys.

I heard you asking questions of each: Who killed the pork chops? What price bananas? Are you my Angel?

I wandered in and out of the brilliant stacks of cans following you, and followed in my imagination by the store detective.

We strode down the open corridors together in our solitary fancy tasting artichokes, possessing every frozen delicacy, and never passing the cashier.

Where are we going, Walt Whitman? The doors close in an hour. Which way does your beard point tonight?

(I touch your book and dream of our odyssey in the supermarket and feel absurd.)

Will we walk all night through solitary streets? The trees add shade to shade, lights out in the houses, we'll both be lonely.

Will we stroll dreaming of the lost America of love past blue automobiles in driveways, home to our silent cottage?

Ah, dear father, graybeard, lonely old courage-teacher, what America did you have when Charon quit poling his ferry and you got out on a smoking bank and stood watching the boat disappear on the black waters of Lethe? [2]

Berkeley 1955

[1] Federico García Lorca (1898–1936), Spanish poet and playwright.
[2] In classical mythology Charon was the ferryman of the River Styx in Hades. Lethe is a river of Hades where all the dead drink and forget what happened to them while they were alive.

America

America I've given you all and now I'm nothing.
America two dollars and twentyseven cents January 17, 1956.
I can't stand my own mind.
America when will we end the human war?
Go fuck yourself with your atom bomb.
I don't feel good don't bother me.
I won't write my poem till I'm in my right mind.
America when will you be angelic?
When will you take off your clothes?
When will you look at yourself through the grave?
When will you be worthy of your million Trotskyites? [1]
America why are your libraries full of tears?
America when will you send your eggs to India?
I'm sick of your insane demands.
When can I go into the supermarket and buy what I need with my
    good looks?
America after all it is you and I who are perfect not the next world.
Your machinery is too much for me.
You made me want to be a saint.
There must be some other way to settle this argument.
Burroughs is in Tangiers I don't think he'll come back it's sinister.
Are you being sinister or is this some form of practical joke?
I'm trying to come to the point.
I refuse to give up my obsession.
America stop pushing I know what I'm doing.
America the plum blossoms are falling.
I haven't read the newspapers for months, everyday somebody goes
    on trial for murder.
America I feel sentimental about the Wobblies.[2]
America I used to be a communist when I was a kid I'm not sorry.
I smoke marijuana every chance I get.
I sit in my house for days on end and stare at the roses in the closet.
When I go to Chinatown I get drunk and never get laid.
My mind is made up there's going to be trouble.
You should have seen me reading Marx.
My psychoanalyst thinks I'm perfectly right.
I won't say the Lord's Prayer.
I have mystical visions and cosmic vibrations.

[1] Supporters of Leon Trotsky (1877–1940), a leader of the Russian Revolution who
was ultimately purged by Stalin.
[2] Industrial Workers of the World, a federation of industrial unions dedicated to the
overthrow of capitalism by direct means.

America I still haven't told you what you did to Uncle Max after
      he came over from Russia.

I'm addressing you.
Are you going to let your emotional life be run by Time Magazine?
I'm obsessed by Time Magazine.
I read it every week.
Its cover stares at me every time I slink past the corner candystore.
I read it in the basement of the Berkeley Public Library.
It's always telling me about responsibility. Businessmen are serious.
      Movie producers are serious. Everybody's serious but me.
It occurs to me that I am America.
I am talking to myself again.

Asia is rising against me.
I haven't got a chinaman's chance.
I'd better consider my national resources.
My national resources consist of two joints of marijuana millions of
      genitals an unpublishable private literature that goes 1400
      miles an hour and twentyfive-thousand mental institutions.
I say nothing about my prisons nor the millions of underprivileged
      who live in my flowerpots under the light of five hundred
      suns.
I have abolished the whorehouses of France, Tangiers is the next
      to go.
My ambition is to be President despite the fact that I'm a Catholic.

America how can I write a holy litany in your silly mood?
I will continue like Henry Ford my strophes are as individual as
      his automobiles more so they're all different sexes.
America I will sell you strophes $2500 apiece $500 down on your
      old strophe
America free Tom Mooney
America save the Spanish Loyalists
America Sacco & Vanzetti must not die
America I am the Scottsboro boys.[1]

[1] In this section, Ginsberg lists famous leftist "cases" that were considered extremely
"unpatriotic" by most Americans. The Spanish Loyalists fought against Franco in Spain.
Sacco and Vanzetti were Italian anarchists who were executed for murder, but whom
many supporters felt were actually persecuted for their radical political views. The
Scottsboro boys were eight Blacks convicted in Scottsboro, Alabama, in March 1931, of
raping two white women. There were several retrials and the case ultimately went to the
Supreme Court.
    Tom Mooney, along with Warren Billings, was convicted of murder in the San Fran-
cisco Preparedness Day bombing July 22, 1916. After much litigation, he was finally freed
in 1939. For the radical left, he became a symbol of American capitalist oppression of
militant labor.

America when I was seven momma took me to Communist Cell
    meetings they sold us garbanzos a handful per ticket a
    ticket costs a nickel and the speeches were free everybody
    was angelic and sentimental about the workers it was all so
    sincere you have no idea what a good thing the party was
    in 1935 Scott Nearing was a grand old man a real mensch
    Mother Bloor made me cry I once saw Israel Amter plain.
    Everybody must have been a spy.
America you don't really want to go to war.
America it's them bad Russians.
Them Russians them Russians and them Chinamen. And them
    Russians.
The Russia wants to eat us alive. The Russia's power mad. She
    wants to take our cars from out our garages.
Her wants to grab Chicago. Her needs a Red Readers' Digest.
    Her wants our auto plants in Siberia. Him big bureaucracy
    running our fillingstations.
That no good. Ugh. Him make Indians learn read. Him need big
    black niggers. Hah. Her make us all work sixteen hours a
    day. Help.
America this is quite serious.
America this is the impression I get from looking in the television
    set.
America is this correct?
I'd better get right down to the job.
It's true I don't want to join the Army or turn lathes in precision
    parts factories, I'm nearsighted and psychopathic anyway.
America I'm putting my queer shoulder to the wheel.

QUESTIONS

1. In "A Supermarket in California" what poetic techniques does Ginsberg use to convey a sense of a world influenced by drugs? What
other poetic devices are apparent in his verse?
2. Why is the spirit of Walt Whitman invoked in the supermarket in
California? Does Ginsberg think of himself as similar to Whitman?
3. Why might "America" be classified as a satiric poem? In what ways
does Ginsberg parody himself in it?
4. What is the effect of Ginsberg's deliberate flippancy about traditional
American values? How does he combine frivolity and seriousness?

QUESTIONS FOR STUDY AND WRITING (PART III)

1. Analyze the character of Baldwin's Elizabeth. What are the sources of Elizabeth's personal strength?
2. What is the difference in mood and tone between the poetry of Larry Neal and Allen Ginsberg? Do they share any poetic strategies and devices?
3. What are the motives of Kerouac's Sal Paradise and Terry for their affair?
4. In what ways can Whitman's influence be seen in Ginsberg's verse? Support your position by analyzing a short poem by each poet.
5. Do the selections by Baldwin and Isherwood disclose any problems common to both Blacks and homosexuals in our society?
6. Compare Mailer's characterization of General Cummings with Isherwood's George. How does each man try to confront the problem of aging? Write a dialog that might take place were the two men (both in their 50's) introduced to each other at an elegant cocktail party. What would each surmise about the other's sexual identity?

IV

The Struggle for Self-Awareness

HENRY DAVID THOREAU

HENRY DAVID THOREAU (1817–62) was born in Concord, Massachusetts, and ultimately settled there permanently. Today he is probably most famous for his essay, "On the Duty of Civil Disobedience" (1849), in which he uncompromisingly asserts the supremacy of an individual's conscience while he condemns the majority of Americans for supporting government when it sinned against justice. Nor did Thoreau shy away from personal political involvement; he defended John Brown and published his views on the slavery issue. Although he also wrote a great deal of poetry, students of American literature usually focus on two of his books that describe his experiences with nature: *A Week on the Concord and Merrimack Rivers* (1849) and *Walden: or, Life in the Woods* (1854).

Thoreau was first impelled to move to Walden Pond by a sense of emptiness and waste in his life and by the conviction that people devoted too much time and energy to industry and the accumulation of wealth. Feeling the need to detach himself from everyday preoccupations and responsibilities, he sought an environment free from most external demands, in which he could concentrate on discovering himself in nature. In "Where I Lived and What I Lived For," he states, "I went to the woods because I wished to live deliberately, to front only the essential facts of life, and see if I could not learn what it had to teach, and not, when I came to die, discover that I had not lived." Like many young people today who seek to flee cities and suburbs, Thoreau felt he had to slow his life to the speed of nature, that he had to divest it of the complexities of modern times in order to "suck all the marrow out of life." Probably nobody of his generation had a richer sense of the potentiality for a fresh, free, and uncluttered existence. Like Whitman, Thoreau cut himself off from the bondage of tradition. He insisted that individuals could find a fresh start for themselves if they would only wake to what was really important. And, although Thoreau sought out a life of contemplation and read much about Eastern religion, he was not basically passive. His primary predisposition was to act; he was unshakable in his belief that the individual did have free will and the right to self-determination.

Even though Thoreau lived at Walden Pond from July 1845 to September 1847, he limits the chronology of his book to a single year, structuring it to follow the mythic cycle of the seasons, and concluding with Spring, the time of rebirth. Despite his allusions to classical literature, which now strike us as highly intellectual and obscure, Thoreau's spirit is essentially that of Whitman's innocent child. In the chapter reprinted here, his playfulness of mind and imagination are evident everywhere. "Where I Lived, and What I Lived For" cannot give a sense of Thoreau's total experience in nature at Walden or of his transcendental philosophy; it does, however, suggest ways of preparing for a period of contemplation during which we may begin to discover ourselves, so that we can return to the world with some sense of direction. According to Thoreau, modern civilization and outmoded traditions can only obscure the way. By turning to nature we may find a sense of time and beauty that answers some need deep within us and that may continue to nourish us as we continue to grow.

[FROM Walden]

2. Where I Lived, and What I Lived For

At a certain season of our life we are accustomed to consider every spot as the possible site of a house. I have thus surveyed the country on every side within a dozen miles of where I live. In imagination I have bought all the farms in succession, for all were to be bought, and I knew their price. I walked over each farmer's premises, tasted his wild apples, discoursed on husbandry with him, took his farm at his price, at any price, mortgaging it to him in my mind; even put a higher price on it,—took everything but a deed of it,—took his word for his deed, for I dearly love to talk,—cultivated it, and him too to some extent, I trust, and withdrew when I had enjoyed it long enough, leaving him to carry it on. This experience entitled me to be regarded as a sort of real-estate broker by my friends. Wherever I sat, there I might live, and the landscape radiated from me accordingly. What is a house but a *sedes*, a seat?—better if a country seat. I discovered many a site for a house not likely to be soon improved, which some might have thought too far from the village, but to my eyes the village was too far from it. Well, there I might live, I said, and there I did live, for an hour, a summer and a winter life; saw how I could let the years run off, buffet the winter through, and see the spring come in. The future inhabitants of this region, wherever they may place their houses, may be sure that they have been anticipated. An afternoon sufficed to lay out the land into orchard, wood-lot, and pasture, and to decide what fine oaks or pines should be left to stand before the door, and whence each blasted tree could be seen to the best advantage; and then I let it lie, fallow perchance, for a man is rich in proportion to the number of things which he can afford to let alone.

My imagination carried me so far that I even had the refusal of several farms,—the refusal was all I wanted,—but I never got my fingers burned by actual possession. The nearest that I came to actual possession was when I bought the Hollowell place, and had begun to sort my seeds, and collected materials with which to make a wheelbarrow to carry it on or off with; but before the owner gave me a deed of it, his wife—every man has such a wife—changed her mind and wished to keep it, and he offered me ten dollars to release him. Now, to speak the truth, I had but ten cents in the world, and it surpassed my arithmetic to tell, if I was that man who had ten cents, or who had a farm, or ten dollars, or all together. However, I let him keep the ten dollars and the farm too, for

From WALDEN: OR, LIFE IN THE WOODS, 1854.

I had carried it far enough; or rather, to be generous, I sold him the farm for just what I gave for it, and, as he was not a rich man, made him a present of ten dollars, and still had my ten cents, and seeds, and materials for a wheelbarrow left. I found thus that I had been a rich man without any damage to my poverty. But I retained the landscape, and I have since annually carried off what it yielded without a wheelbarrow. With respect to landscapes,—

> "I am monarch of all I *survey*,
> My right there is none to dispute."

I have frequently seen a poet withdraw, having enjoyed the most valuable part of a farm, while the crusty farmer supposed that he had got a few wild apples only. Why, the owner does not know it for many years when a poet has put his farm in rhyme, the most admirable kind of invisible fence, has fairly impounded it, milked it, skimmed it, and got all the cream, and left the farmer only the skimmed milk.

The real attractions of the Hollowell farm, to me, were: its complete retirement, being about two miles from the village, half a mile from the nearest neighbor, and separated from the highway by a broad field; its bounding on the river, which the owner said protected it by its fogs from frosts in the spring, though that was nothing to me; the gray color and ruinous state of the house and barn, and the dilapidated fences, which put such an interval between me and the last occupant; the hollow and lichen-covered apple trees, gnawed by rabbits, showing what kind of neighbors I should have; but above all, the recollection I had of it from my earliest voyages up the river, when the house was concealed behind a dense grove of red maples, through which I heard the house-dog bark. I was in haste to buy it, before the proprietor finished getting out some rocks, cutting down the hollow apple trees, and grubbing up some young birches which had sprung up in the pasture, or, in short, had made any more of his improvements. To enjoy these advantages I was ready to carry it on; like Atlas, to take the world on my shoulders,—I never heard what compensation he received for that,—and do all those things which had no other motive or excuse but that I might pay for it and be unmolested in my possession of it; for I knew all the while that it would yield the most abundant crop of the kind I wanted, if I could only afford to let it alone. But it turned out as I have said.

All that I could say, then, with respect to farming on a large scale—I have always cultivated a garden—was, that I had had my seeds ready. Many think that seeds improve with age. I have no doubt that time discriminates between the good and the bad; and when at last I shall plant, I shall be less likely to be disappointed. But I would say to my fellows, once for all, As long as possible live free and uncommitted. It makes but little difference whether you are committed to a farm or the county jail.

Old Cato, whose "De Re Rusticâ" is my "Cultivator," says,—and the only translation I have seen makes sheer nonsense of the passage,— "When you think of getting a farm turn it thus in your mind, not to buy greedily; nor spare your pains to look at it, and do not think it enough, to go round it once. The oftener you go there the more it will please you, if it is good." I think I shall not buy greedily, but go round and round it as long as I live, and be buried in it first, that it may please me the more at last.

The present was my next experiment of this kind, which I purpose to describe more at length, for convenience putting the experience of two years into one. As I have said, I do not propose to write an ode to dejection, but to brag as lustily as chanticleer in the morning, standing on his roost, if only to wake my neighbors up.

When first I took up my abode in the woods, that is, began to spend my nights as well as days there, which, by accident, was on Independence Day, or the Fourth of July, 1845, my house was not finished for winter, but was merely a defence against the rain, without plastering or chimney, the walls being of rough, weather-stained boards, with wide chinks, which made it cool at night. The upright white hewn studs and freshly planed door and window casings give it a clean and airy look, especially in the morning, when its timbers were saturated with dew, so that I fancied that by noon some sweet gum would exude from them. To my imagination it retained throughout the day more or less of this auroral character, reminding me of a certain house on a mountain which I had visited a year before. This was an airy and unplastered cabin, fit to entertain a travelling god, and where a goddess might trail her garments. The winds which passed over my dwelling were such as sweep over the ridges of mountains, bearing the broken strains, or celestial parts only, of terrestrial music. The morning wind forever blows, the poem of creation is uninterrupted; but few are the ears that hear it. Olympus is but the outside of the earth everywhere.

The only house I had been the owner of before, if I except a boat, was a tent, which I used occasionally when making excursions in the summer, and this is still rolled up in my garret; but the boat, after passing from hand to hand, has gone down the stream of time. With this more substantial shelter about me, I had made some progress toward settling in the world. This frame, so slightly clad, was a sort of crystallization around me, and reacted on the builder. It was suggestive somewhat as a picture in outlines. I did not need to go outdoors to take the air, for the atmosphere within had lost none of its freshness. It was not so much within-doors as behind a door where I sat, even in the rainiest weather. The

Harivansa says, "An abode without birds is like a meat without seasoning." Such was not my abode, for I found myself suddenly neighbor to the birds; not by having imprisoned one, but having caged myself near them. I was not only nearer to some of those which commonly frequent the garden and the orchard, but to those wilder and more thrilling songsters of the forest which never, or rarely, serenade a villager,—the wood thrush, the veery, the scarlet tanager, the field sparrow, the whip-poor-will, and many others.

I was seated by the shore of a small pond, about a mile and a half south of the village of Concord and somewhat higher than it, in the midst of an extensive wood between that town and Lincoln, and about two miles south of that our only field known to fame, Concord Battle Grounds; but I was so low in the woods that the opposite shore, half a mile off, like the rest, covered with wood, was my most distant horizon. For the first week, whenever I looked out on the pond it impressed me like a tarn high up on the side of a mountain, its bottom far above the surface of other lakes, and, as the sun arose, I saw it throwing off its nightly clothing of mist, and here and there, by degrees, its soft ripples or its smooth reflecting surface was revealed, while the mists, like ghosts, were stealthily withdrawing in every direction into the woods, as at the breaking up of some nocturnal conventicle. The very dew seemed to hang upon the trees later into the day than usual, as on the sides of mountains.

This small lake was of most value as a neighbor in the intervals of a gentle rain-storm in August, when, both air and water being perfectly still, but the sky overcast, mid-afternoon had all the serenity of evening, and the wood thrush sang around, and was heard from shore to shore. A lake like this is never smoother than at such a time; and the clear portion of the air above it being shallow and darkened by clouds, the water, full of light and reflections, becomes a lower heaven itself so much the more important. From a hill-top near by, where the wood had been recently cut off, there was a pleasing vista southward across the pond, through a wide indentation in the hills which form the shore there, where their opposite sides sloping toward each other suggested a stream flowing out in that direction through a wooded valley, but stream there was none. That way I looked between and over the near green hills to some distant and higher ones in the horizon, tinged with blue. Indeed, by standing on tiptoe I could catch a glimpse of some of the peaks of the still bluer and more distant mountain ranges in the northwest, those true-blue coins from heaven's own mint, and also of some portion of the village. But in other directions, even from this point, I could not see over or beyond the woods which surrounded me. It is well to have some water in your neighborhood, to give buoyancy to and float the earth. One value even of the smallest well is, that when you look into it you see that earth is not continent but insular. This is as important as that it keeps butter cool. When I looked across the pond from this peak toward the Sudbury meadows, which in time of flood I distinguished elevated perhaps by a mirage in their seething valley, like a coin in a basin, all the earth beyond the pond appeared like a thin crust insulated and floated even by this small sheet of intervening water, and I was reminded that this on which I dwelt was but *dry land*.

Though the view from my door was still more contracted, I did not feel crowded or confined in the least. There was pasture enough for my imagination. The low shrub oak plateau to which the opposite shore arose stretched away toward the prairies of the West and the steppes of Tartary, affording ample room for all the roving families of men. "There are none happy in the world but beings who enjoy freely a vast horizon,"—said Damodara, when his herds required new and larger pastures.

Both place and time were changed, and I dwelt nearer to those parts of the universe and to those eras in history which had most attracted me. Where I lived was as far off as many a region viewed nightly by astronomers. We are wont to imagine rare and delectable places in some remote and more celestial corner of the system, behind the constellation of Cassiopeia's Chair, far from noise and disturbance. I discovered that my house actually had its site in such a withdrawn, but forever new and unprofaned, part of the universe. If it were worth the while to settle in those parts near to the Pleiades or the Hyades, to Aldebaran or Altair, then I was really there, or at an equal remoteness from the life which I had left behind, dwindled and twinkling with as fine a ray to my nearest neighbor, and to be seen only in moonless nights by him. Such was that part of creation where I had squatted;—

> "There was a shepherd that did live,
>   And held his thoughts as high
> As were the mounts whereon his flocks
>   Did hourly feed him by."

What should we think of the shepherd's life if his flocks always wandered to higher pastures than his thoughts?

Every morning was a cheerful invitation to make my life of equal simplicity, and I may say innocence, with Nature herself. I have been as sincere a worshipper of Aurora as the Greeks. I got up early and bathed in the pond; that was a religious exercise, and one of the best things which I did. They say that characters were engraven on the bathing tub of King Tching-thang to this effect: "Renew thyself completely each day; do it again, and again, and forever again." I can understand that. Morning brings back the heroic ages. I was as much affected by the faint hum of a mosquito making its invisible and unimaginable tour through my apartment at earliest dawn, when I was sitting with door and windows

open, as I could be by any trumpet that ever sang of fame. It was Homer's
requiem; itself an Iliad and Odyssey in the air, singing its own wrath
and wanderings. There was something cosmical about it; a standing advertisement, still forbidden, of the everlasting vigor and fertility of the
world. The morning, which is the most memorable season of the day, is
the awakening hour. Then there is least somnolence in us; and for an
hour, at least, some part of us awakes which slumbers all the rest of the
day and night. Little is to be expected of that day, if it can be called a
day, to which we are not awakened by our Genius, but by the mechanical
nudgings of some servitor, are not awakened by our own newly acquired
force and aspirations from within, accompanied by the undulations of
celestial music, instead of factory bells, and a fragrance filling the air—to
a higher life than we fell asleep from; and thus the darkness bear its
fruit, and prove itself to be good, no less than the light. That man who
does not believe that each day contains an earlier, more sacred, and
auroral hour than he has yet profaned, has despaired of life, and is
pursuing a descending and darkening way. After a partial cessation of his
sensuous life, the soul of man, or its organs rather, are reinvigorated each
day, and his Genius tries again what noble life it can make. All memorable
events, I should say, transpire in morning time and in a morning atmosphere. The Vedas say, "All intelligences awake with the morning." Poetry
and art, and the fairest and most memorable of the actions of men, date
from such an hour. All poets and heroes, like Memnon, are the children
of Aurora, and emit their music at sunrise. To him whose elastic and
vigorous thought keeps pace with the sun, the day is a perpetual morning.
It matters not what the clocks say or the attitudes and labors of men.
Morning is when I am awake and there is a dawn in me. Moral reform
is the effort to throw off sleep. Why is it that men give so poor an account of their day if they have not been slumbering? They are not such
poor calculators. If they had not been overcome with drowsiness, they
would have performed something. The millions are awake enough for
physical labor; but only one in a million is awake enough for effective
intellectual exertion, only one in a hundred millions to a poetic or divine
life. To be awake is to be alive. I have never yet met a man who was
quite awake. How could I have looked him in the face?

We must learn to reawaken and keep ourselves awake, not by mechanical aids, but by an infinite expectation of the dawn, which does not
forsake us in our soundest sleep. I know of no more encouraging fact
than the unquestionable ability of man to elevate his life by a conscious
endeavor. It is something to be able to paint a particular picture, or to
carve a statue, and so to make a few objects beautiful; but it is far more
glorious to carve and paint the very atmosphere and medium through
which we look, which morally we can do. To affect the quality of the day,
that is the highest of arts. Every man is tasked to make his life, even in

its details, worthy of the contemplation of his most elevated and critical hour. If we refused, or rather used up, such paltry information as we get, the oracles would distinctly inform us how this might be done.

I went to the woods because I wished to live deliberately, to front only the essential facts of life, and see if I could not learn what it had to teach, and not, when I came to die, discover that I had not lived. I did not wish to live what was not life, living is so dear; nor did I wish to practise resignation, unless it was quite necessary. I wanted to live deep and suck out all the marrow of life, to live so sturdily and Spartanlike as to put to rout all that was not life, to cut a broad swath and shave close, to drive life into a corner, and reduce it to its lowest terms, and, if it proved to be mean, why then to get the whole and genuine meanness of it, and publish its meanness to the world; or if it were sublime, to know it by experience, and be able to give a true account of it in my next excursion. For most men, it appears to me, are in a strange uncertainty about it, whether it is of the devil or of God, and have *somewhat hastily* concluded that it is the chief end of man here to "glorify God and enjoy him forever."

Still we live meanly, like ants; though the fable tells us that we were long ago changed into men; like pygmies we fight with cranes; it is error upon error, and clout upon clout, and our best virtue has for its occasion a superfluous and evitable wretchedness. Our life is frittered away by detail. An honest man has hardly need to count more than his ten fingers, or in extreme cases he may add his ten toes, and lump the rest. Simplicity, simplicity, simplicity! I say, let your affairs be as two or three, and not a hundred or a thousand; instead of a million count half a dozen, and keep your accounts on your thumb nail. In the midst of this chopping sea of civilized life, such are the clouds and storms and quicksands and thousand-and-one items to be allowed for, that a man has to live, if he would not founder and go to the bottom and not make his port at all, by dead reckoning, and he must be a great calculator indeed who succeeds. Simplify, simplify. Instead of three meals a day, if it be necessary eat but one; instead of a hundred dishes, five; and reduce other things in proportion. Our life is like a German Confederacy, made up of petty states, with its boundary forever fluctuating, so that even a German cannot tell you how it is bounded at any moment. The nation itself, with all its so-called internal improvements, which, by the way are all external and superficial, is just such an unwieldly and overgrown establishment, cluttered with furniture and tripped up by its own traps, ruined by luxury and heedless expense, by want of calculation and a worthy aim, as the million households in the land; and the only cure for it, as for them, is in a rigid economy, a stern and more than Spartan simplicity of life and elevation of purpose. It lives too fast. Men think that it is essential that the *Nation* have commerce, and export ice, and talk through a telegraph, and ride thirty miles an hour, without a doubt, whether *they* do or not; but whether we should live like baboons or like men, is a little uncertain. If we do not get out sleepers, and forge rails, and devote days and nights to the work, but go to tinkering upon our *lives* to improve *them*, who will build railroads? And if railroads are not built, how shall we get to heaven in season? But if we stay at home and mind our business, who will want railroads? We do not ride on the railroad; it rides upon us. Did you ever think what those sleepers are that underlie the railroad? Each one is a man, an Irishman, or a Yankee man. The rails are laid on them, and they are covered with sand, and the cars run smoothly over them. They are sound sleepers, I assure you. And every few years a new lot is laid down and run over; so that, if some have the pleasure of riding on a rail, others have the misfortune to be ridden upon. And when they run over a man that is walking in his sleep, a supernumerary sleeper in the wrong position, and wake him up, they suddenly stop the cars, and make a hue and cry about it, as if this were an exception. I am glad to know that it takes a gang of men for every five miles to keep the sleepers down and level in their beds as it is, for this is a sign that they may sometime get up again.

Why should we live with such hurry and waste of life? We are determined to be starved before we are hungry. Men say that a stitch in time saves nine, and so they take a thousand stitches to-day to save nine to-morrow. As for *work*, we haven't any of any consequence. We have the Saint Vitus' dance, and cannot possibly keep our heads still. If I should only give a few pulls at the parish bell-rope, as for a fire, that is, without setting the bell, there is hardly a man on his farm in the outskirts of Concord, notwithstanding that press of engagements which was his excuse so many times this morning, nor a boy, nor a woman, I might almost say, but would forsake all and follow that sound, not mainly to save property from the flames, but, if we will confess the truth, much more to see it burn, since burn it must, and we, be it known, did not set it on fire,—or to see it put out, and have a hand in it, if that is done as handsomely; yes, even if it were the parish church itself. Hardly a man takes a half-hour's nap after dinner, but when he wakes he holds up his head and asks, "What's the news?" as if the rest of mankind had stood his sentinels. Some give directions to be waked every half-hour, doubtless for no other purpose; and then, to pay for it, they tell what they have dreamed. After a night's sleep the news is as indispensable as the breakfast. "Pray tell me anything new that has happened to a man anywhere on this globe,"—and he reads it over his coffee and rolls, that a man has had his eyes gouged out this morning on the Wachito River; never dreaming the while that he lives in the dark unfathomed mammoth cave of this world, and has but the rudiment of an eye himself.

For my part, I could easily do without the post office. I think that there are very few important communications made through it. To speak critically, I never received more than one or two letters in my life—I wrote this some years ago—that were worth the postage. The penny-post is, commonly, an institution through which you seriously offer a man that penny for his thoughts which is so often safely offered in jest. And I am sure that I never read any memorable news in a newspaper. If we read of one man robbed, or murdered, or killed by accident, or one house burned, or one vessel wrecked, or one steamboat blown up, or one cow run over on the Western Railroad, or one mad dog killed, or one lot of grasshoppers in the winter,—we never need read of another. One is enough. If you are acquainted with the principle, what do you care for a myriad instances and applications? To a philosopher all *news*, as it is called, is gossip, and they who edit and read it are old women over their tea. Yet not a few are greedy after this gossip. There was such a rush, as I hear, the other day at one of the offices to learn the foreign news by the last arrival, that several large squares of plate glass belonging to the establishment were broken by the pressure,—news which I seriously think a ready wit might write a twelvemonth, or twelve years, beforehand with sufficient accuracy. As for Spain, for instance, if you know how to throw in Don Carlos and the Infanta, and Don Pedro and Seville and Granada, from time to time in the right proportions,—they may have changed the names a little since I saw the papers,—and serve up a bullfight when other entertainments fail, it will be true to the letter, and give us as good an idea of the exact state or ruin of things in Spain as the most succinct and lucid reports under this head in the newspapers: and as for England, almost the last significant scrap of news from that quarter was the revolution of 1649; and if you have learned the history of her crops for an average year, you never need attend to that thing again, unless your speculations are of a merely pecuniary character. If one may judge who rarely looks into the newspapers, nothing new does ever happen in foreign parts, a French revolution not excepted.

What news! how much more important to know what that is which was never old! "Kieou-he-yu (great dignitary of the state of Wei) sent a man to Khoung-tseu to know his news. Khoung-tseu caused the messenger to be seated near him, and questioned him in these terms: What is your master doing? The messenger answered with respect: My master desires to diminish the number of his faults, but he cannot come to the end of them. The messenger being gone, the philosopher remarked: What a worthy messenger! What a worthy messenger!" The preacher, instead of vexing the ears of drowsy farmers on their day of rest at the end of the week,—for Sunday is the fit conclusion of an ill-spent week, and not the fresh and brave beginning of a new one,—with this one other draggle-tail of a sermon, should shout with thundering voice, "Pause! Avast! Why so seeming fast, but deadly slow?"

Shams and delusions are esteemed for soundest truths, while reality is fabulous. If men would steadily observe realities only, and not allow themselves to be deluded, life, to compare it with such things as we know, would be like a fairy tale and the Arabian Nights' Entertainments. If we respected only what is inevitable and has a right to be, music and poetry would resound along the streets. When we are unhurried and wise, we perceive that only great and worthy things have any permanent and absolute existence, that petty fears and petty pleasures are but the shadow of the reality. This is always exhilarating and sublime. By closing the eyes and slumbering, and consenting to be deceived by shows, men establish and confirm their daily life of routine and habit everywhere, which still is built on purely illusory foundations. Children, who play life, discern its true law and relations more clearly than men, who fail to live it worthily, but who think that they are wiser by experience, that is, by failure. I have read in a Hindoo book, that "there was a king's son, who, being expelled in infancy from his native city, was brought up by a forester, and, growing up to maturity in that state, imagined himself to belong to the barbarous race with which he lived. One of his father's ministers having discovered him, revealed to him what he was, and the misconception of his character was removed, and he knew himself to be a prince. So soul," continues the Hindoo philosopher, "from the circumstances in which it is placed, mistakes its own character, until the truth is revealed to it by some holy teacher, and then it knows itself to be *Brahme*." I perceive that we inhabitants of New England live this mean life that we do because our vision does not penetrate the surface of things. We think that that *is* which *appears* to be. If a man should walk through this town and see only the reality, where, think you, would the "Mill-dam" go to? If he should give us an account of the realities he beheld there, we should not recognize the place in his description. Look at a meeting-house, or a court-house, or a jail, or a shop, or a dwelling-house, and say what that thing really is before a true gaze, and they would all go to pieces in your account of them. Men esteem truth remote, in the outskirts of the system, behind the farthest star, before Adam and after the last man. In eternity there is indeed something true and sublime. But all these times and places and occasions are now and here. God himself culminates in the present moment, and will never be more divine in the lapse of all the ages. And we are enabled to apprehend at all what is sublime and noble only by the perpetual instilling and drenching of the reality that surrounds us. The universe constantly and obediently answers to our conceptions; whether we travel fast or slow, the track is laid for us. Let us spend our lives in conceiving then. The poet or the artist never yet had so fair and noble a design but some of his posterity at least could accomplish it.

Let us spend one day as deliberately as Nature, and not be thrown off the track by every nutshell and mosquito's wing that falls on the rails. Let us rise early and fast, or break fast, gently and without perturbation; let company come and let company go, let the bells ring and the children cry,—determined to make a day of it. Why should we knock under and go with the stream? Let us not be upset and overwhelmed in that terrible rapid and whirlpool called a dinner, situated in the meridian shallows. Weather this danger and you are safe, for the rest of the way is down hill. With unrelaxed nerves, with morning vigor, sail by it, looking another way, tied to the mast like Ulysses. If the engine whistles, let it whistle till it is hoarse for its pains. If the bell rings, why should we run? We will consider what kind of music they are like. Let us settle ourselves, and work and wedge our feet downward through the mud and slush of opinion, and prejudice, and tradition, and delusion, and appearance, that alluvion which covers the globe, through Paris and London, through New York and Boston and Concord, through Church and State, through poetry and philosophy and religion, till we come to a hard bottom and rocks in place, which we can call *reality*, and say, This is, and no mistake; and then begin, having a *point d'appui*, below freshet and frost and fire, a place where you might found a wall or a state, or set a lamp-post safely, or perhaps a gauge, not a Nilometer, but a Realometer, that future ages might know how deep a freshet of shams and appearances had gathered from time to time. If you stand right fronting and face to face to a fact, you will see the sun glimmer on both its surfaces, as if it were a cimeter, and feel its sweet edge dividing you through the heart and marrow, and so you will happily conclude your mortal career. Be it life or death, we crave only reality. If we are really dying, let us hear the rattle in our throats and feel cold in the extremities; if we are alive, let us go about our business.

Time is but the stream I go a-fishing in. I drink at it; but while I drink I see the sandy bottom and detect how shallow it is. Its thin current slides away, but eternity remains. I would drink deeper; fish in the sky, whose bottom is pebbly with stars. I cannot count one. I know not the first letter of the alphabet. I have always been regretting that I was not as wise as the day I was born. The intellect is a cleaver; it discerns and rifts its way into the secret of things. I do not wish to be any more busy with my hands than is necessary. My head is hands and feet. I feel all my best faculties concentrated in it. My instinct tells me that my head is an organ for burrowing, as some creatures use their snout and fore paws, and with it I would mine and burrow my way through these hills. I think that the richest vein is somewhere hereabouts; so by the divining-rod and thin rising vapors I judge; and here I will begin to mine.

QUESTIONS

1. Describe Thoreau's prose style. Is it essentially literary or conversational?
2. For what kind of symbol does Thoreau search in a farmhouse? Why does the Hollowell Farm answer his purposes so well?
3. Thoreau calls his daily bathing at dawn a "religious exercise." What myths, Christian and pagan, could such a practice echo? Why is Thoreau so attracted to the idea of an eternal dawn within each of us?
4. Explain Thoreau's use of the metaphor of the German confederacy. Why is this metaphor a particularly well-chosen one?
5. How does Thoreau make use of such institutions of civilization as the railroad and the U.S. Post Office to illustrate his themes?

HENRY JAMES

HENRY JAMES (1843–1916), writing both as a novelist and critic, initiated many important techniques of narration and basically established the modern critical vocabulary for the novel. He dedicated his life to affirming that fiction was as respectable an art as any other literary form. Among his important early works are *The American* (1877), *Daisy Miller* (1879), and *Portrait of a Lady* (1881), all of which are stories about young, innocent Americans who are initiated into the sophisticated, corrupt cultures of Europe. The best novels of his later period (*The Wings of the Dove*, 1902, *The Ambassadors*, 1903, and *The Golden Bowl*, 1904) continue this theme but work it out in highly complex ways. These late novels are written in a difficult style that deliberately makes great demands on the reader's attention. "The Jolly Corner" (1908) has a somewhat easier style whose almost poetic rhythmic qualities are revealed when one reads it aloud. It has some characteristics of a ghost story, a genre James liked and made use of throughout his long career. Perhaps his best ghost story is *The Turn of the Screw* (1898).

As a novelist, James has many critics, especially those who object to the narrowness of his subject matter, which may be attributable to his background. James's father was a Swedenborgian, and his elder brother, William, became America's most distinguished exponent of the philosophy of pragmatism. As a child in a family of comfortable means, he had no worries about food or survival and, like himself, his characters do not have to struggle to survive physically. They also have little concern with either politics or the law, although James himself was an uncompromising libertarian.

Early in his career James emigrated from America to Europe. For most of his life he identified with no one country, although in his later years he settled in Britain and became a citizen there. Many of his characters have this same international identity and mobility. Moreover, he often deliberately grants his characters wealth so they can concentrate on such "luxuries" as individual development and personal relationships. Thus, James's protagonists resemble the current generation of young, affluent Americans. And, like many young Americans, James is concerned above all with awareness. However, awareness for James (he called it "consciousness") is not just verbal awareness or the ability to intellectualize, but always has a fundamentally emotional basis and is crucial in determining the sense of *felt* life one gets.

Toward the end of his career no theme was more important to James than that of the man who discovers awareness late in life and realizes how much he has missed. And yet, no matter how late this discovery comes, it always has a redeeming power. In "The Jolly Corner" we are not sure what Spencer Brydon has done with his life nor do we know how much consciousness he has. We do know that he has spent most of his life in Europe and that he has lived amidst the charm, the esthetic sensitivity, and the sophistication of European culture. We also know that he is appalled by the vulgar commercialism of New York, which has destroyed, in its devouring expansiveness, almost all the buildings of his Manhattan childhood —with the major exception of his family home.

While visiting New York, Brydon becomes obsessed with the idea of "the road not taken"—what he would have been had he stayed in New York and used his considerable powers to become a businessman. He intuits that the "ghost" of such a person still stalks his old home and decides that he would like to confront that side of himself. Thus the story is a kind of psychic suspense tale. James is acute at describing Brydon's sense of fear and self-doubt. (The experience is not unlike the kind of self-testing often undergone in encounter groups or certain drug experiences.) As the story progresses, we realize that Brydon is not simply satisfying a curiosity; he is searching not only for the ghost that haunts the house, but also for the true self he has never really known. Thus the story becomes an account of the terrifyingly powerful process by which Brydon comes to be reborn, to realize the emptiness of his former life, and to acknowledge the importance of human love.

The Jolly Corner

1

"Every one asks me what I 'think' of everything," said Spencer Brydon; "and I make answer as I can—begging or dodging the question, putting them off with any nonsense. It wouldn't matter to any of them really," he went on, "for, even were it possible to meet in that stand-and-deliver way so silly a demand on so big a subject, my 'thoughts' would still be almost altogether about something that concerns only myself." He was talking to Miss Staverton, with whom for a couple of months now he had availed himself of every possible occasion to talk; this disposition and this resource, this comfort and support, as the situation in fact presented itself, having promptly enough taken the first place in the considerable array of rather unattenuated surprises attending his so strangely belated return to America. Everything was somehow a surprise; and that might be natural when one had so long and so consistently neglected everything, taken pains to give surprises so much margin for play. He had given them more than thirty years—thirty-three, to be exact; and they now seemed to him to have organised their performance quite on the scale of that licence. He had been twenty-three on leaving New York—he was fifty-six today: unless indeed he were to reckon as he had sometimes, since his repatriation, found himself feeling; in which case he would have lived longer than is often allotted to man. It would have taken a century, he repeatedly said to himself, and said also to Alice Staverton, it would have taken a longer absence and a more averted mind than those even of which he had been guilty, to pile up the differences, the newnesses, the queernesses, above all the bignesses, for the better or the worse, that at present assaulted his vision wherever he looked.

The great fact all the while however had been the incalculability; since he *had* supposed himself, from decade to decade, to be allowing, and in the most liberal and intelligent manner, for brilliancy of change. He actually saw that he had allowed for nothing; he missed what he would have been sure of finding, he found what he would never have imagined. Proportions and values were upside-down; the ugly things he had expected, the ugly things of his far-away youth, when he had too promptly waked up to a sense of the ugly—these uncanny phenomena placed him rather, as it happened, under the charm; whereas the "swagger" things, the modern, the monstrous, the famous things, those he had more particularly, like thousands of ingenuous enquirers every year, come over to see, were exactly his source of dismay. They were as so many set traps

From THE JOLLY CORNER, 1908.

for displeasure, above all for reaction, of which his restless tread was constantly pressing the spring. It was interesting, doubtless, the whole show, but it would have been too disconcerting hadn't a certain finer truth saved the situation. He had distinctly not, in this steadier light, come over *all* for the monstrosities; he had come, not only in the last analysis but quite on the face of the act, under an impulse with which they had nothing to do. He had come—putting the thing pompously—to look at his "property," which he had thus for a third of a century not been within four thousand miles of; or, expressing it less sordidly, he had yielded to the humour of seeing again his house on the jolly corner, as he usually, and quite fondly, described it—the one in which he had first seen the light, in which various members of his family had lived and had died, in which the holidays of his overschooled boyhood had been passed and the few social flowers of his chilled adolescence gathered, and which, alienated then for so long a period, had, through the successive deaths of his two brothers and the termination of old arrangements, come wholly into his hands. He was the owner of another, not quite so "good"—the jolly corner having been, from far back, superlatively extended and consecrated; and the value of the pair represented his main capital, with an income consisting, in these later years, of their respective rents which (thanks precisely to their original excellent type) had never been depressingly low. He could live in "Europe," as he had been in the habit of living, on the product of these flourishing New York leases, and all the better since, that of the second structure, the mere number in its long row, having within a twelvemonth fallen in, renovation at a high advance had proved beautifully possible.

These were items of property indeed, but he had found himself since his arrival distinguishing more than ever between them. The house within the street, two bristling blocks westward, was already in course of reconstruction as a tall mass of flats; he had acceded, some time before, to overtures for this conversion—in which, now that it was going forward, it had been not the least of his astonishments to find himself able, on the spot, and though without a previous ounce of such experience, to participate with a certain intelligence, almost with a certain authority. He had lived his life with his back so turned to such concerns and his face addressed to those of so different an order that he scarce knew what to make of this lively stir, in a compartment of his mind never yet penetrated, of a capacity for business and a sense for construction. These virtues, so common all round him now, had been dormant in his own organism—where it might be said of them perhaps that they had slept the sleep of the just. At present, in the splendid autumn weather—the autumn at least was a pure boon in the terrible place—he loafed about his "work" undeterred, secretly agitated; not in the least "minding" that the whole proposition, as they said, was vulgar and sordid, and ready to climb ladders, to walk the plank, to handle materials and look wise about them, to ask questions, in fine, and challenge explanations and really "go into" figures.

It amused, it verily quite charmed him; and, by the same stroke, it amused, and even more, Alice Staverton, though perhaps charming her perceptibly less. She wasn't however going to be better off for it, as *he* was—and so astonishingly much: nothing was now likely, he knew, ever to make her better off than she found herself, in the afternoon of life, as the delicately frugal possessor and tenant of the small house in Irving Place to which she had subtly managed to cling through her almost unbroken New York career. If he knew the way to it now better than to any other address among the dreadful multiplied numberings which seemed to him to reduce the whole place to some vast ledger-page, overgrown, fantastic, of ruled and criss-crossed lines and figures—if he had formed, for his consolation, that habit, it was really not a little because of the charm of his having encountered and recognised, in the vast wilderness of the wholesale, breaking through the mere gross generalisation of wealth and force and success, a small still scene where items and shades, all delicate things, kept the sharpness of the notes of a high voice perfectly trained, and where economy hung about like the scent of a garden. His old friend lived with one maid and herself dusted her relics and trimmed her lamps and polished her silver; she stood off, in the awful modern crush, when she could, but she sallied forth and did battle when the challenge was really to "spirit," the spirit she after all confessed to, proudly and a little shyly, as to that of the better time, that of *their* common, their quite far-away and antediluvian social period and order. She made use of the street-cars when need be, the terrible things that people scrambled for as the panic-stricken at sea scramble for the boats; she affronted, inscrutably, under stress, all the public concussions and ordeals; and yet, with that slim mystifying grace of her appearance, which defied you to say if she were a fair young woman who looked older through trouble, or a fine smooth older one who looked young through successful indifference; with her precious reference, above all, to memories and histories into which he could enter, she was as exquisite for him as some pale pressed flower (a rarity to begin with), and, failing other sweetnesses, she was a sufficient reward of his effort. They had communities of knowledge, "their" knowledge (this discriminating possessive was always on her lips) of presences of the other age, presences all overlaid, in his case, by the experience of a man and the freedom of a wanderer, overlaid by pleasure, by infidelity, by passages of life that were strange and dim to her, just by "Europe" in short, but still unobscured, still exposed and cherished, under that pious visitation of the spirit from which she had never been diverted.

She had come with him one day to see how his "apartment-house" was rising; he had helped her over gaps and explained to her plans, and while they were there had happened to have, before her, a brief but lively discussion with the man in charge, the representative of the building-firm that had undertaken his work. He had found himself quite "standing-up" to this personage over a failure on the latter's part to observe some detail of one of their noted conditions, and had so lucidly urged his case that, besides ever so prettily flushing, at the time, for sympathy in his triumph, she had afterwards said to him (though to a slightly greater effect of irony) that he had clearly for too many years neglected a real gift. If he had but stayed at home he would have anticipated the inventor of the sky-scraper. If he had but stayed at home he would have discovered his genius in time really to start some new variety of awful architectural hare and run it till it burrowed in a gold-mine. He was to remember these words, while the weeks elapsed, for the small silver ring they had sounded over the queerest and deepest of his own lately most disguised and most muffled vibrations.

It had begun to be present to him after the first fortnight, it had broken out with the oddest abruptness, this particular wanton wonderment: it met him there—and this was the image under which he himself judged the matter, or at least, not a little, thrilled and flushed with it—very much as he might have been met by some strange figure, some unexpected occupant, at a turn of one of the dim passages of an empty house. The quaint analogy quite hauntingly remained with him, when he didn't indeed rather improve it by a still intenser form: that of his opening a door behind which he would have made sure of finding nothing, a door into a room shuttered and void, and yet so coming, with a great suppressed start, on some quite erect confronting presence, something planted in the middle of the place and facing him through the dusk. After that visit to the house in construction he walked with his companion to see the other and always so much the better one, which in the eastward direction formed one of the corners, the "jolly" one precisely, of the street now so generally dishonoured and disfigured in its westward reaches, and of the comparatively conservative Avenue. The Avenue still had pretensions, as Miss Staverton said, to decency; the old people had mostly gone, the old names were unknown, and here and there an old association seemed to stray, all vaguely, like some very aged person, out too late, whom you might meet and feel the impulse to watch or follow, in kindness, for safe restoration to shelter.

They went in together, our friends; he admitted himself with his key, as he kept no one there, he explained, preferring, for his reasons, to leave the place empty, under a simple arrangement with a good woman living in the neighbourhood and who came for a daily hour to open windows and dust and sweep. Spencer Brydon had his reasons and was growingly aware of them; they seemed to him better each time he was there, though he didn't name them all to his companion, any more than he told her as yet how often, how quite absurdly often, he himself came. He only let her see for the present, while they walked through the great blank rooms, that absolute vacancy reigned and that, from top to bottom, there was nothing but Mrs. Muldoon's broomstick, in a corner, to tempt the burglar. Mrs. Muldoon was then on the premises, and she loquaciously attended the visitors, preceding them from room to room and pushing back shutters and throwing up sashes—all to show them, as she remarked, how little there was to see. There was little indeed to see in the great gaunt shell where the main dispositions and the general apportionment of space, the style of an age of ampler allowances, had nevertheless for its master their honest pleading message, affecting him as some good old servant's, some lifelong retainer's appeal for a character, or even for a retiring-pension; yet it was also a remark of Mrs. Muldoon's that, glad as she was to oblige him by her noonday round, there was a request she greatly hoped he would never make of her. If he should wish her for any reason to come in after dark she would just tell him, if he "plased," that he must ask it of somebody else.

The fact that there was nothing to see didn't militate for the worthy woman against what one *might* see, and she put it frankly to Miss Staverton that no lady could be expected to like, could she? "craping up to thim top storeys in the ayvil hours." The gas and the electric light were off the house, and she fairly evoked a gruesome vision of her march through the great grey rooms—so many of them as there were too!—with her glimmering taper. Miss Staverton met her honest glare with a smile and the profession that she herself certainly would recoil from such an adventure. Spencer Brydon meanwhile held his peace—for the moment; the question of the "evil" hours in his old home had already become too grave for him. He had begun some time since to "crape," and he knew just why a packet of candles addressed to that pursuit had been stowed by his own hand, three weeks before, at the back of a drawer of the fine old sideboard that occupied, as a "fixture," the deep recess in the dining-room. Just now he laughed at his companions—quickly however changing the subject; for the reason that, in the first place, his laugh struck him even at that moment as starting the odd echo, the conscious human resonance (he scarce knew how to qualify it) that sounds made while he was there alone sent back to his ear or his fancy; and that, in the second, he imagined Alice Staverton for the instant on the point of asking him, with a divination, if he ever so prowled. There were divinations he was unprepared for, and he had at all events averted enquiry by the time Mrs. Muldoon had left them, passing on to other parts.

There was happily enough to say, on so consecrated a spot, that could be said freely and fairly; so that a whole train of declarations was precipitated by his friend's having herself broken out, after a yearning look

round: "But I hope you don't mean they want you to pull *this* to pieces!"
His answer came, promptly, with his re-awakened wrath: it was of course
exactly what they wanted, and what they were "at" him for, daily, with the
iteration of people who couldn't for their life understand a man's liability
to decent feelings. He had found the place, just as it stood and beyond
what he could express, an interest and a joy. There were values other
than the beastly rent-values, and in short, in short—! But it was thus
Miss Staverton took him up. "In short you're to make so good a thing of
your sky-scraper that, living in luxury on *those* ill-gotten gains, you can
afford for a while to be sentimental here!" Her smile had for him, with
the words, the particular mild irony with which he found half her talk
suffused; an irony without bitterness and that came, exactly, from her
having so much imagination—not, like the cheap sarcasms with which
one heard most people, about the world of "society," bid for the reputation of cleverness, from nobody's really having any. It was agreeable to
him at this very moment to be sure that when he had answered, after a
brief demur, "Well yes: so, precisely, you may put it!" her imagination
would still do him justice. He explained that even if never a dollar were
to come to him from the other house he would nevertheless cherish this
one; and he dwelt, further, while they lingered and wandered, on the fact
of the stupefaction he was already exciting, the positive mystification he
felt himself create.

He spoke of the value of all he read into it, into the mere sight of the
walls, mere shapes of the rooms, mere sound of the floors, mere feel, in
his hand, of the old silver-plated knobs of the several mahogany doors,
which suggested the pressure of the palms of the dead; the seventy years
of the past in fine that these things represented, the annals of nearly three
generations, counting his grandfather's, the one that had ended there,
and the impalpable ashes of his long-extinct youth, afloat in the very air
like microscopic motes. She listened to everything; she was a woman who
answered intimately but who utterly didn't chatter. She scattered abroad
therefore no cloud of words; she could assent, she could agree, above all
she could encourage, without doing that. Only at the last she went a
little further than he had done himself. "And then how do you know?
You may still, after all, want to live here." It rather indeed pulled him
up, for it wasn't what he had been thinking, at least in her sense of the
words. "You mean I may decide to stay on for the sake of it?"

"Well, *with* such a home—!" But, quite beautifully, she had too much
tact to dot so monstrous an *i*, and it was precisely an illustration of the
way she didn't rattle. How could any one—of any wit—insist on any
one else's "wanting" to live in New York?

"Oh," he said, "I *might* have lived here (since I had my opportunity
early in life); I might have put in here all these years. Then everything
would have been different enough—and, I dare say, 'funny' enough. But

that's another matter. And then the beauty of it—I mean of my perversity, of my refusal to agree to a 'deal'—is just in the total absence of a reason. Don't you see that if I had a reason about the matter at all it would *have* to be the other way, and would then be inevitably a reason of dollars? There are no reasons here *but* of dollars. Let us therefore have none whatever—not the ghost of one."

They were back in the hall then for departure, but from where they stood the vista was large, through an open door, into the great square main saloon, with its almost antique felicity of brave spaces between windows. Her eyes came back from that reach and met his own a moment. "Are you very sure the 'ghost' of one doesn't, much rather, serve—?"

He had a positive sense of turning pale. But it was as near as they were then to come. For he made answer, he believed, between a glare and a grin: "Oh ghosts—of course the place must swarm with them! I should be ashamed of it if it didn't. Poor Mrs. Muldoon's right, and it's why I haven't asked her to do more than look in."

Miss Staverton's gaze again lost itself, and things she didn't utter, it was clear, came and went in her mind. She might even for the minute, off there in the fine room, have imagined some element dimly gathering. Simplified like the death-mask of a handsome face, it perhaps produced for her just then an effect akin to the stir of an expression in the "set" commemorative plaster. Yet whatever her impression may have been she produced instead a vague platitude. "Well, if it were only furnished and lived in—!"

She appeared to imply that in case of its being still furnished he might have been a little less opposed to the idea of a return. But she passed straight into the vestibule, as if to leave her words behind her, and the next moment he had opened the house-door and was standing with her on the steps. He closed the door and, while he re-pocketed his key, looking up and down, they took in the comparatively harsh actuality of the Avenue, which reminded him of the assault of the outer light of the Desert on the traveller emerging from an Egyptian tomb. But he risked before they stepped into the street his gathered answer to her speech. "For me it *is* lived in. For me it *is* furnished." At which it was easy for her to sigh "Ah yes—!" all vaguely and discreetly; since his parents and his favourite sister, to say nothing of other kin, in numbers, had run their course and met their end there. That represented, within the walls, ineffaceable life.

It was a few days after this that, during an hour passed with her again, he had expressed his impatience of the too flattering curiosity—among the people he met—about his appreciation of New York. He had arrived at none at all that was socially producible, and as for that matter of his "thinking" (thinking the better or the worse of anything there) he was wholly taken up with one subject of thought. It was mere vain egoism, and it was moreover, if she liked, a morbid obsession. He found all things come back to the question of what he personally might have been, how he might have led his life and "turned out," if he had not so, at the outset, given it up. And confessing for the first time to the intensity within him of this absurd speculation—which but proved also, no doubt, the habit of too selfishly thinking—he affirmed the impotence there of any other source of interest, any other native appeal. "What would it have made of me, what would it have made of me? I keep for ever wondering, all idiotically; as if I could possibly know! I see what it has made of dozens of others, those I meet, and it positively aches within me, to the point of exasperation, that it would have made something of me as well. Only I can't make out *what*, and the worry of it, the small rage of curiosity never to be satisfied, brings back what I remember to have felt, once or twice, after judging best, for reasons, to burn some important letter unopened. I've been sorry, I've hated it—I've never known what was in the letter. You may of course say it's a trifle—!"

"I don't say it's a trifle," Miss Staverton gravely interrupted.

She was seated by her fire, and before her, on his feet and restless, he turned to and fro between this intensity of his idea and a fitful and unseeing inspection, through his single eye-glass, of the dear little old objects on her chimney-piece. Her interruption made him for an instant look at her harder. "I shouldn't care if you did!" he laughed, however; "and it's only a figure, at any rate, for the way I now feel. Not to have followed my perverse young course—and almost in the teeth of my father's curse, as I may say; not to have kept it up, so, 'over there,' from that day to this, without a doubt or a pang; not, above all, to have liked it, to have loved it, so much, loved it, no doubt, with such an abysmal conceit of my own preference: some variation from *that*, I say, must have produced some different effect for my life and for my 'form.' I should have stuck here —if it had been possible; and I was too young, at twenty-three, to judge, *pour deux sous*, whether it *were* possible. If I had waited I might have seen it was, and then I might have been, by staying here, something nearer to one of these types who have been hammered so hard and made so keen by their conditions. It isn't that I admire them so much—the question of any charm in them, or of any charm, beyond that of the rank money-passion, exerted by their conditions *for* them, has nothing to do with the matter: it's only a question of what fantastic, yet perfectly possible, development of my own nature I mayn't have missed. It comes over me that I had then a strange *alter ego* deep down somewhere within me, as the full-blown flower is in the small tight bud, and that I just took the course, I just transferred him to the climate, that blighted him for once and for ever."

"And you wonder about the flower," Miss Staverton said. "So do I, if you want to know; and so I've been wondering these several weeks. I believe in the flower," she continued, "I feel it would have been quite splendid, quite huge and monstrous."

"Monstrous above all!" her visitor echoed; "and I imagine, by the same stroke, quite hideous and offensive."

"You don't believe that," she returned; "if you did you wouldn't wonder. You'd know, and that would be enough for you. What you feel —and what I feel *for* you—is that you'd have had power."

"You'd have liked me that way?" he asked.

She barely hung fire. "How should I not have liked you?"

"I see. You'd have liked me, have preferred me, a billionaire!"

"How should I not have liked you?" she simply again asked.

He stood before her still—her question kept him motionless. He took it in, so much there was of it; and indeed his not otherwise meeting it testified to that. "I know at least what I am," he simply went on; "the other side of the medal's clear enough. I've not been edifying—I believe I'm thought in a hundred quarters to have been barely decent. I've followed strange paths and worshipped strange gods; it must have come to you again and again—in fact you've admitted to me as much—that I was leading, at any time these thirty years, a selfish frivolous scandalous life. And you see what it has made of me."

She just waited, smiling at him. "You see what it has made of *me*."

"Oh you're a person whom nothing can have altered. You were born to be what you are, anywhere, anyway: you've the perfection nothing else could have blighted. And don't you see how, without my exile, I shouldn't have been waiting till now—?" But he pulled up for the strange pang.

"The great thing to see," she presently said, "seems to me to be that it has spoiled nothing. It hasn't spoiled your being here at last. It hasn't spoiled this. It hasn't spoiled your speaking—" She also however faltered.

He wondered at everything her controlled emotion might mean. "Do you believe then—too dreadfully!—that I *am* as good as I might ever have been?"

"Oh no! Far from it!" With which she got up from her chair and was nearer to him. "But I don't care," she smiled.

"You mean I'm good enough?"

She considered a little. "Will you believe it if I say so? I mean will you let that settle your question for you?" And then as if making out in his face that he drew back from this, that he had some idea which, however absurd, he couldn't yet bargain away: "Oh you don't care either— but very differently: you don't care for anything but yourself."

Spencer Brydon recognised it—it was in fact what he had absolutely professed. Yet he importantly qualified. "*He* isn't myself. He's the just so totally other person. But I do want to see him," he added. "And I can. And I shall."

Their eyes met for a minute while he guessed from something in hers that she divined his strange sense. But neither of them otherwise expressed it, and her apparent understanding, with no protesting shock, no easy derision, touched him more deeply than anything yet, constituting for his stifled perversity, on the spot, an element that was like breathable air. What she said however was unexpected. "Well, *I've* seen him."

"You—?"

"I've seen him in a dream."

"Oh a 'dream'—!" It let him down.

"But twice over," she continued. "I saw him as I see you now."

"You've dreamed the same dream—?"

"Twice over," she repeated. "The very same."

This did somehow a little speak to him, as it also gratified him. "You dream about me at that rate?"

"Ah about *him!*" she smiled.

His eyes again sounded her. "Then you know all about him." And as she said nothing more: "What's the wretch like?"

She hesitated, and it was as if he were pressing her so hard that, resisting for reasons of her own, she had to turn away. "I'll tell you some other time!"

2

It was after this that there was most of a virtue for him, most of a cultivated charm, most of a preposterous secret thrill, in the particular form of surrender to his obsession and of address to what he more and more believed to be his privilege. It was what in these weeks he was living for—since he really felt life to begin but after Mrs. Muldoon had retired from the scene and, visiting the ample house from attic to cellar, making sure he was alone, he knew himself in safe possession and, as he tacitly expressed it, let himself go. He sometimes came twice in the twenty-four hours; the moments he liked best were those of gathering dusk, of the short autumn twilight; this was the time of which, again and again, he found himself hoping most. Then he could, as seemed to him, most intimately wander and wait, linger and listen, feel his fine attention, never in his life before so fine, on the pulse of the great vague place: he preferred the lampless hour and only wished he might have prolonged each day the deep crepuscular spell. Later— rarely much before midnight, but then for a considerable vigil—he watched with his glimmering light; moving slowly, holding it high, playing it far, rejoicing above all, as much as he might, in open vistas, reaches of communication between rooms and by passages; the long straight chance or show, as he would have called it, for the revelation he pretended to invite. It was practice he found he could perfectly "work" without exciting remark; no one was in the least the wiser for it; even Alice Staverton, who was moreover a well of discretion, didn't quite fully imagine.

He let himself in and let himself out with the assurance of calm proprietorship; and accident so far favoured him that, if a fat Avenue "officer" had happened on occasion to see him entering at eleven-thirty, he had never yet, to the best of his belief, been noticed as emerging at two. He walked there on the crisp November nights, arrived regularly at the evening's end; it was as easy to do this after dining out as to take his way to a club or to his hotel. When he left his club, if he hadn't been dining out, it was ostensibly to go to his hotel; and when he left his hotel, if he had spent a part of the evening there, it was ostensibly to go to his club. Everything was easy in fine; everything conspired and promoted: there was truly even in the strain of his experience something that glossed over, something that salved and simplified, all the rest of consciousness. He circulated, talked, renewed, loosely and pleasantly, old relations—met indeed, so far as he could, new expectations and seemed to make out on the whole that in spite of the career, of such different contacts, which he had spoken of to Miss Staverton as ministering so little, for those who might have watched it, to edification, he was positively rather liked than not. He was a dim secondary social success—and all with people who had truly not an idea of him. It was all mere surface sound, this murmur of their welcome, this popping of their corks—just as his gestures of response were the extravagant shadows, emphatic in proportion as they meant little, of some game of *ombres chinoises*. He projected himself all day, in thought, straight over the bristling line of hard unconscious heads and into the other, the real, the waiting life; the life that, as soon as he had heard behind him the click of his great house-door, began for him, on the jolly corner, as beguilingly as the slow opening bars of some rich music follows the tap of the conductor's wand.

He always caught the first effect of the steel point of his stick on the old marble of the hall pavement, large black-and-white squares that he remembered as the admiration of his childhood and that had then made in him, as he now saw, for the growth of an early conception of style. This effect was the dim reverberating tinkle as of some far-off bell hung who should say where?—in the depths of the house, of the past, of that mystical other world that might have flourished for him had he not, for weal or woe, abandoned it. On this impression he did ever the same thing; he put his stick noiselessly away in a corner—feeling the place once more in the likeness of some great glass bowl, all precious concave crystal, set delicately humming by the play of a moist finger round its edge. The concave crystal held, as it were, this mystical other world, and the indescribably fine murmur of its rim was the sigh there, the scarce audible pathetic wail to his strained ear, of all the old baffled forsworn possibilities. What he did therefore by this appeal of his hushed presence was to wake them into such measure of ghostly life as they might still enjoy. They were shy, all but unappeasably shy, but they weren't really sinister; at least they weren't as he had hitherto felt them—before they had taken the Form he so yearned to make them take, the Form he at moments saw himself in the light of fairly hunting on tiptoe, the points of his evening-shoes, from room to room and from storey to storey.

That was the essence of his vision—which was all rank folly, if one would, while he was out of the house and otherwise occupied, but which took on the last verisimilitude as soon as he was placed and posted. He knew what he meant and what he wanted; it was as clear as the figure on a cheque presented in demand for cash. His *alter ego* "walked"— that was the note of his image of him, while his image of his motive for his own odd pastime was the desire to waylay him and meet him. He roamed, slowly, warily, but all restlessly, he himself did—Mrs. Muldoon had been right, absolutely, with her figure of their "craping"; and the presence he watched for would roam restlessly too. But it would be as cautious and as shifty; the conviction of its probable, in fact its already quite sensible, quite audible evasion of pursuit grew for him from night to night, laying on him finally a rigour to which nothing in his life had been comparable. It had been the theory of many superficially-judging persons, he knew, that he was wasting that life in a surrender to sensations, but he had tasted of no pleasure so fine as his actual tension, had been introduced to no sport that demanded at once the patience and the nerve of this stalking of a creature more subtle, yet at bay perhaps more formidable, than any beast of the forest. The terms, the comparisons, the very practices of the chase positively came again into play; there were even moments when passages of his occasional experience as a sportsman, stirred memories, from his younger time, of moor and mountain and desert, revived for him—and to the increase of his keenness—by the tremendous force of analogy. He found himself at moments—once he had placed his single light on some mantel-shelf or in some recess—stepping back into shelter or shade, effacing himself behind a door or in an embrasure, as he had sought of old the vantage of rock and tree; he found himself holding his breath and living in the joy of the instant, the supreme suspense created by big game alone.

He wasn't afraid (though putting himself the question as he believed gentlemen on Bengal tiger-shoots or in close quarters with the great bear of the Rockies had been known to confess to having put it); and this indeed—since here at least he might be frank!—because of the impression, so intimate and so strange, that he himself produced as yet a dread, produced certainly a strain, beyond the liveliest he was likely to feel. They fell for him into categories, they fairly became familiar, the signs, for his own perception, of the alarm his presence and his vigilance created; though leaving him always to remark, portentously, on his probably having formed a relation, his probably enjoying a consciousness, unique in the experience of man. People enough, first and last, had been in terror of apparitions, but who had ever before so turned the tables and become himself, in the apparitional world, an incalculable terror? He might have found this sublime had he quite dared to think of it; but he didn't too much insist, truly, on that side of his privilege. With habit and repetition he gained to an extraordinary degree the power to penetrate the dusk of distances and the darkness of corners, to resolve back into their innocence the treacheries of uncertain light, the evil-looking forms taken in the gloom by mere shadows, by accidents of the air, by shifting effects of perspective; putting down his dim luminary he could still wander on without it, pass into other rooms and, only knowing it was there behind him in case of need, see his way about, visually project for his purpose a comparative clearness. It made him feel, this acquired faculty, like some monstrous stealthy cat; he wondered if he would have glared at these moments with large shining yellow eyes, and what it mightn't verily be, for the poor hard-pressed *alter ego*, to be confronted with such a type.

He liked however the open shutters; he opened everywhere those Mrs. Muldoon had closed, closing them as carefully afterwards, so that she shouldn't notice: he liked—oh this he did like, and above all in the upper rooms!—the sense of the hard silver of the autumn stars through the window-panes, and scarcely less the flare of the street-lamps below, the white electric lustre which it would have taken curtains to keep out. This was human actual social; this was of the world he had lived in, and he was more at his ease certainly for the countenance, coldly general and impersonal, that all the while and in spite of his detachment it seemed to give him. He had support of course mostly in the rooms at the wide front and the prolonged side; it failed him considerably in the central shades and the parts at the back. But if he sometimes, on his rounds, was glad of his optical reach, so none the less often the rear of the house affected him as the very jungle of his prey. The place was there more subdivided; a large "extension" in particular, where small rooms for servants had been multiplied, abounded in nooks and corners, in closets and passages, in the ramifications especially of an ample back staircase over which he leaned, many a time, to look far down—not deterred from his gravity even while aware that he might, for a spectator, have figured some solemn simpleton playing at hide-and-seek. Outside in fact he might himself make that ironic *rapprochement*; but within the walls, and in spite of the clear windows, his consistency was proof against the cynical light of New York.

It had belonged to that idea of the exasperated consciousness of his victim to become a real test for him; since he had quite put it to himself from the first that, oh distinctly! he could "cultivate" his whole perception. He had felt it as above all open to cultivation—which indeed was but another name for his manner of spending his time. He was bringing it on, bringing it to perfection, by practice; in consequence of which it had grown so fine that he was now aware of impressions, attestations of his general postulate, that couldn't have broken upon him at once. This was the case more specifically with a phenomenon at last quite frequent for him in the upper rooms, the recognition—absolutely unmistakable, and by a turn dating from a particular hour, his resumption of his campaign after a diplomatic drop, a calculated absence of three nights—of his being definitely followed, tracked at a distance carefully taken and to the express end that he should the less confidently, less arrogantly, appear to himself merely to pursue. It worried, it finally quite broke him up, for it proved, of all the conceivable impressions, the one least suited to his book. He was kept in sight while remaining himself—as regards the essence of his position—sightless, and his only recourse then was in abrupt turns, rapid recoveries of ground. He wheeled about, retracing his steps, as if he might so catch in his face at least the stirred air of some other quick revolution. It was indeed true that his fully dislocalised thought of these manœuvres recalled to him Pantaloon, at the Christmas farce, buffeted and tricked from behind by ubiquitous Harlequin; but it left intact the influence of the conditions themselves each time he was re-exposed to them, so that in fact this association, had he suffered it to become constant, would on a certain side have but ministered to his intenser gravity. He had made, as I have said, to create on the premises the baseless sense of a reprieve, his three absences; and the result of the third was to confirm the after-effect of the second.

On his return, that night—the night succeeding his last intermission —he stood in the hall and looked up the staircase with a certainty more intimate than any he had yet known. "He's *there*, at the top, and waiting—not, as in general, falling back for disappearance. He's holding his ground, and it's the first time—which is a proof, isn't it? that something has happened for him." So Brydon argued with his hand on the banister and his foot on the lowest stair; in which position he felt as never before the air chilled by his logic. He himself turned cold in it, for he seemed of a sudden to know what now was involved. "Harder pressed?—yes, he takes it in, with its thus making clear to him that I've come, as they say, 'to stay.' He finally doesn't like and can't bear it, in the sense, I mean, that his wrath, his menaced interest, now balances with his dread. I've hunted him till he has 'turned': that, up there, is what has happened—he's the fanged or the antlered

animal brought at last to bay." There came to him, as I say—but determined by an influence beyond my notation!—the acuteness of this certainty; under which however the next moment he had broken into a
sweat that he would as little have consented to attribute to fear as he
would have dared immediately to act upon it for enterprise. It marked
none the less a prodigious thrill, a thrill that represented sudden dismay, no doubt, but also represented, and with the selfsame throb, the
strangest, the most joyous, possibly the next minute almost the proudest, duplication of consciousness.

"He has been dodging, retreating, hiding, but now, worked up to
anger, he'll fight!"—this intense impression made a single mouthful,
as it were, of terror and applause. But what was wondrous was that
the applause, for the felt fact, was so eager, since, if it was his other
self he was running to earth, this ineffable identity was thus in the
last resort not unworthy of him. It bristled there—somewhere near at
hand, however unseen still—as the hunted thing, even as the trodden
worm of the adage *must* at last bristle; and Brydon at this instant tasted
probably of a sensation more complex than had ever before found itself consistent with sanity. It was as if it would have shamed him that
a character so associated with his own should triumphantly succeed in
just skulking, should to the end not risk the open, so that the drop of
this danger was, on the spot, a great lift of the whole situation. Yet
with another rare shift of the same subtlety he was already trying to
measure by how much more he himself might now be in peril of fear;
so rejoicing that he could, in another form, actively inspire that fear,
and simultaneously quaking for the form in which he might passively
know it.

The apprehension of knowing it must after a little have grown in
him, and the strangest moment of his adventure perhaps, the most
memorable or really most interesting, afterwards, of his crisis, was the
lapse of certain instants of concentrated conscious *combat*, the sense of
a need to hold on to something, even after the manner of a man slipping and slipping on some awful incline; the vivid impulse, above all,
to move, to act, to charge, somehow and upon something—to show
himself, in a word, that he wasn't afraid. The state of "holding-on"
was thus the state to which he was momentarily reduced; if there had
been anything, in the great vacancy, to seize, he would presently have
been aware of having clutched it as he might under a shock at home
have clutched the nearest chair-back. He had been surprised at any rate
—of this he *was* aware—into something unprecedented since his original
appropriation of the place; he had closed his eyes, held them tight, for
a long minute, as with that instinct of dismay and that terror of vision.
When he opened them the room, the other contiguous rooms, extraor-
dinarily, seemed lighter—so light, almost, that at first he took the change

for day. He stood firm, however that might be, just where he had paused; his resistance had helped him—it was as if there were something he had tided over. He knew after a little what this was—it had been in the imminent danger of flight. He had stiffened his will against going; without this he would have made for the stairs, and it seemed to him that, still with his eyes closed, he would have descended them, would have known how, straight and swiftly, to the bottom.

Well, as he had held out, here he was—still at the top, among the more intricate upper rooms and with the gauntlet of the others, of all the rest of the house, still to run when it should be his time to go. He would go at his time—only at his time: didn't he go every night very much at the same hour? He took out his watch—there was light for that: it was scarcely a quarter past one, and he had never withdrawn so soon. He reached his lodgings for the most part at two—with his walk of a quarter of an hour. He would wait for the last quarter—he wouldn't stir till then; and he kept his watch there with his eyes on it, reflecting while he held it that this deliberate wait, a wait with an effort, which he recognised, would serve perfectly for the attestation he desired to make. It would prove his courage—unless indeed the latter might most be proved by his budging at last from his place. What he mainly felt now was that, since he hadn't originally scuttled, he had his dignities—which had never in his life seemed so many—all to preserve and to carry aloft. This was before him in truth as a physical image, an image almost worthy of an age of greater romance. That remark indeed glimmered for him only to glow the next instant with a finer light; since what age of romance, after all, could have matched either the state of his mind or, "objectively," as they said, the wonder of his situation? The only difference would have been that, brandishing his dignities over his head, as in a parchment scroll, he might then— that is in the heroic time—have proceeded downstairs with a drawn sword in his other grasp.

At present, really, the light he had set down on the mantel of the next room would have to figure his sword; which utensil, in the course of a minute, he had taken the requisite number of steps to possess himself of. The door between the rooms was open, and from the second another door opened to a third. These rooms, as he remembered, gave all three upon a common corridor as well, but there was a fourth, beyond them, without issue save through the preceding. To have moved, to have heard his step again, was appreciably a help; though even in recognising this he lingered once more a little by the chimney-piece on which his light had rested. When he next moved, just hesitating where to turn, he found himself considering a circumstance that, after his first and comparatively vague apprehension of it, produced in him the start that often attends some pang of recollection, the violent shock of having ceased happily to forget. He had come into sight of the door in which the brief chain of communication ended and which he now surveyed from the nearer threshold, the one not directly facing it. Placed at some distance to the left of this point, it would have admitted him to the last room of the four, the room without other approach or egress, had it not, to his intimate conviction, been closed *since* his former visitation, the matter probably of a quarter of an hour before. He stared with all his eyes at the wonder of the fact, arrested again where he stood and again holding his breath while he sounded its sense. Surely it had been *subsequently* closed—that is it had been on his previous passage indubitably open!

He took it full in the face that something had happened between —that he couldn't not have noticed before (by which he meant on his original tour of all the rooms that evening) that such a barrier had exceptionally presented itself. He had indeed since that moment undergone an agitation so extraordinary that it might have muddled for him any earlier view; and he tried to convince himself that he might perhaps then have gone into the room and, inadvertently, automatically, on coming out, have drawn the door after him. The difficulty was that this exactly was what he never did; it was against his whole policy, as he might have said, the essence of which was to keep vistas clear. He had them from the first, as he was well aware, quite on the brain: the strange apparition, at the far end of one of them, of his baffled "prey" (which had become by so sharp an irony so little the term now to apply!) was the form of success his imagination had most cherished, projecting into it always a refinement of beauty. He had known fifty times the start of perception that had afterwards dropped; had fifty times gasped to himself "There!" under some fond brief hallucination. The house, as the case stood, admirably lent itself; he might wonder at the taste, the native architecture of the particular time, which could rejoice so in the multiplication of doors—the opposite extreme to the modern, the actual almost complete proscription of them; but it had fairly contributed to provoke this obsession of the presence encountered telescopically, as he might say, focussed and studied in diminishing perspective and as by a rest for the elbow.

It was with these considerations that his present attention was charged —they perfectly availed to make what he saw portentous. He *couldn't*, by any lapse, have blocked that aperture; and if he hadn't, if it was unthinkable, why what else was clear but that there had been another agent? Another agent?—he had been catching, as he felt, a moment back, the very breath of him; but when had he been so close as in this simple, this logical, this completely personal act? It was so logical, that is, that one might have *taken* it for personal; yet for what did Brydon take it, he asked himself, while, softly panting, he felt his eyes almost leave their sockets. Ah this time at last they *were*, the two, the opposed projections of him, in presence; and this time, as much as one would, the question of danger loomed. With it rose, as not before, the question of courage—for what he knew the blank face of the door to say to him was "Show us how much you have!" It stared, it glared back at him with that challenge; it put to him the two alternatives: should he just push it open or not? Oh to have this consciousness was to *think*—and to think, Brydon knew, as he stood there, was, with the lapsing moments, not to have acted! Not to have acted—that was the misery and the pang—was even still not to act; was in fact *all* to feel the thing in another, in a new and terrible way. How long did he pause and how long did he debate? There was presently nothing to measure it; for his vibration had already changed—as just by the effect of its intensity. Shut up there, at bay, defiant, and with the prodigy of the thing palpably provably *done*, thus giving notice like some stark signboard—under that accession of accent the situation itself had turned; and Brydon at last remarkably made up his mind on what it had turned to.

It had turned altogether to a different admonition; to a supreme hint, for him, of the value of Discretion! This slowly dawned, no doubt—for it could take its time; so perfectly, on his threshold, had he been stayed, so little as yet had he either advanced or retreated. It was the strangest of all things that now when, by his taking ten steps and applying his hand to a latch, or even his shoulder and his knee, if necessary, to a panel, all the hunger of his prime need might have been met, his high curiosity crowned, his unrest assuaged—it was amazing, but it was also exquisite and rare, that insistence should have, at a touch, quite dropped from him. Discretion—he jumped at that; and yet not, verily, at such a pitch, because it saved his nerves or his skin, but because, much more valuably, it saved the situation. When I say he "jumped" at it I feel the consonance of this term with the fact that—at the end indeed of I know not how long—he did move again, he crossed straight to the door. He wouldn't touch it—it seemed now that he might *if* he would: he would only just wait there a little, to show, to prove, that he wouldn't. He had thus another station, close to the thin partition by which revelation was denied him; but with his eyes bent and his hands held off in a mere intensity of stillness. He listened as if there had been something to hear, but this attitude, while it lasted, was his own communication. "If you won't then—good: I spare you and I give up. You affect me as by the appeal positively for pity: you convince me that for reasons rigid and sublime—what do I know?—we both of us should have suffered. I respect them then, and, though moved and privileged as, I believe, it has never been given to man, I retire, I renounce—never, on my honour, to try again. So rest for ever—and let *me!*"

That, for Brydon was the deep sense of this last demonstration—

solemn, measured, directed, as he felt it to be. He brought it to a close, he turned away; and now verily he knew how deeply he had been stirred. He retraced his steps, taking up his candle, burnt, he observed, well-nigh to the socket, and marking again, lighten it as he would, the distinctness of his footfall; after which, in a moment, he knew himself at the other side of the house. He did here what he had not yet done at these hours—he opened half a casement, one of those in the front, and let in the air of the night; a thing he would have taken at any time previous for a sharp rupture of his spell. His spell was broken now, and it didn't matter—broken by his concession and his surrender, which made it idle henceforth that he should ever come back. The empty street—its other life so marked even by the great lamplit vacancy—was within call, within touch; he stayed there as to be in it again, high above it though he was still perched; he watched as for some comforting common fact, some vulgar human note, the passage of a scavenger or a thief, some night-bird however base. He would have blessed that sign of life; he would have welcomed positively the slow approach of his friend the policeman, whom he had hitherto only sought to avoid, and was not sure that if the patrol had come into sight he mightn't have felt the impulse to get into relation with it, to hail it, on some pretext, from his fourth floor.

The pretext that wouldn't have been too silly or too compromising, the explanation that would have saved his dignity and kept his name, in such a case, out of the papers, was not definite to him: he was so occupied with the thought of recording his Discretion—as an effect of the vow he had just uttered to his intimate adversary—that the importance of this loomed large and something had overtaken all ironically his sense of proportion. If there had been a ladder applied to the front of the house, even one of the vertiginous perpendiculars employed by painters and roofers and sometimes left standing overnight, he would have managed somehow, astride of the window-sill, to compass by outstretched leg and arm that mode of descent. If there had been some such uncanny thing as he had found in his room at hotels, a workable fire-escape in the form of notched cable or a canvas shoot, he would have availed himself of it as a proof—well, of his present delicacy. He nursed that sentiment, as the question stood, a little in vain, and even—at the end of he scarce knew, once more, how long—found it, as by the action on his mind of the failure of response of the outer world, sinking back to vague anguish. It seemed to him he had waited an age for some stir of the great grim hush; the life of the town was itself under a spell—so unnaturally, up and down the whole prospect of known and rather ugly objects, the blankness and the silence lasted. Had they ever, he asked himself, the hard-faced houses, which had begun to look livid in the dim dawn, had they ever spoken so little to any need of his spirit? Great builded voids, great crowded stillnesses put on, often, in the heart of cities, for the small hours, a sort of sinister mask, and it was of this large collective negation that Brydon presently became conscious—all the more that the break of day was, almost incredibly, now at hand, proving to him what a night he had made of it.

He looked again at his watch, saw what had become of his time-values (he had taken hours for minutes—not, as in other tense situations, minutes for hours) and the strange air of the streets was but the weak, the sullen flush of a dawn in which everything was still locked up. His choked appeal from his own open window had been the sole note of life, and he could but break off at last as for a worse despair. Yet while so deeply demoralised he was capable again of an impulse denoting—at least by his present measure—extraordinary resolution; of retracing his steps to the spot where he had turned cold with the extinction of his last pulse of doubt as to there being in the place another presence than his own. This required an effort strong enough to sicken him; but he had his reason, which over-mastered for the moment everything else. There was the whole of the rest of the house to traverse, and how should he screw himself to that if the door he had seen closed were at present open? He could hold to the idea that the closing had practically been for him an act of mercy, a chance offered him to descend, depart, get off the ground and never again profane it. This conception held together, it worked; but what it meant for him depended now clearly on the amount of forbearance his recent action, or rather his recent inaction, had engendered. The image of the "presence," whatever it was, waiting there for him to go—this image had not yet been so concrete for his nerves as when he stopped short of the point at which certainty would have come to him. For, with all his resolution, or more exactly with all his dread, he did stop short—he hung back from really seeing. The risk was too great and his fear too definite: it took at this moment an awful specific form.

He knew—yes, as he had never known anything—that, *should* he see the door open, it would all too abjectly be the end of him. It would mean that the agent of his shame—for his shame was the deep abjection—was once more at large and in general possession; and what glared him thus in the face was the act that this would determine for him. It would send him straight about to the window he had left open, and by that window, be long ladder and dangling rope as absent as they would, he saw himself uncontrollably insanely fatally take his way to the street. The hideous chance of this he at least could avert; but he could only avert it by recoiling in time from assurance. He had the whole house to deal with, this fact was still there; only he now knew that uncertainty alone could start him. He stole back from where he had checked himself—merely to do so was suddenly like safety—and, making blindly for the greater staircase, left gaping rooms and sounding passages behind. Here was the top of the stairs, with a fine large dim descent and three spacious landings to mark off. His instinct was all for mildness, but his feet were harsh on the floors, and, strangely, when he had in a couple of minutes become aware of this, it counted somehow for help. He couldn't have spoken, the tone of his voice would have scared him, and the common conceit or resource of "whistling in the dark" (whether literally or figuratively) have appeared basely vulgar; yet he liked none the less to hear himself go, and when he had reached his first landing— taking it all with no rush, but quite steadily—that stage of success drew from him a gasp of relief.

The house, withal, seemed immense, the scale of space again inordinate; the open rooms to no one of which his eyes deflected, gloomed in their shuttered state like mouths of caverns; only the high skylight that formed the crown of the deep well created for him a medium in which he could advance, but which might have been, for queerness of colour, some watery under-world. He tried to think of something noble, as that his property was really grand, a splendid possession; but this nobleness took the form too of the clear delight with which he was finally to sacrifice it. They might come in now, the builders, the destroyers—they might come as soon as they would. At the end of two flights he had dropped to another zone, and from the middle of the third, with only one more left, he recognised the influence of the lower windows, of half-drawn blinds, of the occasional gleam of street-lamps, of the glazed spaces of the vestibule. This was the bottom of the sea, which showed an illumination of its own and which he even saw paved—when at a given moment he drew up to sink a long look over the banisters—with the marble squares of his childhood. By that time indubitably he felt, as he might have said in a commoner cause, better; it had allowed him to stop and draw breath, and the ease increased with the sight of the old black-and-white slabs. But what he most felt was that now surely, with the element of impunity pulling him as by hard firm hands, the case was settled for what he might have seen above had he dared that last look. The closed door, blessedly remote now, was still closed—and he had only in short to reach that of the house.

He came down further, he crossed the passage forming the access to the last flight; and if here again he stopped an instant it was almost for the sharpness of the thrill of assured escape. It made him shut his eyes —which opened again to the straight slope of the remainder of the stairs. Here was impunity still, but impunity almost excessive; inasmuch as the side-lights and the high fan-tracery of the entrance were glimmering straight into the hall; an appearance produced, he the next instant saw, by the fact that the vestibule gaped wide, that the hinged halves of the inner door had been thrown far back. Out of that again the *question* sprang at him, making his eyes, as he felt, half-start from his head, as they had done, at the top of the house, before the sign of the other door. If he had left that one open, hadn't he left this one closed, and wasn't he now in *most* immediate presence of some inconceivable occult activity? It was as sharp, the question, as a knife in his side, but the answer hung fire still and seemed to lose itself in the vague darkness to which the thin admitted dawn, glimmering archwise over the whole outer door, made a semicircular margin, a cold silvery nimbus that seemed to play a little as he looked—to shift and expand and contract.

It was as if there had been something within it, protected by indistinctness and corresponding in extent with the opaque surface behind, the painted panels of the last barrier to his escape, of which the key was in his pocket. The indistinctness mocked him even while he stared, affected him as somehow shrouding or challenging certitude, so that after faltering an instant on his step he let himself go with the sense that here *was* at last something to meet, to touch, to take, to know—something all unnatural and dreadful, but to advance upon which was the condition for him either of liberation or of supreme defeat. The penumbra, dense and dark, was the virtual screen of a figure which stood in it as still as some image erect in a niche or as some black-vizored sentinel guarding a treasure. Brydon was to know afterwards, was to recall and make out, the particular thing he had believed during the rest of his descent. He saw, in its great grey glimmering margin, the central vagueness diminish, and he felt it to be taking the very form toward which, for so many days, the passion of his curiosity had yearned. It gloomed, it loomed, it was something, it was somebody, the prodigy of a personal presence.

Rigid and conscious, spectral yet human, a man of his own substance and stature waited there to measure himself with his power to dismay. This only could it be—this only till he recognised, with his advance, that what made the face dim was the pair of raised hands that covered it and in which, so far from being offered in defiance, it was buried as for dark deprecation. So Brydon, before him, took him in; with every fact of him now, in the higher light, hard and acute—his planted stillness, his vivid truth, his grizzled bent head and white masking hands, his queer actuality of evening dress, of dangling double eye-glass, of gleaming silk lappet and white linen, of pearl button and gold watch-guard and polished shoe. No portrait by a great modern master could have presented him with more intensity, thrust him out of his frame with more art, as if there had been "treatment," of the consummate sort, in his every shade and salience. The revulsion, for our friend, had become, before he knew it, immense—this drop, in the act of apprehension, to the sense of his adversary's inscrutable manœuvre. That meaning at least, while he gaped, it offered him; for he could but gape at his other self in this other anguish, gape as a proof that *he*, standing there for the achieved, the enjoyed, the triumphant life, couldn't be faced in his triumph. Wasn't the proof in the splendid covering hands, strong and completely spread?— so spread and so intentional that, in spite of a special verity that surpassed every other, the fact that one of these hands had lost two fingers, which were reduced to stumps, as if accidentally shot away, the face was effectually guarded and saved.

"Saved," though, *would* it be?—Brydon breathed his wonder till the very impunity of his attitude and the very insistence of his eyes produced, as he felt, a sudden stir which showed the next instant as a deeper portent, while the head raised itself, the betrayal of a braver purpose. The hands, as he looked, began to move, to open; then, as if deciding in a flash, dropped from the face and left it uncovered and presented. Horror, with the sight, had leaped into Brydon's throat, gasping there in a sound he couldn't utter; for the bared identity was too hideous as *his*, and his glare was the passion of his protest. The face, *that* face, Spencer Brydon's?—he searched it still, but looking away from it in dismay and denial, falling straight from his height of sublimity. It was unknown, inconceivable, awful, disconnected from any possibility—! He had been "sold," he inwardly moaned, stalking such game as this: the presence before him was a presence, the horror within him a horror, but the waste of his nights had been only grotesque and the success of his adventure an irony. Such an identity fitted his at *no* point, made its alternative monstrous. A thousand times yes, as it came upon him nearer now —the face was the face of a stranger. It came upon him nearer now, quite as one of those expanding fantastic images projected by the magic lantern of childhood; for the stranger, whoever he might be, evil, odious, blatant, vulgar, had advanced as for aggression, and he knew himself give ground. Then harder pressed still, sick with the force of his shock, and falling back as under the hot breath and the roused passion of a life larger than his own, a rage of personality before which his own collapsed, he felt the whole vision turn to darkness and his very feet give way. His head went round; he was going; he had gone.

3

What had next brought him back, clearly—though after how long?— was Mrs. Muldoon's voice, coming to him from quite near, from so near that he seemed presently to see her as kneeling on the ground before him while he lay looking up at her; himself not wholly on the ground, but half-raised and upheld—conscious, yes, of tenderness of support and, more particularly, of a head pillowed in extraordinary softness and faintly refreshing fragrance. He considered, he wondered, his wit but half at his service; then another face intervened, bending more directly over him, and he finally knew that Alice Staverton had made her lap an ample and perfect cushion to him, and that she had to this end seated herself on the lowest degree of the staircase, the rest of his long person remaining stretched on his old black-and-white slabs. They were cold, these marble squares of his youth; but *he* somehow was not, in this rich return of consciousness—the most wonderful hour, little by little, that he had ever known, leaving him, as it did, so gratefully, so abysmally passive, and yet as with a treasure of intelligence waiting all round him for quiet appropriation; dissolved, he might call it, in the air of the place and producing the golden glow of a late autumn afternoon. He had come back, yes—come back from further away than any man but himself had ever travelled; but it was strange how with this sense what he had come back *to* seemed really the great thing, and as if his prodigious journey had been all for the sake of it. Slowly but surely his consciousness grew, his vision of his state thus completing itself: he had been miraculously *carried* back—lifted and carefully borne as from where he had been picked up, the uttermost end of an interminable grey passage. Even with this he was suffered to rest, and what had now brought him to knowledge was the break in the long mild motion.

It had brought him to knowledge, to knowledge—yes, this was the beauty of his state; which came to resemble more and more that of a man who has gone to sleep on some news of a great inheritance, and then, after dreaming it away, after profaning it with matters strange to it, has waked up again to serenity of certitude and has only to lie and watch it grow. This was the drift of his patience—that he had only to let it shine on him. He must moreover, with intermissions, still have been lifted and borne; since why and how else should he have known himself, later on, with the afternoon glow intenser, no longer at the foot of his stairs—situated as these now seemed at that dark other end of his tunnel —but on a deep window-bench of his high saloon, over which had been spread, couch-fashion, a mantle of soft stuff lined with grey fur that was familiar to his eyes and that one of his hands kept fondly feeling as for its pledge of truth. Mrs. Muldoon's face had gone, but the other, the second he had recognised, hung over him in a way that showed how he was still propped and pillowed. He took it all in, and the more he took it the more it seemed to suffice: he was as much at peace as if he had had food and drink. It was the two women who had found him, on Mrs. Muldoon's having plied, at her usual hour, her latch-key—and on her having above all arrived while Miss Staverton still lingered near the house. She had been turning away, all anxiety, from worrying the vain bell-handle—her calculation having been of the hour of the good woman's visit; but the latter, blessedly, had come up while she was still there, and they had entered together. He had then lain, beyond the vestibule, very much as he was lying now—quite, that is, as he appeared to have fallen, but all so wondrously without bruise or gash; only in a depth of stupor. What he most took in, however, at present, with the steadier clearance, was that Alice Staverton had for a long unspeakable moment not doubted he was dead.

"It must have been that I *was*." He made it out as she held him. "Yes—I can only have died. You brought me literally to life. Only," he wondered, his eyes rising to her, "only, in the name of all the benedictions, how?"

It took her but an instant to bend her face and kiss him, and something in the manner of it, and in the way her hands clasped and locked his head while he felt the cool charity and virtue of her lips, something in all this beatitude somehow answered everything. "And now I keep you," she said.

"Oh keep me, keep me!" he pleaded while her face still hung over him: in response to which it dropped again and stayed close, clingingly close. It was the seal of their situation—of which he tasted the impress for a long blissful moment in silence. But he came back. "Yet how did you know—"

"I was uneasy. You were to have come, you remember—and you had sent no word."

"Yes, I remember—I was to have gone to you at one today." It caught on to their "old" life and relation—which were so near and so far. "I was still out there in my strange darkness—where was it, what was it? I must have stayed there so long." He could but wonder at the depth and the duration of his swoon.

"Since last night?" she asked with a shade of fear for her possible indiscretion.

"Since this morning—it must have been: the cold dim dawn of today. Where have I been," he vaguely wailed, "where have I been?" He felt her hold him close, and it was as if this helped him now to make in all security his mild moan. "What a long dark day!"

All in her tenderness she had waited a moment. "In the cold dim dawn?" she quavered.

But he had already gone on piecing together the parts of the whole prodigy. "As I didn't turn up you came straight—?"

She barely cast about. "I went first to your hotel—where they told me of your absence. You had dined out last evening and hadn't been back since. But they appeared to know you had been at your club."

"So you had the idea of *this*—?"

"Of what?" she asked in a moment.

"Well—of what has happened."

"I believed at least you'd have been here. I've known, all along," she said, "that you've been coming."

" 'Known' it—?"

"Well, I've believed it. I said nothing to you after that talk we had a month ago—but I felt sure. I knew you *would*," she declared.

"That I'd persist, you mean?"

"That you'd see him."

"Ah but I didn't!" cried Brydon with his long wail. "There's somebody—an awful beast; whom I brought, too horribly, to bay. But it's not me."

At this she bent over him again, and her eyes were in his eyes. "No—it's not you." And it was as if, while her face hovered, he might have made out in it, hadn't it been so near, some particular meaning blurred by a smile. "No, thank heaven," she repeated—"it's not you! Of course it wasn't to have been."

"Ah but it *was*," he gently insisted. And he stared before him now as he had been staring for so many weeks. "I was to have known myself."

"You couldn't!" she returned consolingly. And then reverting, and as if to account further for what she had herself done, "But it wasn't only *that*, that you hadn't been at home," she went on. "I waited till the hour at which we had found Mrs. Muldoon that day of my going with you; and she arrived, as I've told you, while, failing to bring any one to the door, I lingered in my despair on the steps. After a little, if she hadn't come, by such a mercy, I should have found means to hunt her up. But it wasn't," said Alice Staverton, as if once more with her fine intention—"it wasn't only that."

His eyes, as he lay, turned back to her. "What more then?"

She met it, the wonder she had stirred. "In the cold dim dawn, you say? Well, in the cold dim dawn of this morning I too saw you."

"Saw *me*—?"

"Saw *him*," said Alice Staverton. "It must have been at the same moment."

He lay an instant taking it in—as if he wished to be quite reasonable. "At the same moment?"

"Yes—in my dream again, the same one I've named to you. He came back to me. Then I knew it for a sign. He had come to you."

At this Brydon raised himself; he had to see her better. She helped him when she understood his movement, and he sat up, steadying himself beside her there on the window-bench and with his right hand grasping her left. "*He* didn't come to me."

"You came to yourself," she beautifully smiled.

"Ah I've come to myself now—thanks to you, dearest. But this brute, with his awful face—this brute's a black stranger. He's none of *me*, even as I *might* have been," Brydon sturdily declared.

But she kept the clearness that was like the breath of infallibility. "Isn't the whole point that you'd have been different?"

He almost scowled for it. "As different as *that*—?"

Her look again was more beautiful to him than the things of this world. "Haven't you exactly wanted to know *how* different? So this morning," she said, "you appeared to me."

"Like *him?*"

"A black stranger!"

"Then how did you know it was I?"

"Because, as I told you weeks ago, my mind, my imagination, had worked so over what you might, what you mightn't have been—to show you, you see, how I've thought of you. In the midst of that you came to me—that my wonder might be answered. So I knew," she went on; "and believed that, since the question held you too so fast, as you told me that day, you too would see for yourself. And when this morning I again saw I knew it would be because you had—and also then, from the first moment, because you somehow wanted me. *He* seemed to tell me of that. So why," she strangely smiled, "shouldn't I like him?"

It brought Spencer Brydon to his feet. "You 'like' that horror—?"

"I *could* have liked him. And to me," she said, "he was no horror. I had accepted him."

" 'Accepted'—?" Brydon oddly sounded.

"Before, for the interest of his difference—yes. And as *I* didn't disown him, as *I* knew him—which you at last, confronted with him in his difference, so cruelly didn't, my dear—well, he must have been, you see, less dreadful to me. And it may have pleased him that I pitied him."

She was beside him on her feet, but still holding his hand—still with her arm supporting him. But though it all brought for him thus a dim light, "You 'pitied' him?" he grudgingly, resentfully asked.

"He has been unhappy; he has been ravaged," she said.

"And haven't I been unhappy? Am not I—you've only to look at me! —ravaged?"

"Ah I don't say I like him *better*," she granted after a thought. "But hc's grim, he's worn—and things have happened to him. He doesn't make shift, for sight, with your charming monocle."

"No"—it struck Brydon: "I couldn't have sported mine 'downtown.' They'd have guyed me there."

"His great convex pince-nez—I saw it, I recognised the kind—is for his poor ruined sight. And his poor right hand—!"

"Ah!" Brydon winced—whether for his proved identity or for his lost fingers. Then, "He has a million a year," he lucidly added. "But he hasn't you."

"And he isn't—no, he isn't—*you!*" she murmured as he drew her to his breast.

QUESTIONS

1. What is the meaning of James's title? What are some of the ironic overtones of such a title?
2. How would you characterize Henry James's style? How does he construct his paragraphs?
3. What is the literary function of Alice Staverton in the story? Is her love for Brydon too uncritical? Are her dreams about his "ghost" psychologically believable or are they merely an aid for James's plot?
4. What devices does James use to increase the sense of suspense? How do the attitudes of Mrs. Muldoon make us more aware of Brydon's fears? How does James's treatment of time near the end of the tale maximize our sense of Brydon's terror?
5. What is the effect of the "ghost's" having a maimed hand?
6. How does the ghost's behavior toward Brydon overturn most of our preconceptions about supernatural spirits?
7. What is the difference between a psychic and a supernatural story? Which kind is this, and what techniques does James use to indicate its kind?

KEN KESEY

BESIDES *One Flew Over the Cuckoo's Nest* (1962), Ken Kesey (b. 1935) has had published one other novel, *Sometimes a Great Notion* (1964). Tom Wolfe's *The Electric Kool-Aid Acid Test* (1968) is a biographical account of the period in Kesey's life when he experimented with LSD and led a group of young people, called the Merry Pranksters, on a colorful bus trip (in a colorful bus) around the country. Kesey currently lives with his wife and children in Springfield, Oregon.

The narrator of *One Flew Over the Cuckoo's Nest* is Chief Broom, a patient at a mental hospital in Oregon. The Chief, half-Indian, is a giant of a man, like his father, who was cheated of his home and fishing grounds as well as of his name (he changed it to his White wife's name in an effort to adjust to the White man's world). The loss of his name and his culture makes the father a "small" man— someone who has virtually no sense of self—and he resorts to alcohol as an escape. His son, fear-struck by his father's loss of stature, is dominated by a sense of inadequacy. During World War II he is drafted and sent to Europe, where he experiences the terror of air raids. Upon returning to the United States, he continues to imagine that the world is dominated by air raids and fog machines, and when he is frightened he retreats into the fog and air raids that exist in his mind. (Pretended deafness also allows him to retreat from the risk of contact with others.) Kesey's use of these metaphorical devices makes the Chief's emotions almost palpable.

The mental hospital is dominated by the Big Nurse, Miss Ratched, an unmarried ex-Army nurse who controls every aspect of life in the hospital. Her repression, which she calls "treatment," prevents the patients from recovering any sense of self-respect. The patients are categorized according to the seriousness of their condition—from the least ill, the "Acutes," through the "Chronics" to the worst afflicted, the "Vegetables." A troublesome patient is sent to "Disturbed" for "treatment"; should he continue in disobedience, he is sent to the "Shock Shop" for "therapy." And the Big Nurse has one final horrifying power to use against the most recalcitrant patients, a type of psychic castration called lobotomy, an operation in which a portion of the brain is severed, leaving the victim, in effect, a vegetable.

The atmosphere in the hospital is lethargic, hopeless, devoid of spirit. The first episode introduces R. P. McMurphy, who has feigned insanity in order to avoid a work detail in prison. He is a giant of a man who in some ways resembles the Chief's father, but whose spirit is still full-blooded and tenacious and who injects new life into the ward.

The second episode, climax of the first major section of the novel, depicts McMurphy's first victory over the Big Nurse. (Each victory increases her resentment of him and the severity of her retaliation which she justifies by declaring that his resistance to her is proof of his illness.) It also depicts the Chief's abandonment of his pretended deafness and his concomitant realization that he is now vulnerable.

The final episode follows a fight that pitted some of the hospital staff against McMurphy and the Chief and results in shock therapy for the Chief. During this shock treatment—perhaps the most crucial section of the book—the Chief recalls his childhood, especially the incident of his grandmother's burial. He searches the past and emerges with a better sense of his own identity. At the end the Chief, whose mind has been liberated by McMurphy, mercifully kills his friend, whom the Big Nurse has had lobotomized. (The Indian flees the hospital, a free man.)

Kesey's novel contains much implicit social criticism of both mental institutions and the United States as a whole—the latter represented in microcosm by the ward. The Big Nurse is a matriarchal autocrat trying to diminish the inmates' sense of manhood. McMurphy's sanity is contrasted with her insane, mechanistic approach to curing the sick. However, Kesey does not exempt us by blaming society. Through his story he does not urge us to complain and despair, but to confront and overcome our fears so we can let ourselves be vulnerable to new experiences.

[FROM One Flew Over the Cuckoo's Nest]

This morning the lockworks rattle strange; it's not a regular visitor at the door. An Escort Man's voice calls down, edgy and impatient, "Admission, come sign for him," and the black boys go.

Admission. Everybody stops playing cards and Monopoly, turns toward the day-room door. Most days I'd be out sweeping the hall and see who they're signing in, but this morning, like I explain to you, the Big Nurse put a thousand pounds down me and I can't budge out of the chair. Most days I'm the first one to see the Admission, watch him creep in the door and slide along the wall and stand scared till the black boys come sign for him and take him into the shower room, where they strip him and leave him shivering with the door open while they all three run grinning up and down the halls looking for the Vaseline. "We *need* that Vaseline," they'll tell the Big Nurse, "for the thermometer." She looks from one to the other: "I'm *sure* you do," and hands them a jar holds at least a gallon, "but mind you boys don't group up in there." Then I see two, maybe all three of them in there, in that shower room with the Admission, running that thermometer around in the grease till it's coated the size of your finger, crooning, "Tha's right, mothah, tha's right," and then shut the door and turn all the showers up to where you can't hear anything but the vicious hiss of water on the green tile. I'm out there most days, and I see it like that.

But this morning I have to sit in the chair and only listen to them bring him in. Still, even though I can't see him, I know he's no ordinary Admission. I don't hear him slide scared along the wall, and when they tell him about the shower he don't just submit with a weak little yes, he tells them right back in a loud, brassy voice that he's already plenty damn clean, thank you.

"They showered me this morning at the courthouse and last night at the jail. And I *swear* I believe they'd of washed my ears for me on the taxi ride over if they coulda found the vacilities. Hoo boy, seems like everytime they ship me someplace I gotta get scrubbed down before, after, and during the operation. I'm gettin' so the sound of water makes me start gathering up my belongings. And *get* back away from me with that thermometer, Sam, and give me a minute to look my new home over; I never been in a Institute of Psychology before."

The patients look at one another's puzzled faces, then back to the door, where his voice is still coming in. Talking louder'n you'd think he needed to if the black boys were anywhere near him. He sounds like he's way above them, talking down, like he's sailing fifty yards overhead, hollering at those below on the ground. He sounds big. I hear him coming down the hall, and he sounds big in the way he walks, and he sure don't slide; he's got iron on his heels and he rings it on the floor like horseshoes. He shows up in the door and stops and hitches his thumbs in his pockets, boots wide apart, and stands there with the guys looking at him.

"Good *morn*in', buddies."

There's a paper Halloween bat hanging on a string above his head; he reaches up and flicks it so it spins around.

"Mighty nice fall day."

He talks a little the way Papa used to, voice loud and full of hell, but he doesn't look like Papa; Papa was a full-blood Columbia Indian—a chief—and hard and shiny as a gunstock. This guy is redheaded with long red sideburns and a tangle of curls out from under his cap, been needing cut a long time, and he's broad as Papa was tall, broad across the jaw and shoulders and chest, a broad white devilish grin, and he's hard in a different kind of way from Papa, kind of the way a baseball is hard under the scuffed leather. A seam runs across his nose and one cheekbone where somebody laid him a good one in a fight, and the stitches are still in the seam. He stands there waiting, and when nobody makes a move to say anything to him he commences to laugh. Nobody can tell exactly why he laughs; there's nothing funny going on. But it's not the way that Public Relation laughs, it's free and loud and it comes out of his wide grinning mouth and spreads in rings bigger and bigger till it's lapping against the walls all over the ward. Not like that fat Public Relation laugh. This sounds real. I realize all of a sudden it's the first laugh I've heard in years.

He stands looking at us, rocking back in his boots, and he laughs and laughs. He laces his fingers over his belly without taking his thumbs out of his pockets. I see how big and beat up his hands are. Everybody on the ward, patients, staff, and all, is stunned dumb by him and his laughing. There's no move to stop him, no move to say anything. He laughs till he's finished for a time, and he walks on into the day room. Even when he isn't laughing, that laughing sound hovers around him, the way the sound hovers around a big bell just quit ringing—it's in his eyes, in the way he smiles and swaggers, in the way he talks.

"My name is McMurphy, buddies, R. P. McMurphy, and I'm a gambling fool." He winks and sings a little piece of a song: " '. . . and

whenever I meet with a deck a cards I lays . . . my money . . . down,' "
and laughs again.

He walks to one of the card games, tips an Acute's cards up with a
thick, heavy finger, and squints at the hand and shakes his head.

"Yessir, that's what I came to this establishment for, to bring you
birds fun an' entertainment around the gamin' table. Nobody left in
that Pendleton Work Farm to make my days interesting any more, so
I requested a *transfer*, ya see. Needed some new blood. Hooee, look at
the way this bird holds his cards, showin' to everybody in a block; man!
I'll trim you babies like little lambs."

Cheswick gathers his cards together. The redheaded man sticks his
hand out for Cheswick to shake.

"Hello, buddy; what's that you're playin'? Pinochle? Jesus, no wonder
you don't care nothin' about showing your hand. Don't you have a
straight deck around here? Well say, here we go, I brought along my
own deck, just in case, has something in it other than face cards—and
check the pictures, huh? Every one different. Fifty-two positions."

Cheswick is pop-eyed already, and what he sees on those cards don't
help his condition.

"Easy now, don't smudge 'em; we got lots of time, lots of games
ahead of us. I like to use my deck here because it takes at least a week
for the other players to get to where they can even see the *suit*. . . ."

He's got on work-farm pants and shirt, sunned out till they're the
color of watered milk. His face and neck and arms are the color of ox-
blood leather from working long in the fields. He's got a primer-black
motorcycle cap stuck in his hair and a leather jacket over one arm, and
he's got on boots gray and dusty and heavy enough to kick a man half
in two. He walks away from Cheswick and takes off the cap and goes
to beating a dust storm out of his thigh. One of the black boys circles
him with the thermometer, but he's too quick for them; he slips in among
the Acutes and starts moving around shaking hands before the black boy
can take good aim. The way he talks, his wink, his loud talk, his swagger
all remind me of a car salesman or a stock auctioneer—or one of those
pitchmen you see on a sideshow stage, out in front of his flapping banners, standing there in a striped shirt with yellow buttons, drawing the
faces off the sawdust like a magnet.

"What happened, you see, was I got in a couple of hassles at the
work farm, to tell the pure truth, and the court ruled that I'm a psychopath. And do you think I'm gonna argue with the court? Shoo, you can
bet your bottom dollar I don't. If it gets me outta those damned pea
fields I'll be whatever their little heart desires, be it psychopath or mad
dog or werewolf, because I don't care if I never see another weedin' hoe
to my dying day. Now they tell me a psychopath's a guy fights too much
and fucks too much, but they ain't wholly right, do you think? I mean,

whoever heard tell of a man gettin' too much poozle? Hello, buddy, what do they call you? My name's McMurphy and I'll bet you two dollars here and now that you can't tell me how many spots are in that pinochle hand you're holding *don't* look. Two dollars; what d'ya say? God *damn*, Sam! can't you wait half a minute to prod me with that damn thermometer of yours?"

.   .   .

I know how they work it, the fog machine. We had a whole platoon used to operate fog machines around airfields overseas. Whenever intelligence figured there might be a bombing attack, or if the generals had something secret they wanted to pull—out of sight, hid so good that even the spies on the base couldn't see what went on—they fogged the field.

It's a simple rig: you got an ordinary compressor sucks water out of one tank and a special oil out of another tank, and compresses them together, and from the black stem at the end of the machine blooms a white cloud of fog that can cover a whole airfield in ninety seconds. The first thing I saw when I landed in Europe was the fog those machines make. There were some interceptors close after our transport, and soon as it hit ground the fog crew started up the machines. We could look out the transport's round, scratched windows and watch the jeeps draw the machines up close to the plane and watch the fog boil out till it rolled across the field and stuck against the windows like wet cotton.

You found your way off the plane by following a little referee's horn the lieutenant kept blowing, sounded like a goose honking. Soon as you were out of the hatch you couldn't see no more than maybe three feet in any direction. You felt like you were out on that airfield all by yourself. You were safe from the enemy, but you were awfully alone. Sounds died and dissolved after a few yards, and you couldn't hear any of the rest of your crew, nothing but that little horn squeaking and honking out of a soft furry whiteness so thick that your body just faded into white below the belt; other than that brown shirt and brass buckle, you couldn't see nothing but white, like from the waist down you were being dissolved by the fog too.

And then some guy wandering as lost as you would all of a sudden be right before your eyes, his face bigger and clearer than you ever saw a man's face before in your life. Your eyes were working so hard to see in that fog that when something did come in sight every detail was ten times as clear as usual, so clear both of you had to look away. When a man showed up you didn't want to look at his face and he didn't want to look at yours, because it's painful to see somebody so clear that it's like looking inside him, but then neither did you want to look away and lose him completely. You had a choice: you could either strain and look at things that appeared in front of you in the fog, painful as it might be, or you could relax and lose yourself.

When they first used that fog machine on the ward, one they bought from Army Surplus and hid in the vents in the new place before we moved in, I kept looking at anything that appeared out of the fog as long and hard as I could, to keep track of it, just like I used to do when they fogged the airfields in Europe. Nobody'd be blowing a horn to show the way, there was no rope to hold to, so fixing my eyes on something was the only way I kept from getting lost. Sometimes I got lost in it anyway, got in too deep, trying to hide, and every time I did, it seemed like I always turned up at that same place, at that same metal door with the row of rivets like eyes and no number, just like the room behind that door drew me to it, no matter how hard I tried to stay away, just like the current generated by the fiends in that room was conducted in a beam along the fog and pulled me back along it like a robot. I'd wander for days in the fog, scared I'd never see another thing, then there'd be that door, opening to show me the mattress padding on the other side to stop out the sounds, the men standing in a line like zombies among shiny copper wires and tubes pulsing light, and the bright scrape of arcing electricity. I'd take my place in the line and wait my turn at the table. The table shaped like a cross, with shadows of a thousand murdered men printed on it, silhouette wrists and ankles running under leather straps sweated green with use, a silhouette neck and head running up to a silver band goes across the forehead. And a technician at the controls beside the table looking up from his dials and down the line and pointing at me with a rubber glove. "Wait, I *know* that big bastard there—better rabbit-punch him or call for some more help or something. He's an awful case for thrashing around."

So I used to try not to get in too deep, for fear I'd get lost and turn up at the Shock Shop door. I looked hard at anything that came into sight and hung on like a man in a blizzard hangs on a fence rail. But they kept making the fog thicker and thicker, and it seemed to me that, no matter how hard I tried, two or three times a month I found myself with that door opening in front of me to the acid smell of sparks and ozone. In spite of all I could do, it was getting tough to keep from getting lost.

Then I discovered something: I don't have to end up at that door if I stay still when the fog comes over me and just keep quiet. The trouble was I'd been finding that door my own self because I got scared of being lost so long and went to hollering so they could track me. In a way, I was hollering for them *to* track me; I had figured that anything was better'n being lost for good, even the Shock Shop. Now, I don't know. Being lost isn't so bad.

All this morning I been waiting for them to fog us in again. The last few days they been doing it more and more. It's my idea they're doing it on account of McMurphy. They haven't got him fixed with controls yet, and they're trying to catch him off guard. They can see he's due to be a problem; a half a dozen times already he's roused Cheswick and Harding and some of the others to where it looked like they might actually stand up to one of the black boys—but always, just the time it looked like the patient might be helped, the fog would start, like it's starting now.

I heard the compressor start pumping in the grill a few minutes back, just as the guys went to moving tables out of the day room for the therapeutic meeting, and already the mist is oozing across the floor so thick my pants legs are wet. I'm cleaning the windows in the door of the glass station, and I hear the Big Nurse pick up the phone and call the doctor to tell him we're just about ready for the meeting, and tell him perhaps he'd best keep an hour free this afternoon for a staff meeting. "The reason being," she tells him, "I think it is past time to have a discussion of the subject of Patient Randle McMurphy and whether he should be on this ward or not." She listens a minute, then tells him, "I don't think it's wise to let him go on upsetting the patients the way he has the last few days."

That's why she's fogging the ward for the meeting. She don't usually do that. But now she's going to do something with McMurphy today, probably ship him to Disturbed. I put down my window rag and go to my chair at the end of the line of Chronics, barely able to see the guys getting into their chairs and the doctor coming through the door wiping his glasses like he thinks the blurred look comes from his steamed lenses instead of the fog.

It's rolling in thicker than I ever seen it before.

I can hear them out there, trying to go on with the meeting, talking some nonsense about Billy Bibbit's stutter and how it came about. The words come to me like through water, it's so thick. In fact it's so much like water it floats me right up out of my chair and I don't know which end is up for a while. Floating makes me a little sick to the stomach at first. I can't see a thing. I never had it so thick it floated me like this.

The words get dim and loud, off and on, as I float around, but as loud as they get, loud enough sometimes I know I'm right next to the guy that's talking, I still can't see a thing.

I recognize Billy's voice, stuttering worse than ever because he's nervous. ". . . fuh-fuh-flunked out of college be-be-cause I quit ROTC. I c-c-couldn't take it. Wh-wh-wh-whenever the officer in charge of class would call roll, call 'Bibbit,' I couldn't answer. You were s-s-supposed to say heh—heh—heh . . ." He's choking on the word, like it's a bone in his throat. I hear him swallow and start again. "You were supposed to say, 'Here sir,' and I never c-c-could get it out."

His voice gets dim; then the Big Nurse's voice comes cutting from the left. "Can you recall, Billy, when you first had speech trouble? When did you first stutter, do you remember?"

I can't tell is he laughing or what. "Fir-first stutter? First stutter? The first word I said I st-stut-tered: m-m-m-m-mamma."

Then the talking fades out altogether; I never knew that to happen before. Maybe Billy's hid himself in the fog too. Maybe all the guys finally and forever crowded back into the fog.

A chair and me float past each other. It's the first thing I've seen. It comes sifting out of the fog off to my right, and for a few seconds it's right beside my face, just out of my reach. I been accustomed of late to just let things alone when they appear in the fog, sit still and not try to hang on. But this time I'm scared, the way I used to be scared. I try with all I got to pull myself over to the chair and get hold of it, but there's nothing to brace against and all I can do is thrash the air, all I can do is watch the chair come clear, clearer than ever before to where I can even make out the fingerprint where a worker touched the varnish before it was dry, looming out for a few seconds, then fading on off again. I never seen it where things floated around this way. I never seen it this thick before, thick to where I can't get down to the floor and get on my feet if I wanted to and walk around. That's why I'm so scared; I feel I'm going to float off someplace for good this time.

I see a Chronic float into sight a little below me. It's old Colonel Matterson, reading from the wrinkled scripture of that long yellow hand. I look close at him because I figure it's the last time I'll ever see him. His face is enormous, almost more than I can bear. Every hair and wrinkle of him is big, as though I was looking at him with one of those microscopes. I see him so clear I see his whole life. The face is sixty years of southwest Army camps, rutted by iron-rimmed caisson wheels, worn to the bone by thousands of feet on two-day marches.

He holds out that long hand and brings it up in front of his eyes and squints into it, brings up his other hand and underlines the words with a finger wooden and varnished the color of a gunstock by nicotine. His voice is deep and slow and patient, and I see the words come out dark and heavy over his brittle lips when he reads.

"Now . . . The flag is . . . Ah-mer-ica. America is . . . the plum. The peach. The wah-ter-mel-on. America is . . . the gumdrop. The pump-kin seed. America is . . . tell-ah-vision."

It's true. It's all wrote down on that yellow hand. I can read it along with him myself.

"Now . . . The cross is . . . Mex-i-co." He looks up to see if I'm paying attention, and when he sees I am he smiles at me and goes on. "Mexico is . . . the wal-nut. The hazelnut. The ay-corn. Mexico is . . . the rain-bow. The rain-bow is . . . wooden. Mexico is . . . woo-den."

I can see what he's driving at. He's been saying this sort of thing for the whole six years he's been here, but I never paid him any mind, figured he was no more than a talking statue, a thing made out of bone and arthritis, rambling on and on with these goofy definitions of his that didn't make a lick of sense. Now, at last, I see what he's saying. I'm trying to hold him for one last look to remember him, and that's what makes me look hard enough to understand. He pauses and peers up at me again to make sure I'm getting it, and I want to yell out to him Yes, I see: Mexico *is* like the walnut; it's brown and hard and you feel it with your eye and it *feels* like the walnut! You're making sense, old man, a sense of your own. You're not crazy the way they think. Yes . . . I see . . .

But the fog's clogged my throat to where I can't make a sound. As he sifts away I see him bend back over that hand.

"Now . . . The green sheep is . . . Can-a-da. Canada is . . . the fir tree. The wheat field. The cal-en-dar . . ."

I strain to see him drifting away. I strain so hard my eyes ache and I have to close them, and when I open them again the colonel is gone. I'm floating by myself again, more lost than ever.

This is the time, I tell myself. I'm going for good.

There's old Pete, face like a searchlight. He's fifty yards off to my left, but I can see him plain as though there wasn't any fog at all. Or maybe he's up right close and real small, I can't be sure. He tells me once about how tired he is, and just his saying it makes me see his whole life on the railroad, see him working to figure out how to read a watch, breaking a sweat while he tries to get the right button in the right hole of his railroad overalls, doing his absolute damnedest to keep up with a job that comes so easy to the others they can sit back in a chair padded with cardboard and read mystery stories and girlie books. Not that he ever really figured to keep up—he knew from the start he couldn't do that —but he had to try to keep up, just to keep them in sight. So for forty years he was able to live, if not right in the world of men, at least on the edge of it.

I can see all that, and be hurt by it, the way I was hurt by seeing things in the Army, in the war. The way I was hurt by seeing what happened to Papa and the tribe. I thought I'd got over seeing those things and fretting over them. There's no sense in it. There's nothing to be done.

"I'm tired," is what he says.

"I know you're tired, Pete, but I can't do you no good fretting about it. You know I can't."

Pete floats on the way of the old colonel.

Here comes Billy Bibbit, the way Pete come by. They're all filing by for a last look. I know Billy can't be more'n a few feet away, but he's so tiny he looks like he's a mile off. His face is out to me like the face of a beggar, needing so much more'n anybody can give. His mouth works like a little doll's mouth.

"And even when I pr-proposed, I flubbed it. I said 'Huh-honey, will you muh-muh-muh-muh-muh . . . till the girl broke out l-laughing."

Nurse's voice, I can't see where it comes from: "Your mother has spoken to me about this girl, Billy. Apparently she was quite a bit beneath you. What would you speculate it was about her that frightened you so, Billy?"

"I was in luh-love with her."

I can't do nothing for you either, Billy. You know that. None of us can. You got to understand that as soon as a man goes to help somebody, he leaves himself wide open. He *has* to be cagey, Billy, you should know that as well as anyone. What could I do? I can't fix your stuttering. I can't wipe the razorblade scars off your wrists or the cigarette burns off the back of your hands. I can't give you a new mother. And as far as the nurse riding you like this, rubbing your nose in your weakness till what little dignity you got left is gone and you shrink up to nothing from humiliation, I can't do anything about that, either. At Anzio, I saw a buddy of mine tied to a tree fifty yards from me, screaming for water, his face blistered in the sun. They wanted me to try to go out and help him. They'd of cut me in half from that farmhouse over there.

Put your face away, Billy.

They keep filing past.

It's like each face was a sign like one of those "I'm Blind" signs the dago accordion players in Portland hung around their necks, only these signs say "I'm tired" or "I'm scared" or "I'm dying of a bum liver" or "I'm all bound up with machinery and people *pushing* me alla time." I can read all the signs, it don't make any difference how little the print gets. Some of the faces are looking around at one another and could read the other fellow's if they would, but what's the sense? The faces blow past in the fog like confetti.

I'm further off than I've ever been. This is what it's like to be dead. I guess this is what it's like to be a Vegetable; you lose yourself in the fog. You don't move. They feed your body till it finally stops eating; then they burn it. It's not so bad. There's no pain. I don't feel much of anything other than a touch of chill I figure will pass in time.

I see my commanding officer pinning notices on the bulletin board, what we're to wear today. I see the US Department of Interior bearing down on our little tribe with a gravel-crushing machine.

I see Papa come loping out of a draw and slow up to try and take aim at a big six-point buck springing off through the cedars. Shot after shot puffs out of the barrel, knocking dust all around the buck. I come out of the draw behind Papa and bring the buck down with my second shot just as it starts climbing the rimrock. I grin at Papa.

I never knew you to miss a shot like that before, Papa.

Eye's gone, boy. Can't hold a bead. Sights on my gun just now was shakin' like a dog shittin' peach pits.

Papa, I'm telling you: that cactus moon of Sid's is gonna make you old before your time.

A man drinks that cactus moon of Sid's boy, he's already old before his time. Let's go gut that animal out before the flies blow him.

That's not even happening now. You see? There's nothing you can do about a happening out of the past like that.

Look there, my man . . .

I hear whispers, black boys.

Look there that old fool Broom, slipped off to sleep.

Tha's right, Chief Broom, tha's right. You sleep an' keep outta trouble. Yasss.

I'm not cold any more. I think I've about made it. I'm off to where the cold can't reach me. I can stay off here for good. I'm not scared any more. They can't reach me. Just the words reach me, and those're fading.

Well . . . in as much as Billy has decided to walk out on the discussion, does anyone else have a problem to bring before the group?

As a matter of fact, ma'am, there does happen to be something . . .

That's that McMurphy. He's far away. He's still trying to pull people out of the fog. Why don't he leave me be?

". . . remember that vote we had a day or so back—about the TV time? Well, today's Friday and I thought I might just bring it up again, just to see if anybody else has picked up a little guts."

"Mr. McMurphy, the purpose of this meeting is therapy, group therapy, and I'm not certain these petty grievances—"

"Yeah, yeah, the hell with that, we've heard it before. Me and some of the rest of the guys decided—"

"One moment, Mr. McMurphy, let me pose a question to the group: do any of you feel that Mr. McMurphy is perhaps imposing his personal desires on some of you too much? I've been thinking you might be happier if he were moved to a different ward."

Nobody says anything for a minute. Then someone says, "Let him vote, why dontcha? Why ya want to ship him to Disturbed just for bringing up a vote? What's so wrong with changing time?"

"Why, Mr. Scanlon, as I recall, you refused to eat for three days until we allowed you to turn the set on at six instead of six-thirty."

"A man needs to see the world news, don't he? God, they coulda bombed Washington and it'd been a week before we'd of heard."

"Yes? And how do you feel about relinquishing your world news to watch a bunch of men play baseball?"

"We can't have both, huh? No, I suppose not. Well, what the dickens—I don't guess they'll bomb us this week."

"Let's let him have the vote, Miss Ratched."

"Very well. But I think this is ample evidence of how much he is upsetting some of you patients. What is it you are proposing Mr. Mc-Murphy?"

"I'm proposing a revote on watching the TV in the afternoon."

"You're certain one more vote will satisfy you? We have more important things—"

"It'll satisfy me. I just'd kind of like to see which of these birds has any guts and which doesn't."

"It's that kind of talk, Doctor Spivey, that makes me wonder if the patients wouldn't be more content if Mr. McMurphy were moved."

"Let him call the vote, why dontcha?"

"Certainly, Mr. Cheswick. A vote is now before the group. Will a show of hands be adequate, Mr. McMurphy, or are you going to insist on a secret ballot?"

"I want to see the hands. I want to see the hands that don't go up, too."

"Everyone in favor of changing the television time to the afternoon, raise his hand."

The first hand that comes up, I can tell, is McMurphy's, because of the bandage where that control panel cut into him when he tried to lift it. And then off down the slope I see them, other hands coming up out of the fog. It's like . . . that big red hand of McMurphy's is reaching into the fog and dropping down and dragging the men up by their hands, dragging them blinking into the open. First one, then another, then the next. Right on down the line of Acutes, dragging them out of the fog till there they stand, all twenty of them, raising not just for watching TV, but against the Big Nurse, against her trying to send McMurphy to Disturbed, against the way she's talked and acted and beat them down for years.

Nobody says anything. I can feel how stunned everybody is, the patients as well as the staff. The nurse can't figure what happened; yesterday, before he tried lifting that panel, there wasn't but four or five men might of voted. But when she talks she don't let it show in her voice how surprised she is.

"I count only twenty, Mr. McMurphy."

"Twenty? Well, why not? Twenty is all of us there—" His voice hangs as he realizes what she means. "Now hold on just a goddamned minute, lady—"

"I'm afraid the vote is defeated."

"Hold on just one goddamned *minute!*"

"There are forty patients on the ward, Mr. McMurphy. Forty patients, and only twenty voted. You must have a majority to change the ward policy. I'm afraid the vote is closed."

The hands are coming down across the room. The guys know they're whipped, are trying to slip back into the safety of the fog. McMurphy is on his feet.

"Well, I'll be a sonofabitch. You mean to tell me that's how you're gonna pull it? Count the votes of those old birds over there too?"

"Didn't you explain the voting procedure to him, Doctor?"

"I'm afraid—a majority *is* called for, McMurphy. She's right, she's right."

"A majority, Mr. McMurphy; it's in the ward constitution."

"And I suppose the way to change the damned constitution is with a majority vote. Sure. Of all the chicken-shit things I've ever seen, this by God takes the *cake!*"

"I'm sorry, Mr. McMurphy, but you'll find it written in the policy if you'd care for me to—"

"So this's how you work this democratic bullshit—hell's bells!"

"You seem upset, Mr. McMurphy. Doesn't he seem upset, Doctor? I want you to note this."

"Don't give me that noise, lady. When a guy's getting screwed he's got a right to holler. And we've been damn well screwed."

"Perhaps, Doctor, in view of the patient's condition, we should bring this meeting to a close early today—"

"Wait! Wait a minute, let me talk to some of those old guys."

"The vote is closed, Mr. McMurphy."

"Let me talk to 'em."

He's coming across the day room at us. He gets bigger and bigger, and he's burning red in the face. He reaches into the fog and tries to drag Ruckly to the surface because Ruckly's the youngest.

"What about you, buddy? You want to watch the World Series? Baseball? Baseball games? Just raise that hand up there—"

"Fffffffuck da wife."

"All right, forget it. You, partner, how about you? What was your name—Ellis? What do you say, Ellis, to watching a ball game on TV? Just raise your hand. . . ."

Ellis's hands are nailed to the wall, can't be counted as a vote.

"I said the voting is closed, Mr. McMurphy. You're just making a spectacle of yourself."

He don't pay any attention to her. He comes on down the line of Chronics. "C'mon, c'mon, just one vote from you birds, just raise a hand. Show her you can still do it."

"I'm tired," says Pete and wags his head.

"The night is . . . the Pacific Ocean." The Colonel is reading off his hand, can't be bothered with voting.

"*One* of you guys, for cryin' out loud! This is where you get the edge, don't you see that? We have to do this—or we're *whipped!* Don't a one of you clucks know what I'm talking about enough to give us a hand? You, Gabriel? George? No? You, Chief, what about you?"

He's standing over me in the mist. Why won't he leave me be?

"Chief, you're our last bet."

The Big Nurse is folding her papers; the other nurses are standing up around her. She finally gets to her feet.

"The meeting is adjourned, then," I hear her say. "And I'd like to see the staff down in the staff room in about an hour. So, if there is nothing el—"

It's too late to stop it now. McMurphy did something to it that first day, put some kind of hex on it with his hand so it won't act like I order it. There's no sense in it, any fool can see; I wouldn't do it on my own. Just by the way the nurse is staring at me with her mouth empty of words I can see I'm in for trouble, but I can't stop it. McMurphy's got hidden wires hooked to it, lifting it slow just to get me out of the fog and into the open where I'm fair game. He's doing it, wires . . .

No. That's not the truth. I lifted it myself.

McMurphy whoops and drags me standing, pounding my back.

"Twenty-one! The Chief's vote makes it twenty-one! And by God if that ain't a majority I'll eat my hat!"

"Yippee," Cheswick yells. The other Acutes are coming across toward me.

"The meeting was closed," she says. Her smile is still there, but the back of her neck as she walks out of the day room and into the Nurses' Station, is red and swelling like she'll blow apart any second.

But she don't blow up, not right off, not until about an hour later. Behind the glass her smile is twisted and queer, like we've never seen before. She just sits. I can see her shoulders rise and fall as she breathes.

McMurphy looks up at the clock and he says it's time for the game. He's over by the drinking fountain with some of the other Acutes, down on his knees scouring off the baseboard. I'm sweeping out the broom closet for the tenth time that day. Scanlon and Harding, they got the buffer going up and down the hall, polishing the new wax into shining figure eights. McMurphy says again that he guesses it must be game time and he stands up, leaves the scouring rag where it lies. Nobody else stops work. McMurphy walks past the window where she's glaring out at him and grins at her like he knows he's got her whipped now. When he tips his head back and winks at her she gives that little sideways jerk of her head.

Everybody keeps on at what he's doing, but they all watch out of the corners of their eyes while he drags his armchair out to in front of the TV set, then switches on the set and sits down. A picture swirls onto the screen of a parrot out on the baseball field singing razor-blade songs. McMurphy gets up and turns up the sound to drown out the music coming down from the speaker in the ceiling, and he drags another chair in front of him and sits down and crosses his feet on the chair and leans back and lights a cigarette. He scratches his belly and yawns.

"Hoo-*weee!* Man, all I need me now is a can of beer and a red-hot."

We can see the nurse's face get red and her mouth work as she stares at him. She looks around for a second and sees everybody's watching what she's going to do—even the black boys and the little nurses sneaking looks at her, and the residents beginning to drift in for the staff meeting, they're watching. Her mouth clamps shut. She looks back at McMurphy and waits till the razor-blade song is finished; then she gets up and goes to the steel door where the controls are, and she flips a switch and the TV picture swirls back into the gray. Nothing is left on the screen but a little eye of light beading right down on McMurphy sitting there.

That eye don't faze him a bit. To tell the truth, he don't even let on he knows the picture is turned off; he puts his cigarette between his teeth and pushes his cap forward in his red hair till he has to lean back to see out from under the brim.

And sits that way, with his hands crossed behind his head and his feet stuck out in a chair, a smoking cigarette sticking out from under his hatbrim—watching the TV screen.

The nurse stands this as long as she can; then she comes to the door of the Nurses' Station and calls across to him he'd better help the men with the housework. He ignores her.

"I said, Mr. McMurphy, that you are supposed to be working during these hours." Her voice has a tight whine like an electric saw ripping through pine. "Mr. McMurphy, I'm *warning* you!"

Everybody's stopped what he was doing. She looks around her, then takes a step out of the Nurses' Station toward McMurphy.

"You're committed, you realize. You are . . . under the *jurisdiction* of me . . . the staff." She's holding up a fist, all those red-orange fingernails burning into her palm. "Under jurisdiction and *control*—"

Harding shuts off the buffer, and leaves it in the hall, and goes pulls him a chair up alongside McMurphy and sits down and lights him a cigarette too.

"Mr. Harding! You return to your scheduled duties!"

I think how her voice sounds like it hit a nail, and this strikes me so funny I almost laugh.

"Mr. Har-*ding!*"

Then Cheswick goes and gets him a chair, and then Billy Bibbit goes, and then Scanlon and then Fredrickson and Sefelt, and then we all put down our mops and brooms and scouring rags and we all go pull us chairs up.

"You *men*—Stop this. *Stop!*"

And we're all sitting there lined up in front of that blanked-out TV set, watching the gray screen just like we could see the baseball game clear as day, and she's ranting and screaming behind us.

If somebody'd of come in and took a look, men watching a blank TV, a fifty-ycar-old woman hollering and squealing at the back of their heads about discipline and order and recriminations, they'd of thought the whole bunch was crazy as loons.

.   .   .

Up on Disturbed there's an everlasting high-pitched machine-room clatter, a prison mill stamping out license plates. And time is measured out by the di-*dock,* di-*dock* of a Ping-pong table. Men pacing their personal runways get to a wall and dip a shoulder and turn and pace back to another wall, dip a shoulder and turn and back again, fast short steps, wearing crisscrossing ruts in the tile floor, with a look of caged thirst. There's a singed smell of men scared berserk and out of control, and in the corners and under the Ping-pong table there's things crouched gnashing their teeth that the doctors and nurses can't see and the aides can't kill with disinfectant. When the ward door opened I smelled that singed smell and heard that gnash of teeth.

A tall bony old guy, dangling from a wire screwed in between his shoulder blades, met McMurphy and me at the door when the aides brought us in. He looked us over with yellow, scaled eyes and shook his head. "I wash my hands of the whole deal," he told one of the colored aides, and the wire drug him off down the hall.

We followed him down to the day room, and McMurphy stopped at the door and spread his feet and tipped his head back to look things over; he tried to put his thumbs in his pockets, but the cuffs were too tight. "It's a scene," he said out of the side of his mouth. I nodded my head. I'd seen it all before.

A couple of the guys pacing stopped to look at us, and the old bony man came dragging by again, washing his hands of the whole deal. Nobody paid us much mind at first. The aides went off to the Nurses' Station, leaving us standing in the day-room door. McMurphy's eye was puffed to give him a steady wink, and I could tell it hurt his lips to grin. He raised his cuffed hands and stood looking at the clatter of movement and took a deep breath.

"McMurphy's the name, pardners," he said in his drawling cowboy actor's voice, "an' the thing I want to *know* is who's the peckerwood runs the poker game in this establishment?"

The Ping-pong clock died down in a rapid ticking on the floor.

"I don't deal blackjack so good, hobbled like this, but I maintain I'm a fire-eater in a stud game."

He yawned, hitched a shoulder, bent down and cleared his throat, and spat something at a wastepaper can five feet away; it rattled in with a *ting* and he straightened up again, grinned, and licked his tongue at the bloody gap in his teeth.

"Had a run-in downstairs. Me an' the Chief here locked horns with two greasemonkeys."

All the stamp-mill racket had stopped by this time, and everybody was looking toward the two of us at the door. McMurphy drew eyes to him like a sideshow barker. Beside him, I found that I was obliged to be looked at too, and with people staring at me I felt I had to stand up straight and tall as I could. That made my back hurt where I'd fallen in the shower with the black boy on me, but I didn't let on. One hungry looker with a head of shaggy black hair came up and held his hand like he figured I had something for him. I tried to ignore him, but he kept running around in front of whichever way I turned, like a little kid, holding that empty hand cupped out to me.

McMurphy talked a while about the fight, and my back got to hurting more and more; I'd hunkered in my chair in the corner for so long that it was hard to stand straight very long. I was glad when a little Jap nurse came to take us into the Nurses' Station and I got a chance to sit and rest.

She asked if we were calm enough for her to take off the cuffs, and McMurphy nodded. He had slumped over with his head hung and his elbows between his knees and looked completely exhausted—it hadn't occurred to me that it was just as hard for him to stand straight as it was for me.

The nurse—about as big as the small end of nothing whittled to a fine point, as McMurphy put it later—undid our cuffs and gave Mc-Murphy a cigarette and gave me a stick of gum. She said she remembered that I chewed gum. I didn't remember her at all. McMurphy smoked while she dipped her little hand full of pink birthday candles into a jar of salve and worked over his cuts, flinching every time he flinched and telling him she was sorry. She picked up one of his hands in both of hers and turned it over and salved his knuckles. "Who was it?" she asked, looking at the knuckles. "Was it Washington or Warren?"

McMurphy looked up at her. "Washington," he said and grinned. "The Chief here took care of Warren."

She put his hand down and turned to me. I could see the little bird bones in her face. "Are you hurt anywhere?" I shook my head.

"What about Warren and Williams?"

McMurphy told her he thought they might be sporting some plaster the next time she saw them. She nodded and looked at her feet. "It's not all like her ward," she said. "A lot of it is, but not all. Army nurses, trying to run an Army hospital. They are a little sick themselves. I sometimes think all single nurses should be fired after they reach thirty-five."

"At least all single *Army* nurses," McMurphy added. He asked how long we could expect to have the pleasure of her hospitality.

"Not very long, I'm afraid."

"Not very long, you're *afraid?*" McMurphy asked her.

"Yes. I'd like to keep men here sometimes instead of sending them back, but she has seniority. No, you probably won't be very long—I mean—like you are now."

The beds on Disturbed are all out of tune, too taut or too loose. We were assigned beds next to each other. They didn't tie a sheet across me, though they left a little dim light on near the bed. Halfway through the night somebody screamed, "I'm starting to spin, Indian! Look me, look me!" I opened my eyes and saw a set of long yellow teeth glowing right in front of my face. It was the hungry-looking guy. "I'm starting to *spin!* Please look me!"

The aides got him from behind, two of them, dragged him laughing and yelling out of the dorm; "I'm starting to spin, Indian!"—then just *laugh.* He kept saying it and laughing all the way down the hall till the dorm was quiet again, and I could hear that one other guy saying, "Well . . . I wash my hands of the whole deal."

"You had you a buddy for a second there, Chief," McMurphy whispered and rolled over to sleep. I couldn't sleep much the rest of the night and I kept seeing those yellow teeth and that guy's hungry face, asking to Look me! Look me! Or, finally, as I did get to sleep, just asking. That face, just a yellow, starved need, come looming out of the dark in front of me, wanting things . . . asking things. I wondered how McMurphy slept, plagued by a hundred faces like that, or two hundred, or a thousand.

They've got an alarm on Disturbed to wake the patients. They don't just turn on the lights like downstairs. This alarm sounds like a gigantic pencil-sharpener grinding up something awful. McMurphy and I both sat bolt upright when we heard it and were about to lie back down when a loudspeaker called for the two of us to come to the Nurses' Station. I got out of bed, and my back had stiffened up overnight to where I could just barely bend; I could tell by the way McMurphy gimped around that he was as stiff as I was.

"What they got on the program for us now, Chief?" he asked. "The boot? The rack? I hope nothing too strenuous, because, man, am I stove up bad!"

I told him it wasn't strenuous, but I didn't tell him anything else, because I wasn't sure myself till I got to the Nurses' Station, and the nurse, a different one, said, "Mr. McMurphy and Mr. Bromden?" then handed us each a little paper cup.

I looked in mine, and there are three of those red capsules.

This *tsing* whirs in my head I can't stop.

"Hold on," McMurphy says. "These are those knockout pills, aren't they?"

The nurse nods, twists her head to check behind her; there's two guys waiting with ice tongs, hunching forward with their elbows linked.

McMurphy hands back the cup, says, "No sir, ma'am, but I'll forgo the blindfold. *Could* use a cigarette, though."

I hand mine back too, and she says she must phone and she slips the glass door across between us, is at the phone before anybody can say anything else.

"I'm sorry if I got you into something, Chief," McMurphy says, and I barely can hear him over the noise of the phone wires whistling in the walls. I can feel the scared downhill rush of thoughts in my head.

We're sitting in the day room, those faces around us in a circle, when in the door comes the Big Nurse herself, the two big black boys on each side, a step behind her. I try to shrink down in my chair, away from her, but it's too late. Too many people looking at me; sticky eyes hold me where I sit.

"Good morning," she says, got her old smile back now. McMurphy says good morning, and I keep quiet even though she says good morning to me too, out loud. I'm watching the black boys; one has tape on his nose and his arm in a sling, gray hand dribbling out of the cloth like a drowned spider, and the other one is moving like he's got some kind of cast around his ribs. They are both grinning a little. Probably could of stayed home with their hurts, but wouldn't miss this for nothing. I grin back just to show them.

The Big Nurse talks to McMurphy, soft and patient, about the irresponsible thing he did, the childish thing, throwing a tantrum like a little boy—aren't you *ashamed?* He says he guesses not and tells her to get on with it.

She talks to him about how they, the patients downstairs on our ward, at a special group meeting yesterday afternoon, agreed with the staff that it might be beneficial that he receive some shock therapy—unless he realizes his mistakes. All he has to do is *admit* he was wrong, to indicate, *demonstrate* rational contact, and the treatment would be canceled this time.

That circle of faces waits and watches. The nurse says it's up to him.
"Yeah?" he says. "You got a paper I can sign?"

"Well, no, but if you feel it nec—"

"And why don't you add some other things while you're at it and get
them out of the way—things like, oh, me being part of a plot to overthrow the government and like how I think life on your ward is the
sweetest goddamned life this side of Hawaii—you know, that sort of
crap."

"I don't believe that would—"

"*Then*, after I sign, you bring me a blanket and a package of Red
Cross cigarettes. Hooee, those Chinese Commies could have learned a
few things from you, lady."

"Randle, we are trying to help you."

But he's on his feet, scratching at his belly, walking on past her
and the black boys rearing back, toward the card tables.

"O-kay, well well well, where's this poker table, buddies . . . ?"

The nurse stares after him a moment, then walks into the Nurses'
Station to use the phone.

Two colored aides and a white aide with curly blond hair walk us
over to the Main Building. McMurphy talks with the white aide on the
way over, just like he isn't worried about a thing.

There's frost thick on the grass, and the two colored aides in front
trail puffs of breath like locomotives. The sun wedges apart some of the
clouds and lights up the frost till the grounds are scattered with sparks.
Sparrows fluffed out against the cold, scratching among the sparks for
seeds. We cut across the crackling grass, past the digger squirrel holes
where I saw the dog. Cold sparks. Frost down the holes, clear out of
sight.

I feel that frost in my belly.

We get up to that door, and there's a sound behind like bees stirred
up. Two men in front of us, reeling under the red capsules, one bawl-
ing like a baby, saying "It's my cross, thank you Lord, it's all I got,
thank you Lord. . . ."

The other guy waiting is saying, "Guts ball, guts ball." He's the lifeguard from the pool. And he's crying a little too.

I won't cry or yell. Not with McMurphy here.

The technician asks us to take off our shoes, and McMurphy asks
him if we get our pants slit and our heads shaved too. The technician
says no such luck.

The metal door looks out with its rivet eyes.

The door opens, sucks the first man inside. The lifeguard won't
budge. A beam like neon smoke comes out of the black panel in the
room, fastens on his cleat-marked forehead and drags him in like a

dog on a leash. The beam spins him around three times before the door closes, and his face is scrambled fear. "Hut *one*," he grunts. "Hut *two!* Hut *three!*"

I hear them in there pry up his forehead like a manhole cover, clash and snarl of jammed cogs.

Smoke blows the door open, and a Gurney comes out with the first man on it, and he rakes me with his eyes. That face. The Gurney goes back in and brings the lifeguard out. I can hear the yell-leaders spelling out his name.

The technician says, "Next group."

The floor's cold, frosted, crackling. Up above the light whines, tube long and white and icy. Can smell the graphite salve, like the smell in a garage. Can smell acid of fear. There's one window, up high, small, and outside I see those puffy sparrows strung up on a wire like brown beads. Their heads sunk in the feathers against the cold. Something goes to blowing wind over my hollow bones, higher and higher, air raid! air raid!

"Don't holler, Chief. . . ."

Air raid!

"Take 'er easy. I'll go first. My skull's too thick for them to hurt me. And if they can't hurt me they can't hurt you."

Climbs on the table without any help and spreads his arms out to fit the shadow. A switch snaps the clasps on his wrists, ankles, clamping him into the shadow. A hand takes off his wristwatch, won it from Scanlon, drops it near the panel, it springs open, cogs and wheels and the long dribbling spiral of spring jumping against the side of the panel and sticking fast.

He don't look a bit scared. He keeps grinning at me.

They put the graphite salve on his temples. "What is it?" he says. "Conductant," the technician says. "Anointest my head with conductant. Do I get a crown of thorns?"

They smear it on. He's singing to them, makes their hands shake.

" 'Get Wildroot Cream Oil, Cholly. . . .' "

Put on those things like headphones, crown of silver thorns over the graphite at his temples. They try to hush his singing with a piece of rubber hose for him to bite on.

" 'Mage with thoothing lan-o-lin.' "

Twist some dials, and the machine trembles, two robot arms pick up soldering irons and hunch down on him. He gives me the wink and speaks to me, muffled, tells me something, says something to me around that rubber hose just as those irons get close enough to the silver on his temples—light arcs across, stiffens him, bridges him up off the table till nothing is down but his wrists and ankles and out around that crimped black rubber hose a sound like *hooeee!* and he's frosted over completely with sparks.

And out the window the sparrows drop smoking off the wire.

They roll him out on a Gurney, still jerking, face frosted white. Corrosion. Battery acid. The technician turns to me.

Watch that other moose. I know him. Hold him!

It's not a will-power thing any more.

Hold him! Damn. No more of these boys without Seconal.

The clamps bite my wrists and ankles.

The graphite salve has iron filings in it, temples scratching.

He said something when he winked. Told me something.

Man bends over, brings two irons toward the ring on my head.

The machine hunches on me.

AIR RAID.

Hit at a lope, running already down the slope. Can't get back, can't go ahead, look down the barrel an' you dead dead dead.

We come up outa the bullreeds run beside the railroad track. I lay an ear to the track, and it burns my cheek.

"Nothin' either way," I say, "a *hundred* miles. . . ."

"Hump," Papa says.

"Didn't we used to listen for buffalo by stickin' a knife in the ground, catch the handle in our teeth, hear a herd way off?"

"Hump," he says again, but he's tickled. Out across the other side of the track a fencerow of wheat chats from last winter. Mice under that stuff, the dog says.

"Do we go up the track or down the track, boy?"

"We go across, is what the ol' dog says."

"That dog don't heel."

"He'll do. There's birds over there is what the ol' dog says."

"Better hunting up the track bank is what your ol' man says."

"Best right across in the chats of wheat, the dog tells me."

Across—next thing I know there's people all over the track, blasting away at pheasants like anything. Seems our dog got too far out ahead and run all the birds outa the chats to the track.

Dog got three mice.

. . . man, Man, MAN, MAN . . . broad and big with a wink like a star.

Ants again oh Jesus and I got 'em bad this time, prickle-footed bastards. Remember the time we found those ants tasted like dill pickles? Hee? You said it wasn't dill pickles and I said it was, and your mama kicked the living tar outa me when she heard: Teachin' a kid to eat *bugs!*

Ugh. Good Injun boy should know how to survive on anything he can eat that won't eat him first.

We ain't Indians. We're civilized and you remember it.

You told me Papa When I die pin me up against the sky.

Mama's name was Bromden. Still is Bromden. Papa said he was born with only one name, born smack into it the way a calf drops out in a spread blanket when the cow insists on standing up. Tee Ah Millatoona, the Pine-That-Stands-Tallest-on-the-Mountain, and I'm the biggest by God Injun in the state of Oregon and probly California and Idaho. Born right into it.

You're the biggest by God fool if you think that a good Christian woman takes on a name like Tee Ah Millatoona. You were born into a name, so okay, I'm born into a name. Bromden. Mary Louise Bromden.

And when we move into town, Papa says, that name makes gettin' that Social Security card a lot easier.

Guy's after somebody with a riveter's hammer, get him too, if he keeps at it. I see those lightning flashes again, colors striking.

Ting. Tingle, tingle, tremble toes, she's a good fisherman, catches hens, puts 'em inna pens . . . wire blier, limber lock, three geese inna flock . . . one flew east, one flew west, one flew over the cuckoo's nest . . . O-U-T spells out . . . goose swoops down and plucks *you* out.

My old grandma chanted this, a game we played by the hours, sitting by the fish racks scaring flies. A game called Tingle Tingle Tangle Toes. Counting each finger on my two outspread hands, one finger to a syllable as she chants.

Tingle, ting-le, tang-le toes (seven fingers), she's a good fisherman, catches hens (sixteen fingers, tapping a finger on each beat with her black crab hand, each of my fingernails looking up at her like a little face asking to be the *you* that the goose swoops down and plucks out).

I like the game and I like Grandma. I don't like Mrs. Tingle Tangle Toes, catching hens. I don't like her. I do like that goose flying over the cuckoo's nest. I like him, and I like Grandma, dust in her wrinkles.

Next time I saw her she was stone cold dead, right in the middle of The Dalles on the sidewalk, colored shirts standing around, some Indians, some cattlemen, some wheatmen. They cart her down to the city burying ground, roll red clay into her eyes.

I remember hot, still electric-storm afternoons when jackrabbits ran under Diesel truck wheels.

Joey Fish-in-a-Barrel has twenty thousand dollars and three Cadillacs since the contract. And he can't drive none of 'em.

I see a dice.

I see it from the inside, me at the bottom. I'm the weight, loading the dice to throw that number one up there above me. They got the dice loaded to throw a snake eyes, and I'm the load, six lumps around me like white pillows is the other side of the dice, the number six that will always be down when he throws. What's the other dice loaded for? I bet it's loaded to throw one too. Snake eyes. They're shooting with crookies against him, and I'm the load.

Look out, here comes a toss. Ay, lady, the smokehouse is empty and baby needs a new pair of opera pumps. Comin' at ya. *Faw!*

Crapped out.

Water. I'm lying in a puddle.

Snake eyes. Caught him again. I see that number one up above me: he can't whip frozen dice behind the feedstore in an alley—in Portland.

The alley is a tunnel it's cold because the sun is late afternoon. Let me. . . go see Grandma. Please, Mama.

What was it he said when he winked?

One flew east one flew west.

Don't stand in my way.

Damn it, nurse, don't stand in my way Way WAY!

My roll. *Faw.* Damn. Twisted again. Snake eyes.

The schoolteacher tell me you got a good head, boy, be something. . . .

Be what, Papa? A rug-weaver like Uncle R & J Wolf? A basket-weaver? Or another drunken Indian.

I say, attendant, you're an Indian, aren't you?

Yeah, that's right.

Well, I must say, you speak the language quite well.

Yeah.

Well . . . three dollars of regular.

They wouldn't be so cocky if they knew what me and the *moon* have going. No damned regular Indian . . .

He who—what was it?—walks out of step, hears another drum.

Snake eyes again. Hoo boy, these dice are *cold.*

After Grandma's funeral me and Papa and Uncle Running-and-Jumping Wolf dug her up. Mama wouldn't go with us; she never heard of such a thing. Hanging a corpse in a *tree!* It's enough to make a person sick.

Uncle R & J Wolf and Papa spent twenty days in the drunk tank at The Dalles jail, playing rummy, for Violation of the Dead.

But she's our goddanged mother!

It doesn't make the slightest difference, boys. You shoulda left her buried. I don't know when you blamed Indians will learn. Now, where is she? you'd better tell.

Ah go fuck yourself, paleface, Uncle R & J said, rolling himself a cigarette. I'll never tell.

High high high in the hills, high in a pine tree bed, she's tracing the wind with that old hand, counting the clouds with that old chant: . . . three geese in a flock . . .

What did you say to me when you winked?

Band playing. Look—the *sky*, it's the Fourth of July.

Dice at rest.

They got to me with the machine again . . . I wonder . . .

What did he say?

. . . wonder how McMurphy made me big again.

He said Guts ball.

They're out there. Black boys in white suits peeing under the door on me, come in later and accuse me of soaking all six these pillows I'm lying on! Number six. I thought the room was a dice. The number one, the snake eye up there, the circle, the white *light* in the ceiling . . . is what I've been seeing . . . in this little square room . . . means it's after dark. How many hours have I been out? It's fogging a little, but I won't slip off and hide in it. No . . . never again . . .

I stand, stood up slowly, feeling numb between the shoulders. The white pillows on the floor of the Seclusion Room were soaked from me peeing on them while I was out. I couldn't remember all of it yet, but I rubbed my eyes with the heels of my hands and tried to clear my head. I worked at it. I'd never worked at coming out of it before.

I staggered toward the little round chicken-wired window in the door of the room and tapped it with my knuckles. I saw an aide coming up the hall with a tray for me and knew this time I had them beat.

There had been times when I'd wandered around in a daze for as long as two weeks after a shock treatment, living in that foggy, jumbled blur which is a whole lot like the ragged edge of sleep, that gray zone between light and dark, or between sleeping and waking or living and dying, where you know you're not unconscious any more but don't know yet what day it is or who you are or what's the use of coming back at all—for two weeks. If you don't have a reason to wake up you can loaf around in that gray zone for a long, fuzzy time, or if you want to bad enough I found you can come fighting right out of it. This time I came fighting out of it in less than a day, less time than ever.

And when the fog was finally swept from my head it seemed like I'd just come up after a long, deep dive, breaking the surface after being under water a hundred years. It was the last treatment they gave me.

QUESTIONS

1. How effective is Kesey's method of narration? Is believability a problem?
2. What effect does McMurphy's initial appearance have on the ward? On Chief Broom personally?
3. What are some of our everyday, less psychotic equivalents to Chief Broom's "fog machine"? How does McMurphy try to "pull people out of the fog"? What does the Chief mean when he says, "As soon as we try to help someone, we are vulnerable"?
4. On what basis does the Colonel communicate with the Chief? How does this differ from typical human verbal communication?
5. What is the Chief's attitude to shock therapy? How has it affected him in the past? What is McMurphy's attitude?
6. How is the significance of the book's title revealed in the Chief's dreams during shock therapy?
7. What is the nature of the "breakthrough" McMurphy effects on the Chief? What is the source of his power to do it?

CARL ROGERS

IN his autobiographical essay, "This is Me," Carl Rogers (b. 1902) gives us a sense of his own career as well as of his most important accomplishments as a psychotherapist and a teacher. The earlier books he refers to are *The Clinical Treatment of the Problem Child* (1939) and *Counseling and Psychotherapy* (1942). The present article appears at the beginning of *On Becoming a Person* (1961), and we see from this that Rogers is not defensive about using himself as a model for a "person." He has also published *Freedom to Know: A View of What Education Might Become* (1969) and has been associated in recent years with the Center for Studies of the Person, La Jolla, California.

Carl Rogers redefines the importance of a career for young Americans who are no longer interested merely in making money or gaining power. He has spent several decades pursuing work that is fulfilling to him and that has remained so because he has constantly redefined his self and his deepest desires. In every man's work there is a possible tension between the individual's direction and that imposed by institutions and society. Rogers's career is a good but unusual example of a person whose self has never been imprisoned because he has rejected external definitions of who he was and what he was going to do. He admits that the course of his life was determined to some extent by intuition; he had enough self-knowledge to realize that those choices with which he was most comfortable were the ones that would be most fulfilling. Carl Rogers's career, in fact, resembles in miniature the archetypal American's search for identity. He began as the bright, young American innocent who wanted to help people. Because of his parents' values this resulted in his turning to religion. Later, he transferred his interests to psychology, but underwent a period of disillusionment with the established theories in that field, experiencing self-doubt and the pain of alienation from established authority. He decided that all systems of psychotherapy are subject to challenge and that one should adhere slavishly to none. A researcher accepting this idea will be subject to much painful reorganization of concepts and methods, but Rogers feels that such reorganizations are the essence of learning. Thus, in this article, we can share the satisfaction of a man who can look back on a life's work that never stagnated.

Rogers's attitude to his work is highly appealing because of his frankly emotional bias. Brought up by parents who held a strong belief in the virtue of "work" and were undemonstrative and "very controlling of (their children's) behavior," it was probably relatively easy for Rogers to become a fine worker, though difficult and painful to achieve this openness as a person. If family values inhibited him in the full exercise of feelings or the senses, he was able, at least, to use his strong work ethic in the field of psychology to help others do so.

Rogers's gently assertive, nondefensive tone reflects a sense of benevolent power and self-confidence attained by one who has broken through his defenses and found and accepted his inner self. The excitement of reading Rogers is not that he is a therapist, but that he is a therapist and a person, a remarkably whole person for a man of such professional success (which usually implies a very narrow focus). One feels from his writing that he would never mechanically apply psychological theory to his patients, but that he would deliberately emphasize the warmth of the personal relationship that develops in the therapist's office. Rogers feels that in such a favorable psychological climate, a "process of becoming" can take place, "that here the individual drops one after another the defensive masks with which he has faced life; that he experiences fully the hidden aspects of himself; that he discovers in these experiences the stranger who has been living behind these masks, the stranger who is himself." The same impulse is behind all his "significant learnings" in this section—to release in us a strong sense of our own potential and to facilitate human communication.

"This is Me"
The Development of My Professional Thinking and Personal Philosophy

This chapter combines two very personal talks. Five years ago I was asked to speak to the senior class at Brandeis University to present, not my ideas of psychotherapy, but myself. How had I come to think the thoughts I had? How had I come to be the person I am? I found this a very thought-provoking invitation, and I endeavored to meet the request of these students. During this past year the Student Union Forum Committee at Wisconsin made a somewhat similar request. They asked me to speak in a personal vein on their "Last Lecture" series, in which it is assumed that, for reasons unspecified, the professor is giving his last lecture and therefore giving quite personally of himself. (It is an intriguing comment on our educational system that it is assumed that only under the most dire circumstances would a professor reveal himself in any personal way.) In this Wisconsin talk I expressed more fully than in the first one the personal learnings or philosophical themes which have come to have meaning for me. In the current chapter I have woven together both of these talks, trying to retain something of the informal character which they had in their initial presentation.

The response to each of these talks has made me realize how hungry people are to know something of the person who is speaking to them or teaching them. Consequently I have set this chapter first in the book in the hope that it will convey something of me, and thus give more context and meaning to the chapters which follow.

I have been informed that what I am expected to do in speaking to this group is to assume that my topic is "This is Me." I feel various reactions to such an invitation, but one that I would like to mention is that I feel honored and flattered that any group wants, in a personal sense, to know who I am. I can assure you it is a unique and challenging sort of invitation, and I shall try to give to this honest question as honest an answer as I can.

So, who am I? I am a psychologist whose primary interest, for many years, has been in psychotherapy. What does that mean? I don't intend to bore you with a long account of my work, but I would like to take a few paragraphs from the preface to my book, *Client-Centered*

Therapy, to indicate in a subjective way what it means to me. I was trying to give the reader some feeling for the subject matter of the volume, and I wrote as follows. "What is this book about? Let me try to give an answer which may, to some degree, convey the living experience that this book is intended to be.

"This book is about the suffering and the hope, the anxiety and the satisfaction, with which each therapist's counseling room is filled. It is about the uniqueness of the relationship each therapist forms with each client, and equally about the common elements which we discover in all these relationships. This book is about the highly personal experiences of each one of us. It is about a client in my office who sits there by the corner of the desk, struggling to be himself, yet deathly afraid of being himself—striving to see his experience as it is, wanting to *be* that experience, and yet deeply fearful of the prospect. This book is about me, as I sit there with that client, facing him, participating in that struggle as deeply and sensitively as I am able. It is about me as I try to perceive his experience, and the meaning and the feeling and the taste and the flavor that it has for him. It is about me as I bemoan my very human fallibility in understanding that client, and the occasional failures to see life as it appears to him, failures which fall like heavy objects across the intricate, delicate web of growth which is taking place. It is about me as I rejoice at the privilege of being a midwife to a new personality—as I stand by with awe at the emergence of a self, a person, as I see a birth process in which I have had an important and facilitating part. It is about both the client and me as we regard with wonder the potent and orderly forces which are evident in this whole experience, forces which seem deeply rooted in the universe as a whole. The book is, I believe, about life, as life vividly reveals itself in the therapeutic process—with its blind power and its tremendous capacity for destruction, but with its overbalancing thrust toward growth, if the opportunity for growth is provided."

Perhaps that will give you some picture of what I do and the way I feel about it. I presume you may also wonder how I came to engage in that occupation, and some of the decisions and choices, conscious and unconscious, which were made along the way. Let me see if I can give you some of the psychological highlights of my autobiography, particularly as it seems to relate to my professional life.

MY EARLY YEARS

I was brought up in a home marked by close family ties, a very strict and uncompromising religious and ethical atmosphere, and what amounted to a worship of the virtue of hard work. I came along as the fourth of six children. My parents cared a great deal for us, and had our welfare almost constantly in mind. They were also, in many subtle and affectionate ways, very controlling of our behavior. It was assumed by them and accepted by me that we were different from other people —no alcoholic beverages, no dancing, cards or theater, very little social life, and *much* work. I have a hard time convincing my children that even carbonated beverages had a faintly sinful aroma, and I remember my slight feeling of wickedness when I had my first bottle of "pop." We had good times together within the family, but we did not mix. So I was a pretty solitary boy, who read incessantly, and went all through high school with only two dates.

When I was twelve my parents bought a farm and we made our home there. The reasons were twofold. My father, having become a prosperous business man, wanted it for a hobby. More important, I believe, was the fact that it seemed to my parents that a growing adolescent family should be removed from the "temptations" of suburban life.

Here I developed two interests which have probably had some real bearing on my later work. I became fascinated by the great night-flying moths (Gene Stratton-Porter's books were then in vogue) and I became an authority on the gorgeous Luna, Polyphemus, Cecropia and other moths which inhabited our woods. I laboriously bred the moths in captivity, reared the caterpillars, kept the cocoons over the long winter months, and in general realized some of the joys and frustrations of the scientist as he tries to observe nature.

My father was determined to operate his new farm on a scientific basis, so he bought many books on scientific agriculture. He encouraged his boys to have independent and profitable ventures of our own, so my brothers and I had a flock of chickens, and at one time or other reared from infancy lambs, pigs and calves. In doing this I became a student of scientific agriculture, and have only realized in recent years what a fundamental feeling for science I gained in that way. There was no one to tell me that Morison's *Feeds and Feeding* was not a book for a fourteen-year-old, so I ploughed through its hundreds of pages, learning how experiments were conducted—how control groups were matched with experimental groups, how conditions were held constant by randomizing procedures, so that the influence of a given food on meat production or milk production could be established. I learned how difficult it is to test an hypothesis. I acquired a knowledge of and a respect for the methods of science in a field of practical endeavor.

COLLEGE AND GRADUATE EDUCATION

I started in college at Wisconsin in the field of agriculture. One of the things I remember best was the vehement statement of an agronomy professor in regard to the learning and use of facts. He stressed the futility of an encyclopedic knowledge for its own sake, and wound up with the injunction, "Don't be a damned ammunition wagon; be a rifle!"

During my first two college years my professional goal changed, as the result of some emotionally charged student religious conferences, from that of a scientific agriculturist to that of the ministry—a slight shift! I changed from agriculture to history, believing this would be a better preparation.

In my junior year I was selected as one of a dozen students from this country to go to China for an international World Student Christian Federation Conference. This was a most important experience for me. It was 1922, four years after the close of World War I. I saw how bitterly the French and Germans still hated each other, even though as individuals they seemed very likable. I was forced to stretch my thinking, to realize that sincere and honest people could believe in very divergent religious doctrines. In major ways I for the first time emancipated myself from the religious thinking of my parents, and realized that I could not go along with them. This independence of thought caused great pain and stress in our relationship, but looking back on it I believe that here, more than at any other one time, I became an independent person. Of course there was much revolt and rebellion in my attitude during that period, but the essential split was achieved during the six months I was on this trip to the Orient, and hence was thought through away from the influence of home.

Although this is an account of elements which influenced my professional development rather than my personal growth, I wish to mention very briefly one profoundly important factor in my personal life. It was at about the time of my trip to China that I fell in love with a lovely girl whom I had known for many years, even in childhood, and we were married, with the very reluctant consent of our parents, as soon as I finished college, in order that we could go to graduate school together. I cannot be very objective about this, but her steady and sustaining love and companionship during all the years since has been a most important and enriching factor in my life.

I chose to go to Union Theological Seminary, the most liberal in the country at that time (1924), to prepare for religious work. I have never regretted the two years there. I came in contact with some great scholars and teachers, notably Dr. A. C. McGiffert, who believed devoutly in freedom of inquiry, and in following the truth no matter where it led.

Knowing universities and graduate schools as I do now—knowing their rules and their rigidities—I am truly astonished at one very significant experience at Union. A group of us felt that ideas were being fed to us, whereas we wished primarily to explore our own questions and doubts, and find out where they led. We petitioned the administration that we be allowed to set up a seminar for credit, a seminar with no instructor, where the curriculum would be composed of our own questions. The seminary was understandably perplexed by this, but they granted our petition! The only restriction was that in the interests of the institution a young instructor was to sit in on the seminar, but would take no part in it unless we wished him to be active.

I suppose it is unnecessary to add that this seminar was deeply satisfying and clarifying. I feel that it moved me a long way toward a philosophy of life which was my own. The majority of the members of that group, in thinking their way through the questions they had raised, thought themselves right out of religious work. I was one. I felt that questions as to the meaning of life, and the possibility of the constructive improvement of life for individuals, would probably always interest me, but I could not work in a field where I would be required to believe in some specified religious doctrine. My beliefs had already changed tremendously, and might continue to change. It seemed to me it would be a horrible thing to *have* to profess a set of beliefs, in order to remain in one's profession. I wanted to find a field in which I could be sure my freedom of thought would not be limited.

BECOMING A PSYCHOLOGIST

But what field? I had been attracted, at Union, by the courses and lectures on psychological and psychiatric work, which were then beginning to develop. Goodwin Watson, Harrison Elliott, Marian Kenworthy all contributed to this interest. I began to take more courses at Teachers' College, Columbia University, across the street from Union Seminary. I took work in philosophy of education with William H. Kilpatrick, and found him a great teacher. I began practical clinical work with children under Leta Hollingworth, a sensitive and practical person. I found myself drawn to child guidance work, so that gradually, with very little painful readjustment, I shifted over into the field of child guidance, and began to think of myself as a clinical psychologist. It was a step I eased into, with relatively little clearcut conscious choice, rather just following the activities which interested me.

While I was at Teachers' College I applied for, and was granted a fellowship or internship at the then new Institute for Child Guidance, sponsored by the Commonwealth Fund. I have often been grateful that I was there during the first year. The organization was in a chaotic beginning state, but this meant that one could do what he wanted to do. I soaked up the dynamic Freudian views of the staff, which included David Levy and Lawson Lowrey, and found them in great conflict with the rigorous, scientific, coldly objective, statistical point of view then prevalent at Teachers' College. Looking back, I believe the necessity of resolving that conflict in me was a most valuable learning experience. At the time

I felt I was functioning in two completely different worlds, "and never the twain shall meet."

By the end of this internship it was highly important to me that I obtain a job to support my growing family, even though my doctorate was not completed. Positions were not plentiful, and I remember the relief and exhilaration I felt when I found one. I was employed as psychologist in the Child Study Department of the Society for the Prevention of Cruelty to Children, in Rochester, New York. There were three psychologists in this department, and my salary was $2,900 per year.

I look back at the acceptance of that position with amusement and some amazement. The reason I was so pleased was that it was a chance to do the work I wanted to do. That, by any reasonable criterion it was a dead-end street professionally, that I would be isolated from professional contacts, that the salary was not good even by the standards of that day, seems not to have occurred to me, as nearly as I can recall. I think I have always had a feeling that if I was given some opportunity to do the thing I was most interested in doing, everything else would somehow take care of itself.

THE ROCHESTER YEARS

The next twelve years in Rochester were exceedingly valuable ones. For at least the first eight of these years, I was completely immersed in carrying on practical psychological service, diagnosing and planning for the delinquent and underprivileged children who were sent to us by the courts and agencies, and in many instances carrying on "treatment interviews." It was a period of relative professional isolation, where my only concern was in trying to be more effective with our clients. We had to live with our failures as well as our successes, so that we were forced to learn. There was only one criterion in regard to any method of dealing with these children and their parents, and that was, "Does it work? Is it effective?" I found I began increasingly to formulate my own views out of my everyday working experience.

Three significant illustrations come to mind, all small, but important to me at the time. It strikes me that they are all instances of disillusionment—with an authority, with materials, with myself.

In my training I had been fascinated by Dr. William Healy's writings, indicating that delinquency was often based upon sexual conflict, and that if this conflict was uncovered, the delinquency ceased. In my first or second year at Rochester I worked very hard with a youthful pyromaniac who had an unaccountable impulse to set fires. Interviewing him day after day in the detention home, I gradually traced back his desire to a sexual impulse regarding masturbation. Eureka! The case was solved. However, when placed on probation, he again got into the same difficulty.

I remember the jolt I felt. Healy might be wrong. Perhaps I was learning something Healy didn't know. Somehow this incident impressed me with the possibility that there were mistakes in authoritative teachings, and that there was still new knowledge to discover.

The second naïve discovery was of a different sort. Soon after coming to Rochester I led a discussion group on interviewing. I discovered a published account of an interview with a parent, approximately verbatim, in which the case worker was shrewd, insightful, clever, and led the interview quite quickly to the heart of the difficulty. I was happy to use it as an illustration of good interviewing technique.

Several years later, I had a similar assignment and remembered this excellent material. I hunted it up again and re-read it. I was appalled. Now it seemed to me to be a clever legalistic type of questioning by the interviewer which convicted this parent of her unconscious motives, and wrung from her an admission of her guilt. I now knew from my experience that such an interview would not be of any lasting help to the parent or the child. It made me realize that I was moving away from any approach which was coercive or pushing in clinical relationships, not for philosophical reasons, but because such approaches were never more than superficially effective.

The third incident occurred several years later. I had learned to be more subtle and patient in interpreting a client's behavior to him, attempting to time it in a gentle fashion which would gain acceptance. I had been working with a highly intelligent mother whose boy was something of a hellion. The problem was clearly her early rejection of the boy, but over many interviews I could not help her to this insight. I drew her out, I gently pulled together the evidence she had given, trying to help her see the pattern. But we got nowhere. Finally I gave up. I told her that it seemed we had both tried, but we had failed, and that we might as well give up our contacts. She agreed. So we concluded the interview, shook hands, and she walked to the door of the office. Then she turned and asked, "Do you ever take adults for counseling here?" When I replied in the affirmative, she said, "Well then, I would like some help." She came to the chair she had left, and began to pour out her despair about her marriage, her troubled relationship with her husband, her sense of failure and confusion, all very different from the sterile "case history" she had given before. Real therapy began then, and ultimately it was very successful.

This incident was one of a number which helped me to experience the fact—only fully realized later—that it is the *client* who knows what hurts, what directions to go, what problems are crucial, what experiences have been deeply buried. It began to occur to me that unless I had a need to demonstrate my own cleverness and learning, I would do better to rely upon the client for the direction of movement in the process.

PSYCHOLOGIST OR ?

During this period I began to doubt that I was a psychologist. The University of Rochester made it clear that the work I was doing was not psychology, and they had no interest in my teaching in the Psychology Department. I went to meetings of the American Psychological Association and found them full of papers on the learning processes of rats and laboratory experiments which seemed to me to have no relation to what I was doing. The psychiatric social workers, however, seemed to be talking my language, so I became active in the social work profession, moving up to local and even national offices. Only when the American Association for Applied Psychology was formed did I become really active as a psychologist.

I began to teach courses at the University on how to understand and deal with problem children, under the Department of Sociology. Soon the Department of Education wanted to classify these as education courses, also. [Before I left Rochester, the Department of Psychology, too, finally requested permission to list them, thus at last accepting me as a psychologist.] Simply describing these experiences makes me realize how stubbornly I have followed my own course, being relatively unconcerned with the question of whether I was going with my group or not.

Time does not permit to tell of the work of establishing a separate Guidance Center in Rochester, nor the battle with some of the psychiatric profession which was included. These were largely administrative struggles which did not have too much to do with the development of my ideas.

MY CHILDREN

It was during these Rochester years that my son and daughter grew through infancy and childhood, teaching me far more about individuals, their development, and their relationships, than I could ever have learned professionally. I don't feel I was a very good parent in their early years, but fortunately my wife was, and as time went on I believe I gradually became a better and more understanding parent. Certainly the privilege during these years and later, of being in relationship with two fine sensitive youngsters through all their childhood pleasure and pain, their adolescent assertiveness and difficulties, and on into their adult years and the beginning of their own families, has been a priceless one. I think my wife and I regard as one of the most satisfying achievements in which we have had a part, the fact that we can really communicate in a deep way with our grown-up children and their spouses, and they with us.

OHIO STATE YEARS

In 1940 I accepted a position at Ohio State University. I am sure the only reason I was considered was my book on the *Clinical Treatment of the Problem Child*, which I had squeezed out of vacations, and brief leaves of absence. To my surprise, and contrary to my expectation, they offered me a full professorship. I heartily recommend starting in the academic world at this level. I have often been grateful that I have never had to live through the frequently degrading competitive process of step-by-step promotion in university faculties, where individuals so frequently learn only one lesson—not to stick their necks out.

It was in trying to teach what I had learned about treatment and counseling to graduate students at Ohio State University that I first began to realize that I had perhaps developed a distinctive point of view of my own, out of my experience. When I tried to crystallize some of these ideas, and present them in a paper at the University of Minnesota in December 1940, I found the reactions were very strong. It was my first experience of the fact that a new idea of mine, which to me can seem all shiny and glowing with potentiality, can to another person be a great threat. And to find myself the center of criticism, of arguments pro and con, was disconcerting and made me doubt and question. Nevertheless I felt I had something to contribute, and wrote the manuscript of *Counseling and Psychotherapy*, setting forth what I felt to be a somewhat more effective orientation to therapy.

Here again I realize with some amusement how little I have cared about being "realistic." When I submitted the manuscript, the publisher thought it was interesting and new, but wondered what classes would use it. I replied that I knew of only two—a course I was teaching and one in another university. The publisher felt I had made a grave mistake in not writing a text which would fit courses already being given. He was very dubious that he could sell 2,000 copies, which would be necessary to break even. It was only when I said I would take it to another publisher that he decided to make the gamble. I don't know which of us has been more surprised at its sales—70,000 copies to date and still continuing.

RECENT YEARS

I believe that from this point to the present time my professional life—five years at Ohio State, twelve years at the University of Chicago, and four years at the University of Wisconsin—is quite well documented by what I have written. I will very briefly stress two or three points which have some significance for me.

I have learned to live in increasingly deep therapeutic relationships with an ever-widening range of clients. This can be and has been extremely rewarding. It can be and has been at times very frightening, when a deeply disturbed person seems to demand that I must be more than I am, in order to meet his need. Certainly the carrying on of therapy is something which demands continuing personal growth on the part of the therapist, and this is sometimes painful, even though in the long run rewarding.

I would also mention the steadily increasing importance which research has come to have for me. Therapy is the experience in which I can let myself go subjectively. Research is the experience in which I can stand off and try to view this rich subjective experience with objectivity, applying all the elegant methods of science to determine whether I have been deceiving myself. The conviction grows in me that we shall discover laws of personality and behavior which are as significant for human progress or human understanding as the law of gravity or the laws of thermodynamics.

In the last two decades I have become somewhat more accustomed to being fought over, but the reactions to my ideas continue to surprise me. From my point of view, I have felt that I have always put forth my thoughts in a tentative manner, to be accepted or rejected by the reader or the student. But at different times and places psychologists, counselors, and educators have been moved to great wrath, scorn and criticism by my views. As this furor has tended to die down in these fields it has in recent years been renewed among psychiatrists, some of whom sense, in my way of working, a deep threat to many of their most cherished and unquestioned principles. And perhaps the storms of criticism are more than matched by the damage done by uncritical and unquestioning "disciples"—individuals who have acquired something of a new point of view for themselves and have gone forth to do battle with all and sundry, using as weapons both inaccurate and accurate understandings of me and my work. I have found it difficult to know, at times, whether I have been hurt more by my "friends" or my enemies.

Perhaps partly because of the troubling business of being struggled over, I have come to value highly the privilege of getting away, of being alone. It has seemed to me that my most fruitful periods of work are the times when I have been able to get completely away from what others think, from professional expectations and daily demands, and gain perspective on what I am doing. My wife and I have found isolated hideaways in Mexico and in the Caribbean where no one knows I am a psychologist; where painting, swimming, snorkeling, and capturing some of the scenery in color photography are my major activities. Yet in these spots, where no more than two to four hours a day goes for professional work, I have made most of whatever advances I have made in the last few years. I prize the privilege of being alone.

SOME SIGNIFICANT LEARNINGS

There, in very brief outline, are some of the externals of my professional life. But I would like to take you inside, to tell you some of the things I have learned from the thousands of hours I have spent working intimately with individuals in personal distress.

I would like to make it very plain that these are learnings which have significance for *me*. I do not know whether they would hold true for you. I have no desire to present them as a guide for anyone else. Yet I have found that when another person has been willing to tell me something of his inner directions this has been of value to me, if only in sharpening my realization that my directions are different. So it is in that spirit that I offer the learnings which follow. In each case I believe they became a part of my actions and inner convictions long before I realized them consciously. They are certainly scattered learnings, and incomplete. I can only say that they are and have been very important to me. I continually learn and relearn them. I frequently fail to act in terms of them, but later I wish that I had. Frequently I fail to see a new situation as one in which some of these learnings might apply.

They are not fixed. They keep changing. Some seem to be acquiring a stronger emphasis, others are perhaps less important to me than at one time, but they are all, to me, significant.

I will introduce each learning with a phrase or sentence which gives something of its personal meaning. Then I will elaborate on it a bit. There is not much organization to what follows except that the first learnings have to do mostly with relationships to others. There follow some that fall in the realm of personal values and convictions.

I might start off these several statements of significant learnings with a negative item. *In my relationships with persons I have found that it does not help, in the long run, to act as though I were something that I am not.* It does not help to act calm and pleasant when actually I am angry and critical. It does not help to act as though I know the answers when I do not. It does not help to act as though I were a loving person if actually, at the moment, I am hostile. It does not help for me to act as though I were full of assurance, if actually I am frightened and unsure. Even on a very simple level I have found that this statement seems to hold. It does not help for me to act as though I were well when I feel ill.

What I am saying here, put in another way, is that I have not found it to be helpful or effective in my relationships with other people to try to maintain a façade; to act in one way on the surface when I am experiencing something quite different underneath. It does not, I believe, make me helpful in my attempts to build up constructive relationships with other individuals. I would want to make it clear that while I feel I have learned this to be true, I have by no means adequately profited from it. In fact, it seems to me that most of the mistakes I make in personal relationships, most of the times in which I fail to be of help to other individuals, can be accounted for in terms of the fact that I have, for some defensive reason, behaved in one way at a surface level, while in reality my feelings run in a contrary direction.

A second learning might be stated as follows—*I find I am more effective when I can listen acceptantly to myself, and can be myself.* I feel that over the years I have learned to become more adequate in listening to *myself*; so that I know, somewhat more adequately than I used to, what I am feeling at any given moment—to be able to realize I *am* angry, or that I *do* feel rejecting toward this person; or that I feel very full of warmth and affection for this individual; or that I am bored and uninterested in what is going on; or that I am eager to understand this individual or that I am anxious and fearful in my relationship to this person. All of these diverse attitudes are feelings which I think I can listen to in myself. One way of putting this is that I feel I have become more adequate in letting myself *be* what I *am*. It becomes easier for me to accept myself as a decidedly imperfect person, who by no means functions at all times in the way in which I would like to function.

This must seem to some like a very strange direction in which to move. It seems to me to have value because the curious paradox is that when I accept myself as I am, then I change. I believe that I have learned this from my clients as well as within my own experience—that we cannot change, we cannot move away from what we are, until we thoroughly *accept* what we are. Then change seems to come about almost unnoticed.

Another result which seems to grow out of being myself is that relationships then become real. Real relationships have an exciting way of being vital and meaningful. If I can accept the fact that I am annoyed at or bored by this client or this student, then I am also much more likely to be able to accept his feelings in response. I can also accept the changed experience and the changed feelings which are then likely to occur in me and in him. Real relationships tend to change rather than to remain static.

So I find it effective to let myself be what I am in my attitudes; to know when I have reached my limit of endurance or of tolerance, and to accept that as a fact; to know when I desire to mold or manipulate people, and to accept that as a fact in myself. I would like to be as acceptant of these feelings as of feelings of warmth, interest, permissiveness, kindness, understanding, which are also a very real part of me. It is when I do accept all these attitudes as a fact, as a part of me, that my relationship with the other person then becomes what it is, and is able to grow and change most readily.

I come now to a central learning which has had a great deal of significance for me. I can state this learning as follows: *I have found it of enormous value when I can permit myself to understand another person.* The way in which I have worded this statement may seem strange to you. Is it necessary to *permit* oneself to understand another? I think that it is. Our first reaction to most of the statements which we hear from other people is an immediate evaluation, or judgment, rather than an understanding of it. When someone expresses some feeling or attitude or belief, our tendency is, almost immediately, to feel "That's right;" or "That's stupid;" "That's abnormal;" "That's unreasonable;" "That's incorrect;" "That's not nice." Very rarely do we permit ourselves to *understand* precisely what the meaning of his statement is to him. I believe this is because understanding is risky. If I let myself really understand another person, I might be changed by that understanding. And we all fear change. So as I say, it is not an easy thing to permit oneself to understand an individual, to enter thoroughly and completely and empathically into his frame of reference. It is also a rare thing.

To understand is enriching in a double way. I find when I am working with clients in distress, that to understand the bizarre world of a psychotic individual, or to understand and sense the attitudes of a person who feels that life is too tragic to bear, or to understand a man who feels that he is a worthless and inferior individual—each of these understandings somehow enriches me. I learn from these experiences in ways that change me, that make me a different and, I think, a more responsive person. Even more important perhaps, is the fact that my understanding of these individuals permits them to change. It permits them to accept their own fears and bizarre thoughts and tragic feelings and discouragements, as well as their moments of courage and kindness and love and sensitivity. And it is their experience as well as mine that when someone fully understands those feelings, this enables them to accept those feelings in themselves. Then they find both the feelings and themselves changing. Whether it is understanding a woman who feels that very literally she has a hook in her head by which others lead her about, or understanding a man who feels that no one is as lonely, no one is as separated from others as he, I find these understandings to be of value to me. But also, and even more importantly, to be understood has a very positive value to these individuals.

Here is another learning which has had importance for me. *I have found it enriching to open channels whereby others can communicate their feelings, their private perceptual worlds, to me.* Because understanding is rewarding, I would like to reduce the barriers between others and me, so that they can, if they wish, reveal themselves more fully.

In the therapeutic relationship there are a number of ways by which I can make it easier for the client to communicate himself. I can by my own attitudes create a safety in the relationship which makes such communication more possible. A sensitiveness of understanding which sees him as he is to himself, and accepts him as having those perceptions and feelings, helps too.

But as a teacher also I have found that I am enriched when I can open channels through which others can share themselves with me. So I try, often not too successfully, to create a climate in the classroom where feelings can be expressed, where people can differ—with each other and with the instructor. I have also frequently asked for "reaction sheets" from students—in which they can express themselves individually and personally regarding the course. They can tell of the way it is or is not meeting their needs, they can express their feelings regarding the instructor, or can tell of the personal difficulties they are having in relation to the course. These reaction sheets have no relation whatsoever to their grade. Sometimes the same sessions of a course are experienced in diametrically opposite ways. One student says, "My feeling is one of indefinable revulsion with the tone of this class." Another, a foreign student, speaking of the same week of the same course says, "Our class follows the best, fruitful and scientific way of learning. But for people who have been taught for a long, long time, as we have, by the lecture type, authoritative method, this new procedure is ununderstandable. People like us are conditioned to hear the instructor, to keep passively our notes and memorize his reading assignments for the exams. There is no need to say that it takes long time for people to get rid of their habits regardless of whether or not their habits are sterile, infertile and barren." To open myself to these sharply different feelings has been a deeply rewarding thing.

I have found the same thing true in groups where I am the administrator, or perceived as the leader. I wish to reduce the need for fear or defensiveness, so that people can communicate their feelings freely. This has been most exciting, and has led me to a whole new view of what administration can be. But I cannot expand on that here.

There is another very important learning which has come to me in my counseling work. I can voice this learning very briefly. *I have found it highly rewarding when I can accept another person.*

I have found that truly to accept another person and his feelings is by no means an easy thing, any more than is understanding. Can I really permit another person to feel hostile toward me? Can I accept his anger as a real and legitimate part of himself? Can I accept him when he views life and its problems in a way quite different from mine? Can I accept him when he feels very positively toward me, admiring me and wanting to model himself after me? All this is involved in acceptance, and it does not come easy. I believe that it is an increasingly common pattern in our culture for each one of us to believe, "Every other person must feel and think and believe the same as I do." We find it very hard to permit our children or our parents or our spouses to feel differently than we do about particular issues or problems. We cannot permit our clients or our students to differ from us or to utilize their experience in their own individual ways. On a national scale, we cannot permit another nation to think or feel differently than we do. Yet it has come to seem to me that this separateness of individuals, the right of each individual to utilize his experience in his own way and to discover his own meanings in it,—this is one of the most priceless potentialities of life. Each person is an island unto himself, in a very real sense; and he can only build bridges to other islands if he is first of all willing to be himself and permitted to be himself. So I find that when I can accept another person, which means specifically accepting the feelings and attitudes and beliefs that he has as a real and vital part of him, then I am assisting him to become a person: and there seems to me great value in this.

The next learning I want to state may be difficult to communicate. It is this. *The more I am open to the realities in me and in the other person, the less do I find myself wishing to rush in to "fix things."* As I try to listen to myself and the experiencing going on in me, and the more I try to extend that same listening attitude to another person, the more respect I feel for the complex processes of life. So I become less and less inclined to hurry in to fix things, to set goals, to mold people, to manipulate and push them in the way that I would like them to go. I am much more content simply to be myself and to let another person be himself. I know very well that this must seem like a strange, almost an Oriental point of view. What is life for if we are not going to do things to people? What is life for if we are not going to mold them to our purposes? What is life for if we are not going to teach them the things that *we* think they should learn? What is life for if we are not going to make them think and feel as we do? How can anyone hold such an inactive point of view as the one I am expressing? I am sure that attitudes such as these must be a part of the reaction of many of you.

Yet the paradoxical aspect of my experience is that the more I am simply willing to be myself, in all this complexity of life and the more I am willing to understand and accept the realities in myself and in the other person, the more change seems to be stirred up. It is a very paradoxical thing—that to the degree that each one of us is willing to be himself, then he finds not only himself changing; but he finds that other people to whom he relates are also changing. At least this is a very vivid part of my experience, and one of the deepest things I think I have learned in my personal and professional life.

Let me turn now to some other learnings which are less concerned with relationships, and have more to do with my own actions and values. The first of these is very brief. *I can trust my experience.*

One of the basic things which I was a long time in realizing, and which I am still learning, is that when an activity *feels* as though it is valuable or worth doing, it *is* worth doing. Put another way, I have learned that my total organismic sensing of a situation is more trustworthy than my intellect.

All of my professional life I have been going in directions which others thought were foolish, and about which I have had many doubts myself. But I have never regretted moving in directions which "felt right," even though I have often felt lonely or foolish at the time.

I have found that when I have trusted some inner non-intellectual sensing, I have discovered wisdom in the move. In fact I have found that when I have followed one of these unconventional paths because it felt right or true, then in five or ten years many of my colleagues have joined me, and I no longer need to feel alone in it.

As I gradually come to trust my total reactions more deeply, I find that I can use them to guide my thinking. I have come to have more respect for those vague thoughts which occur in me from time to time, which *feel* as though they were significant. I am inclined to think that these unclear thoughts or hunches will lead me to important areas. I think of it as trusting the totality of my experience, which I have learned to suspect is wiser than my intellect. It is fallible I am sure, but I believe it to be less fallible than my conscious mind alone. My attitude is very well expressed by Max Weber, the artist, when he says, "In carrying on my own humble creative effort, I depend greatly upon that which I do not yet know, and upon that which I have not yet done."

Very closely related to this learning is a corollary that, *evaluation by others is not a guide for me.* The judgments of others, while they are to be listened to, and taken into account for what they are, can never be a guide for me. This has been a hard thing to learn. I remember how shaken I was, in the early days, when a scholarly thoughtful man who seemed to me a much more competent and knowledgeable psychologist than I, told me what a mistake I was making by getting interested in psychotherapy. It could never lead anywhere, and as a psychologist I would not even have the opportunity to practice it.

In later years it has sometimes jolted me a bit to learn that I am, in the eyes of some others, a fraud, a person practicing medicine without a license, the author of a very superficial and damaging sort of therapy, a power seeker, a mystic, etc. And I have been equally disturbed by equally extreme praise. But I have not been too much concerned because I have come to feel that only one person (at least in my lifetime, and perhaps ever) can know whether what I am doing is honest, thorough, open, and sound, or false and defensive and unsound, and I am that person. I am happy to get all sorts of evidence regarding what I am doing and criticism (both friendly and hostile) and praise (both sincere and fawning) are a part of such evidence. But to weigh this evidence and to determine its meaning and usefulness is a task I cannot relinquish to anyone else.

In view of what I have been saying the next learning will probably not surprise you. *Experience is, for me, the highest authority.* The touchstone of validity is my own experience. No other person's ideas, and none of my own ideas, are as authoritative as my experience. It is to experience that I must return again and again, to discover a closer approximation to truth as it is in the process of becoming in me.

Neither the Bible nor the prophets—neither Freud nor research— neither the revelations of God nor man—can take precedence over my own direct experience.

My experience is the more authoritative as it becomes more primary, to use the semanticist's term. Thus the hierarchy of experience would be most authoritative at its lowest level. If I read a theory of psychotherapy, and if I formulate a theory of psychotherapy based on my work with clients, and if I also have a direct experience of psychotherapy with a client, then the degree of authority increases in the order in which I have listed these experiences.

My experience is not authoritative because it is infallible. It is the basis of authority because it can always be checked in new primary ways. In this way its frequent error or fallibility is always open to correction.

Now another personal learning. *I enjoy the discovering of order in experience.* It seems inevitable that I seek for the meaning or the orderliness or lawfulness in any large body of experience. It is this kind of curiosity, which I find it very satisfying to pursue, which has led me to each of the major formulations I have made. It led me to search for the orderliness in all the conglomeration of things clinicians did for children, and out of that came my book on *The Clinical Treatment of the Problem Child.* It led me to formulate the general principles which seemed to be operative in psychotherapy, and that has led to several books and many articles. It has led me into research to test the various types of lawfulness which I feel I have encountered in my experience. It has enticed me to construct theories to bring together the orderliness of that which has already been experienced and to project this order forward into new and unexplored realms where it may be further tested.

Thus I have come to see both scientific research and the process of theory construction as being aimed toward the inward ordering of significant experience. Research is the persistent disciplined effort to make sense and order out of the phenomena of subjective experience. It is justified because it is satisfying to perceive the world as having order, and because rewarding results often ensue when one understands the orderly relationships which appear in nature.

So I have come to recognize that the reason I devote myself to research, and to the building of theory, is to satisfy a need for perceiving order and meaning, a subjective need which exists in me. I have, at times, carried on research for other reasons—to satisfy others, to convince opponents and sceptics, to get ahead professionally, to gain prestige, and for other unsavory reasons. These errors in judgment and activity have only served to convince me more deeply that there is only one sound reason for pursuing scientific activities, and that is to satisfy a need for meaning which is in me.

Another learning which cost me much to recognize, can be stated in four words. *The facts are friendly.*

It has interested me a great deal that most psychotherapists, especially the psychoanalysts, have steadily refused to make any scientific investigation of their therapy, or to permit others to do this. I can understand this reaction because I have felt it. Especially in our early investigations I can well remember the anxiety of waiting to see how the findings came out. Suppose our hypotheses were *dis*proved! Suppose we were mistaken in our views! Suppose our opinions were not justified! At such times, as I look back, it seems to me that I regarded the facts as potential enemies, as possible bearers of disaster. I have perhaps been slow in coming to realize that the facts are *always* friendly. Every bit of evidence one can acquire, in any area, leads one that much closer to what is true. And being closer to the truth can never be a harmful or dangerous or unsatisfying thing. So while I still hate to readjust my thinking, still hate to give up old ways of perceiving and conceptualizing, yet at some deeper level I have, to a considerable degree, come to realize that these painful reorganizations are what is known as *learning*, and that though painful they always lead to a more satisfying because somewhat more accurate way of seeing life. Thus at the present time one of the most enticing areas for thought and speculation is an area where several of my pet ideas have *not* been upheld by the evidence. I feel if I can only puzzle my way through this problem that I will find a much more satisfying approximation to the truth. I feel sure the facts will be my friends.

Somewhere here I want to bring in a learning which has been most rewarding, because it makes me feel so deeply akin to others. I can word it this way. *What is most personal is most general.* There have been times when in talking with students or staff, or in my writing, I have expressed myself in ways so personal that I have felt I was expressing an attitude which it was probable no one else could understand, because it was so uniquely my own. Two written examples of this are the Preface to *Client-Centered Therapy* (regarded as most unsuitable by the publishers), and an article on "Persons or Science." In these instances I have almost invariably found that the very feeling which has seemed to me most private, most personal, and hence most incomprehensible by others, has turned out to be an expression for which there is a resonance in many other people. It has led me to believe that what is most personal and unique in each one of us is probably the very element which would, if it were shared or expressed, speak most deeply to others. This has helped me to understand artists and poets as people who have dared to express the unique in themselves.

There is one deep learning which is perhaps basic to all of the things I have said thus far. It has been forced upon me by more than twenty-five years of trying to be helpful to individuals in personal distress. It is simply this. *It has been my experience that persons have a basically positive direction.* In my deepest contacts with individuals in therapy, even those whose troubles are most disturbing, whose behavior has been most anti-social, whose feelings seem most abnormal, I find this to be true. When I can sensitively understand the feelings which they are expressing, when I am able to accept them as separate persons in their own right, then I find that they tend to move in certain directions. And what are these directions in which they tend to move? The words which I believe are most truly descriptive are words such as positive, constructive, moving toward self-actualization, growing toward maturity, growing toward socialization. I have come to feel that the more fully the individual is understood and accepted, the more he tends to drop the false fronts with which he has been meeting life, and the more he tends to move in a direction which is forward.

I would not want to be misunderstood on this. I do not have a Pollyanna view of human nature. I am quite aware that out of defensiveness and inner fear individuals can and do behave in ways which are incredibly cruel, horribly destructive, immature, regressive, anti-social, hurtful. Yet one of the most refreshing and invigorating parts of my experience is to work with such individuals and to discover the strongly positive directional tendencies which exist in them, as in all of us, at the deepest levels.

Let me bring this long list to a close with one final learning which can be stated very briefly. *Life, at its best, is a flowing, changing process in which nothing is fixed.* In my clients and in myself I find that when life is richest and most rewarding it is a flowing process. To experience this is both fascinating and a little frightening. I find I am at my best when I can let the flow of my experience carry me, in a direction which appears to be forward, toward goals of which I am but dimly aware.

In thus floating with the complex stream of my experiencing, and in trying to understand its ever-changing complexity, it should be evident that there are no fixed points. When I am thus able to be in process, it is clear that there can be no closed system of beliefs, no unchanging set of principles which I hold. Life is guided by a changing understanding of and interpretation of my experience. It is always in process of becoming.

I trust it is clear now why there is no philosophy or belief or set of principles which I could encourage or persuade others to have or hold. I can only try to live by *my* interpretation of the current meaning of *my* experience, and try to give others the permission and freedom to develop their own inward freedom and thus their own meaningful interpretation of their own experience.

If there is such a thing as truth, this free individual process of search should, I believe, converge toward it. And in a limited way, this is also what I seem to have experienced.

QUESTIONS

1. Which of Carl Rogers's personal qualities might have come from his family background? What psychological problems that could be considered typically American might have come from the same source?
2. What fortunate events in Carl Rogers's youth enabled him to widen his perspectives? Could he be considered a member of the privileged class in America?
3. What is "romantic" about Carl Rogers's view of his work? In what way could he be said to be both romantic and realistic about it?
4. There is virtually no irony in Rogers's short autobiography. Why would irony be inappropriate to his purposes? To what criticism does he make himself vulnerable by his lack of self-irony?

GREGORY CORSO

GREGORY CORSO'S (b. 1930) first book of verse, *The Vestal Lady on Brattle,* was brought out in Cambridge, Massachusetts, in 1955. Later, in New York and San Francisco, Corso was associated with Jack Kerouac and Allen Ginsberg in the rise of the "Beat" movement. His famous "Bomb" poem was first published in 1958. "Marriage" appeared in a volume of poetry entitled *The Happy Birthday of Death* in 1960. Other volumes include *Gasoline* (1958), *Long Live Man* (1962), and *Elegiac Feelings American* (1970). He has also published a novel, *The American Express* (1961).

Like Ginsberg and Kerouac, Corso tries to recapture the openness and outrageousness of American experience. Read aloud, his poetry shows not only his attempts to be provocative and shocking, but also the vitality bursting from within it. "How I love to probe life," Corso has written. "That's what poetry is to me, a wondrous prober." In "Marriage" Corso probes his own mind to play out various fantasies he has in response to the social pressures for "settling down and marrying a nice girl." Part of the comedy derives from the image of himself as the bare-footed outsider in a "straight" world, but a good deal of the fun comes from the grotesque picture he paints of typical domestic life. Throughout the poem Corso is aware, but aware primarily of what is not acceptable to him. He tries out various types of women and environments. He acknowledges the profundity of such experiences as becoming a father— "finding myself in the most common of situations a trembling man." And even in dullest suburbia, his imagination erupts to transform its everyday drabness. Perhaps the poem does not resolve its initial question, but it does present us with a consciousness aware of its freedom to choose.

Marriage

Should I get married? Should I be good?
Astound the girl next door with my velvet suit and faustus hood?
Don't take her to movies but to cemeteries
tell all about werewolf bathtubs and forked clarinets
then desire her and kiss her and all the preliminaries
and she going just so far and I understanding why
not getting angry saying You must feel! It's beautiful to feel!
Instead take her in my arms lean against an old crooked tombstone
and woo her the entire night the constellations in the sky –

When she introduces me to her parents
back straightened, hair finally combed, strangled by a tie,
should I sit knees together on their 3rd degree sofa
and not ask Where's the bathroom?
How else to feel other than I am,
often thinking Flash Gordon soap—
O how terrible it must be for a young man
seated before a family and the family thinking
We never saw him before! He wants our Mary Lou!
After tea and homemade cookies they ask What do you do for a
                                                    living?

Should I tell them? Would they like me then?
Say All right get married, we're losing a daughter
but we're gaining a son—
And should I then ask Where's the bathroom?

O God, and the wedding! All her family and her friends
and only a handful of mine all scroungy and bearded
just wait to get at the drinks and food—
And the priest! he looking at me as if I masturbated
asking me Do you take this woman for your lawful wedded wife?
And I trembling what to say say Pie Glue!
I kiss the bride all those corny men slapping me on the back
She's all yours, boy! Ha-ha-ha!
And in their eyes you could see some obscene honeymoon going
                                                    on—

Then all that absurd rice and clanky cans and shoes
Niagara Falls! Hordes of us! Husbands! Wives! Flowers!
Chocolates!
All streaming into cozy hotels
All going to do the same thing tonight
The indifferent clerk he knowing what was going to happen
The lobby zombies they knowing what
The whistling elevator man he knowing
The winking bellboy knowing
Everybody knowing! I'd be almost inclined not to do anything!
Stay up all night! Stare that hotel clerk in the eye!
Screaming: I deny honeymoon! I deny honeymoon!
running rampant into those almost climactic suites
yelling Radio belly! Cat shovel!
O I'd live in Niagara forever! in a dark cave beneath the Falls
I'd sit there the Mad Honeymooner
devising ways to break marriages, a scourge of bigamy
a saint of divorce—

But I should get married I should be good
How nice it'd be to come home to her
and sit by the fireplace and she in the kitchen
aproned young and lovely wanting my baby
and so happy about me she burns the roast beef
and comes crying to me and I get up from my big papa chair
saying Christmas teeth! Radiant brains! Apple deaf!
God what a husband I'd make! Yes, I should get married!
So much to do! like sneaking into Mr. Jones' house late at night
and cover his golf clubs with 1920 Norwegian books
Like hanging a picture of Rimbaud on the lawnmower
like pasting Tannu Tuva postage stamps all over the picket fence
like when Mrs. Kindhead comes to collect for the Community Chest
grab her and tell her There are unfavorable omens in the sky.
And when the mayor comes to get my vote tell him
When are you going to stop people killing whales!
And when the milkman comes leave him a note in the bottle
Penguin dust, bring me penguin dust, I want penguin dust—

Yet if I should get married and it's Connecticut and snow
and she gives birth to a child and I am sleepless, worn,
up for nights, head bowed against a quiet window, the past behind
      me,
finding myself in the most common of situations a trembling man
knowledged with responsibility not twig-smear nor Roman coin
soup—

O what would that be like!
Surely I'd give it for a nipple a rubber Tacitus
For a rattle a bag of broken Bach records
Tack Della Francesca all over its crib
Sew the Greek alphabet on its bib
And build for its playpen a roofless Parthenon

No, I doubt I'd be that kind of father
not rural not snow no quiet window
but hot smelly tight New York City
seven flights up, roaches and rats in the walls
a fat Reichian wife screeching over potatoes Get a job!
And five nose running brats in love with Batman
And the neighbors all toothless and dry haired
like those hag masses of the 18th century
all wanting to come in and watch TV
The landlord wants his rent
Grocery store Blue Cross Gas & Electric Knights of Columbus
Impossible to lie back and dream Telephone snow, ghost parking—
No! I should not get married I should never get married!
But—imagine If I were married to a beautiful sophisticated woman
tall and pale wearing an elegant black dress and long black gloves
holding a cigarette holder in one hand and a highball in the other
and we lived high up in a penthouse with a huge window
from which we could see all of New York and ever farther on
                                                  clearer days
No, can't imagine myself married to that pleasant prison dream—

O but what about love? I forget love
not that I am incapable of love
it's just that I see love as odd as wearing shoes—
I never wanted to marry a girl who was like my mother
And Ingrid Bergman was always impossible
And there's maybe a girl now but she's already married
And I don't like men and—
but there's got to be somebody!
Because what if I'm 60 years old and not married,
all alone in a furnished room with pee stains on my underwear
and everybody else is married! All the universe married but me!

Ah, yet well I know that were a woman possible as I am possible
then marriage would be possible—
Like SHE in her lonely alien gaud waiting her Egyptian lover
so I wait—bereft of 2,000 years and the bath of life.

QUESTIONS

1. How does Corso make use of the sheer sounds of words to emphasize his themes? Give specific examples using both words and phrases that have virtually no meaning and words and phrases that have pointed, clear meanings.
2. In what sense does the flow of Corso's verse seem true to the process of your own fantasies? In what sense does the movement of the poem seem artificial and deliberately literary?
3. Describe a fantasy in which you attempt to counter Corso's negative fantasies of marriage. At what point, if at all, does the real world intrude to spoil your vision?

DAVID CROSBY, GRAHAM NASH, and NEIL YOUNG

DAVID CROSBY currently lives in Sausalito, California. In 1971 Crosby released his recording, *If I Could Remember My Name*. His first recording with Graham Nash and Steve Stills was entitled simply *Crosby, Stills and Nash*. Since then, with the addition of Neil Young, they have released *Déjà Vu* and *Four Way Street*.

As a rock singer David Crosby has had a kind of success and a satisfaction with his work that few young people have. This success has, in turn, conferred a sense of security that allows him to be extremely forthright in his opinions and self-assessment. Since his family is relatively affluent, he is typical of many "hip" people of this generation who can cultivate pleasure and sensuality (as well as wider dimensions of sexuality) because they need not be concerned with economic survival and because they have had enough personal experience to realize that they need not confine themselves in narrowly defined roles. Crosby's financial success also allows him time to "get into" activities such as sailing, which become for him a kind of self-exploration rather than a mere hobby or escape. In fact, one of the most enlightening aspects of Ben Fong-Torres's interview with him is Crosby's exploration of the whole idea of "getting into" things.

Crosby's honesty about himself lets us see how he has changed over the years. His arrogance has lessened; and his aggressiveness has been channeled into productive activity. (He is clearly the catalyst of his group, if not the best musician or the most loved or respected.) He is candid about the losses and tragedies in his life and he achieves a greater dignity by admitting that they still cause him pain. He talks about his carefree, undirected days in a commune where he and his friends tried "doin' exactly as we pleased," and he doesn't hesitate to tell us his political opinions. Crosby discloses a man who is honest with himself and willing to continue exploring the complex nature of his identity.

The songs of Crosby, Stills, Nash, and Young—frankly autobiographical but not overtly personal—are about matters of deep concern to them. The songs here are selected for their poetic and visionary qualities, but the group does, of course, write many that are more traditionally "romantic" and even some that are explicitly political. Perhaps more than any other group, they present the feelings of many intelligent, sensitive members of the new generation.

All the songs here, in some way or another, look forward to a new, human world. In Graham Nash's "Teach Your Children," despite the pain suffered by both generations, old and new, mutual love allows the hope of reconciliation through communication.

> Teach your parents well
> Their children's hell
> Will slowly go by
> And feed them on your dreams.

The visions of these songs, which recall the verses of Whitman, are not naïve so much as innocent. In the Torres interview, David Crosby quotes Steve Stills's line, "Rejoice, rejoice, we have no choice but to carry on" when he recalls his feelings about the death of Christine. Similarly, other songs are characterized by either a quiet desperation or a determined confidence. Neil Young's "After the Gold Rush" pictures a new world emerging out of the holocaust, the miracle of life surviving; he sees "silver space ships flying Mother Nature's/silver seed to a new home in the sun."

Whether or not rock lyrics such as these will some day be considered important American poetry, we can see that in them the spirit of Whitman's self, dark and ominous in Ginsberg's verse (p. 301), has here, a decade after *Howl*, burst through in images of sunshine and light. Regardless of the ultimate value of these lyrics as poetry, the generation growing up today will always remember the emotions engendered by them in their youth and think of them as companions on the journey of their emerging selves.

Interview with David Crosby (Ben Fong-Torres)

In the third year as a Byrd, David Crosby was kicked out of the band. There were a number of reasons, none of them made public, but several of them easy enough to guess. Crosby, rhythm guitarist, singer, and composer, was continually at odds with Roger McGuinn, acknowledged leader of the group. While McGuinn steered the band's uneasy course from "folk-rock" through space-rock to country, Crosby, equally energetic, equally opinionated, equally brilliant, kept tampering with the wheel. Crosby worked out and executed the intricate harmonies for the group's three-part vocal lines, but he went beyond "folk-rock" early in the game. He wrote "Mind Gardens," "Eight Miles High," "Everybody's Been Burned," "Why," and "What's Happening?!?!" He called Byrd music "folk, bossa nova, jazz, Afro."

Away from music, but still on stage, Crosby insisted on speaking out on politics, and he did it articulately and abrasively. At the Monterey Pop Festival in June, 1967, he delivered a rap challenging the credibility of the Warren Report. Four months later, he was no longer a Byrd.

Crosby hasn't changed much. If anything, he's younger than yesterday, freer with his music and with his iconoclastic ideas. Since leaving the Byrds, he produced Joni Mitchell's first album; Jefferson Airplane recorded a love song of his that the Byrds couldn't take: "Triad." And now he is the proudest, loudest member of Crosby, Stills, Nash, and Young. On stage, it is David, Leo/lion round face fronting a neat mane of wild hair, with freak fringes flying from his old Byrd jacket, who dominates the between-song raps. It's like the man can't stand dead air.

Where Steven Stills is the restrained Capricorn virtuoso boy wonder, where Neil Young is the earthly balance to the other three's often-angelic approaches, and where Graham "Willie" Nash is the boyish, stretched-out Englishman, Crosby is the most obvious catalyst, working hardest to keep four adamant individualists together. He does it with looks, grins, vibrancy bouncing off the balls of his feet, and, most of all, with raps.

Introducing a Neil Young tune called "Only Love Can Break Your Heart," Crosby rumbles: "Here's a song about President Johnson, Spiro T. Agnew, Richard Nixon/Ronnie Reagan/Vietnam/Cambodia/the moon and refuse" . . . pause . . . "but it's not a bummer!" Talking about

"*Guinevere*," *a song he'd written for his lady Christine before she was killed last summer, he now says:* "*This is a place that Tricia Nixon doesn't get to go.*" *At the Oakland Coliseum last week, Nash come-nowed:* "*She might be groovy,*" *to which Crosby replied, slowly:* "*The odds are stupendously high against it.*" *Then the irreverent capper:* "*She's the kind of girl that'd give bad head.*" *Nash choked, turned away, and laughed. McGuinn would've kicked him off stage.*

"*Yeah, sometimes I rap too much,*" *he admits. But you gotta understand: Crosby has had a lot of past, and it all stays with him, and he builds on it. All that music, dating back ten years when he started at 19 and made the folkie Troubador/Gate of Horn/Bitter End circuit. All the reading—science-fiction books; books on sea life and survival methods; titles like 'Ice Station Zebra' and 'True Experiences in Telepathy.' All the women who inspire him to weave sex into raps everywhere and anywhere. All the love for the sea, for his 60-foot schooner 'The Mayan.' And of course, all the months of personal crystallization as a person, as a Byrd.*

Crosby was an easy interview; he'd become a friend through past meetings for different stories. He said he'd found a journalist he thought he could trust. I'd found a musician/spokesman I knew I could believe. When the tape machine wasn't running, we spent time on the deck of 'The Mayan,' docked at Marina del Rey, and talked about London, about women, and about trips he had made in the waters and the winds while he planed and sanded down hatch doors and revarnished various pieces of the boat's woodwork. Downstairs, whenever we talked, friends would invariably gather to listen. At dinner at Steven Stills' house in Laurel Canyon, he made pitches for the rest of the band to support campaigns being waged by Jess Unruh, Jane Fonda, and Dr. Benjamin Spock. He taunted and debated Steven and Graham about "Yo-Yo Lennon," and about the impossibility of carving out a perfect male-female relationship. But he conceded that Yo-Yo and John might have one worked out.

A few weeks later, Nixon and the National Guard in Ohio did their numbers, and Crosby, Stills, Nash, and Young fell apart, and David called up to tell about it, to say he thought it'd be together again soon. Days later, Neil Young had written "Ohio," and Crosby's prediction had come true, the band was back on the road. We met again and talked some more, over breakfast at a restaurant in Hollywood, after the waitress had finished hounding him for concert tickets for her kids—promising an incredible blow job in the restroom ("And I've got false teeth," she said).

He spoke, not too specifically or certainly, about the band, and it sounded like maybe Crosby, Stills, Nash, and Young might be staying together just long enough to save their legal necks on the concert tour. Young and Stills were at it again. Broken arrows.

But last week, speaking after the Oakland concert, Crosby, the catalyst, sounded very certain: "The music has been so good," he said, "that as far as I can see, we'll do one tour and one LP a year for the next ten years. Steve and Neil were fuckin' hugging and shaking hands after shows. And if me and Willie and the others can get those two cats up and keep 'em up . . . well, we can work it out." And meanwhile, he and Nash will do a joint LP this summer, and Stills will have a solo album out, and CSN&Y have six Fillmore sets recorded for a possible live album this fall, and so David Crosby has a lot to talk about, indeed.   —B.F.-T.

You were talking, when we first met, about what you hoped Crosby, Stills, and Nash would be. And you were saying something about what a joy it was to be able to not have to just sing three-part harmony, to be able to find your voice. You were hinting at limitations as a Byrd and the whole range of things you went through as a Byrd.

Man, there's limitations inherent in anything, I suppose. The thing you gotta do in a group is fill whatever needs to be filled that you can fill and try not to be too specific about it. No, the limitations worked out usually in the areas of there being nobody else to sing harmony.

The way we did the first three Byrd albums, I guess, was Gene [Clark] and McGuinn would sing the melody together and then I would sing the harmony parts and then finally we got Christopher [Hillman] to start singin' and along about then Gene dropped out. Then we got to singin' parts more. But for most of it, it wound up bein' me singin' harmony because I could sing that high and I could stay in tune, and that's about it. And also I really love singin' harmony and I love thinkin' up weird ones, and they used to enjoy the weird ones. So I wound up never singin' lead. Now, I'm not a great lead singer. But there are songs that I like to sing; and then they could all sing it. So . . . he used to want to, and it used to be a matter of habit within the group to try and keep everybody in roles, you know what I mean? When we started out makin' groups the first time around, we thought it was sorta like *Hard Day's Night*, and we thought everybody had to have a role.

It got to be a matter of habit that I would do that and this would be that and that . . . and it's hard to break habit, man. Habit's even harder to break than some kind of deliberate plot, 'cause it's not maliciousness on anybody's part. There wasn't anybody in that group trying to hold me back. There was no real maliciousness in that group until right near the end, y'know? Along around "Eight Miles High" and Monterey Pop Festival, y'know? They used to get uptight that I was playin' with Steven and Buffalo Springfield. They got uptight behind Monterey, me sayin' that shit about Kennedy and the Warren Report.

What exactly did you say?

"Who killed the President?" basically. It was a standard introduction.

We used to do it—you saw us do it a hundred times. We used to do it every single time we did "He Was a Friend of Mine." The introduction for a year solid was: "We'd like to do a song about this guy who was a friend of ours. And just by way of mentionin' it, he was shot down in the street. And as a matter of strict fact he was shot down in the street by a very professional kind of outfit. Don't it make you sort of wonder? The Warren Report ain't the truth, that's plain to anybody. And it happened in your country. Don't you wonder why? Don't you wonder?"

And then we would sing the song. Now, admittedly that's a little extreme for an artist to get into those areas at all. Got no right talkin' about that. But I was pissed about it, and I'm still pissed about it! I guess I overstepped my bounds as an artist. By rights I shouldn't get into that area at all. I'm sure no political genius. I don't fuckin' know what to do. I sure am sure I was tellin' the truth. But I sure am sure that it didn't fuckin' do no good. I mean he isn't alive, he's dead, and nobody still knows why. Or how or who. And everybody's guessin' and everybody's scared. So I guess it didn't do a hell of a lot of good for me to mouth off.

You say "overstepping your bounds." It sounds like at first, the whole band was with you. They knew just what you were saying.

They all believed the same thing, but I don't think any of them would've said it . . . well, they didn't say it.

Did they feel it was improper for Monterey?

Probably. Maybe they thought the focus was there. I know that everybody was conscious of the cameras because it was the first time anybody was filmin' rock and roll, y'know. We were all very camera-shy. I was camera-shy to an extreme degree.

Steve Stills: Being convinced that you were ugly.

Crosby: Well, there are mirrors in this world. For god's sake, man. I mean, Lord. The truth hurts!

So you're up to Monterey and the uptightness begins. Was Steven really a big part of it?

Steven has been a big part of my life, man, for the last three years. The cat came over to my house and played one evening with me, and it was very clear to me that he was a stoned goddamn genius. And I don't know whether anybody else knew it then, but I was firmly convinced of it. He plays rings around everybody. Everybody! He plays everything better than anybody. So, I wanted to hang out with him.

How'd you meet him?

How the fuck'd I meet you, man? I guess I came and heard you.

Stills: You guys paid us $125 for our first gig.

Crosby: First gig? Were you paid on those Byrds concerts?

Stills: Yes, you . . .

Crosby: No wonder you guys were really loose. I wondered why you were loose. [The Byrds' producer. Jim] Dickson didn't tell us that. That's groovy. You sang really good. You put me uptight, as a matter of fact. I felt competitive.

Stills: I know. We watched. We laughed a lot.

Crosby: Oh, you mean guys. Kicked our plug out, too . . . I caught you, bastard! Yeah, so, but they were good, man. That was early Springfield. I didn't really know what he was, man, until he came over to my house one time and we played acoustic guitars. And then I knew what he was. I wanted to obviously do some of that, 'cause it's groovy. Like, I don't know, we like music, we like a lot of music.

At that point, see, my band was turned off to playing. Everybody goes through that stage some time or another, I guess. Right then they were all really turned off to playing. I mean Roger would stop in the middle of a song to look at his watch and see how much more time he had to do in the set. And I'm not kidding you, he'll tell you it's the truth. He's seen him do it. Maybe you haven't seen him do it. I've *seen* him do it. . . .

Anyway, so I had an intensely bad scene on one side, and then I had Steven on the other side; Springfield was falling apart, too. Neither Steven nor I could wash the taste of bein' in a bad group out of our minds. For us, you gotta remember, these two groups—and they were not bad groups —for us, they were intensely painful psychodramas at the time. A mismatching of purposes, of motivations. Everybody was windin' up doin' it for different reasons. Well, Steven and I hung out, and hung out, and we made some demo tapes and played 'em for Atlantic and Atlantic said "Sure, kid, I'll buy that." And I was shoppin' around. Capitol offered me a better deal. I was gonna sign with Capitol as a single. And when Graham came to the United States . . .

And a twinkle lights up your eye . . .

Yes indeed. At that point it started to get good. Now Graham Nash— this is gonna sound like a hype—Graham Nash is one of the most highly evolved people on the planet. He is my teacher and he's certainly the finest cat I know. Excuse me for usin' that word, because I know a lot of really fine cats. He is just an incredible human being! And don't just trust me. Ask anybody that knows him and they will tell you that he is just one of the major joys in their life. And he started bringing my spirits up.

We started singing together and one night we were at Joni Mitchell's— Ah, there's a story. Cass was there. Steven was there, me, and Willie [Graham Nash], just us five hangin' out. You know how it is this night, I mean this time of night, so we were singin' as you would imagine. We sang a lot. What happened was we started singin' a country song of Steven's called "Helplessly Hoping." And I had already worked out the third harmony. Steven and I started singin' it, Willie looked at the rafters for about ten seconds, listened, and started singin' the other part like he'd been singin' it all his life.

That's how Willie does things. And the feeling of that, man, was like havin' somebody give you head all of a sudden in a sound sleep. It was like waking up on acid. I couldn't begin to tell you how that was. That was a heavy flash, 'cause that's a nice thing. You know it was. Especially if you're a harmony singer and you love singin' harmony. And I am and I do and it got me off. So that's what we were doing.

That time in Chinatown when you were having dinner, you made a comparison between yourself, and your relationship to McGuinn, and the roles adopted in the movie by Dennis Hopper and Peter Fonda, in 'Easy Rider.'

Yeh, well, Dennis and Peter used to watch us a lot. Peter's been a good friend for years, and Dennis, too, for that matter, although I don't know him as well as I know Peter. I wouldn't say that Dennis had me down exactly. He did grow a pretty good mustache, I'll say that for him. And, as a matter of strict fact, although it's a really technical detail, he got the knife right, too. Peter's a sailor, too. Dennis—I really dig Dennis. He's outrageous. I went to a wedding party the other day and he's still outrageous. Michelle Phillips in a girl scout uniform. No underwear. God knows I love her . . .

How about the relationship between Fonda and Hopper in the movie and the relationship between you and McGuinn?

It was frequently that. Brash extrovert that I am, and that I was even more, then. Energy source. And McGuinn, a laid-back, highly complex, good multi-evaluating, highly-trained brain.

And optimistic?

Probably not as much as that praise would have gotten everybody to believe, but certainly intelligent about planning the odds. I think he used me as an ice-breaker more than he used his optimism. I'm naturally going and already moving. Easy enough to slide in and then try and get me to go which way he wanted. McGuinn's really a good one for trying to figure out the least effort way to accomplish something. Me, too, for that matter.

So how did it come to be that you left the Byrds?

Roger and Chris drove up in a pair of Porsches and said that I was crazy, impossible to work with, an egomaniac—all of which is partly true, I'm sure, sometimes—that I sang shitty, wrote terrible songs, made horrible sounds, and that they would do much better without me. Now, I'm sure that in the heat of the moment they probably exaggerated what they thought. But that's what they said. I took it rather much to heart. I just say, "OK. Kinda wasteful, but OK." But it was a drag.

In later interviews, McGuinn would say that the Byrds missed your musicianship and the kind of music you contributed. And later on he said different things again.

Well, I don't know. I wish he'd said it at the time . . . Say, it's OK. Rog's doin' fine.

Compared to the Byrds, does this band offer you something closer to total freedom?

This isn't total freedom, no, of course not. I have to—not only am I not free to just express myself, but that can't even be my main concern. Not if I really want this to be a healthy group, which I really do, 'cause I really love it. And I love the cats and they can really play. That's nice. They all also really get off playing. They're doing it for the right reason, thank god. It's really part of it. Why you do it really affects the flavor, man. And I do it 'cause it gets me off, every time, man, that I get stoned and put on a guitar and somebody points me at a microphone, I have—I can't say every time—99 times out of a hundred—I have as good a time as most people do balling. And wouldn't you want to do that? And wouldn't anybody want to do all they could? I want to do it all I can, 'cause it gets me off. I love it.

I mean—you know, I did it—all I can say is that I've done it for every single reason I've been able to find. I've done it for money and I've done it for the glory and I've done it for the chicks and I've done it 'cause I was 19 years old and I thought I was Woody Guthrie on the road, man, and it was hip to sling my guitar over my shoulder. I've done it 'cause of every reason I've ever heard of, and doin' it 'cause it's fun really is an absolutely out of hand good trip.

Neil Young writing a song about Kent State. He surprised everybody.

Yeah. He said, "I don't know. I never wrote anything like this before, but . . ." There it is. I watched him do it. We were at . . . Actually we were up in Chicago. We all came back and it was really crazy and really a drag. I couldn't get mad at anybody, make myself feel righteous, so I split. We went up to Pescadero, and I watched him do it. It wasn't like he set out as a project to write a protest song. It's a folk song. I'll admit that, it is definitely a folk song. But he didn't set out to write it, man. It's just what came out of havin' Huntley-Brinkley for breakfast. I mean that's really what happens. We've all stopped even watching the TV news, but you read the headlines on the papers going by on the streets.

He didn't seek out his subject matter, it's what forced its way into his consciousness, when he had defended his consciousness against it and tried strongly to keep his head in personal good trips all the time. But it's very hard to ignore that Kent State thing. They were down there, man, ready to do it. You can see them, they're all kneeling there, they're all in the kneeling position and they got their slings tight and they're ready to shoot. And there's this kid, this long-haired kid standing there with a flag wavin' it . . . I mean, I cannot be a man, and be a human, and ignore that. I don't think. I don't *think* I can. And I'm not political. I don't dig politics. I don't think politics is a workable system any more. I think they gotta invent something better. And man, it's really right down to there. It's really not happening for me to live in a country where they gun people down in the streets just for that, for saying they don't dig it that way. You can't do that. President Nixon, you can't do that!

How did Graham and Steven react to the song?

They said, "Well, how soon can we record it?" And there was no question in anybody's mind. We all felt the same way about it. As a matter of fact, as soon as we played it to Steven and Graham we just all went to the studio and recorded it. We cut the whole record, both sides, in one night, and finished it the next day. We went in, we played it like that. Those extra words on the end: "Why?" "Why?" "How many?" "How many more?" . . . you know, that? That wasn't even part of the song, that was just what happened when we got to the end. It was all one live take, man, of cats just reacting to our world, that's all. I don't see any holy word or panacea or answer in what we did, we're just people. We live here, too, and they just kicked us in the face.

Do you think it'll just keep getting worse?

Well, now, the way I see it, the seeds of the better are already here. There's the new ways for people to relate to each other and live with each other and grow up. A whole new society inherent in the way that young people are relating to each other now. And communicating with each other on levels that squares never achieve, man, it's that simple. They do not communicate with each other that well.

The shared experience of people who've been high together, the multiplicity of levels that they can relate on and do relate on is not frequently found in straight people. It's a new way, OK? It's only a matter of degree and not really kind, but it's really quite a change in degree of communication. I mean you and I relate to each other on an awful lot of levels. You're reading my skin temperature, my tension, my stance, my position in the room, my tone, inflection, pitch, attack, rise, fall, tension, my blink-blink, my respiration rate, my heart rate, and in the middle of all of those you're copying me telepathically, and I know it. Empathically, anyway, for sure. If you're not doing that then it's different. I see people doing that, man, I see people relating to each other in ways that haven't happened before for people. There are huge numbers of them doin' it. I see, for me, quite plainly a new humanity, I mean a bunch of people who are concerned with being human. I also think that I can see that it's going to get worse before it gets better.

It's something like we have only this one plot of ground, y'know, and we've built a house on it and it's an old frame house and we didn't use redwood. And it's rotten. And we have propped it and shored it and buttressed it and skyhooked it and everything we can think of to keep it up, man. And I don't think it's happening. I think at least we're gonna have to kind of bust it up for the lumber. And I don't dig it, man, because I don't dig destruction, man, I'm a builder. I've always been a builder. . . .

How about rock and roll?

To a degree. I wouldn't limit it to rock and roll. The artists in every area of art in the United States have been saying what the rock and rollers are now saying, for a lot longer than we have. I mean let's not forget the writers. I mean those are the cats who've laid it out a whole lot more complexly, more heavily, more literately, more multi-valuedly and more multi-leveledly than most of us. For the poets, I mean we can go right on back through the history of artists, man, who were willing to tell the truth about their environment and include *all* the environments. It ain't just us that are doin' it now. What the trick is with us is that we're mass artists, and there's never been that kind of stuff before until Gutenberg, y'know, and that didn't really happen until you get up into the electronic mass. And that's simultaneity and interaction on simultaneity and numbers of a very wide scale. It's far out, man. That's the main difference.

It's a tricky thing. I could be dead wrong, man. Richard Nixon might be right, and I'm crazy enough to admit it. I just don't think so. Gotta do what you believe. I believe that all those cats are wrong. I believe what they say matters is not it. Now, I also believe everybody is underestimating the amount of inertia. I believe that that big conglomerate blob of interlocking systems, all moving down this one big socio-economic path . . . I don't think it can change its course. I'm sorry.

So you can't escape. Now, how does your boat tie into this? Several times in crises—mental crises—when the Byrds fired you; when your lady Christine died—you went to the boat. So in a sense there can be an escape.

Well, try to understand. When the hassles in my head, and confusion, and pain sometimes—and everybody's got confusion and pain, I guess—there's no hiding or running, there's only working it out. That's when the boat helps, because the boat has great beauty and constancy and meaning, on a very, very close-up level. It was grace and comradeship. And all of those things get to your head.

It also keeps you very busy . . .

Yeah, but it's on extremely high levels that it works on you. It's not just the mechanics of keeping yourself busy. It's really, it's truly, right up to the very highest levels of it, a rearrangement of how you think. And it's helped me a lot, each time that I've had to try and put myself together and figure out what to do. I'm like everybody else, man. I walk along and stumble and crash straight to the ground, 'cause I sure don't have it figured out.

I didn't pick the boat as an escape route. When I started wantin' to sail I was eleven and a half years old and I wasn't thinking about escape.

It happens that it is a good way to go elsewhere. But the reason I do it is . . . Well, I tried a lot of different philosophies, and none of them worked. So I came down to "if I can't work out any logical, overall ethic to work by, then I've gotta just do what gets me off—which points of consciousness were the highest ones, the peaks. And do whatever it was that got me there—a lot. I mean, God, sailing puts me in the highest kind of consciousness I have, makes the best person out of me I know how to be. It takes me to the same levels that balling does, and music does, and being high and doing both of those things does. Y'know. It's not a philosophical or a political decision at all. It's just me wanting to enjoy it. . . .

Where do you come from? Maybe you ought to give a quick auto-biographical sketch of yourself.

I was born in L.A., a movie family—my father was a filmmaker—and therefore it was an unstable family. Nice, but unstable. Moved around a lot, most of it in Santa Barbara. Went to a whole bunch of different schools and got thrown out of them. Disciplinary problem. The best one was for being, and I quote, "of dubious moral character." *Dut*-dut-dut-dummm . . .

What'd you do?

It was a note passed between two girls in the junior class, comparing notes, as it were, and it was not appreciated by the faculty. Listed a number of other young ladies in the same manner. It caused some scandal in the school, as a matter of strict fact.

What school was this?

Hmm . . . I have to search for the name. Laguna Blanca. It was high school age. I went through several high schools. Started off in a prep school. Bad place to be, no girls, but a good school. Didn't do a whole hell of a lot of anything until I started acting and singing and started doing that at coffeehouses and little theaters and stuff like that. It got me off some, so I went on doing that. Supporting myself mostly with a life of crime. I was a burglar.

What—mostly house jobs or what?

Yeah.

Where were you singing—mostly around home, too?

Right, in the coffeehouses in Santa Barbara. The first one that I ever started in was called the Noctambulist, the nightwalker. I sang by myself. Thought I was goin' to be an actor, took a long look at movie people and decided I didn't want to have anything to do with that much ass-kissing and copping out.

Are you saying that's among actors in general?

Pretty much anywhere. The channels into acting from the bottom are so lame, man, that I don't blame anybody for quitting. The only way to get into acting is to cross over from another field, like we do, or as we are doing, I should say, or drop into it through some other achievement or through some pipeline. It's not worth it to try and fight your way up through the studios.

What'd you say could be the rewards of an acting career?

Mmm . . . they're not as heavy as the rewards of a career as a film-maker, that's basically what I'm talking about. I'm not trying to knock my medium. All I know how to do in the world right now is sing harmony pretty good and write some songs and play guitar. And I like making records with my friends. But the heaviest art form on the planet is certainly films. Let there be no question about it, it's the heaviest cross-fire on your senses that's possible with our present day technology, so far.

At that point, did you consider, say, acting and films to be more pertinent than music?

I changed my mind when I dug the people in the one and the people in the other. People in music are almost universally crazy but they're really quite a large percentage of really nice people playing music. They *are* all goony, but at least I met a whole bunch of cats that I thought were men and cats I can respect. I met a whole bunch of really nice ladies.

Who were the first music people you met?

The first were . . . God knows, I don't even know where I started listening to music. I started singing when I was a kid with my family. People would pull me into the coffeehouses to see and hear people. Travis Edmondson was the first folk musician that would teach me anything. And it was a good trip.

But North Beach—yeah, it was just before Sausalito, Sausalito was prime, just cream. And then, Dino Valente, who is a great person to be on the same bill with, since he will go up every set and just sing his ass off, y'know. Unless he's on some kind of change, he will usually go up and just really do his level best to stir your brains around with a spoon. He's a very alive cat, y'know.

I was surprised to see him join a rock and roll band, after all those years. He told me he was asked to join the Byrds, at one time.

Yeah. Everybody was very surprised to see him join Quicksilver, even though he's always had that very close friendship with them. He and David Freiberg and I were dropping acid together years ago. And David and I were livin' together for just a long time. David and I and Paul Kantner, in Venice, with several others—Steven Shuster, Ginger Jackson, Sherry Snow . . .

What kind of a scene was that?

It was your basic little keep-your-money-in-a-bowl, share your shit . . . we never wanted for food, nor smoke, nor a guitar to play on, nor fresh strings, for that matter, to string up on it. We had a Volkswagen bus, in the classic manner. And we spent most of our time doin' exactly as we pleased. Which meant mostly laying around on the beach, going back, playing, goofin' off, stuff like that. Kantner's really a fine cat to live by, man, and so's David Freiberg.

Were they into the same thing you were—single folk artists?

Yeah. This was right after Sausalito. We were getting it together here after the scene up there.

In terms of the music around this time, was this during the period of the decline of folk—the hootenanny days?

"Decline of folk." There's a phrase for you.

Or over-commercialization of folk.

There's a better phrase. Folk being eaten alive by the gigantic entertainment monster. I mean the entertainment business is not music. Or theater, or culture, or filmmaking. The entertainment business is the marketplace. Let's somehow desperately struggle to remind ourselves of that fact, 'cause it's the truth, man. And the fuckers are really, really twisting us up, a lot. They are the prime reasons that people fuck up—in bands, anyway. Peripheral trips, man. Money trips, and star trips, and selling-it trips. "You want to really be a hit, this is what you gotta do." [Sings:] "So you wanna be a rock and roll star . . ." . . . .

What would you call yourself in your band now? You said "energy source."

No, it's a slightly different role, frankly. Everybody in this group can communicate to the audience. We all can do it in conjunction with each other and they all can do it by themselves. It's a matter of some kind of personal honesty at some point and the ability to communicate, and the ability to love, or something like it.

Would you dig working with Jerry Garcia?

Man, I would. Now I think Jerry Garcia probably needs me like he needs a third eye. Excuse me, a fourth. He has a third. But I would be just so knocked out to play, or sing, or do any kind of music with that dude. I mean, you know I would! Hey, and he's not the only one. What about Lesh, man? Have you really considered what kind of a musician Phil Lesh is? I would like to make a record sometime with him playing classical music on an electric bass. He is certainly one of the most virtuoso string instrument players on the planet.

Somebody somewhere, sooner or later, has got to realize that the Grateful Dead is one of the best bands in the world. And I hope that it's more than just the people who occasionally see them do a really stupendous set. But they're—man, on a good night the Dead is as good as it gets. Period. I mean they can take people and make 'em just absolutely fucking boogie 'til dawn. And there's very little of that around.

You've called them a magic band, and you've said that the Airplane—and Crosby, Stills, Nash & Young—are magic bands. What's the criterion?

Magic is doin' it so well that you get it up beyond mechanical levels. Magic is making people feel good and stuff. Magic is, if you're high on psychedelics, having a great big love beast crawl out of your amplifiers and eat the audience. I don't know what it is, man. Like, they're magic. Something happens when the Dead get it on that don't happen when Percy Faith gets it on.

The Dead have got an offspring band, now, y'know.

I think it's healthy. I don't think man is naturally monogamous.

You've talked about doing things with Cass and with Kantner, and there are people like Clapton and Harrison moving around with different bands. Is there gonna have to be some new deal to free artists from contracts that tie them up with specific groups and labels?

Yeah, it's gonna have to go the way I think we've gone, for most of the people. And that is that they'll be signed not as a Burrito or a Spoonful or an Airplane; they'll be signed as Michael Santana and Joseph Stalin, Admiral Nimitz, Captain Beefheart, y'know. They'll be signed as different cats, and, well now, the record companies.

I'm certain that for a mutual profit gain these companies can be convinced to allow us to cross-pollinate, particularly if it's put to them in those terms. If it's put to them as a revolutionary, "up against the wall, futher-muckers," it will no doubt fall flat smack on its nose, and they will tighten up on the contracts. Be hard-ass, for four more years. If somebody takes the trouble to convince them that it'll net 'em twice as much money over the next ten years, we'll get it Tuesday.

You mentioned that you had written a number of songs and they all seemed to fall or end up in the same strain.

The trouble is the words all come around to "Why is it like this?" They are all mostly about Christine, and with that . . . and they're good songs. I haven't sung 'em to anybody and I don't think I'm gonna. 'Cause they're pretty sad and they don't draw any useful conclusion. Man, if I had learned something from it yet that I could communicate to people, I would. I got no more understanding than an ant does when you pull off his legs. I mean it's just a blind smash from God. I got no rationale behind it, I got no explanation, I have no way to make sense out of it or any useful wording to communicate from it to people. And what's the point of just communicating to them that I hurt? That doesn't do any good at all.

So what's the point of blues?

The point of blues has been pretty much to communicate it and make it a shared experience, which can lighten it just enough to keep you from going crazy. I'll buy that. But who the hell needs to hear about David Crosby's bummer? It ain't true, man, it just ain't true. Nobody needs to hear about it; nobody needs to go on that trip. It was the most horrible trip of my life and nobody needs to go on it. And the songs that I wrote are some of the best that I ever wrote, as a matter of fact, and I'm still not gonna sing 'em for anybody. I'm waitin' until I got something good to sing about, some joy.

You're saying that you'd like to provide answers as well as questions.

No, I don't need any answers, I don't even think there *are* any answers. I would very much like to talk about something other than the death of my old lady. I don't think that's a good trip for anybody.

That one point you made to me, though, that time, "Well, despite it all, at least you know that it can happen."

Rejoice, rejoice, we have no choice.

Carry on.

Yeah. Willie and I wrote that one. Willie and I are a great combination. That's mostly because of Willie.

That trip from Florida to San Diego . . . You mentioned how quickly Graham learned how to take over the boat.

Typical example, man, of Willie. There he is. Steps on the boat in Fort Lauderdale, bravely, having never been on a boat before in his life, never at all, not one minute. And the cat steps on the boat and casually —Well, man, it was nine weeks, Fort Lauderdale to San Diego, and that's a little under 5000 miles, right? And by the time we got to San Diego the cat was standing three-hour wheel watches, dependably. So intelligently that all of us looked upon it as a good time to go to sleep if it was Willie's watch, 'cause he had it covered. The cat was doing celestial navigation better than I do it. And faster.

What's celestial navigation?

Taking star sights and working out positions. The cat was doing engine maintenance on a diesel, which is machined to tolerances of about 20 times as close as a gas engine or something like that. They're hard to know what to do with, and he was doin' a lot of things that are simple really to a diesel mechanic but relatively complex for a person approaching it from the outside. He got into it, is what I'm trying to say. He got into the whole thing just so totally and so fast it was amazing. But it's typical of him.

How does Graham see you, do you think?

Well, I hope he sees me as a loyal friend. 'Cause I am, man. If I was a chick I'd marry the cat. I think he's one of the most highly evolved beings I ever encountered. That's a heavy thing to say about anybody. I don't know what he thinks of me. I don't know what any of them think of me. They don't tell me. But they play with me, you know, and I can't ask very much more than that. I frankly don't know what anybody thinks of me, 'cept a couple of close friends. I don't know what the public thinks of me. I have no idea what my public image is and I would rather not, you know. 'Cause I got my feet firmly planted in the cheese-burgers, here, man. You can't really do any grandiose numbers with the ocean. It's a bit hard to bullshit the ocean. It's not listening, you know what I mean? So it helps me keep in perspective, I don't know . . . I'd be curious to know what they think of me.

I'd think you would be, because that would probably help to shape or reshape your way of communicating with people.

It would no doubt help me learn some stuff, too, 'cause they're bright cats and they probably see ways that I could improve myself as a person. But the point is, all I ask of them—all I ever want to ask of them—is that they, excuse the words, love and respect me enough to want to play with me. And I don't ask them anything more than that. They don't have to approve of my politics, my sexual attitudes, which I'm sure freak them out, and . . .

What about your sexual attitudes freak people out?

Erk, erk. Excuse me while I eat this napkin . . .

Mr. Crosby . . . what's so strange?

Not strange, not by me . . . The problem is that I've explored about every avenue of sex that I've heard of, OK? The trouble is that I like 'em, most of 'em. I'm not too fond of the bathroom trips, but aside from that in the catalog of sexual history I think that there are very few things that I don't like. Which makes me, by most people's standards, a freak. There are some things that have happened to me in my life, I haven't sought them out, I wasn't trying to freak out anybody, but there were times that it happened that I was part of a triangle, right? And there was one that worked out long and really righteously, and like that changed my attitudes about a lot of things, too. That's the song, that's "Triad."

Is it a matter of when you "impose," let's say, your attitudes on other people that they freak? It's not a matter of them delving into your private life . . .

No. I don't try to proselytize for sex. I'm really not trying to convince anybody else to go my route at all, on anything, least of all that.

It's hard to believe that a group of friends who worked with you would be uptight about the song.

Oh, you got me on that one. All I know is that they were . . . At least one group of people was very uptight by that song. This band is not uptight behind that song at all, having been through similar experiences. At least three of the cats in the band—four of the cats, have been through that same experience.

Well, yes. They were singing "Change Partners" at the dinner table. Now, you're planning an album of your own this summer. Are you going to do more producing?

Producing; I don't know if I'll do any more producing for outside people. There's some people that I would like to help: Dead, Airplane. Not that they need much help, but I love playing with them. There's a cat that I would've liked to have produced an album for and I don't know if I'm gonna get a chance to. I'm sure somebody else will snap him up before I have time to do it: Jackson Browne. I think Jackson Browne is one of the probably ten best songwriters around, maybe. He's from Orange County, and he's a stunner. The cat just sings rings around most people, and he's got songs that'll make your hair stand on end. He's incredible. Yeah, I don't know. There's projects that I'd like to do. You heard McCartney's album, sure, right? What do you think?

Well, Paul himself had said he could achieve the same kind of momentum and excitement that he could get with a group, you know, but it misses the band sound totally, in terms of each person contributing, helping each other work up a certain pace, and drama, and leading to climaxes.

Right. I got the same feeling, and I got that same feeling off records I made by myself. I made a couple of records by myself, band records, y'know, and employed a drummer and a bass player 'cause I don't play either of those instruments, right. But I mean that kind of trip, it doesn't work. There's no bouncing off each other. There's no excitement. And it seems to me Paul fell prey to that.

When I do my own album I won't use anything except my big 12-string. You should hear Steven's. If you want to hear a cat go in and do the "I-can-make-a-record-by-myself" trip, check out Steven Stills, 'cause he happens to be better at it than Paul McCartney or Eric Clapton or anybody else. That's not my trip. I can't do that, man, and I don't want to put anybody on that I'm a band. I'm not.

As you said, Stills' album is a thing like "I can make a record by myself."

But he can! I remember a record that he made of "Mr. Fantasy" that nobody ever heard except a few friends. He made every noise that was on that tape. Played every instrument, sang every note. And goddamn, man, it made Traffic look like a bad second band at the Whisky. I mean it was tight shit. It was incredible, you know. He's better at it than almost anybody would suspect, even knowing how good he is, even knowing the full Captain Manyhands image, y'know.

Well, anyway, me learnin' stuff, yeah, I want to learn stuff. Every kind of instrument, every kind of project, every kind of music I can get into for the rest of my life, but it's not directly related to making an album. And I'm not waiting on the album until I'm not doing something I would rather be doing—namely Crosby, Stills, Nash, and Neil Young, which I would rather do than any other musical trip I can think of.

With people like Stills, Nash, and Young around, do you find yourself playing a particular role in the studio during the sessions—when it comes down to production aspects?

Yeah, we all have things that we do. Like, I would say, if anything, that Steven and Neil are even better record makers than I am. I would say Willie is unquestionably one of the finest mixers around. I let him mix my songs, man. I mean, we work on it together, but when it comes down to the final mix, it's very frequently Graham's, y'know. My role is my role. I don't want to get tagged into it too tight, but on the most basic level I can approach it, its energy source, communication, and focus. And I don't want to get into the techniques of it too close because it's like talking about balling; you can really blow it, y'know. There's that and then there's certain kinds of harmony-thinking that nobody else does except me, that I've found, anyway. Willie don't think the same about harmonies as I do.

What kind of reaction have you run across on your second album? Is it anything close to what ROLLING STONE *said about it, which was a putdown?*

No. See, the point is that for me it's not our second album; it's our first album. We're the new group. I don't know how the other people in the world feel about it, but the first album was Crosby, Stills, and Nash; the second album was Crosby, Stills, Nash, Young, Taylor, and Reeves, and that's from three to six, which means that it's a different group. I think anybody should know that anything Neil Young steps into is different thereafter, y'know. I don't care if it's a bathroom. It wasn't a second album. And it has stuff in it that makes me extremely proud. I figure that the third album that we put out will be maybe two or three times better.

Were you really satisfied with the record?

I wasn't. And also, I probably brought it down by sticking to my guns on one thing. I kept "I Almost Cut My Hair" in there over the protestations of Steven, who didn't want me to leave it in 'cause he thought that it was a bad vocal. And it was a bad vocal in the sense that it slid around and it wasn't polished, but I felt like what I meant when I sang it, and so it always put me on that trip. Now, I don't know whether that communicated through to the people out there or not. See, I don't know whether it communicated anything but just a bunch of raucous guitar and me yelling. If it did communicate, then it was right.

You've said a number of times that there were two dominant images of you that you put out. One was the "troublemaker" thing.

Fits . . .

You said you were the troublemaker of the Byrds. The second thing was, you said that "At one time I used to put people down." Then you said you'd stopped it.

I'm trying to outgrow it. I'm getting better at not doing it.

When was it the very worst?

At the peak of my uptight Byrd, when I thought I should have been really heavy and I knew perfectly well that my band was turning into a shuck and I was paranoid, uptight, and slightly on top of it but very uptight. I was playing a very shaky paranoid king-of-the-mountain. And at that point in my life I used to put people down regularly—everybody, anybody. It was my thing. "Aw, that stupid son-of-a-bitch doesn't know what the fuck he's talking about and I know what's really going on, that cocksucker doesn't really understand what the fuck he is—stupid cunt motherfucker." You know. And I would just rage on and on to everyone, about everything. But, of course, that has something to do with irritability, y'know. There are certain substances which we sometimes ingest through our nose, particularly, that increase one's irritability factor, and they're bad for you. There was a lot of that going on then, too. Mostly just unbalance, a lot of unbalance, man. . . .

So, after all is said, how are you gonna save the human race, number one priority?

You got me. There is no answer that I know of to save us. It's just that that's my highest priority.

But through your music, if you affect the people you come in contact with in public, that's your way of saving the human race.

OK, I'll buy that. But somehow operating on that premise for the last couple of years hasn't done it, see? Somehow *Sergeant Pepper* did not stop the Vietnam War. Somehow it didn't work. Somebody isn't listening. I ain't saying stop trying; I know we're doing the right thing —to live, full on. Get it on and do it good. But the inertia we're up against, I think everybody's kind of underestimated it. I would've thought *Sergeant Pepper* could've stepped the war just by putting too many good vibes in the air for anybody to have a war around.

Now, I am doing my level best as a saboteur of values, as an aider of change, but when it comes down to blood and gore in the streets I'm takin' off and goin' fishin'. It's nice to know that four-fifths of the planet is water and I'm gonna be able to go elsewhere when and if it gets down to streetfighting. Let the cats who are really into it do it. If they really want to.

So your guns and rifles are more of a hobby than anything else?

No. My rifles are mostly for another kind of thing. My rifles are because I plan to live all over the world, not just here in suburban America. And there's an awful lot of points in the world where a rifle is a handy little thing. It's called a lunch gun, you know. It gets you lunch or keeps you from being somebody else's. Now, in this country, a weapon is another thing. In this country my rifles might buy me a great big 20 minutes sometime. I mean, fat chance! You can't fight them on their own ground, man, you can't take on the sheriff's department or the Army. That's their game. They got it covered in spades. Totally. But like, it might buy me ten minutes, and that might be the ten minutes that I got away in.

Look, I don't want to get into it from the level that that's what I expect is happening. I think that we might end up just with "business as usual" for a long time. But, man, "It can't happen here" is number one on the list of famous last words.

Triad (David Crosby)

I want to know how it will be
Me and her or you and me
You both stand there with your long hair flowing
Your eyes alive, your minds are still growing
Saying to me what can we do now that we
Both love you— —I love you too
I don't really see, why can't we go on as three
You are afraid, embarrassed too, no one has ever
Said such a thing to you.
Your mother's ghost stands at your shoulder
A face like ice a little bit colder
Saying to you
You can not do that it breaks all the rules
You learned in school
I don't really see, why can't we go on as three
We love each other it's plain to see
There's just one answer comes to me
Sister lovers— —water brothers
And in time maybe others
So you see what we can do
If we try something new—if you're crazy too
I don't really see why can't we go on as three.

David Crosby
(Guerilla Music © 1968)

Teach Your Children (Graham Nash)

You who are on the road
Must have a code that you can live by
And so become yourself
Because the past is just a good-bye.
Teach your children well
Their father's hell
Will slowly go by
And feed them on your dreams
The one they pick's
The one you'll know by.
Don't you ever ask them why
If they told you, you would cry
So just look at them and sigh
And know they love you.
And you, of tender years
Can't know the fears
That your elders grew by
And so please help them with your youth
They seek the truth
Before they can die.
(Can you hear and do you care
And can't you see we must be free
To teach our children what you believe in
Make a world that we can believe in.)
Teach your parents well
Their children's hell
Will slowly go by
And feed them on your dreams
The one they pick's
The one you'll know by.
Don't you ever ask them why
If they told you, you would cry
So just look at them and sigh
And know they love you.

Graham Nash
(Giving Room Music © 1970)

After the Gold Rush (Neil Young)

Well I dreamed I saw the knights in armor coming
Saying something about a queen.
There were peasants singing and drummers drumming
And the archers split the tree.
There was a fanfare blowing to the sun
That was floating on the breeze;
Look at Mother Nature on the run
In the nineteen seventies.

I was lying in a burned out basement
With the full moon in my eyes
I was hoping for replacement
When the sun burst thru the sky.
There was a band playing in my head
And I felt like getting high
I was thinking about what a friend had said
I was hoping it was a lie.

Well I dreamed I saw the silver space ships lying
In the yellow haze of the sun.
There were children crying
And colors flying
All around the chosen ones
All in a dream
All in a dream
The loading had begun
They were flying Mother Nature's
Silver seed to a new home in the sun.

Broken Arrow / Cotillion Inc.

QUESTIONS

1. Does David Crosby seem honest in his self-conception? What does he see as his strengths? His weaknesses?
2. Is Crosby's idiomatic language creative and necessary to express his ideas, or is it merely faddish?
3. What did Crosby learn about himself and about group behavior in his experience with the Byrds?
4. Why does he constantly compare music to sailing and making love? What does he mean by "magic"?
5. In what ways are Crosby's sexual attitudes very different from those of the other American men we have seen? Have his attitudes changed because of the loss of Christine? Have they helped him overcome the tragedy of her loss?
6. Which lyrics suffer most when they are separated from their music? Which stand alone best as poetry?
7. What does Crosby mean when he says that "Graham Nash is one of the most highly evolved people on the planet?" How is this sense of human evolution communicated in Nash's song, "Teach Your Children"?
8. In the song by Neil Young, what myth does he evoke from old fairy tales? What traditional American myths does he recall?

QUESTIONS FOR STUDY AND WRITING (PART IV)

1. What are Whitman's and Thoreau's attitudes toward nineteenth-century American life? Which writer is ultimately more optimistic about America?
2. Analyze the methods of narration used by Henry James and Ken Kesey. How does James, using his third-person omniscient narrator, evoke the reader's sympathy for Spencer Brydon? Is Brydon the only person in the story through whose consciousness we are permitted to see? How effective is Kesey in conveying his ideas through the consciousness of Chief Broom?
3. Examine the problems of American racial minority groups seen in the selections by Baldwin, Kerouac, and Kesey. What problems are common to all three groups? What problems are unique to a single group?
4. Compare the autobiographical articles of Carl Rogers and David Crosby. What similarities are there of emphasis? Are the dissimilarities the result of more than the gap between their ages?

2
B 3
C 4
D 5
E 6
F 7
G 8
H 9
I 0
J 1